Teesside's Sporting Greats

This book has been kindly sponsored by:

NORTHUMBRIAN
WATER

Teesside's Sporting Greats

Eric Paylor
&
John Wilson

Juniper Publishing

First published in Great Britain by
Juniper Publishing, Juniper House,
3, Sandy Lane, Melling, Liverpool L31 1EJ
2000

ISBN 0952862263

Reprographics
P's and Q's Ltd,. Unit 10, Gibraltar Row
King Edward Industrial Estate, Liverpool L3 7HJ

Printed and bound by:
Albion Graphics, Old Connelly Complex,
Kirkby Bank Road, Knowsley Industrial Park North,
Kirkby, Merseyside L33 7SY

ACKNOWLEDGEMENTS

This book would not have been possible without the full support of the sportsmen and women contained in it, plus the enthusiastic co-operation of their families and friends.

We are deeply indebted to everyone for giving up their valuable time in order to search through old scrapbooks and albums for those elusive cuttings and photographs which have helped to make Teesside's Sporting Greats such a unique local publication.

Special thanks to everybody at the Evening Gazette in Middlesbrough who have wholeheartedly embraced this book from its early inception, and to the management for kindly allowing us to use the newspaper's extensive photographic library.

Although many people have contributed a significant amount of relevant information towards this publication, for which we are very grateful, particular thanks are due to the following individuals:

Martin Neal, John Whitfield, Alice and Stuart Hodgson, Ernie Crust of the Middlesbrough Motor Club, Dennis Clareborough, (Sheffield Utd statistician), Duncan Holley, (Southampton FC statistician), Mike Jackman, (Blackburn FC statistician), Tony Matthews, (West Bromwich Albion FC statistician), Ray Simpson, (Burnley FC statistician), Dave Sullivan and the Millwall FC Press Office, Tottenham Hotspur FC Press Office, David Walford, Tony Stedall, (Somerset CCC museum), Sarah Guthrie and Keith Cook (Warwickshire CCC), Jeff Hancock, (Surrey CCC librarian), Jack Hatfield, Harry Greenmon, John Fitzhugh and Steve Landells for their specialist advice on speedway, football, cricket, swimming, boxing and athletics respectively.

Contents

Introduction

THE original brainwave to write a specialist textbook celebrating the marvellous achievements of Teesside's top sportsmen and women was first mooted a couple of years ago. It seemed a good idea at the time.

Never before had any publication attempted to pay a collective and potent tribute to all of the area's top sporting individuals.

There must be around 25 sporting greats from this area, we thought, in our naivety and to encapsulate their stories in one detailed and expansive volume would be a worthwhile project to undertake.

It proved to be very easy to come up with a list of 25 men and women who could be described as having achieved something out of the ordinary, and who had carried the banner of Teesside sport with great distinction. In fact it wasn't too difficult to think of 50 names.

Then, day by day, the file continued to increase. Every little piece of research about one particular athlete, would throw up another new name.

When the list reached 70, we realised that we had taken on a mammoth task. When it approached 100, the job became enormous.

However, more than ever, the continually expanding index justified our decision to compile this book. We realised very quickly that there was a great story to tell. Many great stories in fact. And a reason for Teesside to feel more proud than ever about its sporting sons and daughters.

Eventually Teesside's Sporting Greats grew so big that it was in danger of overpowering us. We had to dissect the phrase 'sporting great' and decide on an entry criteria. It was not an easy task.

In the event, we decided that the final 95 entries in Teesside's Sporting Greats were fully deserving of their inclusion. Most, if not all, are full internationals, although this was not the hard and fast rule which governed our decision making.

The bottom line is that all of the people in this book are special. Some are even extra special. They have attained something out of the ordinary. And this is how we came to support their right to be called sporting greats.

Initially, we felt that people born only within Teesside's boundaries should be included in this book. But then we decided to relax the rules very slightly.as there were athletes, such as Allison Curbishley and Dennis Coates, who were born elsewhere but knew nothing but Teesside during their formative years. There are others, such as the bowls legend Norma Shaw, who has spent most of her life living here and is regarded by all and sundry as a true Teessider.

Naturally there will be some readers who feel we have omitted some individuals who should have been included. In some cases they may have a very strong argument.

In addition, there will be several athletes well worthy of inclusion, whose achievements we did not discover during the course of our research. On this basis we must emphasise that this list of 95 is by no means the definitive list and could be updated in the future. But at this point in time we feel that we are close to the mark.

In many respects it would have been easier if the index of sporting greats had been smaller. Several people have long left Teesside and were very difficult to trace. Others, we did not manage to contact at all, though we have still worked hard to fully research their stories. We were also working to a strict deadline, which had to be met, and this meant that it was simply not possible to talk to everybody or their families.

However, we are satisfied that the finished product is a fair and honest record of Teesside's sporting heritage. It's also a story which is never ending. The region is producing new athletes every year, who are destined to reach the peak of their sporting potential. And they are emerging from a rapidly increasing number of sports.

When we began compiling the list we never imagined that so many different sports would be involved. Yet we have three canoeists in our book, one of whom, Russ Smith, won the world championship. Another, Ian Raspin, has competed in two summer Olympic Games. In Nicola Lavery we have an athlete who has competed in the Winter Olympics.

There are some truly exhilarating stories to relate. In particular the inspiration performances and gold medal winning achievements of our disabled athletes such as Kenny Churchill and Esther Cruice.

Then there is the legendary Freddie 'Win Or Bust' Dixon, the scourge of the racetracks on two and four wheels between the Wars. Eleanor Robinson, the amazing ultra runner of the century. Frank Hodgson, who braved the speedway tracks with a broken back. Keith Schellenberg, the intrepid sporting adventurer and Olympian and Alan Ransome, who established the best table tennis club in Britain in the back garden of his own Ormesby home. These are just a few of the countless enthralling tales which are revealed in the pages of Teesside's Sporting Greats.

In this respect, we have deliberately concentrated heavily on researching the stories which had rarely been told until the publication of this book.

However, all the household legends are still listed here, like Brian Clough, Alan and Chris Old, Wilf Mannion, Mary Reveley and George Hardwick.

Nothing is more certain than this already impressive list of athletes will continue to expand rapidly in future years. Maybe that's an indication that Teesside Sporting Greats Two will have to be compiled one day. We hope it is.

In the meantime, we feel sure that the reader will enjoy browsing through this informative book as much as we enjoyed writing it.

Teesside really should be proud of its sporting tradition and heritage. Here's to the next 100 years!

ERIC PAYLOR and JOHN WILSON

Willie Applegarth
Athletics

WILLIE Applegarth was a flying postman from Guisborough whose track exploits made him one of the fastest men on the planet early in the 20th Century. He held the world record for the 220 yards sprint and won a relay gold medal and 200 metres bronze at the 1912 Olympics in Stockholm before eventually turning professional.

Born William Reuben Applegarth in Union Street, Guisborough, on May 11, 1890, he joined the Post Office when he left school, and was a keen runner in his spare time. He was initially trained by William Hood in Guisborough, and both men were helped by Applegarth's wife, who clocked his trials. Later he was coached by G Cummins from Middlesbrough.

Willie was only 5ft 6in tall, but he was stocky and very powerful. He was soon acknowledged as the top sprinter in the North-east and first came to national prominence in 1910, when he finished third in the AAAs 100 yards. It was the inspiration he needed to make a name for himself. He quickly established himself as one of Britain's top sprint men, particularly over his best distance of 220 yards.

In 1912 Applegarth won the AAAs 220 yards and finished second at the shorter distance. He could not have chosen a more opportune moment. As a result he was selected to compete for Great Britain in the Stockholm Olympics at both of the sprint distances, and also the sprint relay.

Willie travelled to Sweden with high hopes but suffered a disappointment when he failed to reach the final of the 100 metres, despite having won his first round heat quite comfortably. He finished third in the second round and was eliminated. At that time only the heat winners qualified for the next stage.

However Applegarth fared much better in the 200 metres. He won his first round heat, easing up in 24.7 seconds. Then he took the second round in 21.9 to reach the final, where he came up against some of the greatest names in world sprinting, including the tough American Ralph Craig, who had earlier won the 100 metres gold.

Willie Applegarth, second right, was a gold medallist at the 1912 Olympic Games in Stockholm.

Willie made a cracking start in the Olympic final and ran a superb bend, leaving all of his rivals trailing in his wake. He had a slight lead as they straightened up and could see the finishing line ahead of him. But the other runners were queueing up just behind, with Craig heading the challenge.

As they raced for the line, Craig, with his fellow countryman Donald Lippincott on his shoulder, both eased past Applegarth to take first and second places in 21.7 and 21.8 respectively. Willie held on for third place and the bronze medal in 22.0, with the German Richard Rau, who had made a poor start, coming home a fast finishing fourth in 22.2.

Winning any form of medal was a great moment for Willie, and an achievement which brought great pride to the people of Guisborough. But better was to come in the 4x100 metres relay, which was a new event on the Olympic calendar.

The speed kings of the United States, who included double gold medal winner Craig and Lippincott, were hot favourites to win the event but, amid high drama, they were disqualified in the semi-finals for passing out of zone. It was a major blow for the Americans, because they had stormed home in first place in the semis in 42.2sec. But it was a welcome, if unexpected, bonus for the Britons.

Great Britain, with Applegarth running the final leg, went on to win the gold medal in the final in 42.4, which was a slightly slower time than the Americans had achieved in the semis. However nobody could argue that the Britons had run well. Willie was joined in triumph on the victory rostrum by his compatriots D H Jacobs, H M Macintosh and V H A d'Arcy.

Willie was now a proven world class runner and capable of making an impact at any level of competition. He began to dominate British sprinting at both events, taking the AAAs 100 and 220 yards titles in 1913, in times of 10.0sec and 21.6sec. In doing so, he became the first athlete to achieve the sprint double. In further runs, he twice equalled the British 100 yards record and set a new world record of 14.6 for the 150 yards.

Applegarth repeated the AAAs sprint double on July 4 the following year, again running an even ten seconds in the shorter sprint. However it was his lightning success in the 220 yards which earned him renewed international recognition.

Willie stormed home around the sweeping turn at Stamford Bridge in 21.2sec, equalling the world record, but effectively setting a new one because his run had been made around a curved track. His time was later ratified and accepted as matching the official world record for an event which, at that time, was normally run on straight tracks.

Applegarth's new time beat the previous world record for a 220 yards curved run of 21.4 which had been set by the American James Maybury in Chicago on June 5, 1897.

This record around a curved track was to remain unbeaten for 18 years, before the Australian James Carlton ran a controversial 20.6 in 1932, which was ratified as a world record but not accepted by every country. Amazingly, Willie's time was not beaten by a fellow Briton for 44 years and 92 days.

Breaking records became a regular occurrence for the Guisborough speedster, who was now trained by the outstanding sprint coach of his era, Sam Mussabini, who was later to receive international recognition for his work in coaching Harold Abrahams.

Willie achieved the British record time of 10.8sec for the 100 metres no less than four times in 1912 and ran 9.8sec for the 100 yards in 1913 and 1914. All of these records were set over grass.

Applegarth was also a regular member of the British sprint relay team during this time, and helped set two world records.

After completing the AAAs sprint double in 1914, he was selected by England to run in the inaugural home international athletics championships against Scotland and Ireland at Hampden Park on July 11.

He repeated his double victory in the 100 and 220, and his time of 21.4 for the 220 was a new Scottish record. Within a month, Britain was at war with Germany, which brought to an end many of the organised athletics competitions. However Willie had already made the decision to turn professional, where there was plenty of money to be made. He made an immediate impact in the paid ranks, beating the Australian Jack Donaldson, who was then the world's top professional sprinter, over 100 yards on November 28, 1914.

The head to head was held at Broughton Rangers rugby football ground in Manchester, and attracted a crowd of around 4,000, despite the heavy rain which was falling. The prize money was £300 and the promoter was W H Morton, himself a one-time amateur long distance champion.

It was an interesting race from the point of technique, because Donaldson favoured the straight leg start, whereas Applegarth preferred the familiar crouch method. Donaldson made the better start, but Willie finished with a terrific burst of speed and won, to loud applause.

A return match was arranged between the two, which took place on Salford rugby football ground on April 10, 1915, this time over 220 yards. Again Applegarth won, this time in the very good time of 22.25sec.

In the years following the War, foot handicaps were regularly run at tracks all over Teesside, including South Bank, Normanby, Grangetown, Thornaby and Brotton, and Applegarth was a regular competitor. He often found himself giving up to 20 yards away to seasoned club runners over 110 yards, but more often than not pocketed the prize money on offer for winning the grand final.

In 1922, Willie emigrated to the United States, where he coached football and track and field athletics for three years at the Mercerburg Academy in Pennsylvania.

He also played for Brooklyn in the American Soccer League and, even though he was over 30 by that time, took part in a few exhibition races. On one notable occasion at Fordham University, he beat Bob McAllister, who was one of the leading US sprinters.

After leaving Mercerburg Academy, Applegarth retired from sport and took a job as a welder with the General Electric Company where he remained until his retirement in 1955.

Willie died at the age of 68 in Schenectady, in New York, on December 5, 1958.

Bill Athey

Cricket

BILL Athey was a highly talented Test batsman who achieved the rare distinction of playing his part in an Ashes winning tour Down Under and entered the cricketing record books when sharing an opening stand of 193 with Graham Gooch in a one day international against New Zealand in 1986.

He was a prolific scorer with Yorkshire, amassing more than 6,000 runs, and also proved a bountiful runmaker when he left the Tykes and moved to the South-west to join Gloucestershire, later being appointed captain.

He went on to play in 23 Test matches and 31 one day internationals for England, but did not always fully reproduce his outstanding County Championship form, scoring 919 and 848 runs at an average of 22.97 and 31.42 respectively.

Bill eventually retired from playing, but in 2000 was still heavily involved in the Championship as coach to Worcestershire.

Charles William Jeffrey Athey was born into a cricketing family in Middlesbrough on September 27,1957. His father Peter had played league cricket in the North Yorkshire and South Durham League for 29 years, 25 of them with Middlesbrough.

Bill's cricketing links increased in 1982 when Bill married Janet Cook, who was sister of former Middlesex cricketer Colin Cook. Another brother in law, Martin, played in the Thames Valley League, while Athey's father in law was deeply involved in Middlesex youth cricket.

It was clear from his early days at Linthorpe Junior School, Stainsby Secondary School and later Acklam Hall High School that young Bill had all the makings of a top class cricketer.

At the age of 12, he played for Teesside County Schools Under-16s. He joined up with Saltburn and made his debut in the NYSD League in 1972.

Already nicknamed Bumper because of his schoolboy ability to fearlessly hook bouncers to the boundary, Bill had developed into a very stylish right-handed batsman, a fine close fielder and occasional medium-pace bowler.

Ironically, Athey might have become footballer as well. He played for Middlesbrough Under-16s from 1972-4, and was with the Boro Juniors squad between 1974-75. Eventually he was offered apprenticeship forms at Ayresome Park, but turned them down.

The teenager had made his mind up that he had a future as a cricket player, and he was not wrong. In 1974 he made his breakthrough with Yorkshire by playing for the Colts side. In the same year he gained valuable experience when he was called up for the North of England Young Cricketers against the West Indian tourists at Old Trafford.

He linked up with the Bowling Old Lane club in Bradford to attract the attention of the selectors and boost his push for a county breakthrough.

His efforts were not wasted. It was inevitable that Athey would become a first team player with Yorkshire, and he made his county debut in 1976. The same year, Bill went on a tour of Canada with the DH Robins XI.

In search of further experience, Athey signed for Manly Warringah in 1977 and spent three winters in Sydney playing Australian club cricket. By this time, his talent and correct technique were outstanding enough to mark him as a possible long-term successor to Geoff Boycott, both in the Yorkshire and England sides.

In 1980, at the age of 22, Bill was awarded his county cap by the Tykes and also made his Test match debut for England. He was called up for the drawn game against Australia at Lord's but, batting No.3, did not enjoy an auspicious debut, making scores of nine and one.

The following year he toured the West Indies with England, and played in the final two Tests. Again he failed to do himself justice, and did not reach double figures in either match at St John's and Kingston, both of which were drawn.

Despite his disappointments in the international arena, the runs were flowing freely in the Championship. In

Bill Athey is presented with the Player of the Month award for May 1983 at Acklam Park. Bill also has the distinction of still holding England's record one day opening partnership of 193 with Graham Gooch.

fact Bill was established as one of the biggest names in English cricket. He was one of the mainstays of the Yorkshire side and a batsman of some renown. In seven seasons with the Tykes, he scored more than 6,000 first class runs, including ten centuries, at an average of 28.08.

Athey continued with his cricket education, spending the winter of 1980-81 with the Balmain club in Sydney, and then flying out to play for Bloemfontein in South Africa the following year. Later he spent the winter months in New Zealand with Papatoetoe.

He was however unfortunate to establish himself in the Yorkshire side at the height of the political infighting which bedevilled the county in the early 1980s. Although, to his credit, he never expressed discontent publicly, Athey was said to be unhappy with the atmosphere in the dressing room and in 1984 he moved to Gloucestershire.

He revelled in the switch of clubs, making an immediate impact in the South-west and winning his county cap in 1985. In that same season he recorded the best bowling figures of his career, when his right arm medium pacers produced 3-3 against Hampshire at Bristol.

Bill's fine form earned him selection for an England B tour to Sri Lanka in the winter of 1985-86 and it was while he was playing for England B at Galle that he made a career best 184 against a Sri Lankan XI .

Soon afterwards he regained his place in the England side. Bill played in the Second and Third Tests against the Indian tourists, at Headingley and Edgbaston, making a best score of 38 at Birmingham in a match which was drawn.

The Test selectors were determined to stick by him, and Athey played in the ensuing three Tests against New Zealand, though it was not a happy series for

England because two Tests were drawn, and the other was lost by eight wickets. Bill finally made his first half century for England when scoring 55 in the first innings of the Second Test at Trent Bridge. For the Third Test, at The Oval, he was promoted to opener, but only scored 17 in his one visit to the crease.

Athey's finest moment on the international scene undoubtedly came against New Zealand at Old Trafford in July 1986 when he made a sparkling 143 not out and shared in a record one day opening partnership for England of 193 with Graham Gooch.

His performances that summer ensured his inclusion on the winter tour of 1986-87, where he helped England to win the Ashes series Down Under. He opened the innings in every match and formed a strong partnership with Chris Broad which laid the foundations for some big England scores.

Athey made 76 in the first innings of the First Test in Brisbane, which England won comfortably by seven wickets. The Second Test in Perth will always be very special for Athey, because he shared in an opening partnership of 223 in the first innings with Broad, which was England's highest for any wicket at Perth. Bill's personal tally was 96, which was his best Test score so far. However the match was drawn.

He scored another half century, making 55 in the first innings of the Third Test in Adelaide, which was also drawn. The series was clinched in the Fourth Test at Melbourne, which England won by an innings and 14 runs, though Bill made only 21. England lost the Fifth Test in Sydney by 55 runs, Bill's best score being 31.

The following year he was in superb form for Gloucestershire in the Championship, scoring four hundreds in successive first class innings. Pakistan toured England and Athey opened in the First Test at Old Trafford, making a score of 19 in a drawn match. He was dropped to No.3 for the Second Test at Lord's, and marked the occasion with the best Test score of his career, and his only century at that level. Bill made a rousing 123 in the first innings, though the match was eventually drawn.

Bill and his teammates failed to shine in the rest of the series, England losing by an innings at Headingley.

Athey was then called up for the winter tour to Pakistan, Australia and New Zealand, which produced mixed results. England lost the First Test in Lahore by an innings and then drew the next two, Bill making a top score of 27 in his five innings. In the one-off Test against Australia in Sydney, which was drawn, he

made 37. His final match on the tour was the First Test against the Kiwis in Christchurch, which was drawn. Bill made scores of 22 and 19.

Athey was selected to play for England for the 23rd and final time in 1988, when he lined up against the West Indies in the Fourth Test at Headingley. He made scores of 16 and 11 as England struggled and went down by ten wickets.

In all, Athey scored 919 runs for England at an average of 22.97. He scored one century, and four half centuries. He was also a regular part of the England team in one-day internationals and played in 31 matches. Bill's Test career was more or less ended during the winter of 1989-90 when he took part in the much maligned unofficial England XI tour of South Africa. However the suspension which was placed on the players who made up the touring party was remitted in 1992.

Athey was elected captain of Gloucestershire in 1989 and led them with some distinction. However he joined his third county side in 1993 when he moved on to Sussex. He was still a top quality higher order batsman, passing 25,000 First Class runs with his 138 not out against Somerset at Taunton in 1997.

At the end of that season, Bill decided to hang up his batting gloves. He was almost 40, and there was not much more to achieve as a player.

In his overall career, he scored 25,453 First Class runs at an average of 35.69 and recorded 55 centuries. He had compiled 1,000 runs on 13 occasions.

Fortunately Bill has stayed in the game to pass on his experience and is coach to Worcestershire at New Road. Remarkably he was called into action again during the 1999 season when Worcestershire were badly hit by World Cup calls and injuries shortly before playing a National League First Division game against Lancashire at Old Trafford on May 23.

Once it was clear that Athey was needed to make up the numbers, Worcestershire instigated a hot line to Lord's and he was hastily registered in time to play.

In the event, he did rather well, scoring 22 not out as Worcestershire's patched up side beat Lancashire by six wickets.

In addition to his cricketing exploits Bill did achieve some additional notoriety in his career, because he had a Union Jack tattooed on his shoulder at a time when tattoos were not yet fashionable. It was a subject which greatly interested cricket writers throughout the Eighties.

Sid Barras
Cycling

SID Barras enjoyed a remarkable 18 year career as a top professional cyclist, competing all over Europe and winning the trophy for the top British rider on five occasions.

He was a national road race champion, won several stages of the Milk Race and also triumphed in the Criterium Championships, while he broke the record for the highest number of race wins in a season on two occasions.

Sidney Barras was born in Middlesbrough on April 3, 1948. He spent his formative years growing up in Gresham Road, just a short walk from Ayresome Park, and attended Ayresome Primary and then Langbaurgh School.

Like many young boys in the town, he wanted to grow up to be a footballer with the Boro. In fact one of his earliest memories is watching the thousands of fans walking past his home on their way to Boro home games on Saturday afternoons.

However, it was clear from an early age that cycling was to become his major sporting strength and Sid quickly became much more successful on two wheels than he ever did on two legs with a ball at his feet.

In fact Sid made his first marathon bike ride as a five year old, when he hoisted his girlfriend on to the back of his three-wheeler and rode to Redcar. Fortunately he was eventually traced by his family and brought home.

Sid's dad, also called Sid, was a relatively good cyclist before the Second World War, and did well in local time trials. So Sid Junior was encouraged to develop his interest in cycling. His first bike, a second hand Raleigh Rudge, was bought while he was attending primary school. Soon he was enjoying rides of 10-12 miles out into the surrounding countryside with his friends.

Barras was a natural athlete who enjoyed all sports and represented his school at football, cricket, basketball, swimming, and cross-country running. Cycling, however, was always No.1 and he was often caught by his technical drawing teacher designing bikes when he should have been doing something else.

In 1961 Sid intensified his interest in cycling by joining the Teesside Cyclones Club, following a meeting with club secretary Chris Dixon outside of Matt Newton's shop. Sid's good pal Roger Bage joined at the same time, and other keen young members included Dave Clark, Terry Bashford, Derek Bramley and Alan Topp.

Sid and his friends began competing in races all over the region. A regular hectic weekend jaunt involved cycling up to Ponteland on a Saturday with his best racing wheels strapped to the front of his bike. Spending the night in a cheap bed and breakfast hotel, and then competing in a 50 mile road race before cycling home again on the Sunday.

It was all part of building up physical strength and developing a competitive edge.

In 1963, Sid won the divisional road racing schoolboys championships on Hartlepool Trading Estate and qualified for the national final at Crystal Palace. He was in the leading group in the final and in with a top ten chance until a puncture ruined his hopes.

Cycling now held Sid's undivided attention and he set out every day, training and racing. To improve his physical fitness he embarked on a weight training programme at Clairville Stadium, under the controlled supervision of Colin Bell from Teesside Clarion.

Sid left school at 15 and joined ICI, where he became a messenger. It was the ideal job because he rode many miles every day on his various errands, in addition to cycling to work from his home in Berwick Hills and back, which complemented his evening training sessions.

Eventually he moved on to join Charlie Horne and Co in Dock Street, Middlesbrough, where he served his time as an electrician.

Sid joined the senior ranks as a cyclist in 1966 and won 12 races, the best of which was a stage in a prestigious two-day race at Nottingham. By the winter of 1967-68 he had reached international standard and was determined to ride in the Milk Race. He had read that the top Belgian cyclists built up their stamina by running up and down sand-dunes, so he introduced a training stint in the Marske dunes into his weekly schedule.

The move paid massive dividends, because not only did the 20-year-old Sid win two of the stages in the 1968 Milk Race, but he also finished a very creditable fifth overall.

Now his ambition was to win selection for the Mexico Olympics, and he was placed on the short-list. However, despite winning 19 races that year, including two Star Trophy races, Sid was overlooked by the selectors.

There was a selection event at Newcastle, but Sid had had a series of inoculations beforehand and was so weak that he couldn't finish the race. He regained his strength to win the longest stage of the Scottish Milk Race and, although the Olympic team was selected that very night, he was overlooked.

Worse was to follow the following year when Barras was not included in the world championships squad. He was beginning to think that his face didn't fit and was bitterly disappointed.

As a result of these major setbacks, Barras decided to turn professional and signed for the Bantel team. In his first full season as a paid rider he made an immediate impact, winning seven races, including the arduous London to Holyhead marathon, which was the longest single day event in British cycling at 265 miles.

In 1972 Sid moved his base to Hebden, near Grassington, and enjoyed a superb year. He broke the record number of professional wins in a season with 22 victories, easily eclipsing the previous record of 17 set by Dick Goodman. He also came home in 21st place in the world road race championships in the South of France, after a puncture had ruined his chances of a top ten placing.

The following year Barras out-sprinted some of the sport's top names in the first stage of the Tour of Switzerland, where he wore both the yellow and green jerseys. At home, he would almost certainly have won the national road race championships but for a puncture, yet still did enough over the season to earn the Golden Wheel Trophy for being the most consistent rider in the country.

By this time Sid had realised that it was possible to make a healthy living from pro cycling, as long as he maintained his position as one of the top British riders. In 1974 he joined the TI Rally team and moved to

In 1970, twenty-two year old Sid Barras was the only professional cyclist on Teesside.

Belgium, where he spent the year racing on the Continent. However he also won ten races in Britain.

On his return to England, Barras moved to Steeton near Keighley with his wife Linda, whom he had met at Morecambe while she was in her final year at Lancaster University. Barras enjoyed another good year on the road, winning 19 races in 1975 and again carrying off the Golden Wheel, which was now renamed the Pernod Trophy. In fact he won the trophy for three years in succession.

Sid was agonisingly close to finally breaking his duck in the national road race championships in 1976 when he was beaten to the finish by just six inches. He had led the event for 85 miles in a leading group of three, but they were caught virtually on the line at Blackpool Seafront by the chasing pack. Sid was pipped for the title in the desperate sprint finish by Geoff Wiles.

The following campaign brought Barras his best year ever when he climbed the winner's rostrum on 24 occasions, shattering the record for the number of wins which he himself had previously established. Once again he won the London to Holyhead race. He won the Scottish Milk Race and also gained a notable scalp when he finished second overall in the Glenryck Cup, finishing ahead of the world's top rider Eddie Merckx.

By 1983, "Super Sid" Barras was Britain's most successful professional cyclist, having ridden competitively for 14 years. But he was still good enough to win a stage of the gruelling Milk Race at the age of 35.

In 1987 Sid Barras retired from competition riding and now devotes his time to his rural smallholding.

Despite two punctures in the national championships, he still managed to take fifth place.

Barras finally won the national title in his tenth year as a professional at Telford in 1979, though in controversial circumstances when he overcame the challenge from top ranked rider Barry Hoban, who had won eight Tour de France stages.

The finish was held up a long steep hill, in extremely cold conditions, and Sid got his wheel in front to come home first. Hoban claimed afterwards that Barras had cut him up on the hill and an inquiry was held, though it was eventually agreed that Sid had not committed any offence. The title was his.

It was a sparkling year for Sid because he also won the inaugural national Criterium Championship at Milton Keynes by two lengths, and celebrated in style when he was awarded the Pernod Trophy again.

In 1981 Barras switched clubs to Coventry Eagles and commemorated the move by winning the Criterium Championship again, this time at Flint. He also branched out into coaching and was appointed the director of the Northern Region Cycling Centre of Excellence at Clairville Stadium, where he worked with the amateur riders.

The following year Sid opened a bike shop in Harrogate, but his attempts to establish the business affected his racing, and he had a poor year competitively. Sid bounced back in 1983, winning a stage of the Milk Race for the first time in 14 years. This was the first year that the race had gone 'open', and Sid took the longest stage of 125 miles from Bournemouth to Bristol. He also won the Manchester race in the inaugural Kelloggs City Centre Championship series, and finished fifth overall.

Two years later Sid joined the Moducel Air Handling team. He was now 37, but still a hard man to beat on his day, and again he did well with a switch of sponsors when winning two of the Kelloggs races. He won in Cardiff and also beat the hot favourite Stephen Roche when winning in Dublin.

The following year was not too good because Sid had a bad crash in the Milk Race, on the run-in to Cardiff, and was losing a lot of blood from a gaping head wound. The bleeding was stopped in the ambulance on the way to hospital, but Sid needed 26 stitches to repair the damage.

When he came back, he rode in the Kelloggs race in Dublin, but had another bad crash which made him contemplate his future.

Barras decided to give it one more go, and competed professionally for the final time in 1987, but drew a blank. When he announced his retirement he was only a few months short of his 40th birthday.

It was the beginning of a huge change in Sid's life. He decided to give up the shop, and instead developed the smallholding which had been passed on following the death of his father in law in 1981. The outbuildings were converted into holiday cottages and the land was let to a nearby farmer, and now houses sheep, pigs and a few cows.

Managing the smallholding occupies a good deal of Sid's time, though he also works part-time for Grattan Catalogues, along with his former cycling colleague Keith Lambert, in the after sales service of bikes.

Sid has never stopped cycling for pleasure, and still regularly returns to Teesside for the occasional rendezvous with old cycling pals, particularly at Suggitt's Cafe at Great Ayton.

He lives with his wife Linda and teenage son Bob in the 17th century farmhouse on the smallholding at Steeton. Elder son Tom, who is a cyclist himself and a member of the Linda McCartney team, has just finished his degree course at Loughborough University.

Edward Barratt
Cricket

EDWARD Barratt was one of the very first Teesside sportsman to achieve national recognition.

Born in Stockton-on-Tees on April 21, 1844, he played a conspicuous part in the development of Surrey County Cricket Club during the late 19th Century.

In 1870, cutting a dash boasting his distinctive long mutton-chop whiskers, Barratt initially gained a professional reputation with the Longsight Club in Manchester as an excellent slow left-arm bowler, a hard-hitting lower order batsman and a good fielder. Two years later he joined the staff of the very exclusive Marylebone Cricket Club at Lords and on his debut caused a sensation in the North v South match when he took eight out of the ten wickets to fall, disposing of the last six batsmen in four overs at a cost of only two runs.

In 1874, and unable to gain a regular place in the starting XI at cricket headquarters, he moved the short distance across London to the Oval. However, because of the strict residency qualifications in operation at that time, he had wait two years before he could make his debut for Surrey.

His consistent bowling performances during that initial season, which included ten wickets in a match against Yorkshire, quickly ensured that his name came to the attention of the England selectors. The following season he was chosen to play for an England XI against Gloucestershire at the Oval. But despite taking 4-33 in the first innings, this was his only appearance for the national side.

However, the summer of 1878 proved to be the zenith of Edward Barratt's career. He was selected in the Players team against the Australians at the Oval and turned in a truly remarkable performance by taking all ten of the tourists' first innings wickets for only 43 runs. Seven of his victims were caught and the other three stumped. To mark this outstanding personal achievement, at the end of the match, which Australia eventually recovered to win by only eight runs, Barratt was given a £5 note and the match ball suitably inscribed by the Australian manager Mr J Conway.

Victorian cricketer, Edward Barratt, was one of the first Teesside sportsmen to be nationally recognised.

During the same season Edward also took 100 wickets for the first time in his career. This was a feat which he was to repeat on two other occasions with his most successful summer being 1883 when he secured 148 victims at an average of 17.25.

At the time it was recorded in the cricketing journals that on his day, and given the right wicket conditions, Barratt had few superiors in the art of slow left arm bowling. It was noted that his vicious leg break was a particularly effective weapon and his "Chinaman" at times totally unplayable.

Barratt continued to take the field for Surrey until 1885, eventually taking 790 wickets and playing in 130 matches for his adopted county before moving to Rugby as a cricket coach and becoming a first-class umpire. Although he never returned to his native Teesside before his premature death in Kennington, Surrey, at the age of 47, he will be remembered as one of the earliest cricketing professionals from our area to make an impression on the game.

Stuart Braye
Athletics

STUART Braye overcame the handicap of having his right leg amputated below the knee to set a series of British sprint records and win a bronze medal in the 400 metres at the 1992 Paralympics in Barcelona.

Stuart, who was working as a regional development officer for the British Sports Association for the Disabled at the Darlington Dolphin Centre at the time, set a new personal best of 1min 0.92sec in coming home in third place in the Paralympics.

Stuart, who was born in Middlesbrough on April 21, 1958, was educated at Linthorpe Junior School, and later Mill Hill and Middlesbrough High schools where he was a keen sportsman who always kept himself extremely fit.

At the age of 16 he joined the Army for six years before leaving the services to become a lorry driver.

It was while driving a lorry on the M6 in Cumbria that he lost his leg in a road accident. The brakes failed on his lorry when he was approaching a traffic jam, and he ploughed into the stationary vehicles.

Stuart had to be cut from his lorry and his leg was amputated. He was 26. Once he had recovered, he built up his fitness again by weightlifting and swimming.

It was while he was attending Stoke Mandeville on a British Amputees Association training weekend that he was given the inspiration to start running competitively. He met the then British champion Robert Barratt, who gave him details of his own training programmes.

Stuart began running wearing his British-made artificial leg, but realised that it was not suited to speed, so he travelled to the USA and paid $6,000 for a specially made Flexi-foot leg.

Braye trained at Clairville Stadium, where he was helped by coach Ralph Smith, and began to increase his speeds dramatically in competitive events. He became the fastest man in Britain, with times of 12.6sec for the 100 metres and 26.2 for the 200 metres, and just over a minute for the 400 metres.

In 1989 Braye ran in a major championships at Long Island in the USA and then returned to the same venue

Stuart Braye overcame a horrific road accident to represent Great Britain at the 1992 Paralympics.

two years later for the American Paralympic trials, winning the 400 metres in 62sec.

Stuart set his sights on the Barcelona Paralympics and flew to Spain for the pre-Olympic event in 1991, returning home with a bronze medal from the 100 m. However, he was disappointed with his time of 13.11sec. The following year he competed in both sprints and the 400 metres in the Paralympics, but the competition was much tougher and Stuart was relieved to return home with his bronze medal in a personal best 400 metres time of 60.92sec.

Once back in England, Stuart surprisingly decided to quit competitive running, while still retaining a keen interest in keeping fit.

He took a masters degree in sports management at Newcastle and later worked at Durham University as a regional manager for disabled people in sport and also at Teesside University as a lecturer.

In 2000 Stuart is based on Teesside and works for the charity Scope. He lives in Ingleby Barwick with his wife Marion, and sons Andrew and Michael. He still maintains his fitness by hill walking and cycling.

Watched by his two proud sons, Michael and Andrew, Stuart Braye demonstrates to the pupils of Christ the King school in Thornaby the sprinting capabilities of his new " bionic" foot. The specialist artificial limb, which was made in the USA at a cost of $6,000, enabled Stuart to participate in the Barcelona Paralympics of 1992, where he performed with great credit winning a bronze medal in the 400 metres.

John Calvey
Football

FOR more than 90 years, stocky centre-forward John Calvey had the distinction of being Millwall's all-time top goalscorer.

He held on to the club record until former Lions favourite, and Manchester United striker, Teddy Sheringham, finally managed to surpass his total in the late 1980s.

Born in South Bank on June 23, 1875, Calvey first played his football for South Bank Juniors before heading south at the age of 19 to join Millwall Athletic for the 1894-95 season. Initially he had reservations about signing for the dockers' club after watching the swift pace of a match from the touchline. His fears, however, were totally groundless because the following week he scored a hat trick on his debut in an 8-1 victory.

The following year he bagged 33 goals in only 34 Southern League and FA Cup games, including five in Millwall's record 12-0 win against the railway works team, Wolverton, in November 1896.

A fast and clever ball-player, which belied his stocky build of 12st and 5ft 11in, the Teessider used his weight to good effect to bustle through opposing defences. His prolific strike rate was officially recognised when he was chosen for The South v The North trial match at Crystal Palace in February, 1899. He then managed to score another five times in the United League match against Luton in April, 1899, and again finished as leading marksman with 33 goals. His outstanding goals per game ratio, 90 in only 116 appearances, alerted First Division Nottingham Forest, who eventually acquired Calvey's services at the turn of the 20th Century.

Playing in a higher grade of football didn't diminish Calvey's ability to hit the back of the net and he finished Forest's leading scorer in his initial season. The following year he won an England cap against Ireland in Belfast on March 22, 1902, but for some reason was never selected to represent his country again.

After four seasons at the City Ground, during which

South Bank's John Calvey moved to Millwall in 1894 and for over 90 years was their record goalscorer.

time he had scored 50 goals in 150 appearances and helped Forest maintain their First Division status with ease, Calvey returned south to Millwall for the 1904-05 campaign.

Following his departure from the banks of the River Trent, Nottingham Forest's fortunes declined rapidly and within a couple of years they had been relegated. Back on his old stamping ground, Calvey was not the same player who had scored goals so freely earlier in his career. He was now slow and overweight as a result of personal indiscipline away from the pitch. In fact it was rumoured that he had sold his international cap in order to subsidise an alcohol habit. So, after a solitary season of playing on his past reputation, and managing to score only eight times in 36 appearances, Calvey was signed by Chelsea but never made the Blues' starting line up.

Once his playing days were over, John Calvey found employment as a dock worker. He eventually died in Poplar, London, in January 1937 and sadly, according to East End historians, is buried in an unmarked grave in a local cemetery.

Cornelius Carr
Boxing

CORNELIUS Carr was a high class amateur who turned professional when he was 18, and started out on a long hard road which was to lead to him becoming Teesside's first ever world champion 11 years later.

On the way he won the British super-middleweight title, which made him the first boxer from the region to win a domestic title for 80 years.

After one brave failed attempt to win the WBO super-middleweight crown from the durable Irishman Steve Collins, Carr turned his attentions to the WBF middleweight crown, which he won in front of his own fans at Thornaby Pavilion in 1999. It was the greatest achievement by any boxer from Teesside.

John Carr was born on April 9, 1969, and brought up in Grangetown, where he attended St Mary's Junior School. By the time that he moved on to St Peter's Comprehensive School in South Bank he was already learning his basic technique at Grangetown Amateur Boxing Club.

He had been spotted by the boxing club founder, Martin Turner, who realised his uncanny potential, even at the age of ten. Turner took Carr under his wing, taught him boxing skills and helped turn him into one of the top schoolboy boxers in the country.

John made an immediate impact as a senior boxer, winning an England vest in a multi-nations tournament in Sardinia, where he won the gold medal. Then he blasted his way through to the ABA middleweight final in 1987 when he was just turned 18, and took on the experienced England international Rod Douglas. The Grangetown boxer fought his heart out and many people felt that he did enough to win the contest, but Douglas was handed the points decision.

The defeat meant that Carr was to be overlooked in his dream of winning a place in the 1988 Olympics, especially as Douglas was the English team captain. John then made the tough decision not to wait another four years for a second chance, and decided to turn professional immediately. There were no doubts in his mind that he possessed the necessary qualities to make

it in the lonesome world of the pro game.

The top promoters felt the same way. London based promoter and manager Frank Warren won the battle to sign Carr, who moved to London and began to train under the guidance of Ernie Fossey. A plan was carefully laid down for Carr's career, and he trimmed down to light-middleweight and began to build an unbeaten run. John decided to box professionally under the name of Cornelius Carr, and was a convincing winner on his debut when he stopped Paul Burton in five rounds at the York Hall, Bethnal Green. Carr stayed very busy throughout 1988, but after nine fights without defeat, he was homesick and decided to return to Teesside. Again he linked up with his former amateur coach Turner, who applied for a professional licence in order to continue to coach his protege.

Unfortunately Carr's switch did not pay dividends. He was matched against the little known African Bocco George in his tenth fight at Reading. Cornelius travelled down from Teesside on the day, which he later realised was a big mistake. The African was fresher on the night and Carr was caught by a sucker punch in the third round and stopped.

It was a huge bodyblow at the time, and Carr immediately made the decision to return to London, mainly because of the lack of suitable sparring on Teesside.

He stopped Carlo Colarusso in four rounds in his comeback fight, and then stepped up to middleweight in 1990, continuing to add to his victories. He gained vital extra experience from a trip to the United States, where he temporarily linked up with trainer Beau Williford. Beau sent Carr to prison, arranging two bouts against seasoned fighters in Louisiana State Penitentiary. The Grangetown boxer dispatched them both in the first round.

When Carr parted company with Frank Warren, he again returned to Teesside, signing an eight-fight deal with Middlesbrough based promoter John Spensley and his American associate Cedric Kushner.

In training at Grangetown Amateur Boxing Club, Cornelius Carr hones the skills which were to make him a British super-middleweight champion and the WBF world middleweight title holder.

In his 16th fight, Carr finally fought on home soil, stopping Frank Eubanks from Manchester in the fifth round at Thornaby Pavilion in February, 1991. After a repeat win against old opponent Colarusso, he then knocked out two opponents in Italy.

Injuries and illness led to a frustrating time for Carr over the next 12 months and eventually he returned to the United States for further training with Williford, where he spent three months sparring in Reno, Nevada, alongside world top notcher Roy Jones.

A return to England brought yet more new management. Carr briefly linked up with the Mike Barrett stable before signing a deal with another London based manager in the charismatic Mickey Duff. Cornelius made up for some recent ring rust by winning a couple of quick fights under Duff to take his fight record to 22 wins from 23 contests. However he had not fought for six months when he was matched dramatically with holder James Cook from Peckham for the British super-middleweight crown.

The fight took place at the York Hall in Bethnal Green on March 11, 1994, and Carr was a decisive winner, outjabbing the champion and winning by three rounds on the scorecard of referee Paul Thomas. He became the first Teessider to win a domestic crown since Johnny Summers, who was a triple champion before the First World War.

The early rounds of the fight were cagey but, from the moment that Carr began to open up in the ninth round, there was only one winner.

Carr sent the 34-year-old Cook on to the seat on his pants for a count of eight in the tenth round with a stunning straight right, and was always in control in the final two rounds.

Duff's plan was to defend the title against mandatory challenger Fidel Castro Smith on Teesside, and an appeal was made for backers. A date was set for Thornaby Pavilion on May 26 but, two weeks before the fight was due to take place, Carr tore a muscle in his back and was laid up in bed. The fight had to be postponed.

Contractual problems then developed between Carr and Duff and the Grangetown boxer signed a short-term deal with his original manager Frank Warren, who promised him a world title shot within three fights. At the same time Cornelius made the difficult decision to relinquish his British title and move down to middleweight.

He was back in ring action in February, 1995, when he beat Colin Manners of Leeds on points at Cardiff Ice Rink. Another two wins, a third round stoppage over Chris Richards and a KO victory against Barry Thorogood, were the stepping stone to Cornelius realising his ambitions of fighting for a world title.

Carr was matched with WBO super-middleweight champion Steve Collins at The Point venue in Dublin on November 25, 1995. It was a contest which Carr relished, because he knew all about Collins' style, having sparred with him in the past.

Irishman Collins, certain to have most of the 7,000 partisan crowd behind him, predicted that he would stop Cornelius. But it did not work out that way.

In fact Carr gave the Irishman a very tough and demanding fight. Even so, it was a difficult situation fighting in Collins' own back yard, and there were few complaints when Collins' hand was raised at the end of the fight. The three judges scored it 116-112, 116-112, 117-111.

Collins said afterwards: "Carr has got a lot of heart and an awkward style. He could be a world champion." Those words were to prove prophetic.

After a rest, followed by a warm-up win against Danny Juma from Dublin in Newcastle, Cornelius was given another world title chance. This time he was to fight for unbeaten American Lonnie Bradley's WBO middleweight crown and plans were made for the fight to go ahead at the Herlingshaw Centre in Eston. However Carr suffered a blow when Bradley needed eye surgery following a recent defence against fellow American Simon Brown, and the fight was put on hold. One problem after another led to Carr being inactive for 16 months, though he finally got back into competitive action in March, 1997. Cornelius was nominated to fight for the WBO inter-continental super-middleweight title. He was matched with Basingstoke's Dean Francis at Reading, and it looked a relatively comfortable contest for the Grangetown boxer.

However Carr started sluggishly and was wide open to a couple of strong early punches, from which he never really recovered. No doubt Francis was as surprised as anybody else when he stopped Carr in the seventh round. It was only the second time Cornelius had been stopped in his career, and seemed to be a huge setback at the time.

Fortunately, following a couple of warm-up wins, Carr was back on the world title trail again. Initially he was matched against holder Mpush Makambi for the little known IBO middleweight crown, but this fight failed to materialise, and he was then nominated to meet Simon Brown for the vacant WBF crown. Brown, a former double world welterweight champion who was now campaigning at middleweight, was managed by the legendary Sugar Ray Leonard.

The fight was arranged for Thornaby Pavilion on February 20, 1999, which gave Cornelius the added advantage and incentive of fighting on home soil. In addition Carr, with 33 wins and three losses behind him, had never been beaten as a genuine middleweight.

There was a major blow for the promoters shortly before the fight when Brown was forced to withdraw through injury. A suitable replacement was hastily sought and Carr was matched with the experienced Manchester boxer Steve Foster, who was taking a huge step-up in class. It looked easy for Carr, but Foster was keen not to waste the first world title chance of his career, and the Grangetown man was taken all the way before landing the decision on points.

It was a great night for Cornelius and his supporters.

He became the first Teessider to win a world title, finally gaining just reward for 11 hard years work as a professional.

Later in the year Carr defended his world title when topping the bill at Raynes Park in South London against the South African Dingaan Thobela. As a lightweight, Thobela had been a world champion and, despite having gradually stepped up the weights, he was still a whole-hearted and committed competitor.

So it turned out. Carr was again given a testing fight and occasionally had to draw upon all his years of boxing experience. However he always had a little extra in hand and, despite the majority decision, held on to his crown.

Carr's second defence was arranged against another South African, Ruben Groenewald, at the York Hall, Bethnal Green in March, 2000. But the Grangetown man suffered a hand injury in training and the fight was called off.

Cornelius continues to live in the South, where he has settled in New Malden in Surrey with his wife Amanda and one-year-old son Jake Cornelius. However he regularly returns to Teesside to visit his sister Susan and many boxing friends.

Cornelius Carr, Middlesbrough's first British boxing champion for over 80 years, proudly displays his Lonsdale belt to the Boro fans before a game at Ayresome Park in March 1994.

Jackie Carr
Football

JOHN Carr was the most talented of five outstanding footballing brothers who hailed from South Bank. He was born on November 26, 1891, and attended the local Princess Street School. He played schools football until 1907 when he joined the prestigious local junior side South Bank East End, helping them to win two cups in the same season.

By the age of 18 Jackie had progressed into senior football and had established himself in the successful Northern League side South Bank FC. In 1909-10, along with his brothers Harry and Willie, he was a member of the fine South Bank team which unfortunately lost 2-1 in the final of the FA Amateur Cup to the Royal Marine Light Infantry at Bishop Auckland. However, there was some compensation for that defeat when the North Riding Senior Cup was won a few weeks later

Jackie's outstanding inside-forward displays for South Bank quickly encouraged professional interest, initially from Sunderland, but they eventually considered him physically too small to make an impact in the First Division. Sunderland's loss turned out to be Middlesbrough's gain and the Teessiders signed the talented Carr, after much haggling over his wages, in December, 1910.

He made his league debut almost immediately against Nottingham Forest, scoring twice from inside-right in a 2-2 draw at the City Ground. Local legend has it that prior to his debut the shorts he was given to wear were so large for his slight nine stone frame that they had to be tightened round his middle with numerous safety pins in the dressing-room to preserve his modesty.

His lack of stature didn't inhibit his professional progress and by the end of the 1914-15 season, which saw the suspension of the Football League programme due to the First World War, Jackie had made more than 100 appearances for the Boro and was averaging a goal almost every two games. Moreover, he supplied plenty of ammunition for Boro's great free-scoring England international centre-forward George Elliott.

England international forward Jackie Carr was loyal to Middlesbrough for nearly twenty years.

During the Great War, Carr served his country in the Royal Engineers. When professional league football eventually resumed in 1919, he played in a Middlesbrough side which often included his brothers Billy and George, a family feat which is still unsurpassed today by any other football club in the country.

In October, 1919, he was awarded the first of his two international caps when he played for England in a 1-1 draw against Ireland in Belfast. Also in the side that day was Bob Turnbull another former resident of South Bank who played for Bradford City. Jackie's other honour came in a 2-2 draw against Wales in Cardiff on March 5, 1923.

Unfortunately, during the course of the match he sustained a serious leg injury which put him out of action for the rest of the season.

Towards the latter part of 1923 he was struck down by a debilitating bout of pneumonia but recovered sufficiently to play a leading role in securing Boro's two Second Division titles in 1926-27 and 1928-29 by creating many of the chances which helped George Camsell break all manner of goalscoring records.

In 1929, after almost two decades, 449 appearances and 81 goals for the Boro, Carr moved to Blackpool for £500 and helped the Seasiders win promotion to the First Division in 1930. A year later he returned to his native North-east to become player-coach at Hartlepools United before eventually taking over the managerial role for three years.

He was on the move again in 1935, spending a season in charge at Tranmere Rovers before working as an FA coach. The outbreak of World War Two put an end to what was to be his final job in football management at Darlington.

During the war Jackie Carr worked at Head Wrightson Engineering at Stockton-on-Tees but on May 10, 1942, he died suddenly of a heart attack, at the relatively young age of 51. He is buried in Normanby Cemetery in Middlesbrough.

Jackie Carr, middle of the back row, pictured with the Boro squad of 1921-22 which included such legends as goalkeeper, Tim Williamson, middle of the third row, George Elliott, second right, second row, and long-serving trainer Charlie Cole in the suit. Jackie's brothers, George and Billy, are between Williamson and Cole.

Ted Catlin
Football

ARTHUR Edward Catlin was a talented South Bank born left-back who made five appearances for England between 1936-37.

A gangling figure renowned for his well-timed tackling and subtle positioning, Ted also won an FA Cup winner's medal at Wembley with Sheffield Wednesday.

Ted was born on January 11, 1910, and progressed from Middlesbrough Schools through to South Bank FC, where he was spotted by the Sheffield Wednesday's North-east scout who offered him a contract. He joined the Owls as a 20-year-old in 1930. He made his Wednesday debut against Leicester in March, 1931, but more likely than not, he remembered his second outing in the first team when the Hillsborough side were hammered 9-3 by Everton at Goodison Park.

During the early part of his career at Sheffield, opportunities for Catlin were limited because he was covering for Wednesday's famous England full-back Ernest Blenkinsop. So it was not until the mid 1930s that he finally managed to establish himself as a regular in the side.

His greatest moment for the Owls came when he helped them win the FA Cup Final 4-2 against West Bromwich Albion at Wembley in 1935, the two clinching goals coming from Ellis Rimmer in the last six minutes. The same season, Wednesday finished third in the First Division.

In just over a year, Catlin's performances earned him a place in the England team. He made his debut in a 2-1 defeat by Wales in Cardiff on October 17, 1936. In the next two months he tasted international success in a 3-1 win against Ireland at Stoke, and also a 6-2 drubbing of Hungary at Highbury.

At the end of the season Ted took part in England's mini-tour of Scandinavia, and played in the 6-0 win against Norway in Oslo and the 4-0 victory against Sweden in Stockholm.

Unfortunately, Ted failed to win selection for

Stylish full-back, Ted Catlin, won an FA Cup winners medal with Sheffield Wednesday in 1935.

England's 2-1 win against Wales at Middlesbrough the following season.

During the Second World War, Catlin guested for Charlton while on national service in the south.

Later he helped the Owls reach the Northern Cup Final but in the first leg he was badly injured in a challenge with Jack Dodds of Blackpool. It was thought that the serious damage sustained to his knee would finish his career but he recovered sufficiently to continue playing. However, at the end of the War, he finally announced his retirement. In all he made 227 appearances for Sheffield Wednesday without ever managing to get his name on the scoresheet.

In later years Catlin became a publican at the Magnet hostelry, Southey Green, near Hillsborough football ground.

Kenny Churchill
Athletics

KEN Churchill is an outstanding local athlete who against the odds has overcome cerebral palsy to win medals at two consecutive Paralympics and has also held the world record for the javelin throughout much of the 1990s.

At the age of 17, he took the javelin bronze medal in the Barcelona Paralympics in 1992 and followed that achievement up four years later in Atlanta by taking the gold in the javelin and bronze in the shot.

Kenneth Paul Churchill was born on May 10, 1975, in South Bank. He was encouraged to develop his athletics talents by PE teacher Ian Smith at Ormesby School and, at the age of 13, was selected to represent Great Britain at the world championships for disabled youth in Florida, at discus, javelin and shot. Amazingly, he came back from the United States with all three gold medals.

Churchill went on to become North-east junior champion for the javelin and discus and was also a regular member of the able bodied field athletics training squad under the guidance of top local coach Geoff Mitchell.

Ken made his senior breakthrough at the age of only 17 when he won a place in the British team in the Barcelona Paralympics in 1992.

The competition was much tougher than Ken had encountered in Florida, but he did well against much more experienced athletes and came back with the bronze medal from the javelin. He also took fifth place in the discus and finished ninth in the shot.

Churchill worked hard to build up his body strength after the Barcelona experience. His total commitment paid dividends when, still a teenager two years later, he won javelin and discus gold medals at the world championships in Berlin. In doing so, he set a new world record throw for the javelin of 45.43 metres and a personal best of 37.68 for the discus. He was also fifth in the shot.

His outstanding performances were enough for Ken to be named national cerebral palsy athlete of the year for

the second time, while he also carried off the Northern Rock North-east sportsman of the year in the disabled category.

In 1996, Ken threw 43.14 to win the javelin gold in the UK Pan-Disability athletics championships in Birmingham as a prelude to flying out to Atlanta, Georgia, to compete in the Paralympics.

He was a huge success in Atlanta, taking gold in the javelin and bronze in the shot. In addition, he smashed his own world record for the javelin with his winning throw of 45.54m. Churchill also threw a personal best in the discus to take sixth place.

Ken took part in the world championships in Birmingham in 1998. Unfortunately, the event attracted poor crowds which affected performances. Even so, Kenny was undaunted and took gold in the javelin and silver in the shot, setting a new personal best in the process.

The Middlesbrough and Cleveland Harrier continued to make further progress in all three disciplines, particularly the javelin.

In the British championships in 1999, he broke the world record three times on his way to setting a new best of 45.78m. He was also a clear winner of the prestigious Grand Prix series which took place over several British venues.

This result was another giant step on the ladder towards realising his ambition of competing in the 2000 Paralympics. Ken has always had Sydney in his sights and has been able to increase his training programme at Clairville and the Southlands Leisure Centre as a result of financial support from the National Lottery.

Early in 2000 he was building up strongly for Sydney in the grand prix series and UK Pan Games, and also competed with distinction in international events in France and Germany.

Kenny Churchill eventually realised his ambition to compete in his third Paralymics when he was chosen to represent Great Britain in the javelin.

Encouraged to develop his athletic talents at school in Ormesby by his PE teacher, Kenny Churchill's dedication saw him rewarded with Paralymic gold in the javelin at the Atlanta Games of 1996.

Brian Clough
Football

BRIAN Clough established the highest ever goals per game average in the Football League and went on to become a top manager, winning the European Cup on two occasions with Nottingham Forest.

He was a prolific goalscorer with Middlesbrough, netting 197 league goals for Boro between 1955-61 and a further 54 for Sunderland over the following three years, giving him a total of 251 goals in 274 games.

Remarkably he made only two appearances for England, and was also denied the opportunity to display his talents at the highest level by being restricted to three First Division appearances.

His playing career was tragically ended by a serious knee injury at the age of 29, but he went on to become an inspirational and highly successful manager in his own unique style.

Starting with Hartlepools United, he moved on to Derby County and won the League Championship in 1972. After brief spells with Brighton and Leeds United, he was manager of Nottingham Forest from 1975 until his retirement in 1993, winning the Championship once and the League Cup on four occasions.

Brian Howard Clough was born in Middlesbrough on March 21, 1935. During the early years of his life he lived at 11, Valley Road, along with the other seven members of his family.

Brian's father Joseph was manager of Garnetts sweet factory, which was situated near Middlesbrough's Ayresome Park ground, a place with which he was soon to become very familiar. He was educated at Marton Grove. Although on his own admission, he was not a particularly academic pupil, he did achieve the distinction of becoming head boy.

The school, however, did not have an organised football team so young Brian played local league football with his brothers and brother-in-law for Great Broughton. He also occasionally turned out for South Bank and Billingham Synthonia.

It's 1959 and goal machine Brian Clough signs on for another productive season with the Boro.

His outstanding performances, most notably for Great Broughton, came to the notice of Middlesbrough Football Club, who invited him to sign amateur forms for them in 1951. The following year, the Boro manager, Bob Dennison, had no hesitation in making him a full time professional.

Clough made his Middlesbrough debut in a 1-1 draw against Barnsley on September 17, 1955, at Ayresome Park. He scored his first league goal in his fourth game, netting in a 4-3 home win against Leicester.

The following season he was brought into the side in the second match of the campaign, at Bury, and scored twice in a 3-2 defeat. It was the first of seven consecutive matches in which he scored, and afterwards there was no looking back. Brian established himself from that point and scored a remarkable 38 goals in 41 appearances, playing in every game until the end of the season. In the penultimate match, he scored four times in a 7-2 win against Huddersfield Town at Ayresome Park.

In the late 1950s and early 1960s, Brian was the Second Division's leading marksman by a mile. In five consecutive seasons he scored 38, 40, 43, 39 and 34 league goals and another seven in nine cup appearances. On the first day of the 1958-59 season, he scored five times as Brighton and Hove Albion received a 9-0 walloping at Ayresome Park.

Clough's goalscoring feats were rewarded in October, 1959, with two England caps against Wales at Ninian Park and Sweden at Wembley. England were held 1-1 by the Welsh, and then lost 3-2 against beaten World Cup Finalists Sweden. Brian did not score in the two games.

However, it was still a major surprise that these fleeting international appearances were the only times he was called upon by his country, a snub which was to fester with him for many years to come.

Despite his outstanding goalscoring record for Middlesbrough, scoring 204 goals in 222 matches, his efforts could not help the Boro regain their First Division status.

So it was no surprise when, in July, 1961, he tried to fulfil his professional ambitions by signing for arch North-eastern rivals Sunderland in a deal costing £42,000.

However, 18 months later his playing career was all but over when, on Boxing Day, 1962, he collided with the Bury goalkeeper Chris Harker and irreparably damaged the cruciate ligament in his right knee.

Although he worked tirelessly to try to recover from the injury, he eventually realised it would not stand up to the rigours of professional football. After two years of constant rehabilitation he finally had to accept that his playing days were over.

Even though his career had been cruelly curtailed, the statistics of his achievements still make remarkable reading.

Clough recorded the quickest 250 league goals ever scored, scoring 251 in 274 games. This was a prolific strike rate which has never been, nor is likely to be, eclipsed.

Following his enforced retirement, a testimonial match was held at Roker Park on October 27, 1966, and almost 32,000 fans came to honour a true goalscoring legend.

Now at a crossroads in his life, Clough was encouraged to take up coaching by former England and Middlesbrough captain George Hardwick, who had a brief but successful stay as manager of Sunderland during the 1964-65 season.

It was a suggestion which was to give Clough's flagging morale fresh impetus. Hardwick appointed him youth team coach at Roker Park and despite losing his job along with Gentleman George in the summer of 1965, Clough was eventually appointed manager of the struggling and impoverished Fourth Division outfit Hartlepools United on October 27, 1965.

Pools were the very poor relations of North-east football and perennial re-election candidates. But, with his close friend and former Middlesbrough goalkeeper Peter Taylor as his assistant, Clough improved the club's fortunes dramatically. By the end of his second season in charge, Pool had climbed to the dizzy heights of eighth in the league.

His conscientious work at the Victoria Ground alerted many of the more established clubs throughout the country and in the summer of 1967 he moved to Second Division under-achievers Derby County.

Clough quickly realised he needed a inspirational leader to spearhead his team's promotion drive and he pulled off a considerable transfer coup in his second season by convincing the battle-hardened Scotland and Spurs captain Dave Mackay to sign for the Rams. The signing of the charismatic Scot provided the level of experience his team needed and Derby were promoted to the First Division in 1969.

After a couple of seasons of consolidation Clough led

Brian Clough latches onto a loose ball in the penalty area at Ayresome Park, on his way to the remarkable scoring record of 204 goals in 222 appearances for Middlesbrough.

Derby to their first ever League Championship in 1971-72 and to the European Cup semi-final, where they were beaten by Italian giants Juventus following, by all accounts, some debatable refereeing decisions. Clough's success and abrasive outspoken style helped to foster another career. It made him a popular TV and newspaper pundit. And it was to be this increasingly high profile exposure which would bring him into conflict with Derby's chairman Sam Longson, who accused him of devoting too much time to his media work. A power struggle developed within the Midlands club and both Clough and Taylor resigned in October, 1973, amid acrimonious unproven rumours of financial impropriety.

The Derby players and supporters were outraged that the popular Clough had been forced to resign and several unsuccessful attempts were later made to get him reinstated. They were all to no avail.

Ironically it was to be his former captain Dave Mackay who was appointed the new Derby manager.

After a brief and uninspiring eight months stay at Third Division Brighton and Hove Albion, Clough was offered a lucrative five year contract to become manager of Leeds United, who wanted him to follow in the highly respected and successful footsteps of Don Revie, who had left Elland Road to take charge of England.

Unfortunately, Clough's decision to accept this prestigious position with one of the country's leading clubs led to the most traumatic period in his otherwise distinguished managerial career.

Under Revie, the Leeds dressing room had developed a very strong bond of togetherness and Clough made the fatal mistake of trying to invoke change far too quickly. He immediately encountered a players' revolt, orchestrated by the established stars, which resulted in a vote of no confidence in his leadership.

His position soon became untenable and he was sacked by chairman Manny Cousins " for the good of the club " after just six games and 44 days at the helm. The very generous financial pay-off from Elland Road, however, gave Clough the security and time to choose his next job very carefully.

After a three months break, he was offered the position as manager of struggling Second Division outfit Nottingham Forest in January, 1975.

Success did not come quickly and it was only when he was once again joined by his old sparring partner Peter Taylor, in 1977, that Forest were eventually promoted back to the top flight.

Once there, they had an outstanding initial season, winning the Championship at their first attempt in 1977-78.

Amazingly, they even capped that achievement by winning the European Cup the following two seasons against Malmo and Hamburg. This was a back to back feat which had never been previously accomplished by any other British club.

Just for good measure, between November, 1977, and December, 1978, Forest also completed a remarkable run of 42 First Division games unbeaten and had signed the country's first million pound player when Trevor Francis was bought from Birmingham City.

In January, 1977, following the astonishing defection of Don Revie to coach in Saudi Arabia, Clough was interviewed for the job of England manager. He certainly felt ready to undertake the task and was at the time without doubt the unanimous choice of the footballing public.

However, despite apparently giving an impressive interview, the Football Association, in their infinite wisdom, appointed a safe pair of hands in former West Ham manager Ron Greenwood.

As an undoubted sop, Clough was offered the role as England youth team coach which, it has to be said, he accepted gracefully, managing to marry those international commitments with his everyday duties at the City Ground for more than a year before finally stepping down.

He was never interviewed again for the England job and believed, as do many people, that the FA missed a golden opportunity when they failed to appoint him. On footballing grounds there was certainly no better candidate and the only possible legitimate reason for his failure to secure the prime post seems to have been that the FA were wary of his reputation and feared that they would not be able to control him.

Putting the disappointment of the England situation behind him, Clough, over the next decade, established Nottingham Forest as one of the most competitive outfits in the First Division. He moulded a team built on skill, pace and self-discipline which regularly lifted trophies, particularly the League Cup.

Clough's partnership with Peter Taylor came to end in 1982 in rather acrimonious circumstances, a situation which he was to later publicly regret. He did carry on alone with varying degrees of success until 1992-93 when, in the first season of the Premiership, he announced his intention to retire.

Unfortunately, Forest were relegated at the end of his final season in charge and the ultimate irony was that, as he retired from football management to the Derbyshire countryside, despite all his resounding success at the City Ground, he left them in exactly the same position in which he'd found them.

On reflection it was a rather anti-climatic and personally chastening end to a highly distinguished career for a man acknowledged to be one of the best managers of all time. He is affectionately remembered by the footballing public not only as the character they nicknamed "Old Bighead" but for what he achieved on limited resources at unfashionable clubs. Most of all however, the fans everywhere simply enjoyed the cavalier fashion in which his teams played.

Dennis Coates
Athletics

DENNIS Coates was a hugely talented international athlete who competed in the 1976 Olympics and set a world record for the 2000 metres indoor steeplechase.

He raced regularly for Great Britain, both on the track and in cross country races, and set a new British record in the 3000 metres steeplechase qualifiers in the Montreal Olympic Games in 1976, beating the Olympic record which had been set in Munich four years previously.

An air conditioning engineer from Eston, Coates was fancied to win a Commonwealth Games medal in Edmonton in 1978, but his strong running style was not helped by a slowly run race and he finished a disappointing sixth in the final.

Unfortunately, injury and illness combined to prevent Coates from qualifying for the 1980 Moscow Olympics, where he would have been at the peak of his career.

Although he grew up in South Drive, Ormesby, and recorded all his sporting achievements as a Teessider, Dennis was in fact born in Sunderland on February 11, 1953.

When attending Nunthorpe School he once described himself as a 'plodder' as a 1500 metres runner, but this was a mild understatement because he qualified to run the event in the Junior AAAs.

At the same time, Dennis experimented by running the 2000 metres steeplechase in the Junior AAAs. Although he did not reach the final of the 1500 metres, he did finish a creditable second in the steeplechase, which encouraged him to specialise in the event.

Coates first came to national prominence in August, 1971, when he set a new British record when winning the AAA Under-19 2000 metres steeplechase at Wolverhampton in 5min 38.4sec. This time knocked more than three seconds off the previous best and was almost 11 seconds faster than Dennis's previous best in competition.

The run was good enough to earn the Middlesbrough and Cleveland Harrier a British junior vest for an international against West Germany and Sweden in Landau, where he finished second, just six seconds outside his AAA time.

The following year Dennis was a convincing winner of the 2000 metres steeplechase in an international against Sweden and West Germany in Harnosand.

Coates, who was coached in Middlesbrough by the much respected Gordon Surtees, was just as effective in cross-country events, which helped build up his stamina for track racing. He recorded a sensational win for Britain in an international six miles race in France, when he came home in 31min 0.5sec, ahead of the Frenchman Letonant Cerbay, leading Britain to the team trophy.

Dennis became a senior international in 1974, running in A and B internationals against France. Towards the end of the year, he left Middlesbrough and Cleveland to join Gateshead Harriers. He scored a dramatic win in the Cosford indoor meeting the following January when he missed the 2000 metres steeplechase world record by only one sixth of a second.

Having come so close, Dennis had another attempt at the world mark at Cosford two months later, and this time claimed the new record when winning the event in 5min 30.8sec, knocking two tenths of a second off the previous best.

Dennis was rewarded for his world record achievement by winning a British vest in the 3000 metres in an indoor meeting against Belgium at Cosford.

In the May, he won the Inter Counties 3,000 metres steeplechase at Crystal Palace. As a result, he was called up as a reserve for the Great Britain team for the Europa Cup Final in Nice and, when he was refused permission to travel by his employers, he was forced to quit his job.

By this time Coates was now a regular and experienced international runner, competing throughout Europe. He found more sympathetic employers soon afterwards, but still found it difficult to take adequate time off

For a runner who once harshly described himself as just a " plodder, " top athlete of the 1970s, Dennis Coates, possessed enough talent to break both the world indoor and Olympic Games steeplechase records during his accomplished international career.

work to build up for his bid to qualify for a place in the 1976 Olympics.

He did manage to get away for a week's warm weather training in Gibraltar, and returned to England to win the North of England cross country championships. This victory gained him selection for the forthcoming cross country international event, but he unfortunately suffered a debilitating bout of flu for several days beforehand and finished well down the field.

However, Coates was soon running at peak form again when the summer season meetings began. He stayed at the forefront of the selectors' minds when winning an international 3000 metres steeplechase race for Great Britain in Split.

All the hard work paid dividends when Dennis was selected to run in the Olympics following a runaway victory in the 3000 metres steeplechase in the Kraft Olympic Trials at Crystal Palace.

He left a top class field in his wake to win by around 20 metres in a time of 8min 26.9sec, well inside the qualifying time of 8min 30sec.

The so-called athletic experts did not expect Dennis to pull up any trees in the Canadian city of Montreal, but he proved everybody wrong with a remarkable record breaking run in winning his qualifying heat.

Dennis had celebrated the birth of his son Jason, just days before he left for Montreal, by smashing the British record with a remarkable, gritty front running performance. He slashed eight seconds off his own personal best when coming home in 8min 18.95sec, which was only four hundreds of a second outside the new Olympic record which had been set by the Pole Bronislaw Malinowski in the previous heat. The run also made Dennis the sixth fastest man in the world over the distance that year.

Dennis's time was slightly slower in the final but he still ran the second fastest time of his life, clocking 8min 23sec to gain an impressive ninth place. He discovered afterwards that he had competed in the fastest steeplechase of all time, gold medalist Anders Garderud having broken his own world record.

On his return to his home in Bexley Drive, Eston, Coates revealed that he was unable to hurdle in training during the whole of his time in Montreal because of back pains, which made his achievement all the more remarkable.

Obviously now full of confidence he went from strength to strength the following year, winning the 3000 metres steeplechase event in the European Cup

semi-final at Crystal Palace, and then strolling clear to win the AAAs Championships at the same venue.

In January 1978, Coates lowered his own world indoor record for the 2000 metres steeplechase at the Cosford Games. The Gateshead Harrier romped home in 5min 24.6sec to trim 6.2sec off his three-year-old record. Twenty five minutes later he returned to the track to finish seventh in the 3000 metres!

Dennis ran well to finish ninth in the national cross country championships, but muscle fatigue took its toll and he dropped out of the world championships in Glasgow. Coates made a fine start to the international outdoor season in 1978, winning the 3000 metres steeplechase at the Phillips Night of Athletics at Crystal Palace.

He followed up with a storming victory in the AAA Championships to guarantee his place in the English team for the Commonwealth Games in Edmonton, Canada.

Coates set off for Edmonton with high hopes of a medal, having achieved the third fastest time in the Commonwealth. However, on a slow track which produced disappointing times for all the athletes, Dennis came in a frustrating sixth.

The same year he ran in the European Cup, and had a chance of a victory when several runners fell together at a barrier to leave him clear along with Malinowski. But his exertions in the Commonwealth Games took its toll, and Dennis dropped back.

After a rest, Coates began to build up for the new season, but he encountered problems caused by a mixture of injuries, particularly to his back and to tendons in his leg, and also with his digestive system. His running became inconsistent as he struggled in vain to achieve maximum fitness at such a crucial stage of his career.

As a result, Dennis was unable to reach the level of peak fitness which he desperately wanted to achieve, and he ran poorly in the trials for the 1980 Olympics in Moscow, thus failing to win a place in the team. It was a huge blow because Dennis had expected to reach his sporting peak at that time and it was his long-term ambition to make a major impact at Moscow

Consistency of performance became difficult in the two years which followed, even though Coates worked hard and continued to be selected to run for Britain. He maintained a committed training schedule in the hope of refinding his old form, but reluctantly announced his retirement from international athletics early in 1983.

Louise Collins
Athletics

STOKESLEY speed merchant Louise Collins, nee Stuart, was one of Britain's top 200 metre runners throughout the late 1980s, competing in the Seoul Olympics and travelling to the Commonwealth Games in New Zealand two years later.

She also reached the semi-finals of the European Championships in Split in 1990 and, but for a series of frustrating injuries, would undoubtedly have made a much bigger impact at the top level of international athletics and qualified for at least one further Olympic Games.

Louise was particularly outstanding as a junior. A series of fine performances during 1985, including second place in the 200 metres at the European junior championships, resulted in her being named as Britain's top female junior athlete by the British Athletics Writers Association.

She ran in both the 200 metres and the 4x100 metres relay in the 1988 Olympics, and was a medal prospect in the Auckland Commonwealth Games before being withdrawn at the last minute by the selectors under controversial circumstances.

Overall, Louise made 30 full international appearances for England and Great Britain. She won six Northern titles and amassed 20 gold medals from the North-east athletics championships, in addition to still holding the championship best times for the two sprints and the sprint relay.

Louise, grand-daughter of former Boro footballer Bobby Stuart, was born in Middlesbrough on May, 18, 1967, and grew up in Stokesley, where she attended the local primary and senior schools.

She was a keen swimmer and hockey player at Stokesley School in addition to excelling at sprinting. She reached the final of the English Schools 200 metres for the first time in 1982, finishing sixth, and reached the final in the following three years.

Louise finished fifth in the schools 200 metres final in 1984, and competed in the women's under-21 international at Clairville Stadium in Middlesbrough,

In 1986, talented Stokesley sprinter Louise Collins was named Cleveland's Sportswomen of the Year.

where she represented the North of England. She also won the 100 metres at the AAAs Under-21 Championships.

Her rapid progress earned her a three-week training and racing trip to Australia and New Zealand early in 1985 along with the English junior squad. She also competed in the Olympic Stadium in Melbourne, finishing third in the 200 metres, and led the 4x100 relay team home in 46.1sec.

In Brisbane, Louise finished second in the 200 metres, and then anchored the relay team to victory in 45.7sec, which set a new Australian all-comers junior record. In fact the girls were only one hundredth of a second outside the British junior record.

Back in Europe, Louise maintained her superb form. She won the 200 metres in a junior international in Germany and again anchored the relay team to victory. Then she followed up by winning the 200 metres in the English schools championships at Hull, where she beat the higher ranked Simone Jacobs for the first time, coming home two metres clear of her major rival.

The Middlesbrough and Cleveland Harrier continued

to progress rapidly, thanks to the help of her father Charles, who was her coach. Charles had initially developed his interest in coaching when Louise began to blossom as a runner of some potential, and he guided her throughout her career. Still coaching in 2000, Charles is now regarded as one of the top athletics coaches in the region.

Another major breakthrough for Louise came when she was selected to represent Great Britain in the European Junior Championships at Cottbus in East Germany. She was in sparkling form, producing a remarkable silver medal winning run in the 200 metres, and setting a new personal best of 23.83sec in the process.

The race was won by the East German Kerstin Behrendt in 23.21sec, though it was revealed several years later that Behrendt had been taking performance enhancing drugs. To this day, Louise still only holds the silver medal. However, there was some consolation because her run was the best by any member of the GB team, as she was the only gold or silver medalist.

Louise's marvellous efforts were rewarded when she was voted Britain's top female junior athlete of the year by the British athletics writers association.

After leaving school, she started a course at a business studies school in Leeds in late 1985, from where she was able to use the training facilities at Carnegie College and also benefit from the advice of Gordon Adams, the senior national coach at Leeds.

In 1986 Louise was named Cleveland County women sports personality of the year. By this time she was a seasoned international, regularly running for Britain all over Europe and gaining valuable experience.

Louise was gradually building up towards trying to realise her ambitions of competing in the Seoul Olympics. She ran well in an under-23 international in Norway, finishing third in the 200 metres, and then was just 0.2sec outside the Olympic qualifying time when winning the inter-area match at Corby, when representing the North.

However Louise was now working for a stockbroking firm in Middlesbrough, and her need to study for exams was clashing with her training schedules. She was already a member of the 4x100 Olympic squad, but needed to qualify through the 200 metres to be certain of her ticket to South Korea.

It was hard work, but Louise coped well, setting the Olympic qualifying time when winning the 200 metres in 23.61sec for an England Under-23 team in an international in Holland. She also ran the second leg of the sprint which England won in 44.97sec. As a result, Louise was given an award for the best run by an English athlete at the meeting.

The Olympic trials took place at Birmingham in August, 1988, with the first two in the 200 metres certain to be selected for Seoul. It was a close run thing, though Simone Jacobs had the race tied up on the bend and was a convincing winner. Louise was pushed hard all the way up the straight by Pat Beckford, but eventually held on to second place by 0.2sec. The Olympic place was secured.

Louise continued her build up by setting a new PB of 23.47sec at Crystal Palace, though she set off to the Olympics more in hope than anticipation of a medal.

The British team flew initially to a training camp in Japan. Louise had been having problems with an aching wisdom tooth, which continued to get worse as the Olympics neared. In the event, she lost almost a stone in weight in a matter of a few weeks and this considerably affected her Olympic chances.

She was drawn in a tough heat in the first round, alongside the eventual gold medal winner Florence Griffiths-Joyner, but came through comfortably. However, she found herself facing an even tougher quarter-final when she had Merlene Ottey of Jamaica on one side and the French girl Marie Jose Perec on the other.

Louise still ran well and set a new personal best in finishing fifth, but it was not enough to make the semi-finals. The relay team also finished out of the medals.

The next target on the horizon was the 1990 Commonwealth Games in New Zealand, but Louise spent a frustrating time in 1989. After having the wisdom tooth removed, she struggled to shake off a niggling Achilles tendon injury which hampered her bid to achieve a qualifying time.

Once fully recovered, she then suffered from hamstring trouble. However she dug deep and went on to run well, finishing second in both the AAAs and the UK Championships to earn her ticket to Auckland.

However, after arriving in Auckland, Louise suffered a major blow when she picked up an injury soon after stepping off the plane. She was asked to take part in relay training without having time to recover from her jet-lag, and suffered from cramp, which eventually led to bruising. She was advised by the team's physios to rest, in order to be ready for the Games, but the over impatient selectors insisted that she continued running.

Louise Collins practises the sprint starts that would take her to the Seoul Olympic Games of 1988.

She had no choice but to return to the track, but the problem was aggravated as a result, and then the selectors withdrew her from the English team.

It was a huge shock for Louise and she was very upset. She was particularly disappointed to miss the relay, because the English girls had held genuine medal prospects. Upon returning to England she lodged a formal complaint and later received a written apology. But it was too late. The damage had been done.

Louise proved that the selectors had made a big mistake by showing that she was in peak form once the outdoor season started in Britain. She took second place in the UK Championships behind Phyllis Smith from Wolverhampton and Bilston and earned a place in the Great Britain team for a meeting in Helsinki against Finland.

Louise had completed her stockbroking exams by this time, but found it impossible to get enough time off work for her training, and so she left her post. She worked as an economic and planning officer with Cleveland Council before taking up a degree course in

government politics and policy at Newcastle Poly.

She was able to train at the Gateshead track while at Newcastle, and responded to the change of environment by twice lowering her PB in the AAA trials to 23.36sec. This was good enough to earn her a place in the European Championships in Split, where she ran superbly to reach the semi-finals.

Louise ended her under-23 career in style by winning four gold medals in an international in Prague. She won both sprints and helped the teams win both relays, having made her international debut in the 4x400.

Louise now had her sights set on the Barcelona Olympics, but tragedy struck in the spring of 1991 when she suffered a bad ankle injury in a freak accident on an icy pavement in Newcastle. She was used as a pivot by two lads who were chasing each other and hurt her ankle as she fell. Serious ligament and tendon injuries were diagnosed and Louise was on crutches for some time.

Now with Sale Harriers, Louise battled her way back despite continual problems with her right ankle and excelled herself by reaching the final of the World Student Games in Sheffield, where she finished sixth. She also won a silver medal in the relay, despite hobbling around between races.

Then she travelled to Birmingham for the Olympic trials and ran well in the heats and the semi-final to qualify for the final. However the pain in her ankle was so severe by this time that, totally frustrated, she was forced to withdraw from the final.

At the end of the season Louise went into hospital in Birmingham for laser surgery to try to repair her ankle. The surgeon did a relatively good job, but the damage was so involved that, even today, she feels soreness on occasions in her ankle.

Louise did try to race the following year but achieved little, partly because of her ankle and partly because she was studying for her final exams. She gained a first class honours degree. By this time, she had decided to retire from running.

It will never be known what Louise might have achieved but for the injury, though she has no regrets. Since retiring from athletics, she has worked for the Legal Services Commission, initially in Newcastle, and latterly in London, where she met her husband Richard Collins.

Louise and Richard are now happily settled in Berkhamsted in Hertfordshire with their young son Tom.

Geoff Cook
Cricket

GEOFF Cook was a prolific run-maker for Northamptonshire, winning seven Test caps before becoming Durham's first director of cricket following their elevation to the County Championship.

He was captain of Northants for eight years and made 460 first class appearances, scoring more than 23,000 career runs.

Born in Thorntree, Middlesbrough, on October 9, 1951, Geoffrey Cook was encouraged from an early age to develop his cricket skills. His father Harry devoted his summers to the administration of the local game, being secretary, president and chairman of the Middlesbrough mid-week and Cleveland cricket leagues. Geoff's brother David was also a very capable club cricketer, playing for both Normanby Hall and Guisborough.

Geoff was educated at Thorntree primary and Middlesbrough High schools, where he obtained six O Levels and one A Level. At the age of 19 he escaped the Yorkshire recruiting system when Doug Ferguson, who was in charge of Durham schools cricket, recommended him to Northamptonshire.

Geoff went to Northampton for trials and immediately impressed the coaches with his classical batting style, wide variety of strokes and fielding ability. He was offered the opportunity to sign for the county club, for whom he would score 1,000 runs on no less than 12 occasions during a remarkably consistent career. In 1981 Geoff's organisational and tactical skills were recognised when he was made captain of the county side. It was a position he was to hold for much of the decade.

As an opening batsman with a solid technique and an occasional slow left arm bowler, Geoff also displayed a fearless streak by regularly fielding close to the wicket at short leg, which resulted in a couple of bouts of concussion after receiving blows on the head in the pre-helmet era.

Cook first played for Northants in 1971 and won his county cap in 1975. He established with Wayne Larkins one of the best and most attractive opening partnerships in the whole of county cricket.

In 1978-79 he went to South Africa to captain Eastern Province in the Currie Cup and the following winter he hit 172 against North Transvaal at Port Elizabeth. At this time he was showing great confidence against all types of bowling and the England selectors turned to him for the tour of India in 1981-82. Initially Geoff was seen as the natural replacement for Geoff Boycott but, moreover, his captaincy of Northants suggested that he might have the qualities necessary to lead his country.

Unfortunately for Cook he made a rather inauspicious international debut in Sri Lanka's first official Test match at Colombo in 1982, scoring 11 and nought. However, against India in England, he made two fifties

Geoff Cook displays the solid technique which made him an England Test opener in 1982.

and shared in a couple of century opening stands. He took part in the Ashes tour of Australia in 1982-83 but failed to make any significant impact in the Tests. However Geoff attained the rare distinction of never appearing on the losing side in his seven Test matches. In 13 Test innings he made 203 runs at an average of 15.61. His top score was 66. He also played in six one-day internationals in India and Australia scoring 106 runs at an average of 17.67.

Geoff continued to pile up the runs for Northants and went on to appear in 415 Championship matches, putting him comfortably into the county's all-time top ten. He played in 460 first class games and scored 23,277 runs at an average of 31.97.

His first appearance in a one-day final at Lord's was a winning one, when Northants beat Essex by six runs in the Benson and Hedges Cup Final in 1980. Cook scored 29 as Northants went on to make 209 all out, with the Essex reply falling short with two wickets still remaining.

The following year Geoff was back at Lord's in the NatWest Final and scored a century. But it was not enough to make it a winning day for Northants, who were beaten off the last ball by Derbyshire.

In 1986 Geoff put on a record Northants second wicket stand of 344 with Robin Boyd-Moss. Ironically, his best ever individual innings of 203 was made against his home county, Yorkshire, at Scarborough in 1988.

Geoff again led Northants into the Benson and Hedges Final against Yorkshire in 1987 and, after losing the toss and being put in to bat by Phil Carrick, he was out for one when snapped up at short leg off the bowling of fellow Teessider Paul Jarvis.

Northants still went on to compile a tidy 244-7, but Yorkshire had the last laugh when reaching 244-6 and winning by virtue of having lost fewer wickets.

Cook was a highly competent fielder and took 419 catches throughout his career. His bowling was not so effective, though he took 15 wickets at an average of 53.73. His best bowling performance was 3-47 for an England XI against South Australia at Adelaide in 1982-83.

A sporting all-rounder, Geoff also played football and turned out at centre-forward for South Bank in the Northern League and Wellingborough in the Southern League.

Like his father, Geoff was keen to become involved in the game at all levels, and he was elected chairman of

the Cricketers' Association in 1980.

He was, therefore, a superb choice when he was appointed Durham's director of cricket in December, 1990, which was exactly one week before the TCCB were to vote on officially promoting Durham into the Championship. Durham were looking for someone to develop a strong sense of identity within the club, and to help the county's young players to progress as quickly as possible during the 1991 season, prior to Durham's elevation to first class status the following year. Cook had all the qualities necessary to carry out that role.

David Graveney, who was to become Durham's first Championship captain, said: "Geoff did a smashing job in the 1991 season, because we all knew we would stand or fall on his judgement. Nobody in my lifetime has walked into a club stone cold and had to make so many decisions about who might make it and who would not. Every player was a Minor County player and not only did Geoff have to assess their abilities, he also had to weigh up age, experience and what degree of improvement remained."

Cook also paved the way for the arrival of the established first class players the following year, and eventually plumped for the Australian Test international Dean Jones as Durham's first overseas player. It was to prove an excellent choice. Other big name signings were to include Ian Botham, Paul Parker, and his old partner from Northants, Wayne Larkins.

Geoff had a hands-on approach to Durham's development in 1991. He captained the side and regularly opened the batting in Durham's last Minor Counties season. He played in 24 matches and led by example, scoring 782 runs, at an average of 52.13, including a best score of 101.

However, he was reluctant to play for the first team in the Championship the following year, despite making two appearances in the Sunday League and another in the NatWest Trophy against Leicestershire during a time of player unavailability. His top score in these three games was 49 in the Sunday League against Middlesex.

Geoff was rewarded for Durham's initial success of establishing themselves at the highest level, by being made executive director of the county in 1993.

In 2000 he was the Director of Cricket, overseeing the game at all levels but with particular responsibility for the development of young players at the Riverside.

Harry Craster
Boxing

HARRY Craster never won a boxing title - but he was a courageous and adventurous battler during boxing's Golden Era who took on several of the world's top boxers at different weights.

He was well known on the national boxing scene throughout the late Thirties and early Forties, boxing at lightweight and welterweight, and regularly topped the bill in London towards the end of his career.

If he had been fighting in modern times, Harry would surely have gone on to fight for one of the many versions of the world titles.

He often came close to earning a British title chance, though it never happened for him. He was reaching his peak at the start of the Second World War, and would possibly have been a British champion but for the outbreak of the hostilities.

At 5ft 4in, Craster was small for a boxer, especially when he reached the heavier weights, and he always believed that it was his lack of height which cost him the chance to become an international boxer of some renown. But his British bulldog, all action style and will-to-win spirit made him a great crowd pleaser and a tough opponent.

Craster's greatest moment came in 1939 when he produced a major upset by beating the highly rated French-Algerian Marcel Cerdan, who went on to win the world middleweight crown.

Craster and Cerdan met at Earls Court in London, when both were lightweights, on a show which was sponsored by the National Sporting Club.

Cerdan was unbeaten in 41 fights at the time and was expected to overcome the hustling, harassing Teessider. But Harry had other ideas, and pushed Cerdan all the way before coming out on top in the fifth round when Cerdan was disqualified.

Describing the fight afterwards, Harry said: "I had a bad first round. Cerdan was all over me, hitting me with everything but the bucket. I was knocked down twice and was glad to get back to my corner in one piece."

Craster was knocked down a further three times in the second round, including a count of eight after taking a left hook. However he gradually pulled himself around.

He said: "My seconds urged me to give Marcel some of his own medicine and right away I started throwing punches with both hands. Cerdan was hurting me with his hook punches, but I knew I was hurting him too, so I kept up my non-stop stuff in the third round, which I think I won clearly.

"My handlers told me I was getting on top when I reached my corner after a terrifically fought fourth round. Encouraged, I bounced out for round five and after we had been making it at close quarters, Cerdan let fly with a punch which landed on my groin.

"I dropped to the canvas in severe pain and the referee ordered Cerdan to his corner, disqualified. Cerdan had intended to finish me off with that misdirected punch, because my protector was badly dented."

Harry received a purse of £150 for the fight, which was the biggest of his career.

By the time that Craster fought Cerdan, he was an experienced fighter who had earned his corn in rings around the country throughout the Thirties.

Harry was born in Middlesbrough on September 29, 1915. His father was an engine fitter and his mother ran a boarding house, but Harry took a job hawking coal when he left school. He was taught to box by his cousin Alf Craster, and turned professional at the age of 14 when he signed on for Newcastle-based manager Joe Shepherd. His trainer was Ernie Gordon, a former rugby player from Leeds.

Harry was boxing ten rounders as a flyweight before he was 16, with most of his early bouts taking place in Middlesbrough and Hartlepool. He was a tough customer, even as a teenager, quickly gaining a strong following in the North-east.

In 1933, as an 18-year-old, he dropped only one decision. That was excellent form. Within two years he was fighting some of the region's top notchers, and progressing rapidly. In 1935 he put together a string of

Although he never won a British title, Harry Craster was acknowledged to be one of the best boxers of the 1930's possessing a terrific left jab and a dynamite right hand.

eight consecutive wins, beating Jack Lewis, Kid Clarke, Kid Close, Pat Haley, Mick McKay, Billy Quinlan, Douglas Parker and Sonny Lee.

In his fight at the Middlesbrough Sporting Club against Parker, Craster pounded the Sunderland man to exhaustion, the bout being stopped in round five. Five months later Craster met Parker in a return at the Sunderland Royal and again confirmed his authority, though this time he was taken the full distance.

In February 1936, Harry made his London debut, being outpointed by Alby Day at the Devonshire Club. But he put up such a fine performance that he was invited back again to meet left-hand specialist George Daly. This time Harry earned a draw, though the decision was loudly booed by a large section of the

crowd, who felt that Craster had done enough to win it. The following July, Craster ambitiously challenged British lightweight champion Jimmy Walsh in a non-title fight in front of 14,000 fans at Cleveland Park. But Harry was beaten on points despite putting up a gallant display.

On the strength of this performance, he substituted for Walsh against lightweight contender Jimmy Vaughan at Earls Court in January 1937 and recorded a convincing points victory.

Craster won most of his fights due to his terrific jabbing left hand, though he could unload plenty of dynamite with his right when the opportunity was there. At Belle Vue in Manchester in 1936, he had scored a sensational fourth round win over Liverpool's northern area lightweight champion Jimmy Stewart. However both men weighed in over the lightweight limit, and Stewart's title was not at stake. There were calls for Stewart to defend his crown in a rematch against Craster, and the pair finally met again at Newcastle, just one month after Craster had beaten Vaughan. This time Stewart's title was at stake and Craster was in unstoppable form. He belted Stewart to a first round defeat.

Harry returned in triumph to Teesside with the highly prized championship belt, but increasing weight problems meant that he was unable to defend his title before relinquishing it and moving up to welterweight. There was no graduation process in the new division. Craster moved straight into the big league and was pitched in with the top men in the country, most of the fights taking place at Earls Court in London.

Craster and Harry Mizler met twice in 1938, the first fight coming when Craster was northern area lightweight champion and Mizler was British lightweight champion. Their initial meeting was a non-title affair, but it was a cracking fight as they traded punches toe to toe, with Mizler eventually winning on points.

Both boxers then moved up to welterweight and met again in the October. This time Craster concentrated on strong body punches and Mizler grew weaker as the fight progressed. The former British champ was put down for a count of nine in round five but hung on to the bell. However Craster was a clear winner and was awarded the points decision.

Harry then recorded three consecutive draws at Earls Court, but moved back into top gear to stop Johnny Houlston and Smiling Billy Smith in quick succession. After beating Marcel Cerdan in their epic contest, Craster took on Lionel Gibbs from British Guiana on two occasions but was twice beaten on points, and then had the first of three meetings with Arthur Danahar on the Tommy Farr-Red Burman bill at Harringay. Danahar took the points decision, but the respected view of Boxing News reported that Craster deserved at least a draw.

Harry beat Lefty Flynn on a disqualification, but then was frustrated by being held to draws in two ensuing meetings with the same opponent, despite flooring Flynn in the eighth round of their third clash. When they met for a fourth time, Flynn used his height and extra reach to jab Harry to defeat.

Craster met Danahar for the second time in October 1939. This fight was unique because it was staged to raise funds for the British Red Cross and was sponsored by Frances Day, of stage and screen fame. In fact the contest took place at the Hotel Splendide in London's Park Lane in front of a highly select crowd of only 80 people.

The show was still a financial success, thanks mainly to the amount of cash subscribed by the 80 celebrities, who included members of the Royal Family. Craster and Danahar made sure that their hosts were not disappointed by putting on a sparkling show, with Danahar taking the verdict on points.

They met again over ten rounds, just before Christmas, and again Danahar won on points.

Harry joined the RAF in February, 1940, but continued boxing and was outpointed in March in a non-title fight by welterweight champion Ernie Roderick.

On January 20, 1941, Harry met the legendary former world junior lightweight champion Jack Kid Berg at a packed Cambridge Theatre in London. Harry had a six pounds weight advantage and fought out of his skin. It looked as though he had done enough to take the decision. So there was uproar when Kid Berg's arm was raised by the referee after the final bell. As a result the referee needed a police escort before he could safely leave the ring.

Craster was posted to Egypt with the RAF as a sergeant PTI instructor and met up with a young flyweight from Islington called Terry Allen. Craster, who was in Allen's corner for most of his Middle East fights, had no doubts that his protege would be a future champion. His prophecy was fulfilled when Allen went on to win British and world titles.

Harry's last professional contest took place in February, 1942, at the Albert Hall in London. He was outpointed by Harry Watson, despite causing a large cut over his opponent's left eye in the final round which left Watson struggling to hang on.

After the war, Harry quit the competitive game. He had put on two stones in weight and was not tall enough to step further up the weight divisions. He became boxing instructor to the students at Bede College in Durham and held that post until 1952 when he resigned because he was tired of all the travelling. He worked in various jobs but was best known as a United bus driver in Middlesbrough.

Harry Craster died in September, 1993, at the age of 77, and was survived by his two sons, Derrick and John.

Esther Cruice
Athletics

ESTHER Cruice stormed on to the world stage at the age of 15 when she shattered the world record in the 400 metres at the 1992 Barcelona Paralympics.

The strong running athlete from High Street, Moorsholm, cut three seconds off the previous best world time. She returned home with three medals, having finished second in both the 100 and 200 metres. Esther, who suffers from cerebral palsy, qualified for her second Paralympics in Atlanta in 1996 and flew out with high hopes of another gold medal winning performance. But she suffered a major disappointment when the 400 metres was cancelled and she finished fourth in both sprints.

However, she completed a memorable hat trick after being selected to compete in her third successive Paralympics in Sydney 2000.

Esther was born in Bromsgrove on March 31, 1977, but moved to Moorsholm with her family at the age of three. She attended Rosecroft School in Loftus, where she was a keen netball and hockey player.

She was briefly a member at Mandale Harriers, but then switched to Middlesbrough and Cleveland Harriers, where she was coached by Rita Carless. Esther first emerged as a quality athlete in 1991 at the age of 14, when she won two medals at an international meeting in the Olympic stadium in Barcelona. The youngest member of the squad, she raced to a silver medal in the 400 metres and bronze in the 200.

Esther continued to train with the British squad for the Paralympics the following year and was rewarded by winning her place on the plane.

She warmed up in superb style with a phenomenal performance in the British Sports Association for the Disabled national senior athletics championships at Hull.

Esther grabbed three golds in the sprints and broke three national records at the same time, adding to her tally by taking a silver in the team event.

Cruice was later named BSAD female athlete of the year. She enjoyed a remarkable trip to Barcelona in 1992,

receiving a standing ovation from the 60,000 crowd in the Olympic Stadium as she blasting her way around the track to take the gold medal in the 400 metres. She smashed the world and Paralympic records in the process.

Cruice's golden run slashed almost three seconds off the previous world best, setting a new record time of 1.09.92. It was one of three medal winning runs because Esther also took the silver medals in both the 100 and 200 metres.

Esther returned to England and soon picked up another major award, when being named as the Yardley Gold Parallel sportswoman of the year at a luncheon in the Park Lane Hotel in London. She received an engraved Waterford crystal decanter trophy and £1,000 cheque.

Esther continued to dominate the sprint events in Britain and then made a huge impact in the IPC world athletics championships in Berlin in 1994 when she repeated her Paralympics performances by taking the 400 metres gold in addition to winning silver in both sprints.

There is no doubt that Esther would have won a medal in the 400 metres in the Atlanta Paralympics two years later, and she might even have gone close to breaking her world record. But the event was cancelled at the last minute because it had attracted only a small number of competitors.

Cruice still had the opportunity to earn medals in both the 100 and 200 metres, but her disappointment at being unable to run in her specialist event over 400 metres boiled over, and she finished a disappointing fourth in both finals.

Two years later, Esther banished all her frustrations by breaking her own world record in winning the 400 metres gold in the IPC world championships in Birmingham. She knocked ninth tenths of a second off her previous best.

She was also delighted to take the gold in the 200 metres, especially as she defeated her main rival Alison Quinn from Australia over the distance for the

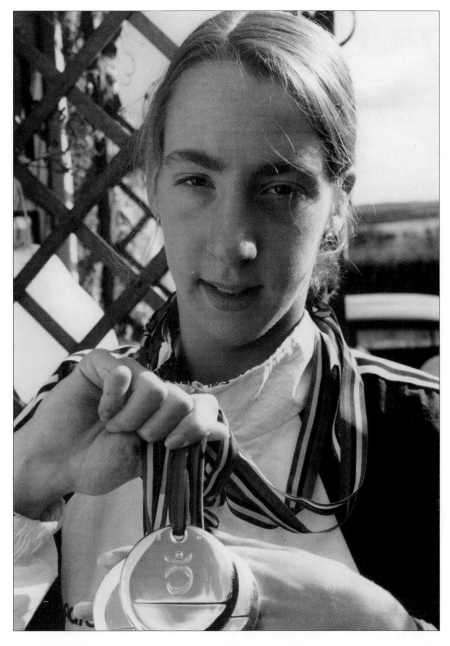

Esther Cruice burst onto the athletics scene as a 15-year-old when, at the Barcelona Paralymics of 1992, she shattered the 400 metre world record by an incredible three seconds to win the gold medal.

first time. The duo had competed against each other on several previous occasions, but Quinn had always come out on top.

Cruice completed a medal winning treble by taking the bronze in the 100 metres.

However in 1999 she suffered a blow losing her 400 metres world record when finishing third in the European Championship Finals at Nottingham.

Even so, Esther achieved a new personal best of 1min 08.3sec, but this was bettered by more than a second by the Portuguese winner. Esther had held the previous world record for a remarkable seven years.

Although she took the silver medals in both sprints, she has since dropped the 100 metres to concentrate on the other two events.

Cruice now lives in Nottingham, where she is coached by her long term advisor Colin Rains. She is a world class funded performer, which allows her to undertake a committed and detailed training programme. She works as a team administrator for Sport England in their East Midlands headquarters in Nottingham.

Esther completed her winter programme on a high note by taking second place in the world cross country challenge in Portugal and in July 2000 was chosen to represent Great Britain in her third Paralympics in Sydney. A remarkable achievement.

Allison Curbishley
Athletics

ALLISON Curbishley is one of Teesside's top sporting talents, having won a silver medal in the 400 metres in the Commonwealth Games in Kuala Lumpur and promising to bring more honours to the area in future years.

She came to the fore as a teenager, becoming a regular international with Great Britain and Scotland, and running for Britain in the Atlanta Olympics 4x400 metres relay while still only 20-years-old.

Allison was born in Newcastle, but is a Teessider through and through, having grown up in Stockton and attended Ian Ramsey School in the town.

A member of Middlesbrough and Cleveland Harriers, she first emerged as a runner of great potential in 1991 when winning the English Schools 300 metres hurdles final at the first attempt, setting a personal best in the process.

Ironically, it was her first serious competitive attempt at the distance, having previously concentrated on the 800 metres, an event in which she had twice failed to reach the final in the schools championships.

The 300 metres hurdles run earned Allison international honours, when she was called up by the Great British and also the Scottish junior teams. Although born in England, she had elected to race for Scotland, much to the delight of her Scottish dad Bill. Allison retained her schools crown at Hull quite comfortably the following year, despite problems with a knee injury, and then stepped up another gear to finish third in the AAAs Under-20 Championships over 400 metres hurdles at Stoke, which sent her straight into the senior rankings at No.18.

Her hard-running performances earned her valuable experience in the English Schools team which competed in a 22-nations competition in Alba, Italy, while she qualified for a place in the European Junior Championships at San Sebastian in Spain soon afterwards. Allison finished seventh in the 400 metres hurdles final in the Europeans, having run a personal best time of 59.04sec in the semi finals. The

Allison Curbishley overcame her long term injury problems to compete in the 2000 Sydney Olympics.

performance was astonishing because it made her the fifth best British senior hurdler of all time.

Under the guidance of coaches Ron and Jean Simmons, Allison was making tremendous strides. In February, 1994, she smashed the British record in winning the 400 metres at the AAAs Under-20 Indoor Championships in Birmingham, clocking 54.78sec.

In the summer Allison, now running in the Edinburgh Woollen Mill club colours, finished second in the 400 metres hurdles in the Scottish Senior Championships at Meadowbank.

The big target of the year was the world junior championships in Lisbon, but Allison suffered a personal nightmare when she fell at the sixth hurdle in the semi-finals. There was another blow soon afterwards, when she failed to make the Scottish team for the Commonwealth Games in Victoria, Canada.

The 1995 season was relatively quiet because Allison's training was hampered by a foot injury, though she did pick up her first international medal when helping the British 4x400 relay team to finish third in the European junior championships.

Curbishley emerged beyond dispute as a top national talent in 1996, after finishing a close third behind second placed Sally Gunnell in the AAAs Indoor Championships 400 metres final at Birmingham, clocking another PB.

Now working with sprints and hurdles coach Keith Antoine in Birmingham, where she was taking a university sports science degree, Allison discovered soon afterwards that she would be part of the British 4x400 metres relay squad for the Atlanta Olympics.

It was a great experience, though the racing ended in disappointment when the girls failed to reach the relay final. They were pipped on the line by the French. Allison ran an excellent second leg, moving Britain up from fourth to third place, but Britain's last leg runner Georgina Olidapo was just edged into fourth place in the last few metres. The first three teams qualified for the final.

Curbishley was concentrating more on the 400 metres at this stage, and broke her personal best when running for Great Britain in an Under-23 international against France and Germany at Hexham in June, 1997. Her new time was 51.79sec.

The new PB did not last long. Allison travelled to Finland for the European Under-23 Championships and stormed to victory in the 400 metres in a new Scottish record of 50.85. She also won a gold medal in the relay, running the anchor leg for Britain.

Curbishley lowered her PB further in the heats of the world championships in Athens, when she stormed home in 50.78sec. However the Stockton girl could not repeat the effort in the semi-finals, and was edged out. There was some consolation when she helped the relay team reach the final, where they finished sixth.

Curbishley, who had progressed well under new coach Malcolm Arnold, put the cap on a fine season by flying out to Sicily to land the gold medal in the 400 metres in the World Student Games. Following the retirement of world star Sally Gunnell, Allison was now Britain's brightest hope over the distance and was rated No.5 in Europe.

The following year, Allison reached the final of the the 400 metres final in the European Championships in Budapest, finishing out of the medal placings. However she came back with a medal when she helped the relay team finish in third place.

The scene was now set for Allison to compete in her first Commonwealth Games in Kuala Lumpur.

The Stockton runner was highly fancied to win a medal, and looked impressive in the qualifying heats. She was always in with a chance of winning the 400 metres final, and ran the race of her life. However she had to settle for the silver medal, blasting across the line in a new personal best and Scottish record of 50.71sec, just behind the top Jamaican Sandie Richards. Curbishley achieved her success despite feeling ongoing problems with her right knee cartilage, and the decision was made afterwards to have an operation.

Allison made a rapid recovery and soon was back on the track, taking second place behind world champion Cathy Freeman in the Sydney Grand Prix meeting in February, 1999.

However Allison continued to endure problems with the knee and flew to Denver for a second operation, which was carried out by leading specialist Dr Richard Steadman. It meant that the season was virtually wiped out, though she was still on course to realise her ambition of running in the Sydney Olympics.

Allison's Olympic dream was still alive when she returned to international competition at the Gateshead Stadium in July 2000 for the European Cup final as a member of the 400m relay team. A few weeks later, and obviously under a great deal of pressure, Allison finished a very creditable second in the 400metres at the British Olympic trials and was automatically selected for Sydney 2000.

Paul Curran
Cycling

THORNABY-born Paul Curran emerged as Britain's No.1 amateur cyclist in the mid-1980s, raced in two Olympic Games, and was a double gold medallist at the Commonwealth Games in Edinburgh in 1986.

A hot competitor who set out to win every race in which he competed, Curran also won a bronze medal at the Commonwealth Games in Brisbane in 1982, and finished fourth and sixth in consecutive Milk Races.

He was honoured by winning the Cleveland Sports Personality of the Year award in 1986 and later joined the professional ranks, continuing to race at the highest level well into the 1990s.

Paul, who was born on January 15, 1961, began cycling mainly in time trials while still a pupil at Dene School. He joined his local club, Stockton Wheelers, and competed in their colours until 1984, when he moved to Manchester Wheelers.

He first came to national prominence as a 16-year-old in 1977, taking honours in both the hard and grass track championship of the English Schools Cycling Association. Then he earned a place in the British junior track team for an international against Holland at the Clairville Stadium in Middlesbrough

Curran also finished third in the Road Time Trial Council's national junior best all-rounder competition. He repeated the feat the following year, and also took second place in the national junior 4k pursuit.

While still a teenager, Paul graduated to the British Cycling Federation's Olympic track squad and made his senior debut for Britain in the European Cup 50k points race in Spain in 1980.

An apprentice turner at ICI Wilton, Paul gained invaluable international experience the following year when selected for the British team which contested the Japanese track championships at Maebashi. Further British selection for races in Frankfurt, Dortmund and Milan quickly followed.

Curran gained his first national title when winning the British Madison Championship at Leicester along with his experienced teammate Stuart Morris from Guisborough.

Having completed his apprenticeship at ICI, Paul served four months as a fully qualified turner but then gave up his job in 1982 to concentrate on a double tilt to try to win selection for the world championships and the Commonwealth Games.

Eventually he was called up by Britain for the 4,000 metres team pursuit for the world championships at Leicester, and warmed up in style by becoming British 50k points champion in a fiercely contested race, also at Leicester. He completed a double by retaining the British Madison crown, though with Manchester Wheeler Hugh Cameron as his partner on this occasion.

Paul went on to finish 13th in the world championship points race and was the top British rider. He had done enough to win his England place for the team pursuit at the Commonwealth Games in Brisbane.

It turned out to be a highly successful trip to Australia because Paul brought back a bronze medal, helping the four-man English team to beat the Canadians by two and a half seconds in the ride-off for third place. In the semis, England had been beaten by eventual winners Australia.

Curran was back in Japan in October, 1983, winning the points race and finishing third in the 75 miles road race, while helping Britain into second place in the 4,000 metres track pursuit.

In June, 1984, Paul, now with Manchester Wheelers, realised his greatest ambition when he was called into Great Britain's 16-man squad for the Los Angeles Olympics.

He prepared with a stint of high-altitude training with the British squad in Colorado.

However Curran's hopes of an individual gold in Los Angeles ended in disappointment when he crashed out of the points final. He was among the leading group, around 30 laps from the finish, when a West German rider fell in front of him, and Paul was unable to avoid

August 1986: Surrounded by celebratory bunting at his parents Thornaby home, Paul Curran proudly displays the two cycling gold medals he won at the Edinburgh Commonwealth Games.

the collision. Despite remounting, all chances of a medal had gone.

In the team pursuit, Britain had been fancied to do well, but they did not progress beyond the qualification round, which was a major disappointment to the whole team.

The following year Paul switched his attentions from the track to road racing and was called up for the England amateur squad for the Milk Race, which kicked off at Bournemouth in May and finished in Birmingham. It was a new experience for the Thornaby

man, but he made a massive impact, being up among the leaders all the way through the race. Eventually he finished fourth overall, 5min 24sec down on Belgian winner Eric van Lancker.

He might have gone close to winning the event, but for losing five minutes in one of the stages, from Richmond to Huddersfield, when van Lancker and an American rider escaped. Although Curran was in the chasing pack, they could not made up the crucial leeway in pouring rain and the break proved to be a winning one. During the race, Curran also held the

King of the Mountains jersey for three days.

Soon afterwards Paul returned to the track to retain his British 50k points title at Leicester.

Curran had now achieved a high level of confidence and maturity. He was a tough competitor who had a good chance of winning every race he entered. He won the Manx International in June, before recording a tremendous victory in the Tour of Normandy, despite suffering from a slow puncture on the final day. Soon afterwards he competed for Great Britain in the world championships in Italy, finishing in the bunch.

Early in 1986, Curran turned down the opportunity to turn professional with the Raleigh team because he wanted to take part in the Commonwealth Games. At that time, both the Commonwealth and Olympic Games were both strictly for amateurs only. So, sticking rigidly to his amateur status, he warmed up in style by winning the six-day Circuit de Mimes event in France, and then finished sixth in the Milk Race, which started in Birmingham and ended in London.

Curran's decision to remain as an amateur paid huge dividends. In the July, he achieved his great moment in cycling when he picked up two gold medals at the Commonwealth Games in Edinburgh.

The weather throughout the two weeks of the Games was dreadful, but it didn't cause too many problems for Curran. The Thornaby man kicked off by helping the England team to win the 100k time trial, storming home ahead of New Zealand, with Northern Ireland third. The four English riders stayed in perfect file until virtually the end of the race when Keith Reynolds lost touch. The other two gold medallists in the British team were Deno Davie and Alan Gornall.

Then Curran produced a sensational sprint finish to win the gold medal in the 105 miles road race, pipping New Zealander Brian Fowler into second place.

Once again riding in pouring rain, Paul made his break for glory after 84 miles when he broke away from the leading pack to build up a 30 seconds lead. He was caught by Fowler and Australian Jeff Leslie with four miles to go, but had kept something in reserve and overcame a painful bout of cramp to finish like a bullet over the final 200 metres to take the gold.

It was a great moment in his life. When he returned to Thornaby he discovered that his parents' home had been bedecked with Union Jacks and there was a fine welcome awaiting from the whole street.

However there was no time for Curran to rest on his laurels. Soon after returning home, he was off to

Belgium for an eight-day stage race, winning one of the stages. Then he spent three weeks at Colorado Springs in preparation for the world championships in Colorado. Both Curran and Dino Davie were in with a chance of a medal in the championships and were in a group of around 15 riders who tried to make a break. However they were caught by the chasing pack, while climbing up a steep hill with less than a mile and a half to go, and missed out in the final shake-up.

Over the following two years, Paul continued to stay at peak fitness as part of his build-up to the road race in the the Seoul Olympics. In fact 1987 was one of his most productive years, winning the national hill climbing championship, the national road racing championship and finally the national team pursuit championship. He was also a clear winner of the Star Trophy series after winning seven of the nine events.

Curran raced very well in the world championships in Austria, and once again was in with a chance of a medal. He was up with the leading pack along with Dino Davie with 13 miles to go, when he was hit by an attack of cramp and fell back. Davie went on to finish sixth.

However a collision with a car in July, 1988, threatened to end his Olympic hopes. Curran was rushed to hospital after being thrown through the windscreen of a car on the North Yorkshire Moors. He had been riding down a hill with a group of cyclists when a car pulled out from the left, colliding with Curran and another rider. He suffered several deep facial cuts after crashing through the windscreen, and needed a massive 64 stitches and a skin graft.

At first it was thought that Paul would not recover in time to fly out to Seoul. But he had other ideas. He was back in full training 13 days after the accident and warmed up for the Olympics by winning the Tour of the Peaks Classic at Buxton.

Paul flew out East with genuine hopes of bringing back an Olympic medal to Teesside. He was fully primed, and riding to the peak of his ability, having made a full recovery from the accident. However he encountered more bad luck in the 123-miles road race in Seoul when one of his spokes snapped as he was about to enter the final 12-mile lap in one of the leading positions.

Curran had led an eight-man splinter group out of the main pack shortly before the loss of his spoke, which left him totally frustrated because he knew that he was handily placed for a medal. Paul was forced to call into the pits for a new bike and, although he managed to get

Teesside's Paul Curran leads the chasing pack as the Milk Race passes through Middlesbrough in 1985.

back into the main pack, it was too late to win a medal. He eventually finished 24 seconds behind the winner, Olaf Ludwig of East Germany.

In December, 1988, Curran finally took the plunge and turned professional with the Percy Bilton team. A bout of chickenpox affected his bid to make an initial impact, but he flew out with the team for a major stage race in America in May and finished 15th overall, after taking third place in what turned out to be the race winning stage.

Paul returned to England to finish a creditable eighth in the Milk Race, and also won the professional criterium championships at Cardiff. He was in superb form at this time finishing sixth in the gruelling Kelloggs stage race from Dundee to Westminster, including taking second place in the prologue.

Curran suffered a blow when the Percy Bilton team folded within 15 months but he was able to link up with the Crown Chase team and again competed in the Milk Race, winning one of the stages. However this team also folded, leaving Paul unsponsored for the rest of the year.

In 1991 he decided to revert to amateur status and linked up with his former club Manchester Wheelers.

The next year he switched clubs to Dinnington RC.

He suffered a bodyblow when he went down with pneumonia in the March and was seriously ill for some time. It was July before he was fully fit again and able to begin competing in major races. However his major achievement that year was winning one of the Star Trophy races at Solihull.

In February 1993, Curran joined up with a Dinnington pro-am team which flew out to Central America to take part in the gruelling Tour of Mexico. However he was struck down by illness and retired after only two days. Later that year Paul won the British motor-paced track title at Leicester, where riders are initially led by a motor bike over two 25k heats. It was to be the first of four consecutive wins by Curran in the event.

In March, 1994, Curran helped the British five-man team finish seventh overall in the Rapport Tour of South Africa. The heat took its toll over the 13-day race, but Curran coped well and won the 55-miles tenth stage.

The following year he spent a lot of time riding on the Continent, particularly in indoor events in Zurich, Dortmund and Nuremburg, where he rode well.

Curran had joined the Optimum Performance team in 1994 and stayed with them for three years, operating as rider-manager in the final two years.

However Paul's 20-year career as one of the top riders ever produced by Britain came to a sudden and disastrous end on September 15, 1996. He was taking part in a road race at Carlisle when a motorbike collided with the back of his machine and he suffered a broken spine.

Paul was rushed to hospital in Carlisle and was later transferred to Newcastle General Hospital, where an operation was performed. Eventually he was moved to the spinal unit at Hexham.

Paul spent a total of nine weeks in hospital, but was grateful for the fact that his injuries did not produce major debilitating effects. However he did suffer permanent damage to his spinal cord, which meant an immediate end to his racing career,

He did return to cycling to manage the Ambrosia Desserts team in 1998, but has never competed in a race since the accident.

Today he enjoys riding on a mountain bike, where the more upright position is easier to cope with, and also occasionally goes swimming.

Paul now lives in Ingleby Barwick with his wife Jackie and son Karl, who was three years old in 2000.

Freddie Dixon
Motor Sport

BETWEEN the two world wars, one Teesside man gained the respect and admiration of the entire motoring world for his courage and fearless determination to win at all costs. His name was Freddie Dixon.

Speedway tracks and motor circuits have their big name riders and drivers, and the pit lanes their top mechanics. Daredevil Dixon encompassed the lot. He was a legendary champion, gifted engineer and charismatic record breaker all in one.

At Donington, Brooklands and in the TTs on the Isle of Man, Freddie's name became the by-word for guts and tenacity. He broke many world records time and time again, and raced all over Europe with great success.

In 1923 he won the very first sidecar TT race in his self-modified Douglas outfit as well as finishing third in the Senior TT. Four years later he achieved the unique feat of being the only rider to win both a solo and a sidecar TT when winning the Junior TT on an HRD. He remains the only man in history to lap Brooklands at 130mph in a car of less than two litres.

Frederick William Dixon was born at 31, Alliance Street, Stockton-on-Tees, on April 21, 1892, one of eight children of John and Martha Dixon. He began his working life upon leaving school at the age of 13 at the cycle shop run by Bob Pennock in Bridge Street, but later moved to Kit McAdam's motor repair shop in Yarm Lane, and then on to another of McAdam's shops in Linthorpe Road, Middlesbrough.

As a 17-year-old garage apprentice, Freddie had developed a love of engines and he paid £6 for a Rex motor cycle left for scrap. Within weeks he had restored it to his own specifications and had it running at hair-raising speeds. It was typical of what was to follow throughout the rest of his life.

From the moment he raced his first bike, this stocky, single minded man was tireless and uncompromising in his pursuit of excellence on speed tracks and motor circuits.

In 1910 he joined Middlesbrough Motor Club and was soon making his mark on local speed trial and hillclimb events. His first Isle of Man Tourist Trophy race was in 1912. For this he rode a Cleveland Precision bike manufactured in Middlesbrough by Egerton Price, who later became mayor of the town in 1922.

During the Great War, Freddie served in the Army Service Corps for four years. His qualities of drive and leadership were quickly recognised and he rose to the rank of staff sergeant major at Grove Park motor transport department.

When he returned to Teesside after the end of the hostilities, Dixon opened his own motor business just off Ayresome Street. Shortly afterwards he moved to bigger premises at Park Street garage in Linthorpe Road.

In addition to selling and repairing machines for his customers, Freddie rebuilt and raced motorcycles at every opportunity and quickly made a name for himself. Manufacturers vied for his services and soon he was riding for Brough Superior and HRD, going on to assist both companies with engineering and design.

In 1919 Dixon earned himself national headlines for the first time when he upset the apple cart by displacing the Scottish favourite to win the Sand Racing Championships at St Andrews.

He became the star member of Middlesbrough Motor Club, representing the club throughout the length and breadth of the country, racing on Harley Davidson, Indian, Brough Superior and Douglas bikes.

Freddie returned to TT racing on the Isle of Man in 1920, as a member of the Indian team, and finished a highly creditable 12th. In the same year he won the Scottish Speed Championship, both solo and with sidecar, and the Sutton Bank Hill Climb.

A breathtaking catalogue of success followed. In 1921 he was riding a big twin American Harley Davidson machine in the 500 miles race at Brooklands, when he suffered a puncture after 300 miles. He was thrown off the bike at 100 mph and rolled for many feet along the concrete track.

Miraculously, gallant Freddie was unharmed. He picked himself up and ignored all offers of assistance to make his way to the pits with his stricken bike, where a new tyre was fitted. Then he resumed the race and went on to complete the full 500 miles, finishing in second place. After the race he discovered that he had set a new 200 miles record. It was the kind of stuff that legendary heroes are made of.

In the same year Freddie produced another sterling performance to finish runner up in the Senior TT at the Isle of Man on an Indian 500cc machine. He took the same bike to the Continent to race in the inaugural Belgian Grand Prix at Francorchamps, and finished third behind Hubert Hassell's Norton over the 188 miles of the race.

The following year Dixon made another strong attempt to win the Senior TT. He was racing neck and neck for first place, just 14 miles from the finish, when a tyre burst. His TT hopes were over for another 12 months.

In 1923 Freddie hit the jackpot by becoming an international sporting celebrity. He captured the world speed record for any class of motor cycle, achieving 106.8mph along the Bois de Boulogne in France on an eight-valve Harley Davidson 1198cc V-twin. This bike had been shipped over to England from the United States specially for Dixon to ride, because the manufacturers were well aware of his increasing prowess in the sport in worldwide circles.

At this time there was no stopping Dixon. In the same year he stormed to victory in both the French and

Isle of Man 1927. Freddie Dixon is surrounded by young admirers after winning the Junior Tourist Trophy Race on his H.R.D. It was his first and only individual TT victory.

Belgian grand prix. He also took first place in the inaugural Isle of Man sidecar TT, bringing home his self-designed Douglas outfit at a speed of 53.15mph despite suffering a broken frame tube two miles from the finish. Freddie's famous banking invention on his sidecar could be raised or lowered to suit the bends. His passenger was Walter Denny.

Dixon made another determined attempt to win the Senior TT at the Isle of Man and rode a great race over the 226 miles, but had to settle for third place.

Freddie set up two new world records at Brooklands in 1924, in addition to breaking two British records, for standing start both solo and with sidecar on his Harley Davidson. At the Isle of Man TT, he set the fastest lap of 63mph on his Douglas and finished third in the Senior event. He would almost certainly have won the TT but for a stroke of bad luck. He was leading by five minutes at the end of the fourth lap, when he skidded through oil lost by another rider and fell off.

Dixon hoped for better luck in the sidecar TT and set the fastest lap of 53.24, but had to retire from this race as well. Worse was to follow. He was leading in the Belgian Grand Prix on his Indian when his machine caught fire. A few flames were not going to unsettle Freddie, even if they did affect the performance of his machine. He ignored the fire and completed the race, finishing fourth. In the same month, July, he was second in the French Grand Prix.

The peak of Dixon's motor cycle career came in 1925, when he established no less than 30 world records, many of them at Brooklands. He was already known as "Fearless Freddie" and "The Wild Indian". Now he earned a new nickname, "Win Or Bust Dixon", which was to stay with him for the remainder of his career.

The year of 1926 was a big one in Freddie's life because he married his sweetheart, a Middlesbrough girl called Margaret Thew who was known to everybody as Dolly. Later they had a daughter, Jean.

The following year Dixon was making headlines again. He set a new record speed of 67.19mph on his HRD in winning the Junior event in the TT race at the Isle of Man. He completed the 264 miles and 300 yards course in three hours, 55 minutes and 54 seconds. However luck was on his side on this occasion because his arch rival Wal Handley, riding a Rex Acme, dropped out through mechanical problems when leading on the last lap.

In the same year, Freddie suffered a nasty experience in France when he was testing a big machine which

George Brough had built with a view to attacking the motor cycle speed record. The back tyre suddenly stripped away and was flailing in the air when Freddie was racing at more than 120mph. It was a life threatening situation so he deliberately rode off the track to try to lessen any effect of a crash. Freddie managed to halve the speed of the bike by riding through long grass before finally coming off as the bike slowed dramatically just in front of a huge block of concrete. Again he walked away unharmed. The following day he was back on the bike, undeterred, and established a new record of 130mph.

In another trip to the Continent, Freddie finished second in the Swiss Grand Prix on his HRD, while he recorded a notable achievement at Brooklands when notching the first ever lap of more than 100mph with motor cycle and sidecar, on his Brough Superior.

It seemed that there was nothing that Freddie could not achieve. So it came as a major shock to fans of the sport when Freddie announced that he was quitting motor cycle racing in 1928. He was at the peak of his career, but he wanted to explore other avenues and spend more time developing engines. He continued working for Douglas and designed and marketed a water cooled four cylinder motor cycle, though it was not a success, largely as a result of the Depression which took hold in the early 1930s.

By this time Dixon was also working on motor cars, and trying to develop a revolutionary new engine.

Finally, in 1932, Freddie returned to competitive racing - in a motor car. Over the next few years he was to become one of the top drivers in the world.

His first car was a Riley Nine, which he bought from former racer Victor Gillow. The vehicle was stripped down and rebuilt to the Dixon design, with new carburettors and camshafts. It was nothing to look at from the outside, and Dixon was laughed at by members of the official Riley racing team when he first unveiled his new project. However Freddie ensured that the laughter soon stopped.

Dixon made an immediate impact in his little Riley, which earned the popular nickname of the Biscuit Tin, in the prestigious Ulster TT on the legendary Ards circuit in 1932. He was leading after 25 of the 30 laps and looked certain to win, when the car spun off the course at Quarry Corner and ended up in a rhubarb field. Freddie was unhurt but his mechanic, Len Ainsley from Middlesbrough, was taken to hospital with a lacerated jaw. Dixon admitted later that he had dozed off at the wheel because he had stayed up working on the car all night!

It has been said of Freddie: "He was no angel. He worked assistant mechanics into the ground. The men slept on the garage floor beside stripped down motors. Often they wouldn't go home for days. Nowadays people wouldn't stand for it."

However Freddie was a winner and he knew how to prepare properly for his races.

In 1933 he carried off the honours in the gruelling Mannin Beg race at the Isle of Man. Then he was controversially disqualified from fourth place in the Ulster TT race for a breach of rules, having finished the course with his exhaust pipe in the back of the car instead of where it should be. Len Ainsley was spotted holding it together with his bare hands and a couple of towels!

As the Thirties progressed and Dixon hit new heights, his mind turned to thoughts of a new land speed record. His ambition was to break the British Empire record of 217mph. Then he intended to visit Daytona Beach, hoping to slash Sir Malcolm Campbell's existing world land speed record of 272.46mph.

Freddie's land speed record hopes became a reality when he purchased the Silver Bullett, a 24 cylinder Sunbeam which speedster Kaye Don had driven in an earlier attempt on the Daytona record. Dixon bought the car from Jack Field of Southport, and spent many long hours working on the vehicle in the hope of being able to launch an assault on the record.

It didn't happen, and neither did the Daytona bid. The Silver Bullett was stripped down to the very last nut and bolt, and completely renovated. Then it was renovated again. For several years the car remained locked up in his garage, regularly being finely tuned. But Dixon never raced the Silver Bullett. Despite many long hours of effort, he could not tune the car to his own high expectations.

However Sir Malcolm was always aware that if anybody might challenge for his world record, then it would be Fearless Freddie Dixon. Sir Malcolm always retained the highest respect for Freddie, describing him as having "the heart of a lion".

Dixon made an ambitious bid to try to win the Le Mans 24-hour endurance race along with his co-driver Cyril Paul in 1934, but they had to settle for third place in their six-cylinder Riley, 16 laps behind the winning Alfa Romeo.

In the same year Freddie was involved in a bad crash at Starkey corner at Donington when he left the track and hit an embankment. He was driving at 100 miles an hour when the brakes and the transmission, both of which were experimental Dixonised parts, failed.

It was a close squeak. Dixon was dragged unconscious from the vehicle just seconds before it burst into flames. He was rushed off to hospital in an ambulance and spent several weeks in Derbyshire Royal Infirmary with a fractured jaw, serious internal injuries and several broken ribs.

However he was made of extra special stuff, was Freddie Dixon. Not only did he make a full and rapid recovery, but he defied medical advice to return to the racetrack and win the 500 miles race at Brooklands in the same year.

In an interview in the Sunday Chronicle, Freddie said: "The doctors thought I had been battered about too badly to want to get up, and imagined my nerve might have suffered. But I knew better. I worried them so much that they were glad to let me out in a month. I'm told I ought to have stayed three."

On February 10, 1935, Dixon was badly injured again, this time in an air crash. He was a passenger in a light aircraft, flying from Leeming to Middlesbrough and piloted by Herbert Barker of Linthorpe, which crashed on to Middlesbrough Golf Club's links.

For several days he remained in a critical condition in a private ward at North Ormesby Hospital with head injuries and a broken upper jaw. There were grave fears that he would not pull through. However Freddie was a battler in everything he did. It was no surprise that the newspapers were claiming that he had more lives than a cat. Gradually he began to improve thanks to expert medical attention and the bedside support of his wife Dolly.

Dixon was eventually moved to a public ward, but spent 30 days in hospital. He was told to rest up at home for some weeks, but defied all warnings by making a swift return to the sport after obtaining a doctor's certificate.

Remarkably, he showed no signs of his injuries when astounding the world of racing yet again by winning the final of the British Mountain Handicap in terrible racing conditions at Brooklands. His little aluminium Riley started in the middle of the field and he won by 400 yards at an average speed of 74.68mph from the speedier Bugatti driven by Flight Lieut. Staniland Eccles. When the race ended, Freddie went on tearing around the track at colossal speed for a further three laps. He

Isle of Man 1927. Always a keen innovator, Freddie Dixon competes in the Senior TT on his H.R.D. which was equipped with an American style flat foot rest.

was carpeted by the stewards afterwards, though they accepted his dubious explanation that he wasn't aware the race was over! More likely he was making a point to the whole of motor racing.

The non-stop series of accidents had left the almost bionic Dixon with many scars. In fact he had only one of his natural teeth remaining in his mouth. But he was still the undisputed master, and was virtually unstoppable at this time, even though he was well into his Forties. He won the Tourist Trophy at Ards in both 1935 and 1936. This made him the first and only person ever to win TTs on two, three and four wheels. Then he came home first in the Brooklands 500 miles event again in 1936.

Another attempt to complete the Le Mans 24-hour race ended in disappointment when his Riley, which he was driving with co-driver Paul, caught fire while being refuelled and was completely destroyed. Neither driver was hurt in the incident.

There was another setback when Dixon got himself into trouble with the law. He was sentenced to three months in Durham Prison for a drink-driving offence and resisting arrest after being stopped by police on the corner of Albert Street and Bridge Street in Middlesbrough. To make matters worse, he was disqualified from driving for six months. However he earned remission for good conduct in prison and was released and returned to his home in Cambridge Road, Middlesbrough, just before Christmas after serving two months.

In 1937, Freddie announced that he was quitting racing to move south to Reigate in Surrey, leaving his brother Frank in charge of the garage business in Linthorpe Road. Freddie had accepted an offer to join the Riley Motor Company on a full-time basis and assist in the development of car engines and design. He was also to manage a team of racers for Riley, signing a contract for a "pretty substantial figure". It was a

Ulster 1935. Having made the successful switch from motorcylcles to racing cars, Freddie Dixon receives the plaudits from the crowd after this victory in Ireland. On his right is his mechanic Walter Maidens.

great opportunity for the man now regarded as one of the leading world experts on motor engines.

Dixon always retained hopes of designing a car with which he could contest the world land speed record. He carried out design work and engine tests on an unorthodox car called The Dart, which it was hoped would reach speeds of 400mph. He also developed the Dixon Special racing car, embodying a new type of independent front wheel suspension.

Unfortunately his ambitious hopes for The Dart failed to materialise, partly because Dixon had his driving licence revoked for two years at Surrey Quarter Sessions following another motoring offence. The incident occurred in Ewell, where he caused a collision between a taxi and another car.

It must have been a major bodyblow for a motoring genius like Freddie to be denied the right to jump behind a driving wheel. By the time he received his driving licence again, the Second World War had arrived. This put paid to any hopes which Freddie held of making a challenge for the land speed record.

However he continued to work in the motor industry throughout the rest of his working life and remained one of the acknowledged world authorities on engines. After the War he worked on developing new engines in an ambitious team of mechanics with Rex McCandless, which was financed by Harry Ferguson. Freddie eventually fell out with Ferguson, though the four wheel drive which the team had been working on eventually saw the commercial light of day as the Ferguson Formula, which was initially used in Jensons.

The world of racing lost one of its greatest pioneers when Freddie Dixon died suddenly in Battersea in London on November 5, 1956.

Bob Dunkley
Pistol Shooting

HOT shot Bob Dunkley used a keen eye, split second reaction and a lightning reflex to carry off a host of British and European practical pistol shooting championships throughout a near 20-year period.

He was virtually without equal in domestic competitions from the late 1970s to the mid 1990s, winning the British crown 17 years out of 18, and notching three European championships.

When he retired from the sport, he was introduced to the American based Western Action Shooting, and has gone on to take three world championships in his class in California in addition to finishing fourth overall on one occasion.

Bob was born in Middlesbrough on December 5, 1948, and grew up in West Lane. He attended Archibald School and was introduced to shooting at a very young age through his family.

His father Ted was a keen competitor, and was a founder member of Guisborough Gun Club and secretary of the Shell Mex-BP rifle club.

Bob joined the Guisborough club when he was 12 and won his first title in his first year as a teenager, when he was successful in the North of England 12-bore pigeon shoot which was held on a farm close to the Redcar Trunk Road.

Bob was able to develop his interest in shooting when he joined the Army Cadets, who were based at Brambles Farm. Teams of lads from the Cadets regularly travelled away to take part in regimental shooting events.

Dunkley usually used his father's shotguns and rifles, though he had his own airgun and practised firing at targets in his back garden every night after school.

As he competed regularly in Guisborough Gun Club competitions on Moorsholm range, Bob gradually took a greater interest in pistol shooting because of the different types of disciplines involved, and began organising competitions between local clubs.

After leaving school, he joined the parachute regiment of the Territorial Army, but did not look for a full career in the army.

Instead Bob became a motor mechanic, working initially for the Cleveland Car Company on Longlands roundabout before working for several other garages. Later he joined the Post Office as a technician and worked for them for 13 years.

By the mid-70s, Bob was now fully immersed in his love of combat and practical pistol shooting, which involved firing at multiple targets from different distances, all against the clock. The object for competitors was to find the perfect balance between accuracy and speed. Bob discovered that he had a natural talent for the sport and developed his skills with regular practice.

In 1978 Bob achieved his major breakthrough when he won the northern area title at Liverpool and then went on to take the national crown at Bisley, beating the previous champion of two years. Following this initial success he would remain almost unbeatable at domestic level until his last title win in 1995.

His first foray into the European Championships in 1979 also coincided with his first ever trip abroad. The event was held in Belgium and was not only a learning experience, but also a personal disaster. Bob suffered from a mix-up in target recognition and shot the 'hostages' instead of the intended targets, finishing well down the field.

However to his credit Bob did not one to dwell on his disappointment, and made a massive impact in his first world championships at Johannesburg when he finished eighth.

He had to take out a bank loan to finance his trip to South Africa, but it was worthwhile, especially as he came into contact with all the top shooters from America and South Africa and discovered that he could match them.

The experience was an invaluable part of Bob's learning curve because he went on to win the European championships three years in succession, in Sweden in 1981, Warminster, England, in 1983 and in France in

Bob Dunkley became a European pistol shooting champion without the help of any central funding.

1985. In the following three European finals, he finished runner-up.

In the early 80s, Dunkley's sporting achievements were recognised when he was runner-up to Sebastian Coe in the Vaux Sports Personality of the Year event. He was also presented with a Sports Aid Foundation award in 1984.

Bob continued to hold off the challenge of the up and coming young shooters by winning the British title in every year except 1987. In the year he missed out, on the British championship the event took place shortly after his wife had given birth to his son James and Bob had suffered several sleepless nights in a row. He then had to drive all the way to Devon to contest the event, but tiredness took its toll on his concentration and he failed to win.

Bob continued to compete in world championships but found not only the level of competition increasing all the time, but also that the hardware was becoming much more sophisticated. New guns were continually being introduced and Bob found it difficult to compete at world level, especially as he had to buy all his own

guns at around £3,000 a time.

Throughout the main part of his career, Bob financed every penny of his involvement in the sport, including paying for all his travelling and hotel bills. He also built up a large collection of guns. It was not until the later stages of his career that Dunkley received any kind of sponsorship, when he competed for three different teams at various times. They were the Springfield, Smith and Wesson and Tan Foglio teams.

Bob branched out to earn a living from his talents by opening a gun-shop business in Redcar in 1984 and initially did quite well. However the infamous Hungerford killings in 1988 gave guns a bad name and business was affected.

He closed the Redcar shop and opened another one in Middlesbrough in 1991, but then the Dunblain massacre led to Bob losing 80 per cent of his business overnight. To make ends meet, he diversified into selling Western style clothing.

Bob had discovered that he had a natural talent for teaching pistol shooting as well as taking part in it, and travelled throughout Europe and America giving coaching lessons.

In his later years as a practical pistol shooter, he also visited the United States twice a year to compete in the Desert Classic in Arizona and the American national open championships at Berryville, Illinois.

In 1994, Dunkley was introduced to Western Action Shooting during a trip to California. The sport involves using traditional 1890s guns from the Wild West, mainly Colts and Winchester rifles.

Bob was immediately bitten by the bug and now travels to the States every year to compete in the world championships, having achieved notable success.

Naturally, as a lover of gun sports, Bob has been frustrated at the criticisms and restrictions which have arrived in recent years, because he believes that enthusiasts are genuine, law abiding people.

He still maintains close links with local shooting, being a committee member at Guisborough Gun Club and secretary of the Tall Trees Gun Club, which normally shoots on the military ranges at Catterick Camp.

Bob, who has two sons from previous marriages, Spencer and James, lives in Redcar with his partner Denise Marshall, who is herself a crack shot. Denise has won the British practical pistol shooting title on three occasions, and has twice won her class in the Western Action Shooting Championships.

Mick Fenton
Football

MICK Fenton was a lethal home-grown striker who went on to spend more than 30 years with Middlesbrough, both as player and coach, and remains fifth on the club's all time list of goalscorers with 162 goals.

He won a single England international cap against Scotland in 1938, when playing against Scotland at Hampden Park, but would certainly have won more if not for the outbreak of the Second World War.

Like his Boro teammates and England contemporaries George Hardwick and Wilf Mannion, Fenton lost seven years of his playing career because of the War and was robbed of the chance of adding at least another 100 goals to his overall tally.

However his playing career spanned three decades and he made his final appearance for the Boro at the age of 36, by which time he had already joined the club's staff.

Michael Fenton was born in Portrack, Stockton-on-Tees, on October 30, 1913. He first played football for Princess Street Juniors before moving to one of Boro's nursery clubs, South Bank East End.

When he left school, he became a butcher, but his ultimate ambition was always to play football. After initially rejecting an approach from Wolverhampton Wanderers, Fenton signed professional forms for the Boro in March, 1933.

He did not have to wait long to make his first team debut, making it a memorable match when scoring in a 4-0 victory against Blackburn Rovers at Ayresome Park on the final day of that season.

Although he was only nine and half stones wringing wet with spindly legs, it was well documented at the time that Fenton was lightning quick and packed a powerful shot in both feet.

In only his eighth game for the first team, Fenton scored a hat trick in a 3-3 home draw with Preston North End. It was the first of several hat tricks.

However he did not fully establish himself in the first team until the 1936-37 season, when he grabbed 22 goals in 35 appearances to finish top scorer. This was the season when Boro showed a marked upturn in their fortunes in the Thirties, finishing seventh overall in the First Division.

Mick's teammates at the time included the likes of goalkeeper Dave Cumming, Billy Brown, Bobby Stuart, the legendary Scottish international Bobby Baxter, Billy Forrest and the top marksman of them all, England international George Camsell.

Fenton was again the top scorer the following season with 24 goals from 36 games, and in fact the only other Boro player to reach double figures was winger Tommy Cochrane, who grabbed ten goals. Such was Mick's immense contribution that Boro moved up a further two places to fifth position.

Mick recorded his best individual pre-war haul in May, 1938, when he grabbed all four goals in a 4-1 home win against West Bromwich Albion.

It wasn't long before Mick proceeded to take over the club's chief goalscoring mantle from Camsell. Fenton was the Boro's top scorer in the three years preceding World War Two with 1938-39 being his best ever season when he hit the back of the net an amazing 34 times from only 33 appearances.

His consistent goalscoring exploits were justly rewarded with an England cap against Scotland at Wembley in 1938, which the Scots won by 1-0. However the war years cruelly cut short any possibility of a long international career and this brief appearance for the national side turned out to be his only major honour for his country.

Mick did play in one wartime international against Wales, at The Hawthorns in October, 1945, which the Welsh won by 1-0.

During the war Fenton joined the technical training command of the RAF and saw service overseas in the North African campaign. On his own admission, however, he saw very little action and spent a good deal of the time playing football for a forces team called the Wanderers, which included such well-known

Like most players of his generation Mick Fenton's career was severely curtailed by World War Two.

players as Tom Finney of Preston North End.

After the cessation of hostilities in 1945, Mick was temporarily posted to Blackpool and played a few games for the Bloomfield Road club, who were so impressed with his ability that they wanted to sign him permanently. However Fenton returned to Teesside and resumed his league career with Boro in August, 1946, at the age of 33.

In the autumn of 1946 the Everton manager, Theo Kelly, made an audacious attempt to sign Fenton as a stop gap replacement for the legendary centre-forward Tommy Lawton, who had been transferred to Chelsea. Fenton declined the rather flattering approach from the

Toffees, preferring to spend the twilight of his career in familiar surroundings at Ayresome Park. In fact he finished up as Boro's leading scorer for the 1946-47 season with 28 goals. He wasted no time in showing that he had lost none of his old spark by scoring four goals in a 5-4 win against Stoke City, which was Boro's first home game after the war .

Mick was a leading player in Boro's magnificent FA Cup run in that same season, netting five goals to help the team reach the quarter-finals. Boro did not have a particularly good Cup record, but there was a belief that this was going to be Boro's year, and a ground attendance record of 53,025 turned up to watch the sixth round tie at home to Burnley on March 1, 1947. Several thousand more fans were locked outside of Ayresome Park.

Boro were leading 1-0 when Fenton seemed to have settled the tie when he scored from a free kick. But the linesman raised a flag for offside against Johnny Spuhler, and the 'goal' was disallowed. The huge crowd was then silenced when Burnley grabbed a late equaliser. Burnley won the replay at Turf Moor in further controversial circumstances, when the winning goal by Billy Morris was allowed to stand despite a clear handball in the goalmouth.

Fenton top scored the following season with 28 goals and again in 1948-49, though his goal tally fell to 12. He was still the only Boro player to reach double figures as the club narrowly avoided the drop to the Second Division.

In the late 1940s Mick took his FA coaching badge at Birmingham University and joined the club's backroom staff in January, 1949, where he worked, primarily with the reserves, although he was pressed into service for one last First Division appearance against Aston Villa in January, 1950, during an injury crisis. It was Mick's 269th appearance for the Boro, having scored 162 goals, which made him the club's third all-time scorer at the time behind Camsell and George Elliott.

After the war Fenton also turned his mind to business, combining his coaching duties at Ayresome Park with establishing a successful local newsagency.

Mick gave Middlesbrough FC more than 30 years loyal service as both a player and coach until his retirement in 1965, but it must be emphasised that he was very unfortunate when, at the height of his goalscoring powers, the Second World War interrupted his burgeoning career.

Tom Fleming
Bowls

TOM Fleming is the most outstanding male bowls player ever to grace the greens of Teesside, winning seven drawing-to-the jack world titles and picking up a gold medal at the Empire Games in Perth in 1962.

He was also the beaten finalist on two occasions in the English Bowling Association singles competition, in addition to playing 14 times for his country and being a regular member of the Yorkshire team.

Tom was also elected president of the Yorkshire Bowling Association in 1966 and served as an executive member of the EBA.

George Thomas Fleming was born in Ferryhill on September 22, 1910. He was educated at Broome Cottage School and later at The Alderman Wraith Secondary School in Spennymoor. He set his heart on becoming a schoolteacher, and trained at St John's College in York from 1929-31.

He had a talent for several sports, though he did not take up bowls until after the Second World War.

Tom played tennis and table tennis for Durham County and was a county bridge player. He also loved football and was a qualified football referee who graduated from taking charge of local schools games to officiate in the Northern League and later as a Football League linesman. In addition, he refereed a schoolboy international at Wembley.

Away from the sporting arena, Tom was a fine pianist. Fleming enlisted in the Army and served with REME, with whom he progressed to the rank of sergeant. He was posted to Egypt during the hostilities and was awarded the African Star on February 27, 1944.

After the War, he taught initially at Fleetham School and later at Marton Grove Junior School. He settled in Glaisdale Avenue in Middlesbrough and took up an interest in bowls in 1950. It was clear from the onset that he had a natural talent for the sport and he joined the Albert Park Club to develop his competitive edge.

Fleming's progress on the greens was dramatic and he became a tough opponent for the most experienced bowlers. He was an unmistakable figure, very tall and lean with an angular frame. He became a regular member of the Yorkshire County team in 1952, playing mainly as lead, and took a major step up the ladder when winning his first county title in 1958 when playing third wood in his club four which was skipped by Joe Lonsdale. Tom went on to reach the county finals over the next four years.

He qualified for the English singles final for the first time in 1959, at Mortlake in Surrey, but was beaten 21-11 in the final by Ken Coulson, an England international from Croydon. However Tom had excelled in reaching the final, having won a marathon semi-final against the legendary Percy Baker from Dorset, who was a former Empire Games competitor and four times English singles champion. The score was 21-19.

The effects of that gruelling game took its toll in the final when Tom trailed by 10-0 after only six ends. Despite working hard to gather his composure, he was unable to make up the lost ground.

The following year Tom was back in the final, but again failed to bring back the championship trophy to Albert Park when being beaten by a young man from Bristol called David Bryant.

However Tom was recompensed when he represented England in the world drawing-to-the-jack championship and won the title. This was an event which was designed to give international competition to bowls players living many miles apart. It involved delivering 32 woods to the jack. The measuring was carried out by a team of independent adjudicators. The total aggregate distance of all 32 woods from the jack decided the world championship.

Fleming became the first ever English winner with a combined distance of 54ft 7in. He pipped the reigning champion, Welshman Bert Evans, by almost three feet. The other six countries represented in the event included Hong Kong, South Africa and the United States.

Twelve months later Fleming won the world title again, this time in competition against ten rivals. His aggregate distance increased to 66ft 10in, which was still good enough to hold off second placed A Pascoe from Rhodesia, who recorded 71ft 4in.

Tom enjoyed a magnificent year in 1962. He became Yorkshire and Northern Counties singles champions, and won the county pairs with Jimmy Scott. Then he helped his club Albert Park to record an overwhelming victory in the Marshall Shield, beating Pickerings United from Hull by more than 50 shots.

In November, 1962, Fleming set off for Perth in West Australia as a member of the English fours team for the Empire Games. It was a highly successful trip, despite searing temperatures which reached 106 degrees in the shade, because the quartet came back with gold medals.

Fleming's teammates were Les Watson from Darlington, who was the Borough Engineer at Thornaby, David Bryant and the skip, Syd Drysdale. They clinched first place following the seven-match series by beating Papua New Guinea by 23-12 in their final game. This gave them a winning total of 16 points, thanks to four victories in the seven games. Scotland and Rhodesia were equal second on 14 points.

Soon after returning home, Fleming was informed that he had won the world drawing-to-the-jack competition for the third successive year. This time his total aggregate was 54ft 10in, just outside his best which he set two years earlier. In second place was Bill

World Champion, Tom Fleming, was quite simply Teesside's best male bowler of the last century.

Woodhard from Guernsey with 64ft 6in. Tom was to win the world title for the following two years, and seven times altogether.

Fleming continued to excel in competition and received the highest domestic accolade in 1964 when he was named as England captain for the home internationals in Belfast.

The following year he linked up with Albert Park teammates Jack Tarren and Joe Lonsdale to win the Northern Counties title.

In 1966 Tom was elected Yorkshire president at the annual meeting in the Guildhall in York, becoming the first Albert Park member ever to achieve this honour.

He went on to play a full part in the Yorkshire County administration. In addition to his year as president, he was assistant secretary for six years. He also served on the EBA Council for eight years and was a leading originator of the National Umpires Scheme, drawing up and marking the inaugural test paper.

Tom was made a Yorkshire life member in 1970. The following year he reached his third national final, in the English Indoor Bowling Association singles championship. However, just as in his previous outdoor final in 1960, Tom was beaten by David Bryant. Fleming later joined the King George V Bowling Club at Guisborough and continued to win major events, even though he was now into his 60s. In 1974, he won the singles and the triples in the Yorkshire Championships. It was his first Yorkshire singles victory since 1962. Throughout his career he was a winner of all the Yorkshire titles.

Remarkably Tom trailed by 14-4 in the singles final to G Lewthwaite from Hull, but then dug deep to put together a remarkable run of winning ends to take the title by 21-15. It was a different kettle of fish in the triples, where Fleming, partnered by Doug Gibson and Hylton Armstrong, was taken to an extra end by Hudson, Brownbridge and Stubbings of the host club Pickering. However Tom kept his nerve and scraped home by one shot.

Fleming then went on to contest the Northern Counties singles event, which he won again, and then he linked up with his triples team of Gibson and Armstrong to reach the semi-finals of the national championships.

It was to be his last major success in an illustrious and unique career. Tom died suddenly at home on July 11, 1977, at the age of 66, and was survived by his widow Anne, and daughter Judy.

Guy Fordham
Hockey

GUY Fordham is a world class midfield player who has been a regular international since the age of 19 and won a bronze medal with England in the 1998 Commonwealth Games in Kuala Lumpur.

He is approaching 100 combined caps for England and Great Britain and was one of the leading candidates to win a place in the British squad for the Sydney Olympics.

Guy Tristan Fordham was born in Stockton on July 19, 1975, but left Teesside at the age of three when his parents moved to London.

He attended Christchurch Junior School in New Malden in Surrey before moving on to Kingston Grammar School. Guy had been playing football since he was eight, but hockey was compulsory at Kingston and he gradually moved away from football and more towards hockey throughout his school years.

He broke into the Surrey Under-16 side at the age of 14 and graduated quickly through the South of England team to England Under-16s. He made his international debut in the home countries under-16 tournament against Scotland, Wales and Ireland at Cardiff. He played well and as a result was selected for the European Under-16 Cup in Holland, where his fine performances helped the England team to win the silver medal.

Guy decided at an early age that he needed to introduce a competitive edge to his game by joining a top club side, and he opted for Hounslow, who were the leading team in the country.

Guy was still at school at the time, but his talents were immediately recognised at Hounslow. In fact he was promoted quickly into their first team squad, before going on to become a regular player in the National Premier League.

In the first year he joined Hounslow, the team completed the double by winning the league and cup, though the young Guy played little part.

However this success qualified Hounslow to play in the European Cup the following season, and Guy

International hockey player Guy Fordham has been capped over 100 times for England and Great Britain.

played in several of the games to help the club take fourth place overall.

Guy was also firmly established as part of the international set-up by this time and earned another silver medal for England Under-18s in the European Cup when the event was held at Cannock. He was the youngest member of the squad when he joined the under-18 squad but he did not hang around long at this level, because he continued to progress and made his debut for England Under-21s as a 17-year-old.

Two years later he was promoted to the England senior

squad when he was selected to travel to India to play in the Indira Ghandi tournament in Delhi. His first full cap came in a match against Kazakhstan, which England surprisingly lost 1-0.

England eventually finished third out of the six countries taking part in the Delhi tournament, which wasn't a bad performance considering that the selectors deliberately took a young squad to the sub-Continent in order to blood several players.

As it was, Guy took full advantage of this opportunity to stay in the full England squad, and has been totally involved on the international scene ever since. The only tournaments which he has missed were usually as a result of work and study commitments.

However he did suffer disappointment by not being selected to compete in the Atlanta Olympics. Guy was already an experienced international with up to 30 caps to his credit, and he had helped Great Britain reach Atlanta via the qualifying tournament. However he was omitted from the squad which travelled to the United States.

If anything, this made him more determined than ever not to miss out on major events in the future. He continued to establish himself and was called up for the squad for the Commonwealth Games at Kuala Lumpur in 1998 when he helped England to win the bronze medal.

The conditions were difficult for the English team in Malaysia because it was hot and humid throughout the tournament. But the team played well and with better luck could have reached the final.

In the event England were beaten in the semi-finals by Australia, in extra time. The match was tied 2-2 at the end of normal time, but the Aussies scored the winning golden goal in the extra period.

This left England facing a play-off with India for the bronze medal, and Guy scored the goal which left this match finely balanced at 1-1 at full-time. The outcome was decided on penalty strokes, which England won.

In the same year Fordham was forced to drop out of the England squad for the World Cup in Utrecht in Holland because he was taking his finals at university. After leaving school, Guy had started a four-year medicine degree course at Southampton University. Two years into the course, he joined the Army, who sponsored him throughout his final two years.

Guy was back in major hockey action the following year and won another medal, taking the bronze again in the European Cup at Padua in Italy.

England finished second in their group behind Holland

to qualify for a semi-final clash against Germany 4-0. This left Guy and his teammates facing a play off match with Belgium for the bronze medal. The English players pulled out all the stops to comfortably win 5-1. The next major tournament on the horizon was the Sydney Olympics, and first of all Britain needed to qualify. Fordham was drafted into the squad which set off for Osaka in Japan in March, 2000, for the qualifying competition.

Britain were drawn in a group of six with the host nation, New Zealand, Poland, Korea and Belgium. The top two teams were guaranteed a place in the Olympics while the third and fourth teams had to play off against similarly placed teams from the second group, in order to qualify for Sydney.

England failed to reach the top two positions in their group, and were paired with Argentina from the second group in a play off for an Olympic place. It was a pressure situation for Fordham and the rest of his teammates, but they dug deep and won 3-1. Guy played in all of the games in the tournament.

Later Guy was called up by Great Britain for the Champions Trophy in Holland, which is regarded as a prestigious pre-Olympics warm-up event. He scored twice as Britain came from two goals down to force a 3-3 draw against Australia, but sadly this was one of the few impressive British performances and they finished last of the six teams.

However, the tournament was all about developing a team pattern and a feeling of togetherness in preparation for Sydney 2000. It left Guy waiting with crossed fingers for several weeks to discover if he would be included in the Olympics squad but he needn't have worried because his place on the plane to Australia was confirmed on July 18th.

After leaving university Guy put down roots on the South Coast and as a result decided to leave Hounslow and join the Guildford club, who also play in the National Premier League.

He has been completing his qualification process as a doctor by working within the National Health Service to gain practical medical experience, in hospitals both in Southampton and Winchester.

He is now officially an Army doctor, with the rank of captain, and intended to start training as a general practitioner, within the Army, after the Olympics.

Guy lives in Southampton with his partner Sarah but regularly returns to Teesside to visits his grandparents, who live in Eaglescliffe.

Peter Gilchrist
Billiards

PETER Gilchrist has been one of the world's leading billiards players since he turned professional in the late 1980s, winning the world championship in Bombay in 1994 and the world matchplay crown in 2000.

He has long been established in the world's top eight, regularly flying out to compete in major international tournaments, particularly to the Indian sub-continent.

Peter was born in Middlesbrough on February 11, 1968, and attended Linthorpe Juniors and later Boynton School.

He played football and was a runner at school, but developed a penchant for billiards when he was given a four foot table as a youngster.

His father Frank was a keen player and a station officer at Middlesbrough Fire Station, and 12-years-old Peter was handed the opportunity to improve his game by practising on the station's full size table.

He joined the Teesside Boys Billiards League squad at the Acklam Steelworks club, where he was coached and taught the finer points of the game by Walter Ormston.

Peter was not a natural cueist, and it was only through his personal dedication and regular practice that he began to progress as a force in the league.

His hard work paid dividends when he won the British Isles Under-16 Championship at the age of 15, beating Simon Snee from Thornaby in the final at the Erimus Club in Middlesbrough. In the quarter-finals. Peter had overcome Mike Russell from Marske, who was to become his good friend and close rival as professionals.

Ironically, at the same time as Peter was winning the under-16 billiards crown, Scottish teenager Stephen Hendry carried off the British under-16 snooker championship at Thornaby Snooker Centre.

When he left school, Peter began working on a YTS placement at ICI, but he found that his billiards game was being adversely affected because his practice time was depleted. So he made the brave decision to quit the job after five months and concentrate purely on his sport.

As a result Peter continued to go from strength to strength and, at the age of 17, he recorded a 107 break while playing for Acklam Steelworks which was believed to be the highest ever made in the world in a boys billiards match.

Gilchrist began playing locally for the North Ormesby Institute, in addition to Acklam Steelworks, and went very close to winning the English Amateur Championship while still only 19. He reached the final at Widnes, after recording his personal best individual break of 332 in beating Des Heald from Peterborough in the semi-finals.

In the final, Peter was paired with David Edwards from Abertillery, and it was the Welshman who led by 96 points at 1247-1151 at the end of the first two sessions.

However Gilchrist fought back on the second day and was leading by 120 points with 45 minutes play left only for Edwards to hit back to take the title by 2474-2244.

Peter did gain some recompense by going on to carry off the CIU title.

His performances were enough to earn Peter a place in the world amateur championships in Belfast. He was far from overawed in the finals and went on to share a three-way tie at the top of his group.

But only two players from each group went through to the finals, and Peter was eliminated on a total points count up behind the more experienced duo, Indian Subhash Agrawal and Joe Grech from Malta.

Ironically Gilchrist had lost only the one game in the group, when he was beaten right at the death by Subhash, who made a match winning late break of 200-plus. Peter overcome Grech in their match. The man from Malta made a break of 400-plus, but Peter held on to win by 40 points.

The world championships proved to be a valuable learning experience for Peter, and during the next 12 months he made massive strides in his overall game. He was helped in no small part by Tony Spensley from the Inn Off The Park, who offered free table time to practise whenever he liked.

The following year Peter emerged from the chrysalis as a top quality player and gained revenge over Edwards when he beat him in the CIU Championships final at Sheffield. The pair met again within a month in the English final and once again Peter came out on top, crushing the Welshman in a one-sided match by 3379-1854.

Having cleaned up on the amateur scene, Peter turned professional immediately. In his first season he made a huge impact, winning the British Open Championship at the Marton Hotel and Country Club when beating fellow Teessider Mike Russell in the five-hour final.

The duo met again in the world championships final in the Blue Mountains near Sydney, but this time Mike had the upper hand and landed the crown.

The British Open was staged again nine months later in Leeds and Peter retained his title, this time beating Norman Dagley from Earl Shilton by 1166-1008 in the final.

There was not a great deal of money in professional billiards at that time, and Peter dabbled with snooker because the rewards were much greater.

However his best achievement was reaching the last 64 of the British Open before losing 5-3 to Alex Hurricane Higgins.

Suddenly there was plenty of prize money on offer in billiards competitions in India, thanks to a £250,000 four-year commitment from the Indian Tobacco Company, and Gilchrist found himself making six journeys a year to the sub-Continent to compete in events. His commitment to billiards was secure in 1994 when he won the Gold Flake world professional title in Bombay, picking up a first prize of £10,000.

In the final he once again came up against his Teesside rival Russell. Gilchrist was in unstoppable form, storming to victory by the convincing margin of 1539-645 after winning the second session 887-209.

The win also gained Gilchrist revenge for his defeat in the UK Championship Final earlier in the year, when Russell won a one-sided match by 1072-330.

Peter won the British Open in 1994 and 1995, but it was still hard to make ends meet despite his successes, and once again he was grateful for help from Inn Off The Park, where he worked as an assistant manager.

Gilchrist proved that he was still developing his snooker by winning the Golden Cue tournament in Delhi in 1996. This was a triangular tournament involving billiards, snooker and pool. The previous

During an impressive billiards career Peter Gilchrist has won both the British and World Championships.

year, former world snooker champion Steve Davis had won the event.

In 1998 Peter won the British Open for the fifth time, at Darley Dale near Matlock, when he defeated the Indian Geet Sethi in the final.

The following year Peter succeeded to the tough job as chairman of the World Professional Billiards Association, taking over from Clive Everton. In addition to looking after the needs of his fellow members, his mandate was to continue to promote the sport and work to generate new prize money for the major events.

Peter reached another final in March, 2000, when he lined up against Russell in the world matchplay championship final at Bath. The match was played 1500-up, and Peter overcame his good pal in a tense battle in which the scores finished exactly on a round number on both sides with Peter winning 1500-1200.

Peter continues to play regularly in all professional invitation tournaments, in addition to playing in exhibitions and also coaching.

He visits Indian several times a year for major events in cities such as Delhi, Bombay, Madras and Bangalore and is approaching his 50th trip to the sub-Continent always being careful to pack his favourite English food for the trip.

Billiards is a huge sport in India and all the major tournaments are televised, making Gilchrist a well known sporting personality in Asia. The sport is also popular in Thailand. However his ambition is to see billiards gain new ground again in Britain and other parts of the world.

Anne Gollogly
Basketball

ANNE Gollogly is one of the finest women basketball players ever produced in Britain and holds a series of records which may never be beaten.

In a distinguished 20-year career, most of it played at the highest level, both internationally and domestically, she made a mammoth 103 appearances for England and another 22 for Great Britain.

Basketball took Anne, who lived in Teesville, to virtually every European country, plus Canada, the United States, New Zealand, Cuba, the Far East and Israel.

She appeared in four consecutive qualifying competitions for the Olympic Games between 1976 and 1988, which is a record, although she never had the opportunity to win a place alongside the top nations in the Olympics proper because the English team was never strong enough.

At 5ft 6in tall, Gollogly was hardly the typical image of a basketball player, being dwarfed by some of the six footers around her. Yet her remarkable number of international caps, many of which were earned as England captain, bears a lasting testament to the full extent of her marvellous achievements.

Anne also won all the major domestic honours, playing club basketball for several different teams throughout the 20 years and appearing in many national cup finals and championship finals. Even towards the end of her outstanding career Anne made a round trip of 400 miles every weekend to train and play for her club Avon Northampton.

Anne Bernadette Gollogly was born in Parkside Hospital, Middlesbrough, on March 4, 1953, and was the youngest of four daughters. She initially attended St Peter's Junior School at South Bank but later moved to St Andrew's School in Teesville when her family moved house before finishing her education at Newlands School in Middlesbrough and St Mary's Convent. In fact it was at Newlands that her sporting involvement took off. She was a member of the highly successful Newlands netball team which won the Yorkshire championship.

Anne was later introduced to basketball by regular players Annie Brown, Eileen Leahy and Linda Gollogly at Sarah Metcalfe Youth Club, and eventually joined the progressive local club Eston Eagles.

As a result, Anne's love of netball was gradually superseded by her commitment to basketball, which was a more physically demanding game and gave players the opportunity to attack as well as committing them to defensive work.

St Mary's Convent developed a very strong basketball team which came from the nucleus of the Newlands netball side. In fact Anne tasted national success for the first time when St Mary's went on to become English Schools Under-19 basketball champions when beating Aspley Grammar School from Hertfordshire in the final.

By this time Anne was playing basketball at every possible opportunity. In 1969 she gained her first international honours when she represented the England Under-19 Schools side during her first year in sixth form. The following year she captained the England Under-19 side.

After leaving school, Anne enrolled at St Mary's College in Twickenham to train as a PE and history teacher. However, such was her commitment to basketball, that she travelled home on almost every weekend during her four years in London to play for Eston Eagles.

The Eagles had a top quality young squad at that time and Gollogly was one of the mainstays of the side. She played her part as the Eagles reached the national club cup final in 1970, before losing to Abbey Wood by 55-53. Undeterred by that reverse they were back in the final again in 1973 when they went down to Turnford Tigers from Hemel Hempstead by 73-64. The Eagles finally turned the tables on the Tigers in the 1974 final when Anne captained them to their first major trophy success by 56-39. Within 12 months they were back to beat the Tigers in the final again, this time by 48-44.

Anne's commitment to the sport took on a new meaning during her second year at St Mary's College when he she spent a full term on a student exchange at Frostburg College in Maryland. She trained and played with basketball teams in the United States and developed a whole new approach towards the sport, mainly as a result of the high level of training and coaching which she encountered. Her experiences in Maryland were to prove beneficial throughout the rest of her career.

In 1972 Gollogly made her full England international debut against Austria in the European Championships qualifiers in Bari, in Italy. It was a huge step up in class for the girl from Teesville, and initially came as a shock to the system. However she gradually came to terms with the rigorous demands at this level and was a regular international from then until the end of her career.

Back in England, Eston Eagles eventually became Cleveland Eagles and achieved a major distinction for Teesside when they carried off the Great Britain Club Championship in 1975, which was contested by the champions from Ireland, Scotland and Wales. Eagles had a cracking side by this time and included seven senior and several junior internationals in their ranks. However they had to work very hard to beat the Irish champions Meteors by 67-61 in the final.

In 1976 Anne was called up for the British squad for the inaugural Olympic qualifiers, which were held in Hamilton, Ontario. It was a major moment in her career. Unfortunately the British women found the opposition very tough and failed in their bid to reach the competition proper in Montreal. They lost all their matches to strong sides from Cuba, South Korea, Bulgaria and Italy.

At the same time, Gollogly was now firmly established as a crucial member of the England team. In the same year, she set a new English points scoring record when she netted 36 in an international against Norway.

The Eagles were as strong as ever. They were runners up in the inaugural Women's National League and reached the national club cup final again, this time losing to their rivals Turnford Tigers. However Anne notched up another major achievement by finishing top scorer in the national cup matches with outstanding contribution of 98 points.

Anne received further top award in 1976 when she was named English player of the year. In the same season she skippered the Eagles to the national club cup final, where Turnford won narrowly by 64-62. Anne had some consolation because she was named most valuable player in the Wembley final. She top scored for Eagles and was third top scorer in the National League with 266 points.

Gollogly led Eagles to the National League Championship in 1978, yet once again they were pipped in the cup final by Turnford, this time by just one point. It had been another excellent season for the Teessider, and in recognition of that fact she received the most votes in being selected as part of the National League All Star team. She had been top scorer for the Eagles and second top scorer in the national league with 352 points.

Anne represented England in the European Championships qualifiers at Wolfenbuttel in Germany in the same year and, although England failed to qualify, Anne's performance in the tournament saw her named in the All Star team at the championships, which was a notable achievement.

She continued to go from strength to strength and was named England captain for the first time for the Home Counties internationals in 1979. It was to be the first of many. She went on to skipper her country for a record 66 times. She led England in their first ever entry into the European Championship Finals at Banja Luka, Yugoslavia, the following year. She also gained her 50th cap during the tournament, against Spain, and top scored for England.

Cleveland Eagles were still a major force in the game and were National League champions again in 1979 and runners up the following season. However the Eagles then made the difficult decision to disband, mainly because many players began drifting away, all at the same time to start families. So Anne linked up with the Newcastle Eagles, who won the Division Two title at the first attempt.

Anne recorded a notable individual achievement in 1979 when she scored the most points by a player in a National League game when netting 58 against Waltham Abbey. Overall she was the league's second top scorer with 398 points.

Anne joined up with Great Britain again for the Olympic qualifiers in Bulgaria in 1980 and the British women were delighted to win one of their matches when beating Mexico by 70-55. Narrow defeats to top sides like Yugoslavia by 64-56 and to South Korea by just 11 points, having lost by 50 to the same country in the 1976 qualifiers, indicated that the British team were making genuine progress.

Former England captain Anne Gollogly was one of the finest female basketball players this country has ever produced, with a career that spanned nearly 20 years at the highest level.

In 1983 Gollogly was selected to compete for England in the Commonwealth Championships in New Zealand, and returned home with a silver medal. The English women played out of their skins to beat the highly fancied home nation in the semi-finals, before going down quite heavily by 85-51 to Australia in the final.

Anne linked up with the British squad again in 1984 and flew out to Cuba for the pre-Olympic qualifying tournament. Once again it was more through hope than belief that Britain took on some of the much stronger countries. England lacked nothing in commitment but failed to qualify for the Atlanta Olympics, being beaten by top nations like Yugoslavia, Canada and Brazil.

There was no disgrace in their reverses at this level. The English association did not have the financial backing which the top countries enjoyed. Anne regularly hitch-hiked to England training sessions, mainly because there was no money to pay expenses. Yet players in many other international teams were virtual professionals in every sense of the word because they lived and trained together with national funding.

When Newcastle Eagles folded, Gollogly joined up with the Ashfield club in Nottingham and helped them to finish runners-up in the national club cup final in 1984 when beaten by Northampton. Later she joined Bolton.

Anne was appointed assistant coach to the England team in 1987, but was still a crucial playing member. She won her 100th cap against Holland in Dublin as England qualified for the European Championships for only the second time. England won two of their three qualifying matches, beating Ireland 54-52 and Denmark 66-55, but lost to fellow qualifiers Holland 74-47. It was Anne's tenth European Championships campaign, which was a record for any individual.

Gollogly had joined the Avon Northampton club at this stage, and in 1986 helped them to reach the finals of both the national championships and the national cup, where they lost 73-65 to Crystal Palace.

Anne was playing as well as ever and in 1987 achieved another notable distinction when she was named England player of the year for the second time. She was also Cleveland sportswoman personality of the year. In the same year she helped Northampton to achieve a remarkable national treble. They won the league, the championship final and the cup final, beating London YMCA Bobcats by 69-63 at Wembley. Anne was also named most valuable player following the cup final.

In 1988 Northampton went close to achieving the treble again, but had to settle for second place in the club championship. In the cup final they had beaten Crystal Palace by 60-53.

In the same season Gollogly took part in her fourth and final Olympic qualifying campaign with Great Britain, still trying to get past the heats for the first time. The qualifiers were held in Kota Kinabulu in Malaysia and Anne was named as British captain. The team won one of their matches when beating Thailand, but they lost to Yugoslavia, France, Bulgaria and Zaire.

As a result of playing in the qualifiers, Anne became the most capped Great Britain player with 22 appearances and is still the only player ever to take part in four pre-Olympic tournaments.

Anne always intended that Britain's Seoul Olympics bid would be her swansong and she announced her retirement from international basketball upon her return home to England, at the age of 35.

At that time Anne was head of PE at Sacred Heart School in Redcar, and she took a year out to travel the world and ease down from the hectic playing and training schedule which had been her life. However, while in Australia, she linked up with the Bankstown club in Sydney and worked as assistant coach. It was a great experience, especially as the Bankstown head coach was also the Australian national coach.

On her return to England, Anne turned down the offer of the job of assistant coach with England, primarily because the national association was unwilling to reimburse her full expenses.

Instead Gollogly devoted herself to coaching the school basketball sides. During the 1980s she had helped teams from Sacred Heart to win four national basketball titles at under-14 and under-16 level, while also helping to produce several individual international players. It gave her a tremendous amount of personal pride to see some of her proteges achieve international success.

However, the end of her playing days also gave Anne the opportunity to develop other interests. Eventually she moved away from basketball completely and now spends her sporting time playing squash for the Redcar club, in addition to enjoying ski-ing trips.

In 2000 she spent a rewarding voluntary stint overseas in Cambodia teaching sport to paraplegics.

George Hardwick
Football

GEORGE Hardwick was one of the greatest post-war England international football captains who also skippered the Great Britain side which took on the Rest of Europe at Hampden Park in 1947.

He came to prominence as a tough tackling young left-back with Middlesbrough in the late 1930s, and went on to become a regular war-time international, appearing many times as a guest player with Chelsea.

As soon as the hostilities were over, George returned to Middlesbrough and was selected as England captain for the first 13 internationals after the War, losing his place only as a result of injury.

In the late 1940s he was regarded as one of the top players in the world and could comfortably hold his own against some of the most feared right-wingers of his time. Stanley Matthews included.

Later he went on to manage several clubs, including Oldham Athletic, the Dutch national side and then Sunderland, where he introduced Brian Clough to coaching.

George Hardwick was born in Garnet Street, Saltburn-by-the-Sea, on February 20, 1920, into a sporting family. His grandfather Francis and father Frank both played football and cricket to a high standard and it was only natural that young George would follow in their footsteps.

His footballing potential was first spotted when the family moved to nearby Lingdale and he attended the local school. The headmaster, Mr Scutt, selected George to play for the school team when he was only seven. As a keen youngster he had the ability to play in variety of positions, once scoring 12 goals in a match, before eventually captaining Lingdale to league and cup success as well as being chosen to represent the local district sides.

From the Lingdale School side he graduated to the Middlesbrough FC nursery team South Bank East End, where he finally settled into the left full-back position which he was eventually to make his own. One of his contemporaries at East End was Harold Shepherdson, who was later to achieve great success as a trainer with Middlesbrough and England.

After leaving school, George worked in the drawing office of the local Dorman Long Steelworks. By this time the family had also moved to Aire Street, South Bank, and on the strength of some eye-catching performances for East End, he was invited to sign amateur forms for Middlesbrough in October, 1935.

Then, following a series of consistent games for the Boro reserves, George was able to secure a full-time professional contract in April, 1937. More solid performances for 'The Stiffs' saw him chosen by Boro manager Wilf Gillow ahead of more experienced players to make his debut at 17 years of age against Bolton Wanderers at Ayresome Park in December, 1937. It turned out to be a game he would never forget as he scored one of the quickest own goals ever recorded in Football League history in the first minute of the match.

However the young Hardwick was still given the opportunity to prove himself at top level and enjoyed a seven match-run run alongside Boro's footballing greats like Bobby Baxter, George Camsell and Mick Fenton, before the more experienced Bobby Stuart returned at left-back.

With the outbreak of World War Two in 1939, George had to drop his hopes of establishing himself in the Boro first team, and he joined the RAF. Early in the conflict he suffered severe leg injuries during an air raid on RAF Eastchurch on the Isle of Sheppey. Such was the extensive damage to the ligaments of his left knee that George feared he might never play football again.

Fortunately an intensive course of rehabilitation at Loughborough, under the watchful eye of tennis stars Dan Maskell and Fred Perry, enabled him to resume his playing career at Stamford Bridge by turning out for Chelsea in the Southern League. His determination to regain his fitness was fully rewarded when he appeared in two wartime cup finals for the Blues.

At the age of 21, George made his England debut in a wartime international against Wales at the City Ground in Nottingham, which England won 4-1. It was to be the first of 17 wartime international appearances for England, including two matches which brought consecutive eight-goal thumpings of Wales and Scotland in 1943.

With the war in Europe already at an end, England began playing Continental opposition and George played war-time games for England against Belgium, Switzerland and France in early 1946, including a 2-1 defeat in Paris in the May of that year.

After being demobbed, he returned to Middlesbrough to resume his First Division career. He was a big name player by this time, and generally acknowledged as one of the top defenders in the country. Immediately he was appointed captain of the club by the new manager David Jack and was also named captain of England.

October 1949. Boro captain George Hardwick, ball at his feet, has the legendary Wilf Mannion on his left.

Hardwick skippered England in 13 consecutive full internationals and also led out Great Britain against the Rest of Europe in May, 1947. It was a great personal honour and an acknowledgement by the football authorities of his sterling leadership qualities. He led Great Britain to a 6-1 victory.

In September 1946, George's first full international after the war produced a 7-2 thrashing of Northern Ireland in Belfast. His Boro teammate Wilf Mannion scored two of the England goals. This resounding victory was followed by a 1-0 win against the Republic of Ireland in Dublin two days later. Before Christmas, England had also beaten Wales by 3-0 at Maine Road

and then hammered Holland by 8-2 at Huddersfield.

The man from Lingdale was at the helm of one of England's best ever sides. A further eight international appearances followed in 1947, including a 10-0 romp against Portugal in Lisbon. With players like Hardwick, Mannion, Tom Finney, Stanley Matthews and Tommy Lawton in their line-up, England were very tough opponents.

Hardwick's 13th and last England game was a 2-0 win against Scotland in Glasgow in April, 1948. In fact he finished on the losing side just once, in a 1-0 defeat by Switzerland in Zurich.

Unfortunately George then lost his England place through injury and, having been replaced as skipper of the international side, was never considered again in accordance with the custom at that time.

Hardwick was still one of the biggest names in world football, a hard and uncompromising defender who always left the opposing right-winger aware of the fact that he had been involved in a game. Unfortunately there had been many changes in the Boro line-up as a result of the war and the Championship honours which George always believed were just around the corner in 1939, no longer promised to come to Teesside.

By 1950, at the age of 30, following several seasons when Middlesbrough had flattered to deceive, George decided to pursue a career in coaching and joined Oldham Athletic as their player-manager.

Although money to improve the quality of the playing staff was in very short supply, he still managed to achieve promotion to Division Two for the Latics in his second season. In all he spent six hard-working years at Boundary Park before eventually resigning in April, 1956, frustrated at continually working on a short shoestring.

George was not out of work long because he was immediately enlisted by the US Army as an honourary colonel and flown to Stuttgart to organise a comprehensive football coaching programme for the GI's who were stationed at German bases.

Teaching football to the Americans may not sound appealing but it proved to be a very successful scheme and on the strength of that success, Hardwick was appointed coach of the Dutch national team in January, 1957.

It was to be in Holland where he laid the coaching foundations of what later became known as Total Football, where players had the ability to interchange positions on the pitch. His training methods came to the attention of top club sides and the following season he was offered the prestigious position as manager of PSV Eindhoven.

Unfortunately, after only one season with PSV, family commitments saw George return to Teesside and he settled in Hutton Rudby. His plan was to sever all his links with football and move into business. He began an alternative career in the motor trade selling cars for Martins and at one time it looked as though his talents might be lost to the game forever.

However it wasn't long before Middlesbrough manager Bob Dennison persuaded Hardwick to take charge of the youth team at Ayresome Park in August, 1961, as successor to Jimmy Gordon. George settled into the job with his usual enthusiasm and enjoyed working with the youngsters, who included the likes of Cyril Knowles, Frank Spraggon and Alec Smith.

Once again bitten by the game he called "a bug without a cure", George then found himself back in the hot seat when he accepted an shock invitation from the Sunderland directors to step into a managerial breach at Roker Park in November, 1964.

Sunderland, who had been promoted to the First Division the previous May, had been without a manager since Alan Brown moved on to Sheffield Wednesday during the summer. George had not managed an English club since 1956, and had been attending Roker Park only through his part-time job as a journalist when he was offered the post out of the blue. However George accepted, and agreed to work without a contract on the understanding that he would be handed a long term deal at the end of the season should he avoid relegation. He proved to be a great success, steering Sunderland to their highest league position since World War Two.

Yet, incredibly, his services were not retained at the end of the season by the Roker Park directors. It was a decision which left George sickened and finished with professional football.

Soon afterwards he was offered the job at Hartlepools United. George turned it down, but he did recommend the right man for the job. That man was Brian Clough, who George had introduced to coaching the previous season when he put him in charge of the Sunderland youth team. Clough took the Hartlepool job, and the rest is history.

Eventually, Hardwick was coaxed out of retirement to manage Gateshead in a part-time capacity from 1968 to 1970, but again a lack of finance denied him the

George Hardwick. The only player to simultaneously captain his club, country and Great Britain.

opportunity to fulfil his ambitions.

In 1983 George's tremendous contribution over the years was recognised at Ayresome Park when he was awarded a well-deserved benefit match together with another Boro legend, Wilf Mannion.

During the intervening years George wasn't totally lost to football as he managed to combine some media work with a series of successful business ventures, particularly in steel fabrication.

Now living happily in Yarm with his wife Jennifer, Hardwick's appetite for watching football is undiminished despite undergoing major heart surgery. He still attends every Boro home match at the BT Cellnet Riverside Stadium, where a suite has quite rightly been named after him.

Dorothy Harrison
Swimming

WORLD class swimmer Dorothy Harrison competed in two Olympic Games for Great Britain, as a teenager in Mexico City in 1968, and then as captain of the women's swimming team in Munich four years later.

During her illustrious career at the very top of international swimming, she was also a Commonwealth Games triple silver medalist in Edinburgh and European Games bronze medalist in Barcelona.

Dorothy was born in North Ormesby on March 16, 1950, and attended North Ormesby primary school and later Stainsby School, where she played hockey, netball and badminton for the school.

She was encouraged to learn to swim by her parents, who used to take her and elder brother William on annual holidays to Staithes and wanted to make sure that both children were experienced in the water.

Dorothy discovered that she had a natural talent for swimming and spent a lot of time at Middlesbrough Baths, where she joined the local swimming club. She excelled at breaststroke and was to concentrate on this style throughout her career.

As a 15-year-old pupil at Stainsby School, she was selected to swim the 200 metres breaststroke for Britain in a junior international in West Germany and was later called up for a further international in Utrecht.

In the same year Dorothy won the English schools 110 yards breaststroke title at Cambridge in 1min 22.5sec. Dorothy, who lived in Westbourne Grove, North Ormesby, continued to carry off domestic titles and win international selection.

She switched to Hartlepool Swimming Club, mainly to link up with talented Hartlepool trio Christine Kindon, Margaret Auton and Judy Turnbull to form a medley team and train together. However it was also a good opportunity to train under the guidance of experienced coach Ron Sharp.

There were few internationals at that time, and it was mainly in the national championships that swimmers were able to take the eye of the selectors.

However Dorothy made a big impact in all competitions. As a result, she was awarded a place in the British team for the Mexico Olympics in 1968. It was her first major senior international, and she was accompanied by her friend Margaret Auton, who was contesting the butterfly event.

In Mexico, Dorothy was competing against many more experienced swimmers with faster times, but she did well to reach the semi-finals of the 110 yards breaststroke and was the fastest of the British girls.

Dorothy also contested the 220 event, and helped the medley relay team reach the final, where they finished a highly creditable sixth. Their time of 4min 38.3sec left them less than two seconds outside a medal. Her teammates in the British quartet were Wendy Burrell, Alexandra Jackson and Margaret Auton.

The next target was the 1970 Commonwealth Games in Edinburgh, and Dorothy virtually secured her place when she won the 220 yards breaststroke in the English trials at Blackpool in 2min 51.5sec.

She went on to win three silver medals in the Games, narrowly missing out on gold on all three occasions. She was second in the 100 and 200 metres breaststroke and helped the medley relay team to the silver medal.

On both occasions in the individual events, Dorothy was pipped by the Australian swimmer Beverley Whitfield. However Dorothy could hardly have done any better because she set personal bests and new British and English records in both races.

Even so, there was some disappointment in the 100, because Dorothy had set the fastest time going into the final. However she was edged out of the gold by Whitfield by two tenths of a second.

Dorothy was swimming to the peak of her ability at this time and followed up her success in the Commonwealth Games by taking a bronze medal in 200 metres in the European Championships in Barcelona. This was a highly satisfactory performance because the competition in Europe was much stiffer than in the Commonwealth.

During an illustrious swimming career Dorothy Harrison represented Great Britain in two Olympic Games and won silver and bronze medals at the Commonwealth and European Championships.

It had been a hectic 12 months for Harrison, having competed in nine international events. At the end of the year it was no surprise when she was voted the Amateur Swimming Association's swimmer of the year. A further major award followed when she was presented with the Vaux North sportswoman of the year trophy in Sunderland.

Now a student teacher at Endsleigh College in Hull, Dorothy was selected to join the British team for a tour of Canada in 1971, competing in Halifax, Montreal, and Toronto, and then taking part in the Canadian Championships in Edmonton, where she won both the 100 and 200 breaststroke events.

Once back in England, she was soon packing her bags again to spend six months training in New South Wales in Australia, thanks to her being awarded a Winston Churchill Travelling Scholarship.

It was no holiday. Dorothy trained solidly every day in Australia under the watchful eye of top coach Don Talbot, who concentrated on altering her technique slightly, getting her to draw breath later in her stroke action.

The intensive coaching paid huge dividends. Dorothy was swimming as well as ever and equalled her British record of 1min 17sec when she won the 100 metres breaststroke in the Australian Open championships in Brisbane in February, 1972. It was a notable moment for the North Ormesby swimmer because she drew clear over the final 25 metres to beat Beverley Whitfield, who had pipped her in both the 100 and 200 metres in the Commonwealth Games. Dorothy followed up with another pulsating victory in the 200 metres breaststroke in 2min 45sec, again beating Whitfield into second place.

However she returned to Teesside in the March with an unexpected injury problem, having picked up infections in both feet while on a riding expedition. Dorothy had not been wearing the proper footwear, and had scraped her feet on the stirrups.

She had walked to the plane, to leave Australia, but her feet swelled during the flight and she could not walk when she returned to England. She needed an immediate course of antibiotics to ease the problem. It was not the best start to her build up towards the Munich Olympics, because her training was badly affected for some time.

Once fully recovered from the feet problem, Dorothy suffered a second blow at the Olympic trials at Crystal Palace when she swam badly. Unfortunately she had been troubled by an ear infection and swollen glands in her neck which also affected her performances. In fact she could finish only fourth in the 200 metres.

However her disappointing swims only partly counted against her. For Dorothy was selected to swim the 100 metres breaststroke in the Olympics. Unfortunately there was no place for her in the 200, which she always regarded as her speciality event.

It was a blow because Harrison was currently rated fifth in the world over 200 metres, third fastest in Europe and quickest in the Commonwealth.

She made a dramatic start to the event in Munich, equalling her British record in winning her heat. She was fourth fastest of the 16 qualifiers for the semi-finals. Then she smashed her British record, coming home in the semis in third place in 1min 16.53sec, to secure a place in the final.

Dorothy knew that she needed to knock two seconds off this time if she was to win a medal, but it wasn't to be and she finished eighth in a highly competitive race in 1:17.49. Her Commonwealth rival Whitfield took the bronze.

Dorothy had high hopes of making a second final, with the medley team, but the British swimmers were not strong enough to reach the last eight.

Dorothy had taken a year out of college to travel for the scholarship in Australia and compete in the Olympics, so she returned to her studies. However she completed them at a college in Coventry, which also gave her the opportunity to train under the watchful eye of Hamilton Bland, who was coaching the Coventry Olympic squad.

Harrison later married John Blake, a Royal Navy engineer, and went to live in Portsmouth, where she became a PE teacher at a secondary school in Gosport. At the same time she stopped swimming competitively at the top level, though she coached swimming in addition to other sports such as hockey, netball and badminton.

She moved on to Pinner, and now lives with John in Oxfordshire, from where she commutes to Hillingdon in London to teach PE.

However Dorothy has lost none of her competitive edge and has become very skilled at boat handling, which she practises regularly on the Thames.

In fact Dorothy and her husband won the European Championship for boat handling at Southampton in 1999, and were due to defend their title in 2000.

Jack Hatfield
Swimming

FEW Teesside sportsmen have achieved so much in their careers and served the local community with such distinction as Jack Hatfield.

He competed in no less than four Olympic Games, from 1912-28, winning silvers at 400 metres and 1,500 metres and a bronze in the 4x200 metres relay at the 1912 Stockholm Games.

On the domestic swimming scene, he was the most prolific English national champion of all time, winning 36 ASA titles in his career from 1912 to 1931. He set four world records, taking the 300 yards record in 1913 in three minutes, 26.4 seconds; the 400 metres in 5:21.6 in 1912; the 500 yards in 6:02.8 in 1913; and the 500 metres in 6:56.8 in 1912.

John Gatenby Hatfield was born on August 15, 1893 in a cottage on the High Green at Great Ayton which his parents had taken for a summer holiday. Jack, as he became popularly known, arrived two months premature on a day of high drama for the family.

His father Thomas, a Wesleyan Methodist preacher, had gone to work at Coatham Pier near Redcar, where he had a concession to sell fruit. During an eventful few hours Tommy had dived into the sea and saved two men who were in difficulties. Then he returned to his stall, after his heroic exploits, only to find that all his fruit had been stolen. At the same time, he was informed that his wife, Hannah, had given birth to a premature baby and that he was needed at her bedside as quickly as possible.

When Tommy arrived at the cottage he found his wife in a critical condition and young Jack very weak and not expected to survive too long.

Thankfully they both recovered, with Jack proving himself to be a real fighter. As he was to be in his career. During the early years of his life he remained rather small and frail but in 1898, when his father was appointed superintendent of Middlesbrough's Gilkes Street Baths and introduced penny admission prices for children, swimming proved to be the ideal activity for Jack to increase both his strength and stamina.

At the turn of the 20th Century Tommy Hatfield was well known in the area for organising large scale swimming exhibitions, particularly in the local parks, and had been bestowed the honourary title of "Professor" by the general public.

It was during these exhibitions that Jack's natural talent was first spotted by his father. The "Professor" wasted no time in developing his son's innate ability and invited elite swimmers to competitions at the Gilkes Street pool so Jack could test himself against the best opposition in the country at that time. By the age of 12 Jack had reached such a high standard that he had already swum in five senior local championships.

During the winter months, when the baths were closed, training was done in a variety of outdoor locations including Smith's Dock on the River Tees, the Blue Lagoon near Great Ayton and Middlesbrough's Albert Park lake.

A century ago, competitive swimming strokes were undergoing constant change, particularly the crawl and its variation which was called the trudgeon crawl. Jack's technical mastery of these overarm strokes combined with excellent leg movements produced a highly efficient swimming style. He seemed to glide effortlessly through the water propelled by his tremendous upper body strength which enabled him to break Northumberland and Durham county records with ease. In order to continue his development, Jack joined Newcastle Swimming Club and was guided by one of the country's leading coaches of that period, Jack Priestley.

By 1912 Priestley's astute training and competitive regime had resulted in Jack winning English national titles at a variety of distances. This success led to his selection, at the age of 19, for the Stockholm Olympic Games.

For one lacking in international experience, Jack's performances for Great Britain in Sweden were a revelation, as he unexpectedly won two silver medals in the 400 and 1500 metres freestyle and a bronze in

London 1913. Jack Hatfield had the amazing ability to race over a wide range of distances. Here he returns triumphant after winning the five mile international championship held on the River Thames.

the 200 metres relay along with William Foster, Henry Taylor and Thomas "Sid" Battersby.

In the individual events, although he broke both the existing world records, he was just beaten on each occasion by George Hodgson of Canada.

In the season following his Olympic triumphs, Jack continued his outstanding level of performance by collecting five English national freestyle titles over varying distances. And in a tremendous run of success he also broke four world and three English records.

In 1913 and 1914, Jack again displayed his versatility by winning the five miles international championship which was held on the River Thames from Kew to Putney.

But just when it appeared he was reaching his peak, Jack's swimming career came to an abrupt halt with the outbreak of World War One.

Jack joined his country's call to arms very early and during his medical, the officer in charge was so impressed by his Olympian physique that he commented on the draft papers that: "Jack Hatfield was the perfect physical specimen." The press quickly picked up on this title and much to his embarrassment he was christened the "Perfect Man".

With his background in sport, Jack was sent to Winchester for training as a saddler before serving with distinction in France, tending to the horses of the Royal Artillery in appalling conditions throughout most of the conflict.

Owing to the Great War, the 1916 Olympic Games were cancelled. And by the time competition resumed in Antwerp in 1920, Jack found himself physically under prepared and unable to do himself justice in both the 400 and 1500 metre freestyle events, and he finished out of the medals.

The realisation of just how much military service had taken away his physical conditioning made Jack determined to regain full competitive fitness. So, in the spring months of 1921, he began a serious training programme specifically aimed at reaching his peak in time for the Paris Olympics of 1924.

He reclaimed all his English national titles in 1921 and also represented England at water polo, initially at centre-forward and later at centre-half.

Jack's dedicated training regime was rewarded in the French capital when he was a very creditable fourth in the final of the 1500 metres and fifth in the 400 metres behind Johnny Weissmuller, who was later to achieve international stardom on the big screen as Tarzan the Apeman.

Throughout the late 1920s, Jack continued to compete at the highest level and was chosen as captain of the swimming team for an amazing fourth Olympiad in Amsterdam in 1928 where, despite being in his thirties, he justified his selection by reaching the semi-finals of both the 400 and 1500 metres freestyle. He also played in the Great Britain water polo team, as he did the following year in the European Championships in Budapest, Hungary.

The final accolade in a glittering international career came in 1930 when he was selected as captain of the England team which attended the inaugural Empire Games in Hamilton, Canada, in 1930.

Looking back over an extraordinary 20 years of competition at the highest possible level, Jack Hatfield won 42 English championships and remarkably held English, European, Empire and world records over every distance from 220 yards to five miles.

Following the Olympics of 1912, "Professor" Tom Hatfield had opened the family's first sports outfitters in Newton Street, Middlesbrough, and when Jack wasn't competing he earned a living working in the shop.

As Jack became more famous so the business thrived, particularly in the promotion of swimwear which bore his trademark. In fact his amateur status was called into question when officials argued that by selling costumes he was a professional. It was a claim that Jack rigorously denied.

In 1968, when plans for the development of the Cleveland Centre were unveiled, the Hatfield retail establishment moved to its present site on Borough Road. For almost 90 years it has become synonymous with supplying top quality equipment and delivering personal customer service to generations of Teesside sports enthusiasts.

Even though he had retired from international competition, swimming was still to play a large part in Jack's life and, in 1930, he competed in an event called the Teesswim from Victoria Bridge, Stockton, to the Transporter Bridge, Middlesbrough, going on to carry off the victor's Northern Echo Cup on several occasions.

In 1952 Jack was invited to become a director of Middlesbrough FC and he served the Ayresome Park club with distinction until the mid 1960s. In fact on one trip abroad to Holland there was a great sense of deja vu when Jack recognised the stadium he had competed in during the 1928 Olympics.

Jack Hatfield was a well-known and much a respected figure throughout the Teesside area who devoted much of his time and energy to the tuition of young swimmers and promoting competitions and charitable events. His marriage to Elsie Darley also proved to be a very happy and lasting liaison.

Jack Hatfield died on March 30, 1965, and in honour of all his achievements a square was named after him near Fry Street in the centre of Middlesbrough.

After his funeral, and in accordance with his wishes, his ashes were scattered on the River Leven at Great Ayton so they would be carried down to the River Tees, passing through all the places where he had swum during his life.

No other person from Teesside has appeared in as many Olympic Games nor achieved so much success at international and national level as John Hatfield.

As a final accolade, his distinguished contribution to the history of swimming was posthumously recognised in the United States when his name was enrolled into the International Swimming Hall of Fame at Fort Lauderdale, Florida in 1984. A fitting tribute to an outstanding career.

Jack Hatfield represented Great Britain with distinction at four Olympiads between 1912 and 1928, winning silver and bronze medals. His remarkable record of securing 36 Amateur Swimming Association titles throughout his eminent career still stands to this day and is very unlikely to be broken in the future.

Gary Havelock
Speedway

GARY Havelock was one of speedway's hottest stars in the late 1980s and throughout the 1990s, winning the world championship in Poland at the age of 23 in 1992. He captained England for six years and made more than 70 international appearances, racing all over the world from the United States to Australia.

Gary has ridden for several teams, including Middlesbrough, Bradford, Eastbourne and his current club Poole. His commitment to the sport is stronger than ever and he regularly flies out to the Continent to compete for Swedish and Polish teams with which he is contracted.

Robert Gary Havelock was born at home in South View, Eaglescliffe, on November 4, 1968, and was educated at Yarm Juniors and Conyers School.

He was expected to play rugby at school by his sportsmaster, but this sport was not his cup of tea. In any case, by this time he was already well established as a junior grasstrack rider.

Gary's father Brian was a motorbike fanatic who started off racing in trials, motorcross and grasstrack events, before progressing to the speedway tracks. Brian quickly became a well known rider on the speedway circuit and went on to race for several teams, including Middlesbrough, Sunderland, Newcastle, Workington, Hull, Berwick and Stoke.

Not only did Gary grow up in a concentrated motorbike environment, but he was given his first bike when he was only three. As soon as he was old enough he began competing in junior grasstrack events.

Initially Gary had very little grasstrack success. He was small and slight, and did not have the physical strength to match some of the bigger lads. As a result, he used to fall off a lot whenever he tried to go faster. However he was blessed with the Havelock family's will-to-win and his attitude and commitment were spot on. With dad helping to mould his riding style, Gary gradually became proficient and learned to fully control his machine. He started winning events when he was 11 and never looked back. His progress was so

dramatic that he won the British junior grasstrack championships in consecutive years from 1981-82.

Gary had never wanted to be anything but a speedway rider, and he finally received a speedway bike at the age of 14. Immediately he began practising on speedway tracks to develop his own riding style.

All speedway riders had to be 16 years or older before they were allowed to race officially, but Gary could not wait, especially as his November birthday ruled him out of the whole of the 1984 season.

So, with a little bit of manipulation of his application form, Gary's birthday was temporarily moved forward from November 4 to September 4. It meant that he was granted a licence, and was able to compete in the junior competitions at the end of the 1984 season.

In fact he went on to win the Suffolk Open Junior Championship at Mildenhall. No doubt he will be the only 15-year-old ever to achieve this feat!

At the beginning of the following year, Gary's dream of becoming a speedway rider was a reality. He signed for Middlesbrough Tigers and went straight into the team as a reserve at the age of 16. Dad Brian was manager of the team at the time, but Gary was very much in there on merit.

In his first season he won a trophy, when he carried off the Pride of the Potteries event at Stoke. Suddenly there was no stopping him. The following year Gary won the British Under-21 Championship and was the National League Grand Slam champion in 1986. In addition, he helped Middlesbrough to win the National League Four-Team tournament in both 1985 and 1986. However, it was obvious that such a prodigious talent was not going to hang around in the National League for too long. All the biggest tracks were in the British League and all the major events were held on those tracks. So, Gary reluctantly made the poignant decision to leave his home-town club and step up into the British League with Bradford Dukes in 1987. Bradford was the obvious choice of destination because Gary had ridden for the Dukes in 15 meetings

At 23, Gary Havelock was one of youngest World Speedway Champions when he won the title in 1992.

at the end of the 1986 season, having doubled up with the Tigers and joined the Dukes as No.8.

However, despite having done well for Bradford at the end of the previous season, his first year with the team was a disappointment. He finished with a seven points average, but had expected much better.

His major problem was a technical one. Upon joining Bradford, he had signed a sponsorship deal with Weslake engines, whereas the GM engines proved to be much faster that particular season.

A change of engine the following season paid massive dividends because Gary was so successful that he was selected for England for the first time. However he suffered a blow in the British Final when he crashed and broke his wrist. He needed an operation to have two screws inserted in the wrist to help it to heal.

Havelock bounced back in the same season and was selected as reserve for England in the World Team Cup Final in Long Beach, California, which brought together all the top riders in the world.

Unexpectedly, because of mechanical problems within the English team, he gained five rides and went on to finish top scorer with eight points. It was a phenomenal achievement under the circumstances, though unfortunately Gary was the only English rider to do himself justice.

But, just as speedway's young pretender was beginning to make his mark, it looked like his career might be over before it had barely begun. For Gary was hit by a five-year ban, with four of the years suspended, after failing a random drugs test.

He admitted smoking cannabis at a party and there were calls for him to be thrown out of the sport for life. While he was suspended, Havelock was hit by a further six months ban for an alleged incident in the Fours final at Peterborough, though this was a charge which he strongly denied. This effectively ruled him out of action for the whole of 1989 and the first two months of 1990.

However, once reinstated, 1990 turned out to be a good year for the Eaglescliffe rider. He was No.1 at Bradford by this time and won the British semi-final and finished fourth in the British Final. However he was very disappointed to go out of the world championships at the Overseas Final stage, because the world finals were being held on his home track at Bradford that year.

Gary still enjoyed plenty of success on the Odsal track and helped Bradford to win the Knockout Cup. It was the first success in an incredible run by Bradford in the competition, who won the cup six times in eight years. The following year was even better. Gary won the British semi-final and then went on to become British champion for the first time when winning the final with a maximum score at Coventry.

His success was partly due to a vast improvement on his engine tuning. Gary had already begun tinkering with his engines himself and everything went well until he suffered a disappointing defeat in the Inter Continental Final.

It was at that time that a rider called Neil Evitts told him that his bike was not fast enough. Havelock gave Evitts one of his engines, and it was later passed on to top German engine tuner Otto Lantanhammer for further improvement.

The results were extraordinary. Suddenly Gary was almost unbeatable. In a three test series against the United States, not only did he take 17 points out of 18 in the first test at Bradford, but he broke the track record. In the second test at Swindon, he gained a maximum.

The scene was now set for a mammoth effort in 1992 and Gary did not disappoint. He won just about everything he could, including the British semi-final, going on to retain his British title at Coventry.

Havelock did suffer a setback, just a few days before

the Commonwealth final, when he crashed in Poland and damaged his shoulder and broke a bone in his hand.

He still insisted on riding in the Commonwealth final at King's Lynn and went on to qualify for a run off for first place, only to finish third.

The following week he bounced back to top form by recording an 18 points maximum in the world pairs semi-final in Germany, when partnering Paul Thorp.

Gary continued to go from strength to strength, moving on to win the Overseas final at Coventry. He finished joint top scorer with the crack Swede Per Jonsson in the world semi-final at Bradford, but was beaten in a run off.

Gary then set off for the world pairs final in Lonigo, Italy, along with Kelvin Tatum, and top scored with 17 points, tieing with the United States for first place. He faced a run off with Greg Hancock, but lost the toss for the gate position and this proved to be crucial, because Hancock took the major honours.

The scene was now set for the World Individual Speedway Final in Wroclaw, Poland. It was Gary's first world final and he did not need reminding that no Englishman had won the competition since Michael Lee triumphed in 1980. In fact the last occasion the final had been won by somebody on his debut was Fred Williams in 1950.

However Gary knew that he had performed well against all of his leading rivals during the past few months, including his major threat, Per Jonsson, and felt confident that he could bring the trophy back to Teesside.

Havelock got off to a great start when, having been drawn in gate four in the second heat which included Jonsson, Henrik Gustafsson from Sweden and American Ronnie Correy, Gary went on to win it.

However, Havelock suffered a blow on his second ride in heat eight, when there was a crash ahead of him. Jimmy Nilsen fell and dislodged Zdenek Tesar from his machine, which spun in front of Havelock. Gary could not manoeuvre out of the way and hit his knee on the loose bike's engine. Immediately he thought he had broken his leg, and fell to the ground in pain as soon as he had returned to the pits.

At this stage the heavens opened. Temperatures during the day had soared to 100 degrees, but black rainclouds had been forming ominously from the moment that racing started. Suddenly there was an almighty deluge. The rain was so heavy that the track was awash within minutes. The water began to form in huge pools, which were several feet deep in some areas. The unexpected break gave Gary time to inspect his leg, which he realised was not broken but only badly bruised. Girlfriend Jayne helped with vital massage and Gary was able to get to his feet again.

It seemed certain for some time that the event would be cancelled, but the combined efforts of the local army detachment and the fire brigade managed to clear the track very quickly once the rain had stopped.

Once back on his bike, Gary finished second in the re-run heat behind the Pole Slawomir Drabik. Then there was no stopping him. He was in electric form in his final three heats, winning them all to take the title. Although the track was still wet, it raced better than it had done when dry.

Havelock's final tally of 14 points was enough to give him the world title by a clear winning margin of three points ahead of Jonsson.

At the age of 23, Gary had achieved a lifetime's ambition. Suddenly he was in big demand. Everybody wanted a slice of Gary Havelock. But, as the euphoria gradually settled, Gary was bitterly disappointed to see that there were no tangible benefits from his world success in Poland. The people running speedway did not take advantage of the fact that they had a world champion in their midst and the sport as a whole in this country did not attempt to reap the rewards in a promotional sense.

Havelock defended his crown the following year in Norden in Germany, but didn't ride as well as he would have hoped and had to settle for fourth place.

Injuries are part and parcel of most sports, and Gary picked up another one in 1994 when he broke his collarbone just a few days before one of the rounds of the Overseas final, which decimated his season.

The following year saw the start of the grand prix series to decide the world individual championship, and Gary worked hard to try to make an impact. But he was rarely in the reckoning. He was unhappy with the quality of his engines and did not feel he was getting the best from them.

A change of engine tuner paid massive dividends and Gary was flying by the end of the season, going on to win the Elite League Riders Championship at Swindon.

He made a much better start to the grand prix series in 1996 and was lying fourth overall after two rounds, and

Gary Havelock displays the distinctive riding style, first seen when he was a teenager with Middlesbrough Tigers, which has helped him stay at the top of the speedway profession for over a decade both at home and abroad.

riding well. Then disaster struck in the July, just three days before the third round.

Havelock was riding in an international match for England against Australia at Poole when he was involved in a bad crash on the first corner. As soon as he hit the track, Gary knew that he had suffered a serious injury to his back.

He was rushed to Poole Hospital, from there to Bournemouth, and finally to the Nuffield Hospital on Teesside. After scans and X-rays the doctors revealed that surgery was necessary to repair his broken back. The operation took six hours, with two screws being drilled into the vertebrae above and below the broken one, while a form of wire 'scaffolding' was inserted to support the top and bottom vertebrae and take all the pressure off the broken one.

The following two days were full of nothing but dreadful pain for Gary, who regularly suffered from muscle spams throughout his whole body which at times gave him the feeling that he could not breathe and that he was suffocating.

However, once the muscle problem had subsided, Gary began to recover. He was allowed home within a week. Even so, it was eight months before he was able to go anywhere near a bike again.

He returned to action for the Bradford Dukes at the start of the new season and initially felt some tentativeness on the first corners of the speedway tracks. However he cut down on his foreign commitments to concentrate on regaining his form and went on to enjoy a good season, helping Bradford to win the championship. It was extra special for Gary because it was his testimonial season.

Havelock was devastated therefore, when the Bradford club folded that winter. After ten years at the top of the sport, Gary might have expected a huge demand for his services. But the only team to show interest was Eastbourne.

Gary was grateful to be offered a contract by the South Coast team but did not have a happy time on the small track at Eastbourne. He did his best and tried different engines to try to improve his riding, but nothing seemed to work and gradually his confidence waned.

To make matters worse Havelock was involved in a bust-up with the England management after being stripped of the captaincy, and quit the international scene in disgust. The previous year he had written to the management, as a representative of several disgruntled riders, airing genuine grievances about favouritism and a lack of professionalism. This seemed to count against him when he found himself labelled as a troublemaker.

Gary's circumstances then took another dive when he was sacked by Eastbourne completely out of the blue. However it turned out to be the best thing which could have happened to him. He moved on loan to struggling Poole Pirates who were tailed off at the bottom of the table and seemingly going nowhere. Something clicked immediately. Gary established a rapport with his new teammates and the club officials. He refound his best form and began to pick up around 13 or 14 points a meeting. Poole even dragged themselves away from the bottom of the league.

The following season produced a complete transformation for Poole. With Matt Ford and Mike Golding now running the team, the atmosphere and the results dramatically improved.

A determination to succeed was generated which had not been previously experienced, and Poole enjoyed a brilliant season. In fact they had a chance of winning the title going into the last match of the season at King's Lynn, only to miss out in the very last heat.

Gary suffered a disappointment when initially he missed out on a place in next season's grand prix series, failing to progress beyond the British final at Coventry in driving rain in May 2000. He was only a reserve for the Overseas final, but gained a late boost when American rider John Cook was declared ineligible to race and Gary was given his Overseas chance on his home track at Poole. He took the opportunity with both hands, racing to four heat wins to book his place in the Intercontinental final in Denmark.

Havelock is 32 at the end of the 2000 season, but has lost none of his love for the sport. In fact he is more committed than ever both from a personal point of view, and for the future well-being of the sport.

In addition to riding for Poole, Gary has contracts to race in not one, but two other European countries. He has been competing in Sweden for Linkoping and in Poland for Rzeszow this year.

Naturally this involves an awful lot of travelling, but Gary loves the life. He leaves two bikes permanently stationed in Sweden, but sends a mechanic on ahead to Poland with his machinery.

Gary continues to use Teesside as his base and lives in Marton with wife Jayne and daughter Holly, who was born in November, 1997. His ambition is to see speedway firmly established as Britain's No.2 sport.

George Hedley
Football

GEORGE Albert Hedley was a robust and aggressive centre-forward who sported a distinctive handlebar moustache. He appeared in no less than four FA Cup Finals in a decade, and collected a winner's medal in three of them. Remarkably he did so, despite having a diagnosed heart condition.

He was born in South Bank on May 3, 1876, and soon made the grade with his local team, South Bank FC in the Northern League.

However, it wasn't long before George's consistent performances were eventually spotted by scouts from one of the country's leading clubs at that time, Sheffield United, and he was invited to join the South Yorkshire club.

Initially he only signed amateur forms for the Blades in 1897, but made such an immediate impact that he was offered full professional terms the following year. Coincidently, it was the season when the Blades won their only First Division Championship.

George quickly established himself in the first team and led the attack in Sheffield United's FA Cup Final appearance against Derby County in 1899. Surprisingly he failed to score, but still won a winner's medal in a 4-1 victory against the Rams. The match was played at Crystal Palace in front of a world record crowd of 73,883.

The following year the Blades followed their cup success by finishing runners-up in the First Division to consolidate their position as one of the country's foremost clubs at that time.

On March 9, 1901, George was awarded his one England cap when he led the attack in a 3-0 victory against Ireland at Southampton. The famous all-round sportsman CB Fry also played for England in the same game.

Later that year, George was again back in the FA Cup Final for Sheffield United against Southern Leaguers Tottenham Hotspur. The teams drew 2-2 in their first meeting in front of a new world record crowd of 110,820. However there was to be disappointment for

South Bank born George Hedley's talent was spotted by Sheffield United in 1897.

Hedley when Spurs won the replay by 3-1 at Bolton's Burnden Park ground. The match made history because it was the first time that a club from outside the Football League had won the Cup.

However, it took the Blades just 12 months to make up for that defeat because they were back in the FA Cup Final the next year and this time were triumphant, against Southampton, another Southern League side. Once again they needed a replay before securing the trophy, the first match having ended 1-1. But George only needed two minutes to fire the Blades ahead in the replay, which they won 2-1.

One of his team-mates in that 1902 winning side was Alf Common who would later enter the record books as the country's first £1,000 player when he moved from Sunderland to Middlesbrough in February 1905. Shortly after his second FA Cup triumph, Hedley suffered a serious injury when he tore some heart muscle tissue. His response was to defy medical advice, which suggested he should retire, by signing for Southern League outfit Southampton in May 1903. At The Dell he switched to inside-right, making 80 appearances and scoring 34 goals which helped the

George Hedley, front row centre, pictured with the Second Division Wolves side which upset all the odds to win the FA Cup Final by comprehensively defeating Newcastle United 3-1 in 1908.

Saints secure the Southern League title.

In 1905-06, Southampton marched through to the quarter-finals of the Cup, with Hedley scoring twice in a 6-1 win at home to Middlesbrough in the third round. It was the last of his three years on the South Coast before being transferred to Wolverhampton Wanderers in May, 1906 where in a six year spell at Molineux he made 214 appearances and scored 74 goals.

Even at the age of thirty George was still one of the most feared forwards in the country and his efforts helped Wolves reach the FA Cup Final in 1908, even though they had only finished half way down the Second Division. On the way to the final, Hedley scored three goals, including one in the 2-0 semi-final victory against his former club Southampton at Stamford Bridge.

Wolves met Newcastle United, whose side was packed with internationals, in the final at Crystal Palace. Prior to the match the Geordies were the hot favourites but Wolves imposed their muscular style of play on their more illustrious opponents and opened the scoring in the 40th minute through the Reverend Kenneth Hunt. Almost immediately Hedley struck an all important second goal and Wolves seemed home and dry. To their credit Newcastle came back strongly in the second half and pulled a goal back through their Scottish international Jim Howie. But the Magpies fate was finally sealed five minutes from the end when

Wanderers grabbed another to take the trophy 3-1 thus condemning Newcastle to their third FA Cup Final defeat in four years.

George Hedley's goal also put him in the record books as he became the first man to score for different teams in football's showpiece. In fact this accomplishment stood alone until 1983, when Frank Stapleton achieved a similar feat for Manchester United against Brighton, having previously netted for Arsenal against Manchester United four years earlier.

Hedley stayed at Molineux until 1913, when he was almost 37. The same year he took over as manager of Second Division Bristol City, where he stayed for two seasons, with moderate success, before the Football League programme was suspended due to the First World War.

Following the armistice he became a publican in Bristol from 1918 to 1941 and later returned to the Black Country to run a small boarding house in Wolverhampton. However, he died soon after his arrival on August 16, 1942.

For George Hedley, defying doctor's orders about his medical condition prolonged his fine football career for almost a decade and enabled him to become unique among Teessiders. No other locally born player has won three FA Cup winner's medals and the fact that this outstanding feat was achieved with different clubs adds to his notoriety.

Frank Hodgson
Speedway

FRANK Hodgson, one of the fastest men on two wheels in the Thirties and Forties, was a daredevil rider from Middlesbrough who went on to captain England speedway team and later unknowingly rode the tracks for two months with a broken back.

He came into the sport rather late in life, at the age of 27, having earlier made a bit of a name for himself as a motor bike gymnast, as well as concentrating on building up his family's painting and decorating business in Linthorpe Road.

Frank had started out as a trials rider, and performed miraculous two-bike gymnastics with Charlie Barker at sports carnivals.

However it was his paintbrush and ladders which opened the door for Frank to make the big breakthrough to the cinder track.

The year was 1935, when Frank received a good tip from his Middlesbrough-born pal Ronnie Parkinson, who was himself a speed king and nationally recognised as one of the top sand racing motor cyclists. Ronnie advised Frank to get himself down to Hackney Wick Stadium, where painting work was badly needed, while adding that there might be the chance of a ride or two on the track.

Ernest Frank Hodgson was born May 2, 1908 and was the son of Charlie Hodgson, who was one of the top officials at Middlesbrough Bowling Club. But bowls was a little sedate for Frank. He had his heart set on a rather faster sport.

He arrived at Hackney Wick to discover that there was a great deal of signwriting needed around the track, and he talked himself into the job. During non-working hours, he managed to climb aboard a speedway bike, and suddenly new horizons opened.

At the age of 27, many speedway riders were considering retiring. But Frank loved the thrill of the race, and was determined to make the grade.

Friends recommended that he stuck to painting, but Hodgson stuck to his guns. He quickly established himself as a valuable and popular member of the

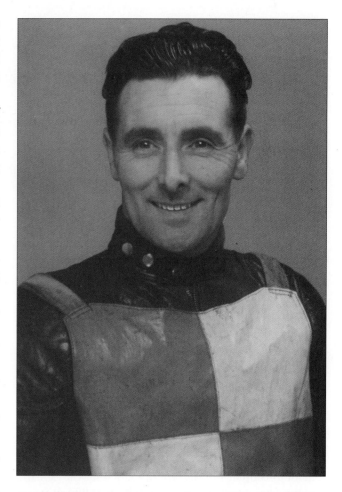

Frank Hodgson came to speedway rather late in life but quickly became one the country's leading riders.

Hackney Wick team. Later he moved on to race for Dagenham, then Nottingham, before returning to the track which gave him his start to captain London.

Hodgson was riding on the crest of a wave when the Second World War arrived. Frank enlisted in the RAF, but there was no competitive speedway racing during active service and he never had the opportunity to race during the hostilities. He did spend some time in the United States with the RAF, where he had the pleasure of meeting singer and actress Gracie Fields in Hollywood, and also served in Canada.

Packed crowds are ready to follow the high speed action as Frank Hodgson moves towards the starting line at Middlesbrough's Cleveland Park track in the summer of 1948.

In 1945, Frank was back in leathers at the ripe old age of 37 and ready to defy the critics again. Immediately he was back in the headlines, but this time thrilling speedway fans on Teesside, where he became a huge favourite at Cleveland Park Stadium.

When the speedway leagues reformed in 1946, Frank was allocated to Borough Bears. But disaster struck a few days before the opening meeting when he fell off his bike in a friendly match against Newcastle and fractured his spine.

A spell in hospital and six weeks in plaster must have seemed like a lifetime to the cinder king, yet it made him all the more determined to race again. The day after his plaster was removed, Frank competed in the preliminary heat of the British Individual Riders Championship at Middlesbrough and qualified for the final in front of an estimated crowd of 10,000. It was a thrilling night for the fans. Frank needed three points in the last heat to qualify, and fought out a terrific duel with Wilf Jay before winning by a wheel.

The same year, Hodgson finished eighth in the British final at Wembley, out of 46 riders. He was the top finisher among the Northern League riders. It was also a great season for the Borough Bears, because Frank skippered them to the Second Division Championship. The following year Frank and the Borough Bears repeated their championship success, with great names like Wilf Plant, Geoff Godwin, Kid Curtis, Tip Mills, Crusty Pye, Herby King and Billy Wilson among those in the squad.

There was a bombshell for Bears fans, however, at the end of that season, when Frank officially asked for a transfer. He did not give his reasons, and stressed that it was with 'great reluctance' that he wanted to get away because of 'circumstances'.

There were reports that Harringay, who were due to resume in the first division in 1948, had been very keen to sign Hodgson and were prepared to pay a record fee. But Harry Whitfield, the Bears' manager, stressed that Frank was definitely not for sale. As the winter passed and the riders were preparing for the new season, it gradually became apparent that Frank would be staying after all. In fact this belief was rubber stamped when Borough turned down a record Second Division transfer fee of £2,000 from Wembley to try to sign Hodgson. The fee consisted of £1,800 cash, plus Wembley rider Bill Kemp.

So Frank stayed and committed himself to the Bears, though this was still to be his last season with the team. The season also brought him another serious back injury. He crashed at Fleetwood in September and rode on for two months without realising he had broken his spine for the second time.

It was thought at first that Hodgson had merely torn spinal muscles in his back. However the pain was horrendous. He raced at Newcastle in agony, and then was driven up to Glasgow for a meeting, while lying on a stretcher! But he still managed to get onto his bike and compete in all his races.

Finally, after eight weeks of pain Frank went for an

Although in constant pain following a serious accident at a meeting in Fleetwood, Frank Hodgson carried on riding for two months unaware that he had broken a bone in his spine.

X-ray, which showed a break in his spine. It brought another spell in hospital, and several weeks in plaster. The injury meant that Frank was unable to accept an offer to skipper the England team on a winter tour of South Africa. However the England selectors did find the perfect replacement in Frank's brother Jack, who had recently taken over the captaincy of the White City Club in Glasgow.

Despite having to miss the England tour, Frank was not to be forced out of the sport by something as minor as a second broken back. Once again he defied the experts by eventually returning to the race saddle. However, as soon as he returned, the death sentence was passed on Middlesbrough's speedway.

Hodgson moved to Newcastle and, after two seasons, he went on to Glasgow to end his racing days. Finally, at the age of 44, he announced his retirement.

During his time as one of the top speedway riders in the country, Frank had led several teams with great distinction, captained England in representative matches, and spent many winters racing in Germany, Belgium and South Africa.

At the end of his racing days, Frank returned to his decorating business, and also continued to tend a small, but productive, market garden in the grounds of his home at Skutterskelfe Hall in Hutton Rudby.

He was occasionally spotted driving around Teesside in his pride and joy, a vintage car. It was a 1927 Galloway, which was the only one of its type in the North-east. The hand built car was manufactured by the private Galloway company in Dumfries, but very few were produced.

Frank died at the age of 74 at his home in Skutterskelfe Hall on May 9, 1983.

Brenda Holliday
Quadrathlon

BRENDA Holliday was a superb long distance swimmer and all-round sportswoman who was the first ever women's world quadrathlon champion at the age of 38 in 1983.

She was a member of the Teesside-dominated team which set a new record for swimming the English Channel in 1965 and she broke several sea and lake individual swimming records in the 1960s.

Arguably Brenda's supreme achievement came in the strength sapping quadrathlon, which involved sea swimming, walking, cycling and marathon running, all of which was held in and around the South East of England.

Brenda, from Middlesbrough, had to complete the four disciplines in 22 hours in order to qualify as a finisher. She swam two miles in the English Channel off the coast at Brighton, walked 31 miles from Brighton to Tunbridge Wells, cycled 100 gruelling miles around the Brands Hatch motor racing circuit in Kent and then ran a 26.2 miles marathon to Gravesend. The event started at 5pm and was held throughout the night.

Not only did Brenda complete the course in the given time, but to her credit she was the only woman competitor to achieve the awesome feat. In the process, she beat 24 of the male competitors, finishing 31st overall. Her aggregate time was 19hr 54min 52sec.

Brenda was born Brenda Evans on August 29, 1944, and grew up in Willow Street in Middlesbrough. She took up swimming while a pupil at Marton Road Secondary School and joined Middlesbrough Ladies, regularly winning local events and also being placed in Northumberland and Durham Schools galas.

In her mid-teens, she was introduced to long distance swimming by Sergeant Martin McNulty, a local policeman and keen swimmer. Brenda discovered that she had a natural aptitude for the sport and joined the Middlesbrough Long Distance Swimming Club to develop that ability.

As a 17-year-old, in her first major event, she crossed the Pennines to Lancashire to win the Morecambe Bay

swim. This was to be the first of several successes in the event. She also finished second in her first attempt at the Sandsend to Whitby race.

The following year Brenda travelled to Torquay for the Torbay eight and a half miles race, but did not finish the course because of the rough seas and cold temperature. However she finished second again in the Sandsend to Whitby race and then retained her Morecambe Bay crown.

In 1964 Brenda won the Sandsend event for the first time and proved her stamina when she triumphed over the gruelling ten miles of the Morecambe Cross Bay event. There was little time for recuperation from her exertions as seven days later she contested the Lake Coniston race.

Not only did she win the event, but she set a new women's record time of 2hr 58min 47sec. It was also the third fastest swim ever on Lake Coniston, the best two having been achieved by men.

Brenda was now ready for the daunting challenge posed by the English Channel. She linked up with a team of six from Middlesbrough Long Distance Swimming Club on June 8, 1965, the others all being men, to make their attempt on the laborious test, competing against uncertain currents. However the team were determined to succeed and set a new record of 10hr 15min, breaking the old time which had stood since 1949.

Brenda was joined in the attempt by Middlesbrough trio Ted Bellerby, 35, a policeman, Peter Hatfield, 28, a sports outfitter and Ron Kellerman, 21, a joiner. The team also included Brian Metcalfe, 16, a Darlington Grammar School pupil, and Tony Heaton, 21, an engineer from Radcliffe.

The team left Cape Gris Nez at 2.40am, led initially into the water by Hatfield, and swam in a strict one-hour rotation before landing both relieved and jubilant on a beach east of Dover at lunchtime. All the swimmers swam twice, except for Metcalfe, and were regularly stung by jellyfish. Bellerby was last man in

June 1965. Brenda Holliday was the only female member of the six strong Middlesbrough Long Distance Swimming Club which broke the cross Channel relay record.

the water, swimming the final 800 yards in 15 minutes and just beating the turning tide, which would have carried him back out to sea.

Brenda continued picking up long distance swimming titles, and made another bid to win the Torbay race in 1965, eventually finishing second in 4hr 11min.

On her 21st birthday, Brenda took first place in the British Long Distance Swimming Association's three-miles Bala Lake swim in Wales. Then she contested the Trentham Lake swim in Derbyshire for the first time and won again.

In 1966 Brenda linked up with the six-man Middlesbrough team and returned to the Channel to double up on her previous achievement by swimming it both ways on September 8 and 9. This was an outstanding accomplishment considering the potential problems which the team faced with the tides. Their time was 26hr 16min.

More long distance titles followed. Brenda won the Douglas Bay event at the Isle of Man, won at Pickmere Lake in Cheshire and dug deep to come home first over the eight miles of the Invergowry Broughty Ferry swim in Scotland in 2hr 21min 22sec.

Brenda eventually became Mrs Brenda Yule and continued her swimming exploits. She made a brave attempt to swim Lake Windermere, but was forced to quit with stomach cramps.

Gradually she turned her attentions towards walking and running and in 1972 won the Lyke Wake Walk women's race in a new record time of 8hr 34min, while wearing hiking boots! She returned to win the event six years later in 7hr 30min.

Brenda also began playing squash, representing the Stockton YMCA club in competitions. She was a regular competitor in the local leagues, winning the Durham and Cleveland county singles championship in 1977 and 1981.

She became a shipping clerk with BSC Shipping

June 1985. Brenda Holliday carried off the world veterans 25k road race championship.

Services in Redcar, and joined Mandale Harriers to concentrate on the local road and moors races. She won the Fennturn Half Marathon in Middlesbrough in August, 1982, in a time of 1hr 21min 35sec.

Less than two months later Brenda competed in her first marathon, winning the Cleveland County race in 2hr 57min. She began building up for the London Marathon and completed the run in 1983 in very creditable 3hr 4min 12sec.

Brenda won the Lyke Wake Walk again in 1983 by regaining the record in an amazing time of 5hr 57min, which knocked 13 minutes off the previous best time.

There was no stopping Brenda at this stage. In the same year, from August 20-21, she recorded her remarkable quadrathlon winning achievement in the world championships, despite having no previous experience of the event. As a result of her success, she was named Cleveland's female sports personality of the year.

Brenda was then invited to join a team of four women to compete in the London to Paris triathlon, which involved swimming the Channel again. The team ran the 100 miles from London to Dover, swam the Channel in rotation, and then cycled 190 miles from Calais to Paris on June 8, 9 and 10. It was another marvellous feat of endurance and the team finished tenth overall. Their best performance came in the Channel swim, where they finished fifth.

Brenda was at the peak of her running and began winning regularly in long distance races, coming home first woman in events such as the Upper Teesdale half marathon, the Loftus Road Run and the Guisborough Moors Race.

On June 8, 1985, at the age of 40, Brenda carried off the world 25k veterans road race championship for the 35-40 age group when comfortably winning the race at Lytham St Annes.

She was now established as one of the top long distance runners in the North. In the same year she came home first in several major races, including the Thirsk, Yorkshire Wolds, Yarmside Holdings, Langbaurgh, Cummins and Kiora Hall half marathons. Her best time of 1min 17min 42sec was set in the Cummins event at Darlington.

Later Brenda competed in the Weatherseal European and British Triathlon Championships. This involved a one-mile swim in the North Sea off Roker beach, followed by a 78-miles bike ride and a 17-miles run into Durham City. However she was unable to complete the event.

In 1987 Brenda suffered a major blow when she snapped her Achilles tendon while playing in the final of the Durham and Cleveland county closed veterans squash championships and was in plaster for three months. She retired from playing squash, but began running again as soon as she'd made recovered from the injury.

Now Mrs Brenda Holliday, she has lost none of her love for physical exercise despite no longer competing in events. She runs regularly in the hills, while also enjoying walking, swimming and cycling.

Kevin Howley
Football

KEVIN Howley was a top FIFA referee who was the youngest man to take charge of an FA Cup Final when officiating between Wolves and Blackburn Rovers at the age of 35 in 1960.

He was on the FIFA list for 14 years from 1957 to 1971, during which time he travelled Europe and America to officiate at major games, and was a linesman during the 1966 World Cup in England.

Before this World Cup competition, Howley was invited to visit South and Central America to give players in countries like Mexico, Peru, Argentina and Brazil experience of taking part in games controlled by an English referee. He travelled 50,000 air miles during this tour.

Kevin, who was known to his close friends as Ken, came from Cargo Fleet. He was a teenager at the outbreak of the Second World War and served all over the world in the Royal Navy as a torpedo operator. It was during the war that he began refereeing while serving with the Navy in Algiers in 1944.

Howley was demobbed in 1946 and took out his ref's certificate with the North Riding FA. He gained employment as an assistant mill foreman at Cargo Fleet Iron and Steel Works and began to officiate in local Teesside leagues. His domestic career as a ref began when he controlled a match between Acklam Parish Church against Sutton Estate at Tollesby. His fee was 2s 6d, out of which he had to pay 3d in bus fares. Kevin did not have a proper ref's outfit at the time, so he turned out in his Navy tropical kit.

It was the first rung of a ladder which was to take Kevin climbing quickly to the top of the tree. Five years later he was running the line in the Football League.

Howley, who now worked as a records clerk for ICI's Nylon Plant at Billingham, made such phenomenal progress that he was promoted to the FIFA list in 1957. In the same year Kevin took charge of the FA Cup semi-final between Aston Villa and West Bromwich, which Villa won. Later in the year he was given control of the Charity Shield match between League Champions Manchester United and FA Cup holders Aston Villa at Old Trafford.

He was also involved in a much publicised incident when he took charge of the first ever floodlit game at Ayresome Park on October 17, 1957, when Boro met Sunderland in a friendly derby.

Howley awarded a penalty when Brian Clough was brought down in full flow. Lindy Delapenha hammered the ball into the net and it came out through a hole in the back. Sunderland immediately claimed that it was no goal, and Kevin awarded a goal kick.

He always stressed that he had not seen the ball enter the net, and therefore had made the right decision. Despite protestations from the 27,241 crowd and the Boro players, he would not change his mind. However it was later discovered that the pegs holding the net had not been fitted correctly, and that the ball could conceivably have escaped under the net. Boro still won the game 2-0. Throughout the rest of his life, Howley was ribbed about the incident.

Kevin received the greatest domestic honour for referees when taking charge of the Wembley final between Wolves and Blackburn, which Wolves won 3-0. He always kept the Cup Final whistle as a treasured memento.

In the same year, Howley took charge of the Germany v Portugal and Scotland v Wales internationals, and also an under-23 game between England and Hungary.

In 1962 Kevin was handed control of a needle match between Nationale Montevideo and Cola Cola of Chile in the semi-finals of the South American Cup. One tremendous fracas brought a ten-minute stoppage in play, during which time simply Howley sat on the ball and waited for the aggravation to subside. Then he calmly dismissed two players and cautioned three others.

The following year Kevin flew to Valencia to take control of the second leg of the Inter Cities Fairs Cup Final between Valencia and Dynamo Zagreb, which

In 1960, at the age of 35, Kevin Howley was the youngest referee to take charge of an FA Cup Final.

the Spanish side won 2-0 and 4-1 on aggregate.

Howley was once in charge of a game at Goodison Park when he awarded a penalty against Everton. At that moment, an apple was thrown at him from the crowd. Kevin calmly took a bite from the apple and then threw it away.

Afterwards, every time that he appeared at Goodison Park, an apple would come flying from the same area of the crowd. Kevin always took a bite, and then tossed it aside.

In 1965, Howley took charge of what he described as the roughest and hardest game of his career between Scotland and Spain and Hampden Park. He sent one player off, and was given a hard time by fans and players alike. Later he described the stadium as a 'referee's graveyard'.

In the build up to the 1966 World Cup, Kevin flew out to join in training with the Chilean national team so they could get used to playing in matches controlled by an English official. He intended to stay for five weeks, but eventually stopped for 63 days as he refereed games in Peru, Bolivia, Ecuador, Brazil, Mexico, Uruguay, Panama, Chile and Argentina.

One one occasion, when refereeing a match between Chile and Uruguay, he was given an armed escort to and from his hotel. Later, when he sent off a Chilean player for punching an opponent, 250 people invaded the pitch, including a radio commentator.

Kevin had hoped to be given charge of one of the 1966 World Cup games in England but eventually had to settle for the distinction of running the line in the third and fourth placed tie between Portugal and Russia.

He was at Brunton Park in 1968, refereeing a match between Carlisle and Chelsea in the League Cup, when a piece of slate was thrown from the crowd and knocked out Chelsea goalkeeper Peter Bonetti.

Howley stopped the game and went into the main stand to make a loudspeaker announcement that if there was a repeat of the incident, he would empty the ground and continue the match behind closed doors. Not surprisingly there were no further problems.

Kevin's very last match, ironically, was as a linesman, when he joined an English trio to officiate in the European Cup Final between Alax and Panathinaikos at Wembley in June, 1971. Jack Taylor was the referee, while Kevin and fellow Teessider Pat Partridge ran the lines. It was the only occasion when Kevin and Pat worked together in the same match.

Howley stepped down from the official refs' list that same year and became an assessor. He had taken charge of 34 internationals, ten representative and 43 European Cup games and more than 600 league and cup games during a distinguished career in the middle. Kevin remained as an assessor until 1981, when he retired to his home in Malvern Road, Billingham. He was a well known character in the town, particularly at Billingham Constitutional Club, where he was treasurer and an occasional snooker player.

He died in North Tees Hospital in July, 1997, aged 73.

Nicky Jarvis
Table Tennis

NICKY Jarvis first played for the full England team at the age of 15 and went on to make more than 250 international appearances.

He competed in three world championships and four European championships, and travelled all over the world to play in major tournaments, including Japan and China.

He was England's No.1 at the age of 20 and reached the final of the English closed championships on three occasions.

Nicky helped the Ormesby club to win the European Cup in 1972 and later played alongside the best players in Europe in the Bundesliga in Germany, before his career was ended prematurely by a back problem at the age of 26.

Nicky was born in Middlesbrough General Hospital on March 7, 1954, and grew up in Redcar. He attended St Mary's Junior School and later St Mary's College in Middlesbrough.

He was a keen footballer at school, playing for Middlesbrough Boys against Redcar, and also won the Redcar swimming championships on two occasions.

He was introduced to table tennis on the dining room table at home, while still at junior school, and began playing seriously on a lunchtime at St Mary's College. Nicky was a keen Boro fan and used to watch the Boro in action on a Saturday afternoon, and then move on to St Joseph's Youth Club in Marton Road to play table tennis.

Later he joined Redcar Boys Club in Coatham Road, initially to play football in the fire station next to the club. Once this particular facility came to an end, he concentrated on table tennis.

Eventually Nicky linked up with another top young player, Peter Able, who played for Teesville, and the duo joined Ormesby together.

Nicky's progress was rapid. He had a natural aptitude for table tennis and became a junior international at the age of 13 when playing for England against West Germany at Barnsley, winning one of his two games against opponents up to the age of 17. The following year he gained valuable experience when competing in the European Junior Championships at Oberstaun in Austria.

Jarvis became the England No.1 junior at the age of 15 and went on to win the inaugural England junior title at Loughborough University.

In the same year he became a senior England international, still aged 15, though feeling very nervous playing in front of 1,500 people against Sweden at Eston Sports Centre. Ormesby teammate Denis Neale played in the same match.

Over the next couple of years Nicky continued to play in both senior and junior internationals, eventually bowing out at junior level with a resounding performance when winning 13 of his 15 matches in a team event in Ostend.

Jarvis was ranked as the No.4 player in England at this time. He was a key member of the cracking Ormesby team which brought major honours to Teesside when carrying off the prestigious European Cup when beating the Swedish club Falkenburg over two legs in the final in 1972.

However Nicky received a shock, shortly after the Ormesby team had qualified for the final, when coach Alan Ransome announced that they would be travelling to Falkenburg by car. Teammate Trevor Taylor had refused to fly and, in order not to weaken the team, Alan had organised a 36-hour road journey - in both directions.

Nicky was learning to play the guitar at the time. He recalled: "Denis and I were furious when we discovered we had to go by car. So I took the guitar along and we composed a song about Alan which we sang all the way. He couldn't stop us because he was driving. But we had a wonderful team spirit, and I suppose this helped us a great deal."

Jarvis won two sets in Ormesby's 6-3 victory in Sweden. He was also in unbeatable form in the 7-2 second leg victory at Ormesby when the Evening

Nicky Jarvis was only 15 when he made his table tennis debut for England.

Gazette reported that "his forehand loop was almost unplayable".

Shortly after leaving school, and still aged only 18, Jarvis jetted off to Tokio to study table tennis under the guidance of the world's top coach, Ogimura. The cost of the trip was met by table tennis equipment manufacturers Stiga, and Jarvis was the first British player given the opportunity to make this trip. It was no holiday. Jarvis played six and a half hours of table tennis every day except Sunday - when he played for four and a half hours.

It was initially a traumatic experience for Nicky, especially when he first arrived and discovered that he had to rise at 6am every morning to take part in a three-miles run. Another problem was the food. It was largely raw, and not for a European palate.

Nicky said: "It was more than just a learning experience. I came back a different person. Beforehand, playing table tennis had been a joyride for me. Now I concentrated on becoming a good player."

The Japanese diet had helped to alter Nicky's eating habits. Instead to sticking rigidly to steak and chips, suddenly he was eating everything and anything.

But the biggest difference was in his training methods. He became more dedicated, and concentrated heavily on fitness and physical strength.

He even trained with Middlesbrough FC in two different spells, initially when Stan Anderson was manager, and then when Jack Charlton was at the helm. He become friendly with several members of the squad.

Jarvis competed in the European Championships in Rotterdam in 1972, and then travelled to Sarajevo for the world championships the following year. Other tournaments took him all over Europe and to China and Russia. He also spent two weeks training in Canada at the invitation of the Canadian TTA.

At the age of 20, in November, 1974, Jarvis became the new England No.1 following victories in the North of England, Humberside and Midland open tournaments. He replaced Denis Neale, his Ormesby colleague, at the top.

The following January, Nicky combined with his former Ormesby teammate Trevor Taylor to form England's second string and win the men's team event at the Norwich Union Open Championships at Brighton. They beat Hungary 3-0, France 3-2, China II 3-2, Russia 3-0 and then China by 3-2 in the final

In the same month Jarvis set off to represent England in the Commonwealth Championships in Melbourne. He helped England to win the team event, but was bitterly disappointed to be knocked out in the quarter-finals of the singles by the Australian No.1 because he had hoped to go all the way.

He set off for his second world championships, this time in Calcutta, but his hopes of doing well ended when he was struck down by a mystery virus and was seriously ill for three days.

Nicky reached the final of the Norwich Union Closed Championships at Crystal Palace in the same year but was beaten by his fellow Teessider Neale. Jarvis had beaten Paul Day by 3-1 in the semi-finals.

He was back in the final the following year after gaining his revenge on Neale in the semis. But this time he was beaten again in the final, by Desmond Douglas.

Jarvis began to suffer painful problems with his back in 1976 and it came to a head during the Yugoslav Open when he broke down completely during a match and was unable to move.

Once back in England, he visited Boro FC doctor Neil Phillips, and was later referred to John Buck, one of the foremost back surgeons in the world. Mr Buck diagnosed a cracked vertebra in his back.

An operation was necessary not only to save Nicky's career, but to prevent more serious problems in years to come. The operation took place in March, 1977, and came at a bad time because it meant that he was unable to compete in the world championships in Birmingham, when he believed he could have made a major impact.

The operation involved a piece of bone being taken from Nicky's hip and used to replace the cracked vertebra. It was secured with two screws.

Jarvis was able to walk out of the hospital ten days later but it was not until the September that he could step up his training to full pace again. Before Christmas he had won the North of England Open and was playing for England again when helping them to beat Sweden in a European League game at Gloucester. He also triumphed in the crucial match, combining with Desmond Douglas to win the doubles.

Jarvis was beginning to return to his peak. He stormed through to the final of the Norwich Union English Closed Championships at Woking in 1978, but was beaten by the extra fitness of Cambridge student Paul Day. It was Nicky's third defeat in the final.

Day won 15-21, 21-15, 21-5, 12-21, 21-15, after Jarvis had avoided a four-sets defeat when fighting back to win the fourth from 7-2 down.

Jarvis then joined a four-man English team for the European Championships in Duisberg. He linked up with Desmond Douglas, Paul Day and John Hilton and the quartet reached the final. The team was hopeful of winning the event, and so they were devastated when Hungary beat them.

The same year Jarvis was offered a lucrative contract to play in the Bundesliga for the Badhamm team, where he replaced his former Ormesby teammate Jimmy Walker, who was moving to the Reutlingen club. He played in Germany for a full season and did well, though he was advised to return to England by the ETTA the following year.

In March. 1979, Jarvis began to suffer trouble with the nerves in his leg, and the problem was eventually traced to his back again.

He recovered sufficiently to travel to North Korea for the world championships in Pyongyang but the leg problem returned, and Nicky was unable to do himself justice.

He did struggle on for another year, but finally hung up his bat after suffering a bout of meningitis which initially put him into hospital for a few days and left him sidelined for three months.

It was a frustrating early end to such a productive sporting career, at the age of 26, though Nicky bears no regrets. He made his mark in table tennis, which he had set out to do, having reached No.14 in Europe and No.22 in the world. Today he is happy to enjoy the occasional round of golf, off a ten handicap.

In 1976 Nicky had moved into business with Tees Sport, and he was able to concentrate on developing his these interests following his retirement.

He also retained an involvement with international table tennis when being appointed as non playing captain of England. This was a role he held for three years.

However Jarvis returned to playing competitive table tennis in the mid-Eighties after accepting an opportunity to coach the younger players at The Grove club in Market Drayton. Eventually he was coaxed out of retirement and began playing again for the club in the British League. However the back problem returned during a match at Maidenhead, near Christmas, and Nicky was in pain for three months. He did not play competitively again.

Nicky is now a partner in Jarvis Sports, which is a specialist table tennis equipment company. However he also spends a great deal of his time coaching.

Table tennis is very much in the family because in 1979 Nicky married Linda Howard, who was England's No.1 women's table tennis player at one time and who reached a highest European ranking of twelve.

In 2000 the family lived in Guildford with sons Ben, 17, and Matthew 14, who is a young footballer with Millwall and a county champion both as an athlete in the 1,500 metres and as a 100 metres breaststroke swimmer.

Paul Jarvis

Cricket

PAUL Jarvis was the youngest player to make his first class debut for Yorkshire at the age of 16 years and 75 days.

He went on to play in nine Tests for England and 16 one-day internationals, though it would have been many more but for unfortunate injury setbacks.

Paul eventually left Yorkshire to join Sussex, and then moved on to Somerset to extend his impressive 20 year career at the highest level of cricket in which he has taken more than 1,000 wickets in all competitions.

Paul William Jarvis, who was born in Redcar on June 29, 1965, attended Bydales Comprehensive School in Marske and showed promise from an early age. In fact he was chosen to play for Marske Under-14 team when only eight. By the time he was 15, he was bowling second change for Marske first XI.

He was born into a real cricketing family, his father Malcolm having played with distinction for Marske for more than 30 years in the North Yorkshire and South Durham League. His brother Andrew played for England Schools Under-15s and had trials with Northamptonshire and Derbyshire.

However Paul had more good fortune in his attempts to earn a first class career, and his impressive efforts soon attracted the interest of Yorkshire. After five notable games for Yorkshire Colts in 1982, Paul became the youngest player ever to represent Yorkshire in a competitive game when he made his debut against Lancashire in the John Player League at the age of 16. His record-breaking first class bow followed soon afterwards against Sussex at Hove. All in a whirlwind fortnight.

A right-arm fast medium bowler and lower order right hand batsman, Paul's career was hampered by a series of breakdowns and illness ranging from severe back problems to blood poisoning. At 5ft10in he was rather short for a fast bowler and suffered from being over bowled when Yorkshire's choice of pace attack was very limited.

Jarvis played for Young England against the West Indies in 1982, and against Australia the following year. He expanded his cricket education by spending three winters playing club cricket overseas. In 1984-85, Paul played for the Mosman Middle Harbour club in Sydney, 12 months later he turned out for Avendale in Cape Town and the following year he played for Manly Warringah in Sydney.

Jarvis played for the Tykes between 1981 and 1993, being awarded his county cap on June 23, 1986. One of the high spots of Paul's career came when he took a hat trick against Derbyshire at Chesterfield in 1985. He was the youngest Yorkshireman ever to achieve the feat. In 1986-87 he toured St Lucia and Barbados with Yorkshire. He returned to England and enjoyed particular success the following season, when he took 81 wickets at an average of 24.58.

Jarvis helped Yorkshire to reach the Benson and Hedges Cup Final in 1987 and his superb performance at Lord's played a major part in the Tykes beating Northants to win the trophy.

The Marske bowler took four wickets for 34 runs off 11 overs as Northants made 244-7. Yorkshire had also totalled 244 by the time the final ball was bowled, but won the trophy because they had lost only six wickets in reaching their tally.

Paul's accuracy and ability to swing the ball away from right-handers in 1987 earned him a call-up to the England side and he took part in the tour to Pakistan, New Zealand and Australia in the winter of 1987-88.

Injury prevented Paul from enjoying an extended run in the Test side, while he joined the 'rebel' tour to South Africa and received an international ban. However he returned to the international arena after his suspension was remitted and played in a tour to India and Sri Lanka in 1992-93.

In 1994 Jarvis left Yorkshire to link up with Sussex and was heralded as the 'final piece in the jig-saw' by the county captain Allan Wells, who was hoping to win trophies.

At the age of 16, Paul Jarvis was the youngest player to make his first class debut for Yorkshire CCC.

Paul certainly made a great start to his career with Sussex and took 49 wickets in his first season, though his later career with the county was plagued by injury. At the end of his first season with Sussex, Jarvis spent another winter overseas when playing for the Onslow club in Wellington.

He stayed with Sussex for five seasons, during which time he took 127 wickets at an average of 35.05, and weighed in with 822 runs at an average of 19.63. In 1999 he moved on to Somerset.

During his career, Paul has taken 50 or more wickets in a season on four occasions and at the end of the 1999 season had amassed 668 first class wickets, including 21 Test and 24 one day victims. His bowling average in the Championship was 29.01 and his best performance was 7-55 for Yorkshire against Surrey at Headingley in 1986.

He has also occasionally been very effective as a hard hitting batsman, having made a highest championship score of 80 for Yorkshire against Northants at Scarborough in 1992. In all competitions he has scored almost 5,000 runs.

Paul Jarvis, who has two children, Alexander, born in 1989, and Isballa, born in 1993, is qualified as an advanced cricket coach and has studied for a degree in sports science.

Alyson Jones
Swimming

ALYSON Jones was a highly talented teenage swimmer, who won a bronze medal at the 1972 Commonwealth Games in Christchurch, New Zealand. Despite years of studying to qualify as a doctor, she never lost her competitive spirit and, at the age of 28, became the oldest winner of a first national crown in the Amateur Swimming Association British national championships in 1985.

Alyson, who swam for the Hartlepool club as a teenager, achieved an international call-up as a 15-year-old when she swam in the 100 metres freestyle relay in the Four Countries competition at Aberavon in Wales. She followed this up by storming home to victory in the individual event in the English Schools Championships.

Jones went on to smash the Northumberland and Durham women's 100 metres freestyle record, winning the event at Hartlepool's new swimming baths in 1min 2.5sec. This was seven tenths of a second inside the Olympic qualifying time.

Alyson, who lived in Lunedale Avenue, Acklam, travelled to Crystal Palace for the Olympic trials with high hopes. Again, she achieved the Olympic qualifying time in her heat. But with three other swimmers achieving the same time, Alyson was the unlucky one to drop out. As a result of failing to reach the final, she was not selected for the British team for the Olympic 4x100 metres freestyle relay squad for Munich.

Although missing the Olympics was undoubtedly a major blow, Alyson still had plenty of time to achieve her ambitions. The following year she again swam in the Four Countries event, and was then selected by Great Britain for the relay in a major four nations match in Dortmund, against West Germany, Holland and Italy. The British girls competed well eventually finishing second to Germany.

Later in the year Alyson, who attended Acklam High School, finished a fine second in the girls' 16-17 years 100 metres freestyle event at the national age group championships at Coventry.

Her excellent form was rewarded with a place in the England swimming team for the Commonwealth Games in Christchurch in January, 1974. After 11 days' intensive training at Crystal Palace, Alyson flew out to New Zealand.

Her trip paid major dividends when she won the bronze medal with the 4x100 metres freestyle relay team. Canada took the gold, and Australia the silver.

Alyson left Acklam High School to study medicine at Nottingham University, and joined the Nova Centurions swimming club in Nottingham. She competed in the World Student Games in Bulgaria in 1977 and in Mexico two years later. She also won the British Universities Championship at both 100 and 200 metres freestyle. Her times of 1min 1.2sec and 2min 13.9sec. were new championship records.

After qualifying as a doctor, Alyson joined a London hospital. Her medical studies continued and limited her training, though she continued swimming and joined the Swiss Cottage club.

Jones became a doctor in Harrow and was able, gradually, to devote more time to building up her competitive edge again. Her love of the sport brought her back into major events. In 1985 she created swimming history when becoming the oldest woman, at the age of 28, to win her first national crown. She outsprinted Fleetwood's 16-year-old Lesley Masters to win the 100 metres freestyle in 59.71sec at the ASA national championships in Leeds.

The next day, Alyson did it again. She won the 50 metres sprint, despite having qualified with only the third fastest time. She edged out the pack in the final few metres to win in 27.68sec, just one hundredth of a second faster than 19-year-old Sarah Garrett from Beckenham.

The following year, Alyson won three gold medals in the Sun Life English Masters Championships at Scarborough. She won the 30-34 years 50 metres butterfly, 100 metres freestyle and individual medley.

Commonwealth bronze medallist Dr Alyson Jones was the oldest woman to win a first ASA title when she won the 100 metres freestyle in 1985.

Gordon Jones
Football

SINCE the Second World War no player made more appearances for Middlesbrough than Gordon Jones.

He was a remarkable club servant for 15 years, going on to play in 528 league and cup games. Only the legendary goalkeeper Tim Williamson played more games in the history of the club.

As a naturally left footed full-back, Gordon was the ideal defender, strong in the tackle, but keen to move forward at every opportunity to deliver his pin-point crosses which created many goals over the years.

Born in Sedgefield on March 6, 1943, Gordon Edward Jones signed amateur forms as a 15-year-old for Boro in August, 1958, after one of the briefest trials of all time. He had played only the first ten minutes of a match at Hutton Road, watched by manager Bob Dennison and trainer Harold Shepherdson, before being removed from the action. Back in the dressing room Gordon disconsolately thought his football career was over before it had even started.

However, to his surprise, Boro coach Jimmy Gordon came in to say that the club wanted to speak·to his father. Apparently he had made such an instant impact with the accuracy of his left footed distribution that the Boro coaching staff immediately knew he was a cut above the rest.

Two years later Jones became a full-time professional, before going on to make his debut in January, 1961, at Southampton as a very late replacement for right-back Derek Stonehouse, who was taken ill prior to the kick-off. Boro lost the game by 3-2. But Gordon made such a big impression in this initial appearance that he never looked back, staying in the side as a permanent fixture eventually making 462 league appearances for Boro in a career spanning 13 seasons.

Jones was always quick to support his attack, but personal goals were a rare occurrence and he scored only four in his Boro career. The first one came in a 2-2 draw at Preston NE in September, 1963. His only goal at Ayresome Park was in a 3-1 win against Bournemouth in the Third Division in February, 1967.

In November, 1961, Gordon's promising performances were quickly rewarded with the first of nine under-23 caps in a 7-1 win against Israel at Elland Road. Although the England team were unbeaten in every match in which he appeared, he was surprisingly never called upon to play at full international level.

Boro fans were hopeful that Jones's strong work up and down the left flank would win him a place in the build up to England's World Cup campaign in 1966, but again he was overlooked.

During the early part of his Boro career, Gordon supplied the ammunition for those prolific goalscorers Brian Clough and Alan Peacock but he acknowledges his favourite Boro player was Welsh international Bill Harris, whose passing ability he greatly admired.

When Bob Dennison was replaced as manager by Raich Carter in January 1963, Boro's fortunes began to slide alarmingly and the once proud club were eventually relegated to the Third Division in 1966.

For Boro's first ever season in the Football League basement Jones was handed the club captaincy by new manager, Stan Anderson. He skippered the side which included John Hickton, John O'Rourke and Dickie Rooks to immediate promotion in one of the club's most nailbiting finales to a season when the final two home games were won to secure the runners up place behind Queens Park Rangers.

During the six years which followed, Gordon was virtually an ever present in the side. Anderson strengthened the team and they were constantly challenging for a return to the top flight. Despite going agonisingly close on a number of occasions, Gordon was never to fulfil his ambition of playing in the First Division with Boro.

Gordon Jones was awarded a much deserved testimonial at Ayresome Park in 1969 and at the end of the 1972-73 season he made the short journey to Darlington where he played 85 games for the Quakers. He retired after two seasons at Feethams to pursue a business career on Teesside where he still lives today.

England Under-23 full-back, Gordon Jones, surprised himself when he was invited to join Middlesbrough as an apprentice, but he would spend 15 years with the club and make over 500 first team appearances.

Carole Knight-Moore
Table Tennis

CAROLE KNIGHT-MOORE was quite simply the best woman table tennis player ever to emerge from Teesside.

She competed regularly against the best in the world and was an established England international for ten years, carrying off the national title on three occasions. She won major tournaments all around the world, including the Commonwealth Championships in Bombay.

Carole Knight was born on June 9, 1957, in Berwick Hills, Middlesbrough, and was educated at Berwick Hills Primary and then Langbaurgh School.

She excelled at athletics at school, being particularly good at sprinting and long jumping. However her best sport was the javelin, in which she competed in the English Schools Championships.

Remarkably Carole had never played table tennis until she was 14 and only then was she introduced to the game by pure chance. In fact football was always Carole's first love. Not only did she play the game, but she was as good as any of the boys and played centre-forward for the local Joe Walton's Youth Club.

However, one evening, a football practice session was called off and Carole was asked to fill in for the table tennis team when one of the players failed to arrive.

Joe Walton's were playing top local team Ormesby that night and, although Carole didn't even fully understand the rules, somehow she managed to win her game. That night was a watershed in her life. Suddenly she was hooked on table tennis. She began playing for the Langbaurgh School side and never looked back.

Her innate talent had already been spotted by representatives from the Ormesby club and she was invited to join them. She agreed at once and, from then on, playing football took a back seat.

The area's top table tennis coach Alan Ransome recognised Carole's potential and encouraged her to fully develop her talents. Such was her appetite to improve, that she regularly went to the club straight from school and practised hard until ten at night, seven nights a week.

Carole left school at 16 and worked during the day as a clerk for a local taxi firm which was run by her father James. However, every evening, she continued developing her table tennis skills at the Ormesby club. In August, 1973, Carole qualified to take part in an England intermediate assessment camp at Lilleshall and beat all the other girls taking part. By the end of the year she was ranked 12th woman in England, and fifth in the juniors.

Carole took another step forward by winning the North of England Junior Open, and made her junior international debut in the March of the following year, helping England to beat Wales by 9-0 in Cardiff. In her singles match she beat Pat Allen of Wrexham by 21-14, 21-19, and combined with Karen Rogers of Leicester to beat Allen and Julie Ralphs 21-15, 21-10. She stayed on in Cardiff to win the junior final of the Stiga Welsh Open, beating Rogers in a three set final. Then she proved her undoubted potential in the women's event before eventually losing to world No.3 Alica Grofova from Czechoslovakia.

Carole was showing dramatic improvement month by month. She marched on to become English Junior Open champion in May, 1974, when she beat Dutch No.1 Marian Wagemaker in an exciting final at Worthing. Carole lost the first set 21-12 and was 17-13 down in the second before fighting back to take the next two sets by 21-19 and 21-18 for the match.

Victory earned Carole a place in the England team for a junior quadrangular match in Glasgow. She went on to reach the final, before losing to Karen Senior from Ireland. However she helped England win the team event.

Carole was now the No.1 ranked junior in England, which was an astonishing achievement considering she had not picked up a tennis bat until two years earlier.

In the August, she reached the quarter-finals of the European youth championships in West Germany and also played a major role in the English girls finishing fourth in the team event.

In January, 1975, she made her senior international debut, playing against China at Thornaby Pavilion. It was very much a learning experience for the Teesside teenager. She lost to Yu Ching Chia by 12-21, 13-21 in the singles and also went down in two sets when combining with Jill Hammersley in the doubles.

Soon afterwards Carole was called up to compete for England in the Commonwealth Championships in Melbourne. Table tennis did not feature on the Commonwealth Games sporting calendar, so the championships were organised in their place.

At 17, Carole was the youngest member of the England party. However she made a huge impact, storming through to the semi-finals where she put up a magnificent fight before eventually going down to the holder and England No.1 Hammersley by 14-21, 21-19, 13-21, 20-22.

She also combined with Karenza Matthews to reach the women's doubles semi-final, before losing in four sets to New Zealanders Ann Stonestreet and Neti Traill.

However the English team of Knight, Hammersley and Linda Howard won the team competition.

Carole was already one of the country's top women players after just three full years in the sport. Back in Britain, she reached the final of the Norwich Union English Closed Championships at Crystal Palace, where she again met Hammersley. Playing superbly, Carole won the first two sets and looked set to pull off a mammoth victory when leading 7-4 in the third. However she then lost the initiative and Hammersley hit back to record an unlikely success.

Carole later admitted that her inexperience probably cost her victory. She said: "Players were allowed to take a break and I needed one. Jill was a good defender and I should have taken the break to upset her rhythm. But I didn't, and I paid for that lack of experience."

There was some consolation when Carole combined with Karenza Matthews from Middlesex to beat Hammersley and Linda Howard in straight sets in the doubles final.

The Ormesby Ladies team was one of the strongest in the country at this time and they achieved a notable landmark when carrying off the national title when beating the hot favourites Guildford by 5-4 in the final at Stroud.

Ormesby, who included Carole, Angela Tierney and

June Williams in their line-up, beat a trio consisting of Linda Howard, Sue Henderson and Judy Williams.

In May 1976, Carole had her first of several brushes with the game's international selectors when she was temporarily withdrawn from the international squad for alleged use of bad language. Carole refuted the allegations but was forced to serve a short period on the sidelines.

However she returned to compete in the European youth championships in Prague, where she helped England to reach the final of the team event, before they were beaten by Russia.

Carole then became the first Teessider ever to win a singles title in the Norwich Union English Open Championships when beating European champion Hammersley in a magnificent final at Thornaby Pavilion. The match went to five sets, with Hammersley saving five match points in a thrilling climax, before Carole finally won the day.

The following month Carole did it again, in another classic. This time she beat Hammersley over five sets in the final of the Norwich Union English Closed Championships at Woking. It was Carole's first domestic title.

Carole was then called up to compete in the world championships at Birmingham, where the competition was hot. However she was not out of her depth and helped England to finish fourth in their Corbillion Cup group. In a great singles match, she came within three points of beating the world No.1 Pak Yung Sun. With the match tied at 2-2, Carole was leading 10-6 in the final set when they had to switch ends. The move somehow affected Carole's concentration and she lost six points in a row and ultimately the match.

Carole was also playing her part in another strong surge by Ormesby in the national championships. The Teesside club eventually retained their title by beating Fellows Cranleigh from Essex by 5-1 in the final in Stroud. Carole won both of her matches.

Her phenomenal performances earned Carole the English No.1 ranking for the first time in May, 1977, when she replaced Jill Hammersley at the top of the tree.

Carole celebrated with a three-week trip to America where she won the Canadian Open before moving on to Kingston to reach the final of the Jamaica Open. There was an invitation for her to fly on to Los Angeles to compete in the US Open, but Carole decided to have a rest and holidayed in Jamaica for a month.

Carol Knight-Moore didn't even pick up a table tennis bat until she was 14 but she soon made up for lost time by the becoming a three times national champion and an established England international.

When she returned home, Carole discovered that she had been named in the world rankings for the first time, coming in at No.28. Her international experience increased when she took part in a two-week tour of China, where she was the only member of the English team to win a match. No sooner had she returned home, than she headed off for Budapest to play in the Hungarian Open, where England were beaten in the team final by Yugoslavia.

Carole was unable to retain her Norwich Union English Open title, going down in the semi-finals to the Yugoslavian Erzebet Palatinus in four sets, by 24-22, 18-21, 11-21, 14-21. However she was unbeaten for England in the team event.

In September, 1978, Carole joined the international jet-set when she signed a lucrative contract to play for Donauworth from Munich in the West German Bundesliga. As a result, she spent every second weekend playing in Germany, where she competed in two club matches and helped Donauworth to third place in the Bundesliga.

However 1979 was a disappointing year for the Teesside girl. Carole competed in the Commonwealth Championships in Edinburgh, and reached the final of the singles, while she also won the doubles along with Linda Howard and helped England to win the team event.

But a series of poor performances sent her hurtling down the national rankings. Severe emotional problems, caused by the sad death of both her father and her brother in law John, within seven weeks of each other, were the major cause of her loss of form.

Carole also needed a cartilage operation on her knee, which put her on the sidelines for some time.

The arrival of 1980 saw an upturn in fortunes. Carole beat Jill Hammersley in an epic five setter in the second round of the Stiga Welsh Open in Cardiff, before going down in three sets to China's Bu Clijman in the quarter-finals.

It was all the warm-up that Carole needed. Eight days later she beat Hammersley 21-13, 20-22, 21-18, 8-21, 21-11 to win the Norwich Union English Closed Championships at Woking for the second time. She was the only player to have beaten Hammersley in the championships since 1973, and so this victory was particularly sweet. Knight also took the doubles, along with Anita Stevenson of Leicester, beating Hammersley and Linda Jarvis by 3-1 in the final.

The same month, Carole reached the quarter-finals of the West German Open before going down to world No.16 Coa Yang Hua from China.

However the England selectors were not over impressed, and Carole was denied the chance to play in crucial international matches, despite winning another final in the Canadian Open in Toronto.

Carole recalled: "Right through my career I had a constant battle with the selection committee. I felt that I had to do three times better than one or two people a bit further south to get the same recognition."

A two-months training programme with the Japanese national team in Tokio enabled Carole to keep physically fit and mentally alert. She also improved her style by developing a safe backhand to enable her to become a more attacking player.

The trip to the Far East paid mammoth dividends in February, 1982, when she won the final of the Commonwealth Championships in Bombay, beating Alison Gordon from Reading by 17-21, 23-21, 21-12, 25-23 in the final. Carole also teamed up with Joy Grundy to beat Indu Puri and Vyoma Shah of India in the doubles final.

The same month, Carole carried off the Norwich Union English Closed title at Basingstoke for the third time when beating Anita Stevenson in straight sets in the final. She was never threatened in winning 21-9, 21-10, 21-16. Anita had earlier made a supreme effort in knocking Jill Hammersley out of the semi-finals.

Carole was now into her fourth season in the Bundesliga, all with different clubs. She had played for Frankfurt and Kronshagen, and was currently playing for the Kaiserburg club in Duisberg. However all the travelling was beginning to take its toll.

In 1983, Carole was offered an ETTA contract for the very first time. The contracts were designed to prevent the top English players from having to ply their trade abroad.

Carole signed the contract but, having married her dentist husband David Moore a few months earlier, it was no longer necessary for her to survive on her table tennis earnings. So she gave the cash from her contract away as a charitable donation.

At the same time, Carole was battling to regain her best form. She had gone into hospital for another knee operation, just two days after getting married, and made the mistake of trying to come back too early.

She lost unexpectedly to Karen Witt in the semi-finals of the English Closed Championships, and was then beaten by a relatively unknown young German girl in the third round of the English Open.

When she failed to gain selection for the world championships, Carole decided to call it a day. She announced her retirement from table tennis live on BBC Grandstand, and gave her forthright reasons why. After the birth of her son, Leigh, Carole switched her attentions to a new sport. She began playing tennis and suddenly became hooked, just as she had done when she first picked up a table tennis bat. She started playing three hours a day on the courts of Tennis World in Middlesbrough and soon became the ladies team captain, going on to play for Durham and Cleveland in county matches.

It was her good friend and long time coach Alan Ransome who finally re-introduced Carole to table tennis. She began coaching at the Ormesby club and then graduated to become captain of the English junior girls team.

Carole switched her attentions to Ormesby for a while before being drafted back on to the international scene. She became a member of the England youth team selection committee for 18 months. Eventually she was offered the England women's team captaincy, but declined because she felt that the task was too big to take on.

Since then Carole has devoted her time to coaching, and is now the regional table tennis coach based at Ormesby. She has helped to build up a new nucleus of top young players, one or two or whom could one day go on to emulate her own magnificent achievements as an international player.

Edwin Latheron
Football

PINKY Latheron was a top class inside-forward from Grangetown who won two Football League Championship medals with Blackburn Rovers, was twice capped by England and represented the Football League on five occasions.

Born in 1887, Edwin Gladstone Latheron arrived at Blackburn almost by accident. He was playing for his local side Grangetown FC when they were drawn against Crosshill in an FA Amateur Cuptie. Representatives of Blackburn attended the match with the intention of watching another member of the North-eastern side but it was the performance of Latheron which caught their eye. So, in March, 1906, a fee of £25 was quickly agreed to take the Teesside teenager to Ewood Park.

Pinky, as he was affectionately known because of his ruddy complexion and red hair, made his debut for Blackburn in December, 1906, in a 4-1 victory over his home town club Middlesbrough.

Latheron developed into a great ball playing inside-forward with dazzling footwork in the Wilf Mannion mould. He had the ability to play on either side of the field and quickly established himself in the Rovers first team. Although only 5ft 5in tall, he was good in the air, but above all he was the perfect team member, being unselfish and willing to graft for others.

It was this enthusiasm which made him a key player in helping Blackburn to win the League title in 1912 and again in 1914.

His outstanding performances at club level were finally rewarded on the international stage when he made his debut for England against Ireland in Belfast on February 15, 1913, and scored the goal in England's 2-1 defeat. The following season he was again called up when England faced Ireland at Middlesbrough. It must have been a proud moment for the Teessider to make an international appearance at Ayresome Park alongside the legendary Boro striker George Elliot. However Pinky and George finished on the losing side as the Irish totally outplayed England to win 3-0.

Edwin Latheron's football career was tragically cut short when he was killed in action in 1917.

As an England international at the peak of his powers, Latheron's engaging personality, style of play and total commitment made him a very popular figure with the Rovers supporters and the footballing public at large for more than a decade.

It was therefore a devastating blow when news was relayed back from France that Latheron had been killed in action for the Royal Field Artillery on October 14, 1917, leaving a widow and child.

Edwin Latheron played the last of his 281 games for Blackburn on March 17, 1917, five days before he marched off to the war. He scored 104 goals for the club. His death was deeply felt not only by his relatives on Teesside but also at Ewood Park, where the Lancashire club was left with the memory of a rare and gifted talent which fate decreed would never have the opportunity to fully mature. It was a tragic loss of such a great player.

Nicola Lavery

Ski-ing

NICOLA Lavery made ski-ing history when she was selected as a member of the first ever British team to compete in the Winter Olympics at the gruelling event of cross country ski-ing.

The Middlesbrough born athlete had previously won the British ski five kilometres championship, which ultimately helped to earn her selection for the British team which took part in the Olympics at Sarajevo in 1984.

Born on November 19, 1960, Nicola attended St Hilda's Boarding School in Whitby, where she excelled in several sports, particularly netball.

Her father was in the Army, and when he was posted to Norway in 1976, Nicola joined up with her parents after leaving school.

The Norwegian barracks were snowbound for much of the winter, so it was only natural for Nicola to take up ski-ing. There were several Britons already actively engaged in the sport, in addition to Norwegian friends. All the ski-ing in the area was cross country, as distinctly opposed to the other sport of downhill racing.

When her father was posted elsewhere, Nicola decided to stay on in Norway and worked at a hotel in Kvitavatin for four hours a day. The rest of her spare time was spent practising her ski-ing technique.

It was from this group of British friends in Norway that the nucleus of the British Olympic women's team was formed. They stayed together as a group for several years, training alongside the Royal Marines. In fact the team was sponsored by the Army.

In the summer Nicola kept fit by running and ski-bounding on roller skis, while she also returned to England to work as an assistant tutor at outward bound centres in the Lake District.

From 1980 onwards, the group began travelling around Europe to race in major events and gain the much needed experience of international competition. Nicola and the team visited countries such as Italy and France in an ageing mini-bus which had previously been used by the British downhill team.

In 1982 Nicola competed in the World Cup Series in Norway, and also won the British 5k title in Germany. She was selected for the Olympics in 1984 competing in both the 20 and 10 kilometres races, and also the relay.

Unfortunately, none of the British ladies were close to winning medals, though it was still a great learning experience to compete at that level.

After Sarajevo, Nicola decided against undergoing another four years of extreme personal sacrifice to train for the 1988 Winter Olympics and moved on to other sports.

She travelled to New Zealand and Australia with her husband Mick Hoffe, where she cycled and took part in triathlons, including the extremely exacting Coast to Coast event.

Once back in England, Nicola turned her attention to serious fell running, while also competing in occasional triathlons.

She won the Lake District triathlon at Loweswater several years in a row and also achieved the distinction of completing the summer Bob Graham Run in less than 24 hours. This lung-bursting event involves climbing up and down 42 peaks and running a total of 72 miles.

In the early 1990s Mick and Nicola sailed a 15-foot yacht across the Atlantic from the Canary Islands to Venezuela, before going on a trekking expedition.

Two years ago Nicola competed in the Bob Graham Run in winter, and again completed the gruelling course in less than 24 hours. It was another major personal achievement.

In the past couple of years she has competed in the team event in the Western Isles Challenge in the Outer Hebrides. This is a quadrathlon involving running, canoeing, swimming and cycling.

Now working as a health visitor, Nicola lives in Kendal with her husband Mick and daughters Alexandra and Joanna.

Having represented Britain in cross country ski-ing at the 1984 Winter Olympics in Sarajevo, Niclola Lavery successfully turned her attention to competing in gruelling long distance triathlon and quadrathlon events at home and abroad.

Geoff McCreesh
Boxing

GEOFFREY McCreesh is one of the strongest pound-for-pound boxers ever produced on Teesside, winning a Lonsdale Belt outright and going on to win four British welterweight title fights before eventually relinquishing the crown.

He also fought for the European welterweight title, making an unsuccessful attempt to beat the reigning champion Michele Piccarillo in Italy.

Geoff was born in North Tees Hospital on June 12, 1970, and grew up in Billingham. He attended Bewley Juniors and Brunner School and made his first impact in sporting circles as a footballer, when he had the notable distinction of playing at Wembley. He was a left-winger at school and was a member of the Bewley Juniors team which played in the Smiths Crisps six-a-side finals at Wembley, prior to the England v Germany Under-21 international.

However Geoff began displaying more natural talents in the boxing ring at the Stockton Amateur Boxing Club, winning the National Association of Boys Clubs Class A Championship in Bristol when he was 15. He earned a unanimous victory over Lewis Reynolds from London in their 7st 7lb final.

Unfortunately, when he left school, Geoff was forced to leave Teesside in search of work, and he settled in Bracknell, Berkshire. He joined the Crown ABC and went on to become Home Counties welterweight champion. He reached a second NABC final, at class C, but this time was beaten by Peter Waudby at Grosvenor House.

McCreesh achieved unwanted national headlines in 1990 when he was involved in a rather unsavoury fracas with a group of yobs when he was fighting Robert McCracken in the ABA welterweight quarter-finals in Birmingham.

Geoff, who had earlier been hit by a beer can thrown into the ring, leapt through the ropes when he saw that his father Doug was pinned to the ground by the yobs after being struck over the head with a chair.

The Billingham boxer's brave act in wading in to defend his dad, led to his disqualification from the championships. However the ABA decided to take no further action at a later hearing.

In 1994, McCreesh turned professional with Reading based manager Jim Evans. He made a fine start to his new career by outpointing Liverpool's Tony Walton, and then stepped up in class to beat former Welsh ABA champion Barry Thorogood.

The route to the top was long and hard, but McCreesh was a never-say-die battler and most opponents could not live with him.

In July, 1997, he won the British welterweight title in a thrilling battle with reigning champion Kevin Lueshing from Beckenham, which had the crowd on its feet from the first bell to the last.

McCreesh's victory was all the more remarkable because he lost almost a stone in weight through grief when his mother and father were involved in a car crash within a month of the fight taking place. Mum Linda was killed in the accident, while father Doug suffered ten broken ribs.

However McCreesh was determined to win the title for his parents, and proud dad Doug defied his injuries to make the trip to Wembley Arena to watch the fight against Lueshing, which was later described as the Fight of the Year.

In mid-September, Geoff defended his title for the first time and recorded a crushing win, stopping Paul 'Scrap Iron' Ryan in devastating style in one minute and 17 seconds of the second round at the North Hall Arena in London.

McCreesh's impressive form earned him a quick tilt at the European title, and he travelled in good heart to Novara, in Italy, to take on the champion Michele Piccarillo.

It turned out to be a difficult contest on the rangy Italian's home soil. Piccarillo opened a cut under Geoff's eye in the first round and scored well with his long left jab. But McCreesh continued to come forward until the fight ended in the ninth round. Geoff

October 1998 and Billingham boxer Geoff McCreesh is the undisputed British welterweight champion.

was floored by a strong right and, after rising at the fifth count, took two more telling punches before the fight was stopped.

Worse was to follow. Not only did McCreesh struggle to obtain his fight fee upon his return to England, but he was informed that he had produced a positive drugs test after the contest.

The Billingham man was found to have the outlawed anabolic steroid Boldenon in his system and was banned from the European rankings for one year by the EBU, and also hit with a £5,000 fine.

McCreesh continued to concentrate on his British crown, and was rewarded on his return to the ring when he won the highly prized Lonsdale Belt outright when successfully defending his title for the second time in July, 1998.

He met Michael Smyth at Reading's Rivermead Centre and stopped the Welshman in seven rounds.

Unfortunately, once again McCreesh found himself unwittingly surrounded by controversy when Smyth's fans started a riot when their man was on the verge of defeat in the sixth round.

The bout had to be suspended for five minutes before police and stewards could restore order. However McCreesh was more determined than ever once the fight resumed, and took just one minute and 11 seconds of round seven to finish off the challenger.

Geoff made a quick defence of his crown in Basingstoke at the end of October when beating Ross Hale, the former British and Commonwealth light-welterweight champion from Bristol. The Billingham man had overcome the cream of the division and was the undisputed best British welterweight boxer.

The following January, McCreesh made the bold decision to relinquish the British belt to concentrate on his world title ambitions.

He had three warm-up fights against mediocre opponents, to keep busy, but eventually fell out with his manager Frank Warren, which led to a parting of the ways.

McCreesh has since signed a deal with the high profile manager Frank Maloney and eventually realised his ambitions to fight for a world title, by tackling the Bristol born but now New Jersey domiciled Adrian Stone for the little known IBO light middleweight crown.

The fight took place on the undercard of the Lennox Lewis-Frans Botha world heavyweight championship bill on 15th July, 2000 at the London Arena and provided the Teessider with a huge opportunity to further enhance his career in front of a worldwide pay per view audience.

Unfortunately, McCreesh who was hoping to use this title as a stepping stone to one of boxing's bigger prizes, never really got into the fight. And although he fought back gamely to recover from two knockdowns in the second round, he sustained a bad cut above his left eye in the fifth, and was eventually beaten when referee James Santa stepped in to stop the fight in the following round to save McCreesh from further punishment from his hard hitting opponent.

This comprehensive defeat was an obvious setback in Geoff's career and it remains to be seen what the future holds for him..

In the meantime he is now happily settled in Bracknell, Berkshire, with his wife Melissa and three year old son Tommy Lee and one year old daughter Mia.

Mick McNeil
Football

MICHAEL McNeil was among the cream of the top quality young players that Middlesbrough produced in the late 1950s, going on to make nine full appearances for England while the club was still rooted in the Second Division.

He was born in Middlesbrough on February 7, 1940, and began his football career as an inside-left or outside-left for Boro Boys and Middlesbrough Tech.

After leaving school he turned out for the works team of Cargo Fleet, where he was working as an analytical chemist. Former Middlesbrough half-back Jimmy Gordon, who was then a coach at the club, spotted Mick's excellent potential, and eventually he was offered the chance to join the Boro.

At first, McNeil was not sure whether or not to give up his job. However, finally he decided to opt for a football career, because he felt that he would have more time off, particularly in the summer months, to help his father on his market garden.

Mike signed for the Boro in May, 1957. He made his league debut away against Brighton on December 20, 1958, as a makeshift left-half in an amazing 6-4 victory in which Brian Clough scored a hat trick. Mick made further appearances that season at centre-half and left-back. At the start of the 1959-60 campaign he was chosen to play left-back and quickly established himself as an ever-present during that season as Middlesbrough finished fifth in the Second Division.

His impressive displays were rewarded with selection for the England Under-23 team against France at Roker Park on November 11, 1959, and in all he received nine caps, playing on the losing side only once.

After helping the Under-23s to beat Holland by 5-2 at Hillsborough, McNeil and teammate Eddie Holliday were selected for a summer tour to the Continent to play East Germany, Poland and Israel. Holliday scored twice as the Under-23s beat East Germany by 4-1 in Berlin, and then they overcame Poland by 3-2 in Warsaw. However the tour finished with a heavy 4-0 defeat in Israel.

Playing in Division Two with the Boro didn't stop Mick McNeil becoming an England international.

Later that year McNeil earned his sixth Under-23 cap in a 1-1 draw against Italy at Newcastle. By that time, he had already moved on to a much bigger stage.

Even though he was playing his football in the Second Division, his forceful displays were rewarded with a full international call-up for England against Northern Ireland in Belfast on October 8, 1960, which England won 5-2. Suddenly Mick was established as one of the top defenders in the country.

He went on to play nine times for his country within a calendar year and played in some of the highest scoring England games ever.

Mick earned his second full cap when he was called up for England's World Cup qualifier in Luxembourg, which England strolled by 9-0. Seven days later he made his debut at Wembley as England beat Spain 4-2. McNeil was settling in well into the England set-up and played his part in a 5-1 trouncing of Wales at Wembley in the November.

The following March, Mick scored his first ever league goal for Middlesbrough in a 2-2 draw at home to

119

Mick McNeil is directly behind manager Raich Carter in this Middlesbrough squad picture of 1963/64. By the end of that season, with the Boro's fortunes very much in the doldrums, he had moved on to Ipswich Town.

Charlton Athletic. He was back on representative duty ten days later when he played for the English League against the Scottish League at Ibrox, which the Scots won by 3-2.

Then Mick returned to the England fold in April in the famous 9-3 hammering of Scotland at Wembley, when the hapless Frank Haffey was in goal for the Scots. Seemingly there was no stopping this England team. With McNeil again in the line-up, they crushed Mexico by 8-0 in May.

The Mexico victory was a warm-up for England's next World Cup qualifier, against Portugal in Lisbon. Mick played his part in helping England earn a 1-1 draw. Three days later the party moved on to Rome and beat Italy 3-2.

Mick continued to be one of the mainstays of the Middlesbrough defence and scored his second goal for the club when hitting home the winner in a 1-0 victory against Preston North End in September, 1961. His last full international appearance was in the return World Cup qualifier against Luxembourg at Highbury less than four weeks later, when England won 4-1. In nine England games, the Middlesbrough man had never featured on the losing side.

Unfortunately it was not enough to keep him in the team. He was to lose his international place to the great Ray Wilson and then suffered double disappointment when he narrowly missed out on selection for England's 1962 World Cup Squad.

The FA tried to make it up to McNeil by including him in the English League side for a 9-1 victory against the League of Ireland at Goodison Park. Then he was awarded another three under-23 caps in 1962. England beat the Scots by 4-2 at Aberdeen, crushed Belgium by 6-1 at Plymouth and hammered Greece by 5-1 at St Andrews in Birmingham. But it was to be the last time that Mick appeared on the international stage at any level. Ironically, he was even edged out of the left-back spot at Middlesbrough due to the rapid emergence of Gordon Jones, who himself was to go on and become an England Under-23 international. Middlesbrough experimented by switching McNeil to right-back and even played him at left-half.

By this time the tide was beginning to turn at Ayresome Park. Middlesbrough finished fourth in the Second Division in 1962-63 but it was becoming an era of frustration for players and fans alike as it looked as though the club would never return to the top flight. In fact they began to fall away the following season.

Eventually McNeil joined the ever increasing exodus of talent leaving Ayresome Park, including Brian Clough and Alan Peacock, when he signed for Ipswich Town in July, 1964. He had made 193 appearances for Middlesbrough and scored three goals. Mick settled well in East Anglia and became an integral part of the Ipswich team which won promotion to the First Division in 1968 under Bobby Robson.

Mick retired from the game in 1971 and now runs a successful sports outfitting business in Suffolk. He lives in Bury St Edmunds.

Willie Maddren
Football

WILLIE Maddren, who witnessed two periods of widely contrasting fortunes at Ayresome Park, was regarded by many leading authorities in the game to be one of the best defenders never to have been capped by England.

As a cultured defender in Jack Charlton's 1970s team he played a major role in some of Middlesbrough's most successful post war seasons in the First Division. Willie's career was eventually ended by a major knee injury after 343 first team appearances but later he returned to the club as manager in the 1980s.

However, he suffered a very rude awakening when he discovered just how far the club had fallen during his absence and, throughout his 18 cash-strapped months at the helm, he could only watch helplessly as the club plummeted towards financial collapse.

Even so, Willie had helped to nurture a blossoming youth programme which was to pay massive dividends once the club rose again from the ashes of liquidation.

Born in Haverton Hill on January 11, 1951, William Dixon Maddren attended Roseberry Primary School in Billingham where he captained the junior team to league and cup success before moving to Faraday Hall on the Billingham School Campus.

While playing in the local Stockton and Billingham League he was invited for trials to Leeds United but two days before the event he broke his ankle in a match for Port Clarence Juniors and was unable to attend.

Leeds' loss was Boro's good fortune when, after a recommendation by local talent scout Freddie Barnes, Maddren signed professional forms at Ayresome Park in June, 1968.

His full debut against Bury in the final home league game of the season proved to be an eventful occasion when he suffered a broken nose after only ten minutes and had to leave the pitch for medical attention. Following extensive treatment he returned to the fray and despite his painful injury managed to score his first Boro goal, with the help of a post, in a 3-2 defeat. The experience of that day had a profound effect on the teenage Maddren, who said: "Playing in my first game

Willie Maddren was acknowledged as one of the best defenders never to have played for England.

was hard to take in at the time. The funny thing was that the ball left a muddy print on the post. During the summer I went into the ground for training and the print was on the post all the time. I used to stand and gaze at it in disbelief."

Maddren proved to be an extremely versatile player, eventually appearing in seven different positions before making real progress as an outstanding central defender. His chance came in this position after Bill Gates broke his jaw in an FA Cup replay at Old Trafford in February, 1970.

In 1971 he was voted Player of the Year by the supporters and his emergence as a defender of the highest calibre was cemented when Boro manager Stan Anderson signed Stuart Boam from Mansfield Town in May, 1971. The two forged an almost telepathic understanding, going on to become one of the best centre-half pairings in the country.

Maddren's consistent displays were eventually rewarded with five England Under-23 caps. He made his Under-23 debut against Czechoslovakia in a 1-0 win at Villa Park in March, 1973.

The following season Willie played a further times at this level, in a 1-1 draw against Denmark at Portsmouth, a 2-1 win against Scotland at Newcastle and a 2-2 draw against France in Valence. He came on as a substitute in a 1-0 defeat by Yugoslavia in Zrenjanin. Boro teammate David Mills also played alongside Willie in the final three under-23 games.

Willie did then progress to call-ups to Don Revie's full England squad although surprisingly, given his standing within the game, he never made the starting line-up.

Maddren enjoyed a phenomenal season as Boro were promoted to the First Division on a wave of euphoria under Jack Charlton in 1973-74 and then settled very comfortably into life in the top flight. He was an ever present in Big Jack's first two years at Ayresome Park, scoring five goals.

In 1975-76 Maddren scored one of the goals at Burnley which helped Boro to reach the semi-finals of the Football League Cup. Boro were paired with Manchester City and were standing on the verge of their first ever Wembley appearance. However the two semi-final matches ended in major disappointment for Willie and his teammates when they lost 4-1 to City on aggregate.

Throughout his career Willie suffered from increasing trouble with a knee injury which at times became so inflamed that he was unable to train between matches. Eventually, in 1977, following an unsuccessful operation, and at an age when most defenders are at their peak, Maddren was forced to retire from the game after making 346 appearances in a Boro shirt.

He still had a great deal to offer the game and quickly began a coaching career at Hartlepool United, combining this with business interests in local sports shops.

Willie soon realised that the future of the smaller clubs was built on the strength of their youth policies, and along with former Boro wing-half of the 1960s, Billy Horner, he gradually introduced top quality youngsters to the North-east's Cinderella club.

In fact he was so successful that Pool went on to win the Northern Intermediate League, which was an unprecedented achievement for a struggling Fourth Division side. Young stars nurtured at the time by Maddren included Peter Beagrie and the Linighan brothers, all of whom went on to play for Premier League clubs.

However, despite his success, Maddren had a difficult working relationship with Vince Barker, the club's chairman, and eventually left the Victoria Ground in frustration.

He moved back to Middlesbrough FC and worked under Malcolm Allison as a physio but was switched to the coaching staff in 1983 by caretaker boss Jack Charlton, who had stepped into the breach following the departure of the former Manchester City boss.

When, at the end of the 1983-84 season, Big Jack made it clear he did not want the manager's job on a full-time basis, he recommended Maddren to take over the Ayresome Park helm.

The former Boro favourite accepted the challenge of rejuvenating the ailing club and stressed at the time that it would be at least a three year job to turn the club round. He said: "You couldn't believe how far things had slipped. It was heartbreaking. And of course the job turned out to be impossible."

Boro were heavily in debt, and Maddren had to work on very limited resources. Although the club was a pale shadow of the great team of the 1970s, Willie tried manfully to change the Boro's fortunes. He brought back former Boro striker David Mills, who ended the 1984-85 season as top scorer and also helped with the coaching.

Maddren spent his limited financial resources very wisely by bringing in Bernie Slaven and Stephen Pears, who were to play a significant part in the club's revival under Bruce Rioch. Willie also introduced the raw talent of Gary Pallister to Ayresome Park and he was later sold to Manchester United for £2.3million.

Although Boro survived the drop on the last day of the season, the fiscal position did not change and try as he might, Maddren couldn't improve the results. Eventually he stepped down as manager in February, 1986, to be replaced by the coach he had appointed, Rioch. There was no bitterness when he left. In fact he reflected: " It was almost a relief ."

Willie returned to managing his sports shops before eventually selling his business interests the 1990s.

Unfortunately, personal tragedy overtook him when he was cruelly struck down with Motor Neurone Disease. For several years he showed great courage in battling the debilitating disease and established a fund which raised £250,000 for research into its causes.

Sadly, Willie Maddren died on August 29, 2000. His funeral at St Cuthberts Church in Billingham was attended by many of his ex-colleagues.

Harry Makepeace
Cricket and Football

JOSEPH William Henry Makepeace, who was born in Middlesbrough on August 22, 1881, was one of a unique breed of sportsman. He was a great sporting all-rounder who played both cricket and football for England.

In fact Harry has achieved a sporting accomplishment which may never be equalled. He is the only man ever to win an FA Cup winner's medal, a League Championship medal, be capped as an England football international, win a County Championship medal and be capped as a cricket international. It's a cornucopia of sporting riches which most people can only dream about.

Unfortunately Harry was not living in Middlesbrough when he achieved his sporting successes. The Makepeace family had left Teesside for Merseyside when he was only ten years old, and it was Everton FC and the Lancashire county cricket team who were to eventually benefit from his uncanny talents with ball and bat.

It was very evident from an early age that Harry was a natural sportsman, and he was attracted to football and cricket when both major sports when enjoying a burgeoning boom period and attracting huge crowds. Queen Victoria was still on the throne when Harry was selected to play football for Liverpool Schools. Later he turned out for the Queens Road Mission FC and also Bootle Amateurs before Everton sat up and took notice of this talented young wing-back.

Off the pitch, Harry was a quiet and unassuming man. On the pitch he went through a transformation. He was a fearsome tackler and great ball winner.

It was these strengths which attracted Everton's scouts, and Harry agreed to sign forms for the Toffees in 1902. He was joining one of the biggest clubs in the country. Makepeace made his first team debut in an FA Cuptie against Manchester United in February, 1903, at the age of 21. He quickly adapted to life in the First Division and established himself as a regular member of the side, going on to became a great and much admired player on Merseyside. His outstanding career at Goodison Park was to last until 1919, after the end of the First World War.

One of the best years of Harry's illustrious football career was 1906. He made his international debut as a footballer, won an FA Cup Winner's medal, and became a county cricket player with Lancashire.

Harry was called up to play at left-half for England in a international against Scotland in Glasgow on April 7, 1906, which the Scots won 2-1. However the best was yet to come. Everton stormed through to the Cup Final, where they met Newcastle United at Crystal Palace. This time Harry was on the winning side playing at right-half as the Magpies were pipped by 1-0. It completed a great season for Merseyside, because Liverpool had won the First Division Championship.

Makepeace had played a vital part in Everton reaching the Cup Final, scoring their only goal in a 1-0 win against Bradford City in the third round.

Harry was back in the Cup Final the following year, this time against Sheffield Wednesday. However the Toffees failed in their bid to retain the trophy and went down narrowly by 2-1.

This was Harry's last appearance in an FA Cup Final, although three further appearances followed for England. However there was a four-year gap before Harry's international career was revived. He was called up by his country to play at left-half in a clash against Scotland at Glasgow, on April 2, 1910, and once again the Scots triumphed, this time by 2-0.

Two years later Harry was chosen to play in two home internationals. Glasgow was a familiar destination for the former Middlesbrough man, but this time England forced a 1-1 draw on February 23, 1912. Seventeen days later came the icing on the cake, when Harry tasted international football success for the first and only time in a 2-0 victory against Wales at Wrexham. All of Harry's four international appearances were made at left-half.

Domestically, the highlight of Harry's career came in 1914-1915, at the age of 34, when he helped Everton to win the Football League Championship. It was one of the tightest title races of all time, with the Toffees

Harry Makepeace, right, was one of the greatest sporting all rounders of the last century winning FA Cup and championship medals with Everton and international caps for England at both football and cricket.

pipping their Lancashire rivals Oldham Athletic by one point. It was a great moment for Harry because Everton had previously been First Division runners-up on three occasions.

This title-winning football season proved to be the last of Harry's professional career. The First World War effectively ended league competition for four years. When the Football League resumed in 1919, Harry had just reached his 38th birthday and his contract at Goodison Park was not renewed.

In 14 consecutive seasons with Everton, Harry was a virtual regular for the Toffees and made more than 300 appearances.

His football career did not end there, because Harry went on to coach in Holland. He also coached at Everton before ending his links with the sport in a coaching capacity at nearby Marine in Crosby.

However, by this time, Harry was already well established as a top cricketer.

Having started out playing cricket in the Liverpool

League for Clubmoor and Wavertree, Makepeace had made his first class debut for Lancashire against Essex at Leyton in 1906. He settled quickly into the county side and formed a famous opening partnership with A H Hornby.

After the Great War, Harry was recognised as one of the top batsmen in the country thanks to his strong impregnable defence and his uncanny ability to play spin. Harry was finally called up by England in his 40th year for their much maligned tour of Australia in 1920-21.

Makepeace played in four Tests, scoring a century in the Fourth Test at Melbourne at the age of 39 years and 173 days. He became - and still remains - the oldest player to score a maiden Test century. Harry made 117 in the first innings and followed this up with 54 in the second innings, but the Aussies won the match by eight wickets.

The other Tests also produced heavy defeats, including a Second Test defeat by an innings and 91 runs, also in Melbourne. Harry scored 60 in the first innings of the Third Test in Adelaide, but the Aussies won by 119 runs. Four of Harry's other five Test innings ended in single figure scores.

England lost all five Tests and the team was heavily criticised back home. The tour had not started well when the team was quarantined in Fremantle for a week because a passenger on the ship had contracted typhus. This was followed by a tiring four-day train journey to Adelaide.

England did recover to fare well against the state sides, but they were no match for the Warwick Armstrong led Aussies in the Tests. The home side were stronger in all areas. Makepeace's tour batting average was a healthy 34.87, which made him one of the more successful batsmen. But surprisingly this was to be the only time when England were to call upon his services. Harry was justly awarded a benefit by Lancashire in 1922, and was presented with the very tidy sum for those days of £2,110.

He continued piling up the runs in the County Championship in the 1920s and passed 1,000 runs in a season on 13 occasions. His best two seasons were 1923 and 1926 when he scored 2,310 and 2,340 runs respectively at averages of 50.8 and 48.75.

Harry recorded the highest individual score of his career in 1923, hammering 203 off the Worcestershire attack at Worcester. In the same year he recorded his only other double ton, making 200 not out against Northamptonshire at Liverpool.

However, despite his ability to score runs, Makepeace is not remembered as an attacking batsman. Just like his footballing style, Harry was a technically solid right-handed batsman, and was described by the Evening Gazette as 'essentially a defensive batsman'. However his style in no way hindered his ability to make runs and, throughout his first class career, Harry scored 25,799 runs at an average of 36.23. He hit 43 centuries and 140 half centuries. On four occasions he carried his bat through completed Lancashire innings.

Harry was also a tidy leg break bowler, though was used very sparingly. He took 41 wickets in his career, including a best of 4-33 against Warwickshire at Old Trafford in 1913. In addition to his ability as an all rounder, he was also a specialist fielder at cover point. When well into his Forties, he was a regular member of the great Lancashire side of the second half of the 1920s which swept all before them. They won the County Championship in four of the five years from 1926-30 and finished second on the other occasion. In the years 1928 and 1930 they did not lose a single match. One of the major strengths of the side was Harry's prolific opening partnership with Charlie Hallows.

Lancashire's first title win during this spell gave Teesside born Makepeace his special niche in the sporting history books. He was the first man to become an international at cricket and football for England and play on winning sides in the major prestigious competitions in both sports.

Harry eventually announced his retirement from first class cricket at the age of 49 in 1930, having played a remarkable 487 matches for the Red Rose county. However this was far from the end of the Lancashire story for Makepeace. Upon his retirement, he was appointed county coach and went on to hold this post for 21 years.

Finally, at the age of 70, and with almost 50 years of top level sport behind him, Harry retired from his position at Old Trafford. He was immediately made an honourary life member of the club he has served so loyally. Few men of his era could possibly have made a greater all-round contribution to sport in this country.

Harry died at home in Bebington, Cheshire, on December 19, 1951.

Wilf Mannion
Football

"HE could dance on cornflakes without making them crackle.....he was artist and a delight to watch!"

Universally known as the Golden Boy because of his distinctive fair hair, Wilf Mannion was undoubtedly not only one of the greatest players in the history of Middlesbrough Football Club but also throughout the whole of the English game.

They say that he needed only to shake his hips with the ball at his feet, and two or three opponents would fall over.

There was magic in his boots. He tormented, tortured and tantalised. Even after beating some players he was happy to go back and beat them all over again before releasing the ball. He was the scourge of opposition defences, was the player who could turn a game at the drop of a hat, and he was Teesside through and through.

It was no wonder that Wilf was idolised. He was a true star. If it hadn't been for the outbreak of the Second World War he could have achieved anything. His football statistics would have been beyond reproach.

As it was, Wilf played 368 games for Boro during his 18 years with the club and scored 110 goals. He created countless more. All of his games for the club came in the top division. In addition he was, and still is, Boro's most capped player, having played 26 times for England.

When he finally quit Boro and First Division football with his 36th birthday approaching, many Boro fans could not believe it.

Wilfred James Mannion was born in South Bank on May 16, 1918, and was one of five brothers in a family of ten. As a small rather waif-like little boy, he attended the local South Bank St Peters School.

Although he displayed an outstanding footballing talent from an early age, there were many doubters who had their reservations about this boy with the slight physique being able to cope with the rigours of such a physical game. In fact he was overlooked for selection by England schoolboys. Despite that setback

Wilf Mannion. Popular opinion believes him to be one of the greatest footballers of all time.

Wilf's continual eye-catching performances for St Peters prompted great interest from a host of top clubs and it was Middlesbrough FC who signed him on professional forms in September, 1936.

He joined a dressing room packed with international stars. Household names like Bob Baxter, Ralph Birkett, Micky Fenton, George Camsell, Jacky Milne and Dave Cumming were all gracing the Ayresome Park turf at that time.

Any fears that Mannion might struggle to make the grade among the top players in the country quickly disappeared. He made his debut in a red shirt as raw 18-year-old in January, 1937, in a 2-2 draw against Portsmouth at Ayresome Park. The following season he began to establish himself in the first team, scoring his first goal for the club on his seasonal debut in a 2-0 win against Leeds United just after Christmas.

He soon became an integral part of the very talented Middlesbrough side which concluded the 1938-39 campaign in a very creditable fourth position and was widely expected to be challenging for major honours the following season.

Wilf achieved a personal peak in December, 1938, scoring four goals in a 9-2 hammering of Blackpool at Ayresome Park, and grabbing a hat trick later in the season when Portsmouth were thumped by 8-2.

Opposition managers were fulsome in their praise of his innate skills and one was prompted to glowingly report: "He is the complete footballer. He cannot get any better." It was a comment with which most Boro fans were already in agreement.

Unfortunately both Mannion and the Boro's title hopes were cruelly curtailed by the outbreak of the Second World War in September, 1939.

At the beginning of the hostilities Wilf initially joined the Auxiliary Fire Service before being drafted into the Green Howards, who were based on the East Yorkshire coast at Bridlington. In a matter of weeks he was on active service overseas. It wasn't long before he was among the thousands of British troops who were being rescued from the Dunkirk beaches as the German war machine sliced through France virtually unopposed.

After arriving back in England aboard a cargo boat, there were still many opportunities to play football as the government recognised the important contribution sport could make to the morale of the nation. Wilf turned out for Middlesbrough and the Army as well as guesting for Tottenham Hotspur and Bournemouth.

In February, 1941, he was chosen for the first of his four war-time England internationals when he played against Scotland at St James' Park, Newcastle. His performance in a 3-2 defeat drew much praise from the press who wrote that he "showed great craftsmanship in his ball play". Remarkably all four of his war-time internationals were played against the Scots, with England winning the other three. He also scored for a Football League XI in a 3-2 victory against a Scottish League XI at Bloomfield Road.

The Green Howards were eventually posted to the Far East and saw active service in Burma before Wilf and his comrades found themselves back in Europe and in the thick of the action in Sicily. It was here, during an intense period of fighting, that half his company, including Yorkshire and England Test cricketer Hedley Verity, lost their lives. From Sicily his unit, in tandem with the Eighth Army, moved north through Italy and took part in the battles of Anzio and Monte Casino before he was reported missing in action.

Wilf was eventually located suffering from malaria and was sent to a convalescent camp in the Middle East to recuperate, before being dispatched home.

He was demobbed in 1946 but, like all his footballing contemporaries, he'd lost the best six years of his life. After a period of readjustment, he returned to Ayresome Park and, despite the effects of his war time experiences, he still proved beyond doubt that he was one of the finest inside-forwards of all-time.

Mannion's first 12 England appearances mirrored those of his Boro teammate George Hardwick, who captained the international side. Mannion scored a hat trick on his debut, which was a 7-2 win against Northern Ireland in Belfast. He scored twice in a 3-0 win against Wales soon afterwards, and added another in an 8-2 drubbing of Holland.

In May, 1947, he had the distinction of scoring twice for Great Britain when they trounced the Rest of Europe 6-1 at Hampden Park, Glasgow, in front of 134,000 spectators.

Wilf played a major role in the legendary 10-0 win against Portugal in Lisbon in 1947 and a 5-2 romp against Belgium in Brussels later that year.

In 1950, Mannion scored a hat trick for the Football League in a 7-0 win against the League of Ireland at Molineux, and again turned out for the League XI soon afterwards in a 3-1 win against the Scottish League at his home ground of Ayresome Park.

Less than a month later, he played for England in the crucial 1-0 win against Scotland in a World Cup qualifier in Glasgow, and then took part in the brief Continental tour prior to the World Cup Finals. He helped England beat Portugal by 5-3 in Lisbon and then scored in a 4-1 against Belgium in Brussels.

Wilf was selected for the England squad for the World Cup Finals in Brazil, and scored in the opening 2-0 victory over Chile in Rio de Janeiro. But it was a hugely disappointing event for the England party, who lost their other two group games and were eliminated. During the late 1940s Wilf Mannion's consistently outstanding performances for both club and country made him a much sought after player. One particular breathtaking exhibition of his considerable talents against Blackpool in November, 1947, is simply remembered to by all those who were privileged to witness it as the "Mannion Match".

Wilf did not score, even though Boro won 4-0, but he ripped the Blackpool rearguard to shreds time after time, and produced an array of tricks and outrageous

Autumn 1950. The Golden Boy hones his close control skills during a training session on Saltburn beach. In those days the Boro players were not allowed to train on the Ayresome Park pitch so they could often be found enjoying the seaside air.

ball control that many top players in the modern game can only dream about.

Later, Wilf revealed the reasons behind his amazing virtuoso display in the book Ayresome Park Memories. He said: "It's simple. I played for me. I had just got engaged to Bernadette and she was sitting in the stand watching me.

"Naturally I wanted to impress her. So I produced all the skills and all the tricks I knew. It was like putting on an act, if you like. The only problem was that

Bernadette came away thinking that I played like that every week."

At that time Middlesbrough, who had failed to recapture their pre-war promise, had received many large offers for Wilf's services. But all approaches, much to Mannion's annoyance, were politely declined. He knew that there were ways and means in which he could rapidly improve his earnings away from Teesside, and gain some recompense for his special talents, instead of taking home the same £10 a week wage as the men he used to leave on the seats of their pants every Saturday afternoon.

As the clamour for his signature steadily intensified, Mannion controversially refused to play for Middlesbrough at the start of the 1948-49 season. He declined to re-sign and demanded an immediate transfer. In those days, clubs technically held a player's registration for life, and Middlesbrough stubbornly refused to accede to his demands. Wilf said: "The maximum wage was still in force but you could earn money in other ways at other clubs. In any case I wanted to play for one of the better teams. But the Boro directors wouldn't listen. I felt insulted."

Mannion eventually left his house on Normanby Road with the intention of starting a business in Lancashire and playing for Oldham Athletic. It was a decision which was made intending to force the hands of the club. Boro, however, increased the pressure on their wayward star by demanding an excessive transfer fee of £25,000, which was way beyond anything Oldham could afford. The situation dragged on for months, but the Boro board would not bend. Eventually Wilf had to return home when it became patently obvious that the directors had no intention of being held to ransom.

This protracted altercation certainly soured his relationship with Middlesbrough Football Club and although he returned to Ayresome Park to help the club avoid relegation, there were those inside the boardroom who never forgave him for what they saw as his intransigence.

Wilf still played for Boro with great honour and pride, and never let them down. He was always up among the top scorers and his goals and creativity were almost carrying the team in the Fifties.

In the first season after the war, Mannion had finished joint top scorer with 18 goals along with Mick Fenton. Boro finished 11th overall, but then they began to struggle the following season as Mannion's form dipped. In the season he stayed away at Oldham, Boro narrowly won a battle against relegation, finishing 19th.

Wilf gradually moved back into gear again and, with better players coming into the club, like Scottish striker Alex McCrae, Boro enjoyed a magnificent campaign in 1950-51 and finished sixth, which is still their highest post-war position. Mannion was second top scorer behind McCrae with 14 goals.

However it was a false dawn for the club. They quickly slipped down the table again, despite a superb

contribution from the 34-year-old Mannion in 1952-53 when he finished top scorer with 18 goals.

Mannion played on for another full season until his retirement. But it was not the way he would have wanted to leave the club, as Boro were relegated into the Second Division for the first time in over 25 years. Surprisingly, six months later he was persuaded to come out of retirement by Hull City. His much heralded Boxing Day debut at Boothferry Park created a huge amount of local interest with a crowd of almost 40,000 in attendance.

By now, at the age of 36, Mannion was obviously well past his England best and spent only one season on Humberside. He also found himself under investigation by the Football League for newspaper articles he had written in which he claimed that illegal payments were being paid to players during his time at the top level. When asked to explain his serious allegations in greater detail, he flatly refused and was duly suspended from the professional game in June, 1955.

Mannion's response to his suspension was to drop down into non-league football and play for Poole Town, before later turning out for King's Lynn, Haverhill Rovers and Earlestown, until he finally retired in 1962.

Wilf became a publican at Stevenage, but it was not a way of life he was looking for, and he returned to Teesside to work in local industry.

There was a growing clamour in Middlesbrough for Wilf to be awarded a testimonial, but the requests were repeatedly turned down by successive boards of directors. However, finally, in 1983, Wilf and his former Boro and England teammate George Hardwick paired up for a special testimonial night at Ayresome Park and walked out to a remarkable wall of noise from generations of appreciative fans.

Wilf continued to follow Boro's progress with great interest and was a regular visitor to Ayresome Park and the BT Cellnet Riverside Stadium until 1999.

He died in hospital on April 14, 2000, and thousands of Teesside people, many of whom had never seen him play, took to the streets to watch the cortege and pay their respects to the Golden Boy on his final journey through Middlesbrough to the cathedral.

At the end of the emotional service the whole of Boro first team squad formed a guard of honour as a tribute to one of the footballing greats.

David Mills
Football

DAVID Mills became Britain's first half million pound footballer when he was sold from Middlesbrough to West Bromwich Albion in January, 1979.

He later returned to Ayresome Park and went on to make 381 appearances for the club in his two stints, scoring 108 goals. He also won eight England Under-23 caps.

David John Mills was born in Whitby on December 6, 1951, but grew up in Thornaby when his father, Jonathan, joined the police and was stationed in Middlesbrough. David attended Westbury Street juniors and the Arthur Head Secondary Modern School, where he developed as an outstanding schoolboy footballer with great pace.

He was selected for Stockton and Billingham Boys before receiving international recognition with England. His attacking potential attracted many of the country's leading clubs, including Manchester United. However Mills' professional career was almost over before it began when a serious back problem in his middle teens kept him out of the game for over a year. In an interview in the book Ayresome Park Memories he recalled the actual moment the injury occurred. He said: "I was running in the Stockton and District Sports when I had a severe pain in my back and couldn't take part in the sprint final.

"I was taken to see a specialist who diagnosed twisted and fractured vertebrae in my lower back. Apparently it was the result of competing in too many sports."

Despite the spinal problems, Middlesbrough manager Stan Anderson always kept in touch with his medical progress and finally signed the blond forward in July, 1968, by which time he had made a full recovery.

David began playing for the youth team, under coach George Wardle, and was a member of a strong side which included future first teamers like Willie Maddren, Pat Cuff, Joe Laidlaw, Alan Murray and Alan Moody.

Mills made his first team debut as a sub in a 3-1 defeat at Birmingham in the last game of the 1968-69 season.

David Mills recovered from a career threatening back injury to become England's most expensive player.

The following season he came off the bench to score his first league goal in a 4-1 win at home to Blackburn, and scored again on his full debut at Swindon in April, 1970. Then a series of consistent displays during the early 1970s helped establish him in the Middlesbrough first team.

His career, however, like so many other Boro players of that era, was to blossom under a new Boro manager, the charismatic Jack Charlton, who deliberately utilised Mills' lightning quick pace to unsettled unwary opposition defences.

Throughout the momentous 1973-74 Second Division promotion season David made a significant contribution towards Boro's record breaking championship campaign by scoring a dozen times. His performances were justly rewarded during this successful period when he was awarded eight England Under-23 caps.

He made his England debut against Scotland on March 13, 1974, and scored one of the goals in a 2-1 victory. Further appearances came at the end of that season on a tour which took in Turkey, Yugoslavia and France.

Later he played against Czechoslovakia, twice, Portugal and Hungary, and scored a further two goals. By that time Mills had emerged as one of the leading front runners in the First Division. Over the next four years with Boro he hardly missed a game and became an integral part of Big Jack's well-drilled playing system which saw Boro firmly established back among the football's elite.

Arguably his best season came in 1976-77, when he was clear top scorer with 15 goals, including a hat trick in a 3-2 home win against Aston Villa. He also scored a further three goals in Boro's fine FA Cup run that season, when he helped Boro reach the sixth round, where they lost 2-0 at Liverpool.

When John Neal became Boro manager in May, 1977, the club went through a period of transition with many changes of personnel. Youth, in the shape of David Hodgson, Craig Johnston and Mark Proctor was given its head. However, in Neal's first full season in charge, Mills was again top scorer with 16 league and cup goals. He scored four times in helping Boro to the sixth round of the FA Cup again but, with the door to the semi-finals wide open, Boro lost to Second Division Orient.

By January, 1979, although still a key member of the first team, Mills' career would change dramatically when West Bromwich Albion's colourful manager Ron Atkinson offered £500,000 for the fair-haired striker. It was an opportunity both the club and player could not afford to turn down. So, after playing more than 300 games for Boro, David unwittingly found himself the country's first half a million pounds player and on his way to The Hawthorns.

The move to the Midlands, however, did not prove to be a success and, after less than 50 appearances, and only half a dozen goals, Mills enjoyed a 15 match loan spell at Newcastle United early in 1982.

His return to WBA was very brief because in January, 1983, Sheffield Wednesday paid £30,000 to take him to Hillsborough. He stayed only six months before moving back to Newcastle United, this time on a permanent transfer. He made 16 further appearances for the Magpies.

In June 1984, the then Middlesbrough manager, Willie Maddren, re-signed Mills as player-coach. David wasted little time in making a big impression in Boro's cash-strapped side, ending the season as the club's top scorer with 15 goals.

On his return to Ayresome Park, however, he was deeply shocked to find how much the club had declined in a decade, observing: "The club was short, numerically and financially. The situation was summed up when the kit man Ken Smith came into the dressing-room before a match and said that there weren't enough tea bags to make a brew at half-time as well as full-time. So we had to choose."

After a period in charge of Boro Juniors, David spent some time at a rehabilitation centre recovering from an Achilles tendon problem before finishing his league career with a non contract spell at Darlington in 1986-87. He later joined Whitby Town in the Northern League.

David's life was changed forever when he was involved in a serious car accident in the Tyne Tunnel which claimed the life of his father and left David dangerously ill in hospital with severe facial and internal injuries.

He fractured his lower and upper jaw, shattered an eye socket, broke an arm, half a dozen ribs and punctured a lung, into which blood was seeping.

He needed several operations, but was allowed to leave hospital after only two weeks with his face fully wired. Eventually the wiring was removed and, remarkably, David was back at work at his job as a salesman for Hill Print in Bishop Auckland three months after the accident.

Later that year, he was approached by Radio Tees, who are now known as TFM, and offered the role as summariser following Middlesbrough FC's exploits around the country. David was pleased to accept the post and worked for the company for almost five years, working in turn with Bernard Gent, John Murray and Dave Roberts.

Then he was approached by Kevin Keegan at Newcastle United and offered the chance to undertake match reports and player assessments for the Tyneside club. David was delighted to have the opportunity to increase his involvement in the game, and gratefully accepted. In 2000 he still carries out this important role for the Magpies travelling all over Europe assessing teams and players.

David also still manages to fit in this work schedule with his full-time job for OCR Colour Print at Team Valley, while still continuing with his media work as a highly respected pundit with Tyne Tees Television.

He lives happily in Middlesbrough with his wife Sandra and family. They have four children, Andrew, Sarah, Steven and Richard.

Stuart Morris
Cycling

STUART Morris was a talented track rider who was surprisingly overlooked for selection in consecutive Olympic Games before going on to win the world masters pursuit championship at the end of his competitive career.

He made a dramatic arrival on the world of cycling by being called into the national training squad when still a junior at the age of 16 and competed at top level throughout the Seventies, including riding for Great Britain in the world championships in Liege in 1975.

Stuart Morris was born in Guisborough on May 2, 1955, but grew up in Grangetown. He attended Lawson Infants School in Cargo Fleet and Smeaton Street Juniors, before returning to the Lawson School's junior section when Smeaton Street closed.

At Langbaurgh School, Stuart represented the school in athletics, both at shot putt and at cross country running.

He came into cycling relatively late, at the age of 14, when he asked his father, George, for a racing bike. His father granted his wish, as long as Stuart agreed to join a cycling club.

Stuart and his pal Keith Robinson, who also had a racing bike, went to watch an Evening Gazette sponsored race at Stokesley, which was won by Sid Barras, and started talking to members of Teesside Clarion.

They were invited to join the club and within weeks Stuart was riding in time trials. He was hooked immediately on cycling and spent every spare hour training and practising. The results were phenomenal. He made such rapid progress that he was the most prolific race winner in the North of England in 1971 with 32 victories.

His incredible performances were enough to earn him a place in the British Olympic training squad, which was the national squad devised to develop the country's top riders.

He was soon making a national impact, and was in a winning position in the British junior road championships in the Isle of Man when he was put out of the running by a puncture with 12 miles to go.

The following year Stuart won the national junior individual pursuit championship at Kirkby in Merseyside. He was also third in the junior sprint event. His rapid progress continued when he was then called up for the English youth team for a five-day event at Gutersloh in West Germany.

Later in the year he won the British Cycling Federation's Peter Buckley Junior Trophy series, which was contested by the country's top junior riders. His performances had not gone unnoticed at the highest level, and he was awarded the BCF Clement Gold Medal for his superb achievements on the track.

In 1973 Stuart was called up for the world junior pursuit championships in Munich but the trip was destined to end in bitter disappointment.

He was training with the squad before the start of the championships when he received a bombshell when informed by the team manager that he would not be included in the team. Instead his place would go to Des Fretwell, who had travelled to Germany to compete in the road racing.

Stuart was a good friend of Fretwell and held no personal bad feelings, but he was absolutely shattered by the decision. He received no consolation when the British team failed to make an impact. Stuart did go on to compete in the road race, but his heart wasn't in it. To make matters worse, the team manager admitted to Stuart afterwards that he had made a big mistake with his selection policy.

Now working at Head Wrightson as an apprentice pattern-maker, Morris returned to England and stepped up to the senior ranks. The following year he raced for Britain in the ten-stage Tour of Newfoundland. He made his presence felt, particularly on the third stage, over 113 miles, when he established a two-minute lead with 25 miles to go. However Stuart was caught ten miles later to finish in eighth position.

The following day Stuart was fourth, over 70 miles,

then fifth and sixth at the end of the next two stages, followed by a round the houses criterium in which he finished eighth. Unfortunately, while lying eighth overall, he was struck down by a virus and was unable to get out of bed, being forced to miss the final stage. However, once fully recovered, Morris accepted invitations to stay in North America and rode competitively in events in Toronto and Boston, where he took fifth place in a 50-miles criterium.

On his return home, Stuart began to prepare for a major international event in San Sebastian in Spain, which was held at the same venue as the recent world championships. Most of the British team in the championships had since turned pro, and Stuart was included in a new look four-man British team to contest the team pursuit event in San Sebastian.

He linked up with Steve Heffernan, Ian Banbury and Robin Croker and the quartet performed very well, going on to take third place.

The squad then continued to work together and set off for the world championships in Belgium in 1975. The British four qualified as the seventh fastest team and knew they needed to improve if they were to get among the medals.

They suffered a blow on the first lap in their battle against the Italians when there was a little jolt through the team which led to a collision and ended with Heffernan hitting Morris's wheel and falling off. The team was supposed to carry on with three riders, but Stuart was advised by members of the British party to fall off as well, and did so, rather awkwardly at 30mph. Once Stuart had dusted himself down and inspected his bruises, the two teams set off again in a re-run and the British quartet raced well. But the Italians had the edge and went through to the semi-finals.

In an attempt to win a place in the British team for the Montreal Olympics, Morris decided to spend the following winter in Holland where he could continue to train thoroughly in the indoor velodromes.

As a result, he gave up his job as a pattern maker and made the difficult decision to pawn many of the gold and silver medals which he had won at various events. He raised almost £95, which was a lot of money at the time and was enough to help finance his trip.

However the visit to Holland was not a success. After a month of competitions, Stuart develop eczema on his feet and was forced to return home because he could not afford the medical fees.

Morris still trained very hard, but failed to win a place

Stuart Morris capped a fine career by winning cycling's world masters pursuit championship.

in the Olympic team, which was a major setback, because he had been working solidly towards this goal. He was more determined than ever to qualify for the Olympics at Moscow, and continued to make an impact at the highest level.

The pre-1980 Olympics squad sessions were held at Leicester, and Morris and his Teesside colleague Hugh Cameron performed consistently well in all the sessions.

The riders were asked to adopt a special carbo-hydrate loading diet, which paid particular benefits for Morris and had him riding to the peak of his ability.

Throughout the training runs, he was rarely out of the top three on times and could not have done any more to achieve Olympic selection.

The selectors delayed making their decision, and Stuart was kept on tenterhooks as he travelled to the Midlands to attend extra sessions. The diet never let him down and he regularly finished in the top two or three. Yet another extra pre-selection session was fitted in rather unexpectedly by the selectors and disaster struck when Stuart was hit by a debilitating virus. Despite his efforts he was unable to race because of bouts of dizziness.

He paid a high price for his illness. The selectors named the Olympic team the following day and Morris was excluded. All of his hard work over four years was wasted.

In disgust at being overlooked, he cut out much of his track racing and decided to spend more time on road racing. He did well, winning a major event in 1982 when coming home first in the prestigious Tour of the Border four-day race, beating several top riders including the notable scalp of Olympic road racer Joe Waugh.

However Stuart did return to Leicester to win the national Madison championships, along with fellow Teessider Paul Curran. He also finished second in the British Eight Kilometres Championship on the track at Leeds, being pipped by Ken Cowdell.

Stuart had a major decision to make when he was offered the chance to turn pro by a Belgian plumbing company called TJ Glemp, who were starting a professional racing team in Britain. Stuart turned to his good friend and professional Sid Barras for advice, and Sid advised against it because the new team was not yet established and if it was to fold, then the riders would not receive their cash.

Morris took his pal's good advice and stayed in the amateur ranks. It was a wise decision because as Barras predicted the team did fold, and the riders did not get paid.

However this period was turbulent for Stuart because he suffered from personal problems and he gradually drifted away from the sport.

In a near 15-year career at the top, he had won many top races throughout the country, in addition to 14 divisional championships.

Morris had already qualified as a joiner on a government training scheme and was earning a living fitting windows. Then he started his own business, initially concentrating on windows, but eventually branching out into all forms of building and property maintenance.

However Stuart had never lost any of his competitive edge and in 1994 he began racing again, though this time on a mountain bike. He started off in local races, but quickly progressed to national events and established himself as one of the top ten veteran riders in the country.

He was going well in the national series, having finished in the top three in every race. As a result he trained hard and was determined to win the overall trophy. However he suffered a blow in a race at Eston when he was leading with a few miles to go, but was directed off course by a marshall and missed the chance of victory. Stuart was disgusted because all of his work over the season was destroyed. As a result he vowed never to race on a mountain bike again.

However the competitive edge was still there and Stuart decided to have another attempt at winning major honours on the track in 1995.

He trained hard throughout the winter and was rewarded with the silver medal in the national veteran points championship at Manchester. Then he stepped up another gear by winning the gold medal in the veterans pursuit.

Now the scene was set for Stuart to attack the ultimate challenge. He returned to Manchester to contest the world masters pursuit championships and came out on top of a thrilling event with the gold medal.

Having achieved a world prize, Stuart again decided to call it a day. In any case, his commitment to the sport had been absolute for the past 12 months and he needed to spend more time on working on developing his business and with his family.

Not that Stuart has lost his will-to-win. He has enjoyed regular ski-ing trips to the Continent for 20 years, but paid the price for being too competitive when breaking his shoulder and hand, suffering a hernia and damaging the cartilages in both knees in a fall at Val D'Isere in France.

Not to be deterred, Stuart still fits in occasional ski-ing trips, along with regular running sessions. He has also developed a new sporting love and is often in action both locally and in the Lake District on water skis.

Stuart also finds some time to continue working on his business, Stuart Morris Window and Door Services. He lives with his wife Ellen and teenage daughter Nicki at their Marton home.

Tony Mowbray
Football

KNOWN simply to all supporters as Mogga, Tony Mowbray was Middlesbrough's defensive bedrock for more than a decade and developed into one of the most respected captains in the history of the club.

He was the epitome of what every fan was looking for in a local player - hard working, courageous and totally committed. Never giving less than 100 per cent for the Boro cause.

Tony gained in stature through adversity, when he was named skipper of Bruce Rioch's young side immediately following the painful liquidation period of 1986. He emerged mentally tougher for the experience, and led the team back to the First Division within two seasons.

In 11 years as a first team player with Boro, Mowbray made 406 appearances and scored 28 goals. He was twice capped by England B, playing in matches in Switzerland and Norway in 1989.

In November 1991, he moved on to Scottish giants Celtic, and performed with distinction in the Scottish League before returning to England and joining Ipswich. He eventually became player-coach at Portman Road, scoring a vital goal at the age of 36 which helped the East Anglian side to return to the Premier League in the summer of 2000.

Anthony Mark Mowbray was born at Saltburn on November 22, 1963. In his youth he stood on the Holgate End at Ayresome Park idolising his hero, Boro legend John Hickton. As a talented youngster he was first spotted playing for Lakes Primary school in Redcar by Boro scout Ray Grant.

Later in his schoolboy career he captained the Langbaurgh and Cleveland Boys Under-15 team and also represented Grangetown Boys, Nunthorpe Athletic and Guisborough Town. Tony was also selected to play in an England schoolboy trial match but his international aspirations were never fulfilled when he sustained a leg fracture in his very first game.

In 1978 he signed schoolboy forms for his home town club, and two years later became an apprentice professional with the Boro.

He said: "It was always Boro for me. My father made me go to Aston Villa for a couple of weeks just so that I knew what it was like at another club but there was never any danger that I wouldn't sign for Boro."

Impressive displays by the strapping 6ft 1in central defender were rewarded with a full debut at St James's Park in September, 1982, when he was detailed to mark some ex-England captain called Kevin Keegan.

Unfortunately Mogga's early playing career also embraced one of the most dismal and turbulent times in the history of Middlesbrough FC, particularly when the club went into liquidation in the summer of 1986 following relegation to Division Three. During that period it seemed that the Boro's mere existence was hanging by an ever-fraying thread on a daily basis. The whole playing staff was given permission by the FA to talk to other clubs.

To his credit, Mowbray set a marvellous example to the rest of the squad by remaining at Ayresome Park. As a result of his loyalty, he was rewarded with the club captaincy by manager Bruce Rioch, with whom he formed the solid bond on which was built Boro's remarkable renaissance in the late 1980s.

Their relationship was publically cemented when, after Mowbray had scored a last minute equaliser in an exhilarating FA match against Everton, Rioch famously observed to the Evening Gazette: "If you were in a rocket ship going to the moon, the man you would want sitting next to you would be Tony Mowbray."

This genuine remark has now become indelibly etched into Teesside's football folklore and provided the long-running independent club fanzine with its unique title, 'Fly Me to the Moon'.

In Rioch and Mowbray, Boro had two very determined characters who proceeded to mastermind successive promotion campaigns which ended in a return to the top flight in 1988 with a team comprising mainly of local players. At the time Mowbray reflected: "I was

Unavailable for selection due to injury, Boro favourite, Tony Mowbray, was given the honour by the club of leading out Middlesbrough for their first Wembley showpiece in the 1990 ZDS cup final against Chelsea.

proud to be captain and I found I thrived on the responsibility. I'm sure that this period will become one of the great moments in Boro history."

By the summer of 1989, Mowbray's outstanding performances at club level were rewarded with an England B tour to Switzerland, Iceland and Norway along with Boro defensive colleague Gary Pallister.

In March 1990, Middlesbrough reached their first Wembley showpiece and, despite being injured, Mowbray was given the honour of leading the team out in the Zenith Data Systems Final by the new manager Colin Todd.

After more than 400 games and another change of management, which saw Lenny Lawrence take over at the helm, Mowbray was sold to Celtic in November, 1991, for £1m. However he did return to Ayresome Park the following season with the Bhoys for a much deserved testimonial match.

Mowbray's time in Glasgow, however, was dogged by injury but more importantly it was filled with personal tragedy when his wife Bernadette died from cancer.

After four seasons and 96 games for Celtic he moved to Ipswich Town in October, 1995, for £300,000 and eventually became player-coach with the East Anglian side.

He has enjoyed a successful time at Portman Road, but suffered along with the rest of the squad when Ipswich were beaten in a series of First Division play-off games which cost them the chance of promotion.

However everything worked out well in 2000 when Ipswich beat Barnsley in the play-off final at Wembley to take Tony and Ipswich back into the Premier League. He also played a big part in the victory, scoring the crucial equalising goal to bring Ipswich back into the game after Craig Hignett had fired Barnsley into the lead.

Denis Neale
Table Tennis

DENIS Neale is Teesside's top table tennis player of all time. He was a natural talent and an outstanding English international who made an incredible 495 appearances for his country.

He was the mainstay of the highly successful Ormesby Club and went on to win 18 titles in the English Closed Championships between 1966 and 1977. These included six men's singles, seven men's doubles and five mixed doubles. This was a record until it was eventually surpassed by Desmond Douglas.

Remarkably Denis had broken his right arm in five places, when he fell from a roof at the age of only five. The arm never set properly as a result, and could have been restrictive to a top sportsman like Neale. Yet, although it never disrupted his table tennis, his elbow did very occasionally spring from its joint and he found it difficult to execute some strokes.

Neale was born in Middlesbrough on December 9, 1944, and grew up in Lamport Street. He attended Newport infants and junior schools, before moving on to Stainsby School, where he was a keen athlete, basketball player and footballer. He also opened the batting for Middlesbrough Schools cricket team along with Alan Old, who was, like Denis, later to make his name internationally at another sport. In Old's case it was rugby union.

There was a sporting background in Denis's upbringing. His father Ernest had been a top footballer in his time and had played for England schoolboys. Neale Senior could have turned professional with several clubs, but did not like the idea of taking the huge gamble which was involved.

Denis's own ambition as a youngster was to be a professional player for the Boro, but his rapid progress as a table tennis player left little doubt about which route he should take in his life. He had taken up the sport at Newport Boys Club in 1958 and discovered that he had an uncanny natural talent. Within two years of picking up a bat he had earned England trials and went on to make his junior international debut against Wales in Cardiff in November, 1961.

When he left school he took a job as a messenger boy in the template shop at Dorman Long, but left after six months to become a full-time table tennis player.

In 1963, Denis became a senior international when he was still only 18, playing in the quadrangular home international tournament in Dublin. The following year he played in the European championships in Malmo, Sweden, gaining valuable experience and helping England to finish eighth in the team event.

He won all three matches in an international against West Germany while still a teenager, and then beat former European champion Zoltan Berczik from Hungary twice in three days before Christmas.

Denis was called up by England for the world championships in Ljubljana in Yugoslavia in April, 1965. It looked at one time that he may have to cry off, after spending a week in bed with a bad bout of bronchitis. But he was encouraged by manager Johnny Leach to travel and he benefitted from the experience, despite feeling weak and tired, which took away his competitive edge.

Denis was now established as a regular in all of England's internationals. During the year, he beat five of the top six men in Europe.

Neale was a committed competitor, and also spent many extra hours working on his physical fitness. In fact he was given permission to train with the Middlesbrough football squad during the time when the club was managed by Raich Carter and later Stan Anderson. Not only did he take part in the same training programme as the players, but also played them at table tennis afterwards.

In January, 1966, Neale, at the age of 21, won the English closed championship at Crystal Palace for the first time. In the semi-finals, Neale came back from 2-1 down to beat his big rival and the three-times champion Chester Barnes from Essex by 21-19, 13-21, 18-21, 21-18, 21-17. In the final he was a comfortable 3-0 winner against 18-year-old Stuart Gibbs.

With nearly 500 international appearances and 18 national titles to his name, Denis Neale is undoubtedly the top table tennis player ever produced on Teesside.

Denis continued to grow from strength to strength. He reached the final of the Expo 67 championships in Montreal and then beat the world rated Pak Sin II of North Korea in the world championships in Sweden.

This latter performance was enough to earn him No.1 spot in the English rankings, above Barnes. Denis celebrated with a world tour, playing in major events in North America, New Zealand and Australia, winning the open championships in both Canada and New Zealand.

In 1971 Neale and Barnes both fell into dispute with the ETTA, refusing to compete in the inaugural Commonwealth Championships in Singapore and the world championships in Japan when the tour to the Far East was extended without their knowledge. The ETTA decided to include an extra two weeks in China, and informed the players at the last moment.

However Neale and Barnes had both signed contracts for a series of exhibition matches back in England, and the promoters had already sold tickets. Their protests were ignored and, when they refused to travel, they were banned from international table tennis. It was a huge disappointment for Neale, who was the No.1 seed for the Commonwealth Championships and hot favourite to win. It was six months before his suspension was finally lifted.

The following year Neale reached the quarter-finals of the European championships in Rotterdam before going down in straight sets to the Hungarian Istvan Joyner by 21-10, 21-15, 21-18. It was the heaviest defeat of Neale's career, though he did receive some vindication later when it was discovered that Joyner had been using speed glue, which was a previously unknown substance which made the bat twice as fast. In the team event at Rotterdam, Neale won ten of his 15 matches.

One of Neale's best individual performances came in the world championships in Sarajevo in 1973, when he reached the last 16. He had pulled off the shock result of the tournament in the first round when beating the reigning world champion Hazagowa from Japan.

Denis won the Norwich Union English closed championship in 1974, and toured Japan with a European representative side. The itinerary included a match between Europe and Japan, who were the world champions.

Neale was now ranked 17th in the world and ninth in Europe and was playing to the peak of his ability. He again won the domestic crown for the fifth time in 1975, beating his friend and Ormesby clubmate Nicky Jarvis in the final at Crystal Palace which was televised live on TV. Denis took a two-set lead, but Jarvis pulled back to level and the fifth was all-square until the change-around, when Neale pulled away to win.

In January, 1977, Denis suffered a shock defeat in the Norwich Union English open tournament at Thornaby Pavilion when he was beaten in the final by 17-year-old Alan Griffiths. However he bounced back in the closed championships at Woking, beating England's No.1 Desmond Douglas from Birmingham by three sets to one to win the final for a record sixth time. Neale and Douglas then combined to beat Nicky Jarvis and Jimmy Walker in straight games in the final.

More controversy was to follow when Neale was dismissed from the England team for the world championships in Birmingham for "being a disruptive influence and undermining the authority of the team trainer".

The incident followed a sponsorship agreement for the England team which had been made between Denis and Ladbrokes bookmakers. He arranged for all the players to receive £3,000 sponsorship each in exchange for wearing the Ladbrokes logo on their international tracksuits.

It seemed a good deal, especially as £3,000 was a lot of money at the time. But the ETTA would not support the agreement, and the Teessider was disciplined.

However Denis, who was a strong campaigner for players' rights, was not prepared to accept the unreasonable decision. He took legal action and following top level negotiations, was reinstated to the five-man squad.

The same year, Neale signed a contract with the Dutch team HIA Panels of Deventer, committing him to playing 20 matches at £350 a match. Two weeks later the deal was off. The Dutch club was bankrupt.

In 1978, Denis played in his last major tournament when flying out for the Australian Masters. When he returned to England, he announced his retirement from top level table tennis, though he was still keen to pass on his many years of experience through his work as a coach.

Neale was only five games away from 500 international appearances, but had had enough of all the travelling and internal wrangling. Table tennis had provided him with a steady income since he first became world ranked, but it was time to move on.

Denis's first enterprise away from the sport was to open a betting shop at Great Harwood, though he sold up after four years and bought a newsagent's in West Dyke Road in Redcar. Later, he ran the Black Swan Inn at Thornton le Moor.

In 1994 Denis was appointed England men's team captain. The team was relatively successful during his year in charge, reaching the semi-finals of the Super League Premier Division, the quarter-finals of the World Cup and the semi-finals of the European Nations Cup.

However he headed off to Australia to compete in the world veterans' championships and ended up staying longer than he had anticipated. He did well in the tournament by reaching the quarter-finals before losing to the eventual winner from China.

He was offered a coaching appointment at Cairns and enjoyed a wonderful 13 months in one of the top holiday resorts in the world, near the Great Barrier Reef. Since his return to England, Neale has concentrated on his coaching work. He has coached the England cadet teams and coaches under the World Performance Scheme, helping to guide the blossoming careers of some of the country's top young players. He also coaches one day each week at the national academy in Nottingham.

Denis is the father of three children, daughter Joanne, and sons David, and Andrew.

Chris Newton
Cycling

CHRIS Newton is a world class racing cyclist who has completed in the last two Olympic Games for Great Britain. At Sydney, 2000, he won a bronze medal in the 4000m team pursuit which added to his silver medal from the 1994 Commonwealth Games in Canada, also in the same event.

A top junior rider as a teenager, Chris developed rapidly and could have been called up for Britain's Olympic team at Barcelona in 1992, but for suffering a bad fall.

However two years later he was selected for England's Commonwealth Games team in Victoria and returned home in triumph with a silver medal.

The following year he finished eighth in the team pursuit in the world championships in Colombia, and then tenth in the same event in the Atlanta Olympics in 1996.

Chris turned professional at the start of the 1998 season and finished eighth in the Prutour, and was 12th the following year. He has won many national titles, both on the track and on the road.

Christopher Malcolm Newton was born in Middlesbrough on September 29, 1973, and grew up in Linthorpe. He attended Linthorpe Juniors and Boynton Comprehensive School, and was a strong all-round sportsman. He was a member of the school football, swimming and athletics teams.

He excelled over the longer distances as a runner and represented Cleveland in the English schools cross country championships at Wadebridge in Cornwall, finishing half-way down the field. However the purpose of running, as far as Chris was concerned, was to build up his fitness for cycling.

He had gained a keen interest in cycling when he was taken by his father, Robert, who was a friend of Middlesbrough rider Sid Barras, to watch the professional races at Stockton Riverside.

Chris was handed his first bike when he was ten, and started racing competitively three years later. He joined local club Teesside Clarion and went on to win the Divisional Track League Under-14 Championship. Chris developed very quickly and proved that he was a top talent by becoming English schools champion in 1990 when winning a multi-stage stage around the North-east which was based at Hetton Lyons. He also won the Cleveland road race and track league championships.

Newton continued to progress and became a regular Great Britain international from the age of 16 in 1990. In the same year he competed in a six-nations event on the Kirkby track on Merseyside.

Then he was called up to take part in the world junior championships in Colorado Springs, narrowly missing out on the bronze medal in the team pursuit. He finished eighth in the points race and also raced in the road race, but retired.

His remarkable progress was rewarded at the end of 1990 when he was named Middlesbrough young sports personality of the year.

The following year, with new club Northern Velo, Chris won a bronze medal in the individual points race at the national track championships at Leicester and finished fourth in the individual 3,000 metres pursuit.

He switched clubs again in 1992, joining Middridge, and continued to work hard in the hope of winning a place in the Barcelona Olympics. He was called up for training with the British Olympic squad, but suffered a bad fall in the May which put him out of action for two months.

He was competing in a time trial on the A66 when he collided with a broken down car and suffered a very badly gashed knee. His leg was in plaster for a month and he was sidelined for a further four weeks, which effectively ended his Olympic hopes.

However Chris still had plenty of time on his side. He had already established himself as one of the top young riders in Britain and won his first national track title in the 20 kilometres race at Leicester in 1993, while still only 19. He also won the gold medal in the national

Olympic bronze and Commonwealth silver medallist and former Teesside Young Sports Personality of the Year, Chris Newton, builds up his cycling stamina on the North Yorkshire Moors.

centre of excellence road race championships over 98 miles at Hull.

In 1994, Chris was called up by England for the Commonwealth Games and enjoyed a memorable trip to Victoria, Canada, by returning with a silver medal from the 4000 metres team pursuit. England were beaten in the final by the powerful Australian team, who had the edge virtually throughout the race.

The following year Chris joined the North Wirral Velo race team. He won the 20k championship at Leicester again, and made a big impression on the road when winning the national under-23 road series. He was voted the best under-23 rider of the year, being awarded the Polar Aspirants Trophy.

Later he went on to win a silver medal in the national team time trial at Abergavenny.

The next major championships in Newton's sights were the world championships in Colombia. He joined the British team for an acclimatising training period in

Colorado, before heading off for South America. It was a great experience for Chris, both in terms of the racing and the different cultural lifestyle in Colombia. However he coped well in the strange surroundings and helped the team to finish eighth in the world championships, in a new British record time of 4.12.03, which guaranteed their place in the Atlanta Olympics.

Newton was by no means a certainty to be selected for the British pursuit team in the 1996 Olympics and had to work laboriously as a member of the pre-Olympics training squad of six riders.

As part of the build-up, the squad travelled to Langkawi in Malaysia to take part in a 12-day international stage race, which covered around 1,700 kilometres. Chris won one of the stages and was King of the Mountains, and finished second overall.

Back home in Britain, the Olympics training squad was eventually reduced to four for the big event in

Atlanta. Fortunately the name of Christopher Newton was included.

His battle to win a place for Atlanta meant that Chris had to make a brave decision in his life. He had been studying for a sports science degree at Teesside University, but had to forego his last year of studies in order to concentrate all his energies towards his Olympic bid.

He headed out to Atlanta with high hopes but the team did not perform as well as they had expected, and finished a disappointing tenth.

Chris also intended to compete in the individual time trial in the Olympics, but was struck down with a throat infection and could not race. He had been unhappy with the general standard of hygiene in the Olympics, which was partly due to the huge size of the event and the difficulties of maintaining it. This was in contrast to the more organised and more sedate Commonwealth Games which Chris had experienced in Canada two years earlier.

Later in 1996, Chris was called up for the British squad for the world championships in Lugano in Italy, and finished in a highly satisfactory 24th position in the time trial. He also competed in the road race, as part of his time trial preparation, but retired early.

During the same year he had won the bronze medal in the national time trial championships, in addition to recording several race wins in the national series.

In 1997, Newton decided to concentrate heavily on the European circuit, and he moved to France, where he lived in a flat in Annamasse and began riding for an amateur team. The sport of cycling had gone open the previous year, allowing amateurs and professionals to compete in the same races, and Chris benefitted from the extra competition. He also won several races, including the Grand Prix of Geneva,

He returned to England occasionally, and took the gold medal in the national team time trial championships in Devon and the silver medal in the national individual time trials on the A19 course at Crathorne.

At the end of the year, Chris decided to leave France to return home to England and he turned professional with the Brite team. He was good enough to make a reasonable living as a professional, and made a major impact in the Prutour when he finished in a very commendable eighth position overall.

The year of 1998 was a big one for Chris, because he won the National Premier Calendar Road Racing Series as a result of a remarkably consistent set of

riding performances which brought him two first places and eight seconds.

He also helped the Brite team to win the national team time trial championships in Suffolk, near Ipswich, and took second place in the national individual time trial in Nottinghamshire.

He flew out with the English team for the Commonwealth Games in Kuala Lumpur at the peak of his form and raced very well, especially considering the humidity, to take seventh place in the time trial.

The following year, and now racing for the Linda McCartney team, Chris was the top British finisher in 12th position in the Prutour.

He recorded a notable double by carrying off the two major time trials, winning the RTTC national event at Boroughbridge and the BCF time trial on the Isle of Man.

He continued to notch up the titles, helping the Linda McCartney team to win the national team time trial and also the national team pursuit event.

In October, 1999, Chris travelled to Treviso in Italy for the world championships and was disappointed to finish no higher than 44th. He rode as well as he could, but felt fatigued, and could not reproduce some of his form from earlier in the year.

Worse was to follow, when he was one of ten riders to be released from his Linda McCartney team contract.

With the 2000 Olympics looming on the horizon, Chris found himself desperately looking for vital sponsorship to help try to realise his long-held ambition of winning a medal. Initially he had to rely on his savings from his two years as a professional and the financial support of his wife Julie as he battled for a place on the flight to Sydney, but then his training programme was given a substantial boost when he was awarded lottery funding through the world class performance plan.

Having linked up with the Middridge team, Chris has enjoyed a good season on the road in 2000, being the dominant rider in the Premier Calendar Series with four wins. He also won two major international races in Belgium and a stage race in Holland.

Chris's main target was to get to Sydney and, after being named as one of seven cyclists in the British team pursuit training squad in Manchester, he was absolutely delighted when he was named in the final squad of five which won a bronze medal at the Olympic Games in Australia.

Alan Old
Rugby Union

ALAN Old is the elder of the two sporting Old brothers and was a world class fly-half who played 16 times for England.

He toured South Africa, both with England and the British Lions, setting individual points records on both occasions.

Alan Gerald Bernard Old was born on September 23, 1945, and was educated at Green Lane Primary School and then Acklam Hall Grammar School from 1957-1964. It was during his time at school that the solid foundations of a highly successful sporting career were laid with appearances for Durham County and North of England Under-15 cricket teams, followed by the Cleveland U15 and U19 rugby teams.

His family, however, always placed a great deal of importance on academic progress and Alan gained a BSc degree in Mathematics from Queen Mary College University of London in 1967.

A post graduate teaching qualification from the University of Durham opened up a career in education and over the next few years Alan was able to combine both sport and teaching commitments.

He made his first appearance for Middlesbrough Cricket Club 1st XI at the age of 16 and went on to become club captain, and eventually their professional.

A fine middle order batsman and pace bowler, Alan might even have made it in the first class game. He signed for Warwickshire and made one appearance in 1969, scoring 34 runs in his only innings, and taking 1-93 with the ball.

However it is with Durham that Alan is best remembered as a cricket player. He played Minor Counties cricket for 11 seasons and was named Durham's player of the year in 1970. That season he was awarded his county cap, having scored 230 runs to head the batting averages with 46.0, and taken 12 wickets at an average of 21.85. His player of the year award was worth 50 guineas and he also received the Sunderland and Shields Building Society Trophy.

At the time, there were regular changes of captaincy, and Alan was in charge for certain games in seasons 1971 and 1972.

Limited over Gillette Cup matches offered him the opportunity to play against first class counties and the highlight of these campaigns was Durham's five wickets victory over Yorkshire in June, 1973, at Harrogate. The win created plenty of family rivalry, and no doubt a little bit of ribbing afterwards, because younger brother Chris ended up on the losing side.

Alan played 45 times for Durham, scoring 1,012 runs at an average of 23.53, including a best score of 82 not out. He also bowled almost 800 overs, taking 95 wickets at an average of 20.66, and including a best analysis of 6-20.

Alan's successful teaching career began in Redcar at the Sir William Turner School from 1968-1972 then on to Worksop College from 1972-1976. Eventually he moved on to Myers Grove School at Sheffield. During these later years he spent three years playing cricket for Doncaster in the competitive Yorkshire League and five years as the professional at Worksop.

It was, however, in the winter sport of rugby that he established himself on the international scene. He made his debut for Middlesbrough RUFC during the 1968-1969 season and played for his home town club until 1972, latterly as captain, when new teaching commitments saw him move to Worksop.

He played his last game in his first spell with Middlesbrough in the club's centenary celebration game against London Welsh at Acklam Park in September, 1972.

From his preferred position of fly half, Alan developed into an excellent place kicker with fine tactical awareness and sound defensive qualities. During the 1969-1970 season he was selected for Yorkshire and over the next ten years he was not only first choice for his county but also he was to gain international recognition and take part in numerous tours around the world.

His first representative appearance was for the North

Although Alan Old was an outstanding club and Minor Counties cricketer with Middlesbrough and Durham it was as a world class rugby fly half that he made his name. On overseas tours in the 1970s with both England and the British Lions he set individual points scoring records.

Eastern Counties against South Africa during their tour which was plagued by anti apartheid demonstrations in 1970. The following season he received his England call-up and made his international debut opposite the legendary Barry John in a tough game against Wales, who had won the Grand Slam the previous season. However England did reasonably well and, in a tight game, Wales won 12-3. Unfortunately England had a very poor Five Nations Championship, finishing with the wooden spoon.

Despite this setback, Alan was chosen for England's tour of South Africa, where he established a record points score of 24 in a 60-21 victory against Griqualand West at Kimberley. He kicked nine conversions, one penalty and a dropped goal. It beat, by one, Bob Hiller's previous tour best for an Englishman, which had been set on the 1968 Lions' visit. Having warmed to the trip, Old helped England to an unexpected victory over the Springboks at Ellis Park, Johannesburg, by 18-9. In fact it was a highly successful tour because England remained unbeaten in their seven matches, winning six and drawing one.

An injury plagued 1972-1973 season prevented further international recognition until England's successful summer tour of 1973 Down Under, when he played in the outstanding team which defeated the mighty All Blacks by 16-10 and secured victory against Australia by 20-3.

In the summer of 1973 Alan was selected for England's six match tour of Argentina, though later suffered disappointment when the tour was cancelled because of threats by guerrillas to kidnap players.

During the 1973-1974 season Alan played in all England's Five Nations matches. On the strength of his consistent performances for his country he was chosen as a member of the British Lions party which toured South Africa. Unfortunately after scoring 37 points in a match against South West Districts, injury prematurely ended his involvement and he returned home in plaster.

After a couple of seasons playing for Leicester he returned to Middlesbrough RUFC for the 1974-1975 season and was also selected for Yorkshire, North East Counties and the North of England, as well as the international match against Ireland, which England lost by 12-9.

In May, 1975, Old was called up as a late replacement for England's tour of Australia. He went straight into the side for the Second Test in Brisbane, with England already one down, and played his part in England levelling the series against the Wallabies.

Alan was living in South Yorkshire at this stage and he switched clubs and joined Sheffield, one of the strongest Yorkshire sides at that time, and he played for them until 1985.

Old was very frustrated in 1978 when he was called up for the first Five Nations match against France in Paris, scoring his country's points from two dropped goals, but was then dropped to the replacements' bench for the following game against Wales. Immediately he wrote to the international selectors informing them that he no longer wanted to be considered for the bench. Effectively, it was the end of the Teessiders international career.

In 1980, Alan scored a try and kicked a penalty for the North in a Bill Beaumont-led thrilling 21-7 victory against the All Blacks at Otley. It was a fitting climax to a distinguished rugby career during which time Alan had played 16 times for his country, scoring 98 points, and made 54 appearances for Yorkshire.

Owing to increased teaching and family responsibilities, Alan announced his retirement from international and county rugby. The following season he was appointed Yorkshire's county coach and then the Northern Division Technical Administrator with overall responsibility for the coaching throughout the region.

However Alan was eventually tempted back out of retirement by the Yorkshire selectors and went on to play in the 1984 County Championship Final against Gloucestershire at Bristol, when the Tykes were beaten on a pitch which Alan described as having the all the qualities of a paddyfield.

In 1985 Alan was appointed deputy headmaster at the King Edward VI School in Morpeth and relinquished his post as technical administrator for the North. He was approaching his 40th year, but was still enjoying playing as much as ever and joined the Morpeth club.

The following year Alan was appointed Northumberland County coach, and held this position until 1991 when he stood down and became a county selector. This is a role which he carries out to this day. However he returned to his Teesside roots in 1988 when he took over as principal of Sir William Turner's Sixth Form College in Redcar. Six years later he was appointed vice-principal of Cleveland Tertiary College, which is now known as Redcar and Cleveland College.

Chris Old
Cricket

IN the words of former England captain Mike Brearley, Chris Old was "a displaced gene away from greatness".

It was a shrewd observation which acknowledged his undoubted natural ability but also suggested the lack of a ruthless streak and a susceptibility to injury.

However this should not be allowed to deflect from the fact that, in the context of Test appearances, Chris Old is quite simply the greatest cricket player that Teesside has ever produced by a mile.

He played in 46 Test matches for England between 1972 and 1981, taking 143 wickets at an average of 28.11.

Old's remarkable achievement of taking four wickets in five balls in the First Test against Pakistan at Edgbaston in 1978 had previously been recorded on only one previous occasion.

Occasionally he was also a dab hand with the bat. His century made for Yorkshire in only 37 minutes against an indifferent Warwickshire attack in 1977 was the third fastest ever in first class cricket. His second 50 took only nine minutes.

Chris also played in 32 one-day internationals, taking 45 wickets at an average of 22.2, and scoring 338 runs. His best one-day score was 57 not out.

Born in Middlesbrough on December 22, 1948, Christopher Middleton Old was educated at Green Lane and Acklam Hall Grammar Schools. He was an outstanding schoolboy cricketer, first representing Middlesbrough Juniors at the young age of 13 before graduating through the Durham, North of England and England Schools teams to the Yorkshire County groundstaff in 1964.

Modest and unassuming, tall and strongly built, Chris was an immensely gifted cricketer in all departments of the game. At 6ft 3in, he had the perfect frame for a bowler, sending down right arm fast medium outswingers and back breaks which occasionally mesmerised batsmen. Using his height, he had a rhythmic approach in his run-up and a classic side-on

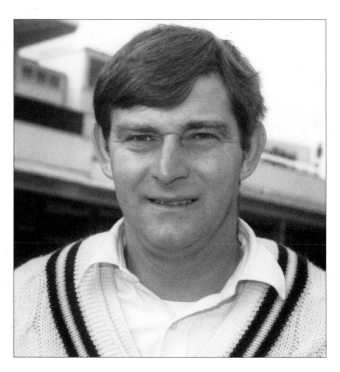

Chris Old, an all-round cricketer of great natural ability with an international record to match .

action which extracted awkward bounce from the deadest of pitches.

He made his first appearance for Yorkshire at the age of 17 and went on to play in 379 first class matches for the Tykes and later Warwickshire, taking 1,070 wickets at an average of 23.48.

No doubt Old would have played in many more than 46 Tests had not his career been dogged by persistent injuries. He had operations on both knees in the early 1970s but seldom failed to justify his selection. His best county bowling figures were recorded on his home ground of Acklam Park in Middlesbrough, when he took 7-20 against Gloucestershire in 1969.

As a hard hitting left-handed batsman he was an effective run-maker against most types of bowling except real pace. He never really picked up as many runs as he should have done in Test cricket, although his tally of 7,756 runs from first class cricket at an

At Edgbaston in 1978 against Pakistan, Chris Old's rhythmic run up and classical side-on delivery action enabled him to become only the second bowler in Test cricket history to capture four wickets in five balls.

average of 20.84 was pretty respectable.

As an all-rounder Chris could be a match winner, and his best individual performance arguably came against the old enemy from across the Pennines when in the Roses match of 1978 at Old Trafford he scored 100 not out and took nine wickets in the game.

He was also a brilliant fielder. He was athletic in the deep and a clinical catcher in the slip cordon.

In his early career Chris was genuinely quick but deliberately slowed down his pace in order to bowl longer, more accurate spells. Over the years cricket commentators have accused him of lacking that mean streak which separates good bowlers from great bowlers but that didn't stop him reaching the pinnacle of his profession.

Chris helped Yorkshire to reach the inaugural Benson and Hedges Cup Final in 1972, but it wasn't a memorable occasion. He was out for six as Yorkshire made 136-9, and then recorded figures of 0-35 off 9.5 overs as Leicestershire won by five wickets.

Chris made his England debut on the winter tour to India and Pakistan in 1972-73, when called up for the Second Test in Calcutta. England lost the match by 28 runs, but Old staked his claim for a permanent place by taking six wickets and carrying his bat in both innings, making a total of 50 runs.

The following summer he played in two Tests against New Zealand, recording his best figures so far when taking 5-113 against the Kiwis in the drawn Test at Lord's.

Tours to the West Indies and Australia followed over the next two winters. In between, Chris hammered 65 off the Pakistan attack in the drawn Third Test at The Oval.

In 1976-77 Chris helped England to win the Test series in India, before travelling on to Australia and taking seven wickets in the legendary one-off Melbourne Test which the Aussies won by 45 runs.

The following winter he improved his best ever Test figures by taking 6-54 in the first innings of the First Test against New Zealand in Wellington, though the Kiwis won the match by 72 runs.

Old's finest moment arrived in the Test series against Pakistan in 1978. In the First Test at Edgbaston, he took his four wickets in five balls in the first innings, bowling a no-ball in the middle of his haul of wickets, Chris finished with figures of 7-50 as England romped home by an innings and 57 runs.

He helped England to win the Second Test by an innings at Lord's, and then produced another remarkable bowling spell in the first innings of the Third Test at Headingley, when taking 4-41 off 41.4 accurate overs.

In 1981 Old also took part in the amazing Headingley Test against Australia when England, magnificently led by Ian Botham and Bob Willis, defied odds of 500-1 to come back from a hopeless position and beat the Aussies by 18 runs.

Chris was to play in just one more Test, in the fourth match of the same series at Birmingham, when England fittingly beat the Aussies by 29 runs. He bowled brilliantly in the first innings to finish with figures of 3-44.

In 1979 Old's loyal service to Yorkshire had been rewarded with a successful benefit season and at the beginning of the 1981 campaign he was appointed captain of Yorkshire during a turbulent time for the White Rose county which surrounded Geoff Boycott's position at the club.

However his career went into a sudden decline when, having spent the 1981-82 winter playing for North Transvaal, he joined the "rebel" tour of South Africa and along with the other English players concerned, like Graham Gooch, was banned from Test cricket for a period of three years.

Following Yorkshire's disappointing season which was continually disrupted by political in-fighting, Old was relieved of the captaincy in June, 1982, and surprisingly replaced by 50-year-old Ray Illingworth. Worse was to follow when, in October of the same year, it was announced that he was not being retained by his home county. He had given them sterling and loyal service since 1964.

Old wasted no time to secure his immediate future and within a month had accepted terms to move to Warwickshire, where he finished his playing career in 1985.

He was back at Lord's for a second Benson and Hedges Cup Final appearance in 1984, but again finished on the losing side. Warwickshire were bowled out for 139, Chris making only five, and then he recorded figures of 0-23 off 10.4 overs as Lancashire won by six wickets.

However Old was still as good as any paceman given the right conditions. He produced fine match figures of 11-99 against Yorkshire at Headingley in 1984 to prove that he had maintained the highest quality right throughout his career.

Gary Pallister

Football

MANCHESTER United manager Sir Alex Ferguson raised more than a few eyebrows in August 1989 when he paid Middlesbrough FC a British record fee of £2.3m for a defender in order to take Gary Pallister from Ayresome Park to Old Trafford.

Many seasoned football writers regarded the transfer with a certain scepticism as Pallister was relatively inexperienced at the highest level.

However, for almost a decade after his transfer, United's raw recruit would become an integral part in one of the most successful sides in English football history.

Gary Andrew Pallister was born in Ramsgate on June 30, 1965, when his parents were working and living in Kent. His family returned to their native Teesside when he was only six months old. As a youngster he attended Fredrick Nattrass and Blakeston schools in Norton where he developed into a fine all round sportsman, excelling particularly at basketball and cricket, gaining representatives honours in both. In 1984 he was voted Norton Cricket Club's Young Player of the Year.

Football, however, was always his first priority and he began his career as an amateur in the Northern League with Billingham Town. It wasn't long before the tall centre-half was attracting the attention of Middlesbrough but he failed to impress manager Malcolm Allison and played only one Central League game before being released.

However, Boro coach Willie Maddren had noted Pallister's potential and when he succeeded Allison in the managerial hot-seat 12 months later, he signed the blond defender in November, 1984.

At that time Boro were in dire financial straits and Maddren needed to find somebody willing to sponsor Pallister's wages if he was to be proved right about the player's ability to make the grade. It was to be a local businessman and Boro director Richard Corden who eventually volunteered to pay Pallister's salary so the club could retain the services of the highly promising prospect.

In order to gain some much needed league experience early in his professional career, Gary spent a period on loan with Darlington. The Quakers were keen to make the move permanent, but Maddren would not sell.

In the second half of the 1985-86 season, Pallister began to sew the seeds of what what to prove a very productive partnership with Tony Mowbray. But Boro were struggling for points and they were relegated to the Third Division following a 2-1 defeat at Shrewsbury Town on the final day of the season. To make matters worse, Pallister was sent off during a stormy second period.

Gary then had to face up to an uncertain future when Boro immediately went into liquidation. Like all the players during that period of instability, he had the opportunity to talk to other clubs and move on. But Gary stayed loyal to the Boro and once the team began to prosper under the inspired leadership of new manager Bruce Rioch, he developed his solid and reliable defensive partnership with Mowbray, with each complementing the other's attributes.

Under Rioch's charismatic guidance, Boro achieved two promotions in quick succession and, by 1988, after a series of nailbiting play-offs against Bradford City and Chelsea, they had regained their First Division status. During that rapid rise back to football's elite, Pallister's elegant performances earned him an England call up in March 1988 against Hungary. It was to be the first of 20 caps for his country.

Unfortunately in 1989, after only one season in the top flight, Boro were relegated. But Pallister's consistency in a struggling team had attracted the attention of many of the leading clubs. And it was Manchester United manager Alex Ferguson who eventually paid a record fee of £2.3million to take him across the Pennines after Rioch and Boro chairman Colin Henderson had hiked up the fee during several hours of negotiations.

Gary had made 180 appearances during this first stint with Boro and scored seven goals.

Unfortunately Pallister had a nightmare debut for United when he gave away a penalty in a 2-0 home

From Middlesbrough to Manchester United and back again. England international Gary Pallister was one of the most outstanding players of the 1990s winning numerous major championship and cup medals.

defeat against Norwich City. But with the public backing of Ferguson he steadily grew in confidence and became a massive influence at the heart of the United defence, where he forged another cohesive partnership, this time with the combative Steve Bruce. Again, their contrasting styles of play complemented each other superbly.

In order to maximise Gary's physical attributes of height and speed, and add a harder edge to his accurate passing game, Manchester United initiated a rigorous programme of weight training designed to increase his stamina and body strength.

This combination of natural ability and physical dominance transformed Pallister into one of the most solid, stylish and accomplished all-round defenders of his generation.

His professional standing among his peers also grew when he was named the PFA player of the year in 1992. Critics have suggested that he had a tendency to lose concentration during matches but this was a flaw in his game he tried hard to eradicate and only very rarely did the opposition profit from his mistakes.

Considering his ability, it is quite surprising that he was capped only 20 times by England. In some cases, however, he was unavailable for selection due to a back problem which robbed him, most significantly, of a place in Euro 96.

During the 1990s, with Manchester United becoming the dominant force in English football, Gary Pallister collected every major domestic winner's medal in the game including four championships, three FA Cups, one League Cup and also a European Cup Winners Cup. A truly outstanding achievement for a player who made an uncertain start to his Old Trafford career but then proceeded to totally vindicate Alex Ferguson's belief in his ability.

During the summer of 1998, Manchester United clinically demonstrated that there was no sentiment in football when they bought outstanding Dutch international central defender Jaap Stam to replace Pallister, who was now 33.

So, after 431 appearances and 15 goals for the Reds, he returned to the North-east to help his old teammate Bryan Robson consolidate Boro's place in the Premier League. This he did to great effect as Boro emerged as a solid and defensively competent side on their return to the top flight, with Pallister regularly running the show from the back.

Cecil Parkin
Cricket

CRICKET comedian Cecil Harry Parkin began his county career with Yorkshire - until shocked officials discovered that he had been born 20 yards outside the county boundary.

There were some red faces at the Tykes' headquarters when it came to light that the highly talented slow bowler was not a true-born Yorkshireman. In fact Parkin had entered this life on the wrong side of the River Tees, in the stationmaster's house at Egglescliffe in County Durham on February 18, 1886.

This was not allowed, of course. The Tykes were steadfast in their determination to use only those players who were born within their own county boundaries.

It was a shame, because the young Parkin was a prodigious talent. A right arm bowler of off breaks and leg breaks, Cecil, who was known affectionately as Ciss, had been a prolific wicket-taker as a teenager with Norton, winning the inaugural Crosby Cup as the club's young player of the year at the age of 19 in 1905. His progress was so rapid that he was only 20 when he made his controversial debut for the Tykes.

Parkin had actually started out as a pace bowler, and a rather skinny one. He was a pretty good opening bowler, but never top notch. His quest for bowling greatness was to lie along another route. The key to Cecil's development as a world class medium-slow bowler came from the support and patience of his mentor. The old leg spinner C L Townsend lived close by in Norton and Cecil regularly visited him for coaching lessons. After many long periods of practice, Cecil mastered the leg break, and then the googly.

However, having been shown the door by Yorkshire, Parkin's Championship career stalled for a number of years. Durham provided Cecil with the opportunity to continue to play representative cricket and he began playing in the Minor Counties the following season, developing his unique bowling style in the competitive world of Lancashire League cricket.

Cecil's career took off again in 1914 when he joined the Lancashire county side. He made his name immediately, taking 14 wickets for 99 runs in his first match against Leicestershire at Liverpool. Wisden, commenting on his debut success, reported that he broke both ways 'on the quick side of medium' and that 'a player of remarkable powers had been found'.

Tall, dark and good looking, Parkin had now laid down the foundations to become one of the most feared bowlers in England over the next ten years. He wasted no time in becoming an integral cog in the Lancashire side, and was a great and much loved character in the dressing room.

Cecil was also acknowledged as one of cricket's great eccentrics. As a talented conjuror, juggler and comedian, he often entertained the crowd, and his fellow players, with his outlandish brand of humour and clowning around. But he also found time to bamboozle even the most accomplished batsmen with his highly unusual repertoire.

Cecil constantly experimented with his high action, loose limbed technique and would try anything with the ball, making it extremely difficult for his captain to set a field to his diverse deliveries.

Parkin's basic delivery was the off break, a ball which he bowled with every conceivable variation of flight, speed and angle, but he also intermingled his overs with leg breaks, flighted slower balls and top spinners. He would perfect his bowling by using his long suffering wife as a dummy batsman. The poor woman would often end these sessions in tears with her fingers black and blue because she had been struck on the hands so frequently. Parkin did acknowledge in later years that without her support he would not have been such an effective bowler.

The seeds of success were nevertheless sewn as a young boy. Naturally his early cricket was played on Teesside, while he was learning to be a pattern maker. However his natural talent earned him the chance to become a cricket professional, and Cecil signed up for Ossett in the Yorkshire League. In July, 1906, after taking more than 100 wickets for Ossett and playing

Between 1905 and 1930 Cecil Parkin, right, gained a reputation as one of cricket's great characters.

several productive games for the Yorkshire Second XI, he was selected to play for the full county side.

Parkin's debut was against Gloucestershire and he duly took a couple of wickets. However his career wearing the White Rose proved to be an all too brief experience when officials discovered he was not qualified to play. In his memoirs, Parkin recorded his feelings: "Imagine my disappointment when, after one match with the White Rose, the news reached me that I had been disqualified from playing for Yorkshire.

"But let me say that Yorkshire captain Lord Hawke was fully aware, when I first played for Yorkshire, that I was born in Durham. I did not get into the Yorkshire XI under false pretences.

"And it was not, as the story goes, that Yorkshire got me disqualified. The MCC did the disqualification from information received from some evidently kind friend of mine."

Parkin cut his links with Yorkshire completely, and began playing in the Lancashire League, which was one of the strongest cricket leagues in the country. Two of the clubs he played for were Tunstall and Church.

Cecil's native county Durham were also keen to utilise his services, and he signed up to play Minor Counties

cricket. Even so, Parkin played only 16 matches for Durham between 1907-13. He took 56 wickets at an average of 13.05, his best figures being 6-37 against Lincolnshire at South Shields in 1912, when he took 10-74 in the match. The following season he took 6-39 against Staffordshire at Stoke.

It was these kind of skilled bowling performances which attracted the attentions of Lancashire, and Cecil was finally offered a route back into the Championship. However it was 1914, and the Great War was looming, and it was not until after the end of hostilities that Parkin went to become one of the biggest names in the game.

At the end of the war, Parkin initially returned to league cricket, playing successfully for Rochdale and Blackpool. In fact he did not turn professional on a full-time basis with Lancashire until he was 36. He made his decision after returning with the MCC from the disastrous Johnny Douglas-led Ashes tour of Australia in 1920-21, when his teammates had included Middlesbrough-born Harry Makepeace.

Despite the problems experienced Down Under by the tourists, Cecil had been voted the pick of the MCC attack by the victorious Aussies. He was top wicket-taker in a woeful attack, dismissing 16 victims at an average of 41.87 runs apiece. His best performance came in the first innings of the Third Test at Adelaide, when he took 5-60. But he had little support and England lost by 119 runs.

Parkin recalled later: "The Governor General sent for Jack Hobbs and gave him a cigarette case or somesuch. Then a message came for me that the Governor General wishes for the presence of Mr Parkin. So I smoothes my hair and puts on my England blazer.

"The Governor General receives me like royalty. 'Congratulations Mr Parkin, well bowled', he said. Then bowed me out and I got nowt."

The hard Aussie wickets were not to the liking of the English bowlers and the home side won all five Tests by convincing margins.

It was a difficult time for everybody on the tour, but no doubt Parkin's England teammates welcomed his unique brand of humour to help relieve the pressure as they struggled from one disaster to another.

Parkin once said to Johnny Douglas: "Here's Macartney coming in to bat sir. You go on for an hour and bowl him in, then I'll come on and bowl him out."

Cecil was a great guy to have in the dressing room and a crowd pleaser in more ways than one because he combined his cricketing exploits by keeping the crowd smiling with a series of japes. He played sport for fun and he liked to see everybody else enjoying themselves.

Once he was full-time with the Red Rose, Parkin was able to commit himself fully to the task of reviving Lancashire's fortunes. He represented the county with great distinction in an illustrious career which lasted for 13 years between 1914 and 1926. Cecil's bowling peak was between 1922-25, when he captured 100 wickets in a season on four consecutive occasions. The best of them all was 1924, when he dismissed 194 hapless victims.

Parkin made ten appearances for England. Nine of them came against Australia, and the other against South Africa. He faced the Aussies in four Tests in England in 1921, and was again the leading wicket-taker with 16 wickets, at a more economical average of 26.25. His best performance came in the Fourth Test at Old Trafford, when he thrilled his own Lancashire fans by taking 5-38 in the Aussie first innings. But the Test was drawn. The tourists went on to win the series.

Unfortunately Cecil was on the losing side in his first seven Test Matches. He contributed towards his own swift international demise by publicly criticising the England captain, Arthur Gilligan, in a newspaper article after the Edgbaston Test of 1924, much to the displeasure of the MCC authorities. This was Parkin's first Test appearance for three years, and his last.

Remarkably South Africa were dismissed for 30 in their first innings by Maurice Tate and Gilligan and Parkin never got on in that innings. Despite being regarded as England's premier spin bowler, he was used sparingly in the second and had figures of 0-38. He voiced his disappointment publicly about Gilligan's captaincy, and the outburst effectively ended his Test career.

Ironically, Lord Hawke, now aged 65, was again to be linked with Parkin following the bowler's newspaper outburst. Hawke told Yorkshire's annual meeting: "Pray God no professional shall ever captain England. I love and admire them all but we have always had an amateur skipper and when the day comes when we shall have no more amateurs captaining England it shall be a thousand pities."

It was proof that Parkin was ahead of his time in more ways than one.

While he had few peers as a slow bowler, Parkin never professed to being a batsman. He enjoyed batting, but was never very good, making just 1,959 runs in his 157 matches for Lancashire at an average of 12.09.

However, as a bowler, he was occasionally unplayable. The best bowling performance of Parkin's career came at Ashby in 1924, when Cecil took nine Leicestershire wickets in an innings for only 32 runs. His best match analysis had been achieved the previous year, when he took 15-95 against Glamorgan at Blackpool.

There is a story handed down through the years about Parkin and his Yorkshire rival Wilfred Rhodes. Apparently for the benefit of an old lady a Yorkshire cricketer was identifying celebrities at a sporting gathering and when told, " That's the great Rhodes, " she exclaimed," Not THE great Rhodes. Not Cecil Rhodes." "No madam came the innocent reply, " Wilfred's HIS name. You're thinking of Parkin."

The rivalry between Yorkshire-Lancashire became particularly intense in the 1920s due to the emergence of the Red Rose county as a cricketing power. It was Parkin and the bulky Richard Tyldesley who made possible Lancashire's first victory in a Roses match in Yorkshire since 1899, when they bowled out reigning champions Yorkshire for a mere 33 on a drying wicket at Leeds. Tyldesley took 6-18 and Parkin 3-15.

In his Lancashire career, Cecil took 901 wickets at an impressive average of 16.12 runs apiece. He signed off in some style, the Red Rose county winning the Championship in his last season with the club.

However his career with Lancashire ended in acrimonious circumstances, when he fell into dispute with the county. This disagreement with Red Rose officialdom was to see him leave the county scene altogether and return to league cricket.

It was a rather sad, but wholly appropriate way, for Parkin's first class career to finish because, according to many who knew him well, he was his own worst enemy. He was an individual who found it difficult to conform to the structure imposed by cricket's establishment and he never really fulfilled his potential at the highest level.

Although Parkin did continue to play in occasional charity matches in the 1930s he became the licensee of a Manchester pub. When he died on August 15, 1943 his ashes were scattered over the wicket at Old Trafford. His son Reginald eventually followed in his footsteps and also played for Lancashire on 20 occasions throughout the Thirties.

Ronnie Parkinson
Motor Sport

FOR a brief period between the First and Second World Wars, motor cycle sand racing was a huge attraction, not only on the local Teesside beaches, but also throughout the country.

Thousands of eager spectators lined the promenades at Saltburn and Redcar to watch the thrills and spills of the high-speed action, and nobody was a better exponent of the sport than 'The White Devil of Pendine', the flamboyant Ronnie Parkinson.

'Parky', as he was known, was born in 1905. His interest in motor cycles began at early age when, as a youngster, he used to clean the Harley Davidson owned by a neighbour, Horace Williams, who was secretary of the Middlesbrough and District Motor Club.

Parkinson started his working life as an apprentice electrical engineer, but later moved into his father's hosiery business which was situated where the Crown Buildings now stand in the centre of Middlesbrough.

After saving hard, he bought a new AJ Stephens machine for £80 which he immediately modified to his personal specifications. When it was finished, the AJS caused quite a stir among the local motor cycling fraternity who called it a 'gem'.

Ronnie began his racing career in the amateur classes on the local hill climbs at Yearby Bank, Ormesby, Legs Cross Flatts and Sutton Bank.

By 1924 he was entering the sand races held at Saltburn and the following year recorded a very respectable time behind another famous local racer, Freddie Dixon.

In a highly successful racing career, which reached its peak between 1928 and 1932, Ronnie carried off many local and national championships. In fact he was placed first on a staggering 360 occasions, winning over a wide range of distances from ten to 50 miles, riding a variety of machines from 350cc to 1000cc, and on beaches all over the country in Yorkshire, Scotland, Lancashire and Wales.

Throughout his racing career Parkinson had the reputation of being a highly organised and meticulous individual. His workshop was always beautifully clean and his machines were presented for competition in pristine condition. On race days he was a great crowd pleaser, often flying to venues in style before changing into his distinctive white overall, an eye-catching outfit, which eventually earned him his 'White Devil' nickname.

Although sand racing was his major priority, he did take part in the Isle of Man TT races but managed to finish only once. He also tried his hand at dirt track riding, which came to England in the late 1920s, but did not take to the confines of the tight circuit.

However, his expert knowledge was put to good use when he initially became mechanical superintendent at Hackney Wick and Wimbledon stadiums in London, and later as head of the experimental and engine testing department of Associated Motor Cycles Ltd, where his pioneering innovations involved the use of supercharges.

As his job became more time consuming, Ronnie decided to retire from sand racing. However he was coaxed out of retirement in 1936 to take part in the very demanding Paradubic Golden Helmet race in Czechoslovakia where, considering his lack of recent competitive riding, he finished in an amazing second place. The trip was also notable because while he was waiting to board a train at Nuremburg, standing on the same platform was the German Chancellor, Adolf Hitler.

While living in London, Ronnie also diversified into car rallying and learned to fly, eventually obtaining his pilot's licence and buying his own two-seater Spartan aeroplane.

In 1936 he moved to Jersey to manage a garage but this excursion to the Channel Islands was short lived, and he returned to Teesside by working his passage on a ship bound for the North-east.

He then started up his own retail business, firstly in Bottomley Street, Middlesbrough, and later in larger

On seaside beaches all over Britain in the late 1920s, Ronnie Parkinson was one of the greatest exponents of motor cycle sand racing. His distinctive outfit earned him the nickname, "The White Devil of Pendine."

extended premises at Eastbourne Road, dealing in cars of distinction such as the Bristol.

In 1949 he accepted an invitation to enter the gruelling Alpine Rally as co-driver to a Czechoslovakian called Treybal. It was a decision which was to almost cost him his life.

During a stage near Cortina in the Italian Dolomites, their Bristol car spun off the road on a hairpin bend and somersaulted two hundred feet down a ravine. Miraculously they both survived but Ronnie sustained severe head and leg injuries and was given only a 2% chance of recovery. In fact if it hadn't been for the swift intervention of the Italian army, who were on

manoeuvres in the area at the time, in transporting them quickly to hospital, Ronnie would certainly have died.

After undergoing extremely delicate and complicated surgery, Ronnie spent seven weeks recuperating in hospital, before he gradually began to pull round. Eventually he was well enough to return home in an air ambulance, very grateful for the medical care he had received in Italy.

As a result of his horrendous injuries Ronnie was forced to tone down his exhilarating lifestyle but he continued to successfully run his car dealership in Middlesbrough until his retirement.

Pat Partridge
Football

PAT Partridge was one of the most respected FIFA referees in the world throughout the 1970s and early 1980s, reaching the pinnacle of his distinguished career when taking charge of two World Club Championship Finals and refereeing in the World Cup Finals in Argentina in 1978.

He became president of the Association of Football League Referees and Linesmen in 1975 and officiated at the FA Cup Final between West Ham United and Fulham in the same year. Three years later he controlled the 1978 League Cup Final between Liverpool and Nottingham Forest.

Pat visited more than 50 countries to officiate in major games in his ten years as a FIFA official. Having initially extended his distinguished refereeing career beyond the normal retiring age of 47, he then took on the important job as a UEFA referees observer and delegate which he carries out to this day.

Patrick Partridge was born at No.37, St Vincent Street, Haverton Hill, on June 30, 1933. However he grew up in Cowpen Bewley and attended St John's School and later Stockton Technical College.

He was a keen schools footballer and was introduced to Middlesbrough FC by his father Patrick, at the age of 12, and became a life-long fan. Eventually he became a regular full-back in the Teesside League for Billingham St John's and could comfortably hold his own against senior players at the age of 16.

He was also a keen swimmer and water-polo player, and spent as much time in the water as he did on the football field.

However Pat began to suffer problems with both ankles as a result of some strong tackles in the Teesside League, and was advised to give up the game by a specialist. It was a devastating blow at the time because Pat was only 18.

He was serving his time as an electrician at Head Wrightson, and his workmates pestered him to fill the football void by taking up refereeing. Two years later he finally applied to take his initial exam. He started out by taking control of games in the Stockton and District Junior League and the Stockton and District Minor League and was to go on to spend 28 years in the middle.

Pat discovered that he had a natural aptitude for controlling football games and thoroughly enjoyed the role. However he was forced to put down his whistle for two years in 1955, when he undertook his national service in the Army. Unlike many young men, those two years were a very happy time for Pat, who took advantage of the various opportunities available to excel in a host of sports including water polo, shooting, basketball and hockey.

Seventeen months of his service were spent in Hong Kong, where he illustrated his prowess in the swimming baths by captaining the British Army swimming and water polo teams. He also successfully passed his class two refereeing exams in the Army.

Once demobbed and back on home soil, Partridge took up refereeing again. He started off in the Teesside League, where he had once been a player. After 12 months he passed his class one exams and continued to rise up the ranks.

Pat also maintained his interest in other sports. In 1959 he was appointed secretary of the inaugural Teesside Basketball League and, to this day, is still the league president. He was also secretary of the North-east water polo league.

In 1966 Pat was refereeing games in the Northern League and later that year became the first ref from an amateur league to be promoted directly to the Football League list. He took charge of his first league game in the Fourth Division at Barrow, where the visitors were Tranmere. He was back at Holker Street later that season to take charge of his first FA Cuptie, between Barrow and Torquay, who were managed at the time by John Bond.

Over the next 15 years, up until his retirement just before his 48th birthday, Pat was to travel the world several times over to take charge of top games.

In March, 1967, Pat earned the nickname Penalty Partridge from the Daily Express in his first ever match in the old First Division when he awarded three spot kicks in a match between Manchester City and Leicester City at Maine Road. He also clashed with England goalkeeper Gordon Banks in the game, having had the 'affrontery' to award the first penalty against Leicester for handball. Banks chased Pat around the penalty area for some time before play was resumed.

At the end of the season, Pat found himself officiating in the 'Battle of Old Trafford' in only his third First Division match. This time it was Manchester United against Stoke City, when Pat had to deal with a flare up involving both sets of players. There was one incident which he missed, but was later highlighted on Match of the Day, when Pat Crerand was seen to spit at another player. Partridge admitted later that had he seen the incident, he would have dismissed the Scottish international.

These games, and the mental strength which Pat gained from the experience, were to give him a great base from which to become a strong and well respected official.

In 1970 Pat achieved a refereeing feat which may never again be repeated. He took charge of the FA Cup third and fourth place play-off match between Manchester United and Watford at Highbury, on the eve of Chelsea and Leeds United meeting in the final at Wembley. This is the only occasion in which there has ever been a play off for third and fourth place in the FA Cup.

Pat was appointed as a FIFA referee at the age of 37 in 1971, shortly after having run the line in two big games - the League Cup Final between Spurs and Aston Villa and the European Cup Final at Wembley when Ajax beat Panathanaikos 2-0.

It was the start of a very hectic period. Pat refereed the Charity Shield between Liverpool and Leicester City and flew out to Turin to take charge of Torino v Spurs, which was an annual match played between the Italian and English Cup holders. A few months later, he was in the middle for the Inter League match between England and Scotland at Ayresome Park.

In May, 1972, Pat flew out to Tokio for a three-week tour of Japan to give lectures and coaching sessions for Japanese refs. He also took control of a couple of domestic matches in the Far East. Further trips to lecture refs in Kuwait and Brazil were to follow.

Partridge's first cup final at Wembley as a ref was the Challenge Trophy Final between Stafford Rangers and Barnet in 1972, which Rangers won 3-0.

Pat made a bold decision in his life the following year when quitting his Acklam home and his work as an electrical sales rep with Arthur Jones Electrical Wholesalers. He accepted an invitation from his father in law Frank to take up farming at Cockfield in County Durham, where he joined a partnership along with his brother in law Stuart in running a 160 acre dairy farm.

It was a completely new venture for Pat, especially as he had no farming experience at the time. Under the arrangements which were agreed, Pat was able to continue to maintain his hectic life as a FIFA referee. Only once did living on the farm cause a problem, when he was snowed in and could not find his way to Darlington station to catch a train to Southampton, where he was due to take charge of an FA Cuptie. There was the chance of being airlifted out by helicopter, but in the end Pat stayed put and this was the only game he ever missed throughout his time as a ref.

Partridge was back in front of the Twin Towers on May 3, 1975, for the FA Cup Final between West Ham United and Fulham. It was the occasion which all top refs aspire to achieve, and it was a very proud moment for Patrick Partridge. The Hammers won the game 2-0 with a brace of goals from Alan Taylor.

Later that summer Pat also officiated in the Home International between Scotland and Northern Ireland at Hampden Park.

The 1976-77 season was a busy one for Pat. He flew to Brazil for the World Club Championship and to Spain, West Germany and East Germany for European games. He also spent two weeks in the Persian Gulf to officiate at the World Cup preliminary tournament in Qatar.

At the end of that season he became the first English referee to take charge of a European Cup Winners Cup Final, between Hamburg and Anderlecht at Amsterdam.

The hectic schedule increased the following season. A European Cuptie between Porto and Cologne was followed by Atletico Bilbao v Ujpest Dozsa, the World Cup clash between Iran and Korea in Teheran and then another European match between Lens and FC Magdeburg.

In February 1978, Pat was informed that he was the only English referee selected to officiate at the World

During the 1970s, Pat Partridge was one of this country's leading football referees. For well over a decade he officiated at many of FIFA's top tournaments, including the World Cup Finals in Argentina. Here he is pictured with some of the memorabilia and mementoes he accumulated throughout his travels both at home and abroad.

Cup Finals in Argentina. It was another big moment in his career. He warmed up by taking charge of an international between Scotland and Bulgaria, European matches in Madrid and Bastia, and then the Football League Cup Final between Liverpool and Nottingham Forest at Wembley.

He also refereed the final group four World Cup qualifying match between Holland and Belgium. Dutch skipper Johan Cruyff had claimed before the game that he would not go to Argentina even if his country went through. They did qualify, but Cruyff was adamant he would not change his decision, and afterwards he presented Pat with his red, white and blue captain's armband.

Partridge went on to referee just one match in the Finals in Argentina, when officiating between Peru and Poland in Mendoza.

It was still an eventful game. Pat had to take his book out and caution Peruvian goalkeeper Ramon 'El Loco' Quiroga for rugby tackling a Polish player on the half-way line. After the game, Quiroga waited for Pat in the tunnel and presented him with a key ring!

At the start of the 1979-80 season, Pat reached the natural retirement age for referees. But he was given a year's extension because of his great experience, and it turned out to be as busy as any other.

Partridge was handed the FA Cup semi-final between Manchester City and Ipswich at Villa Park, and followed up by controlling the European Cup Winners Cup semi-final second leg between Benfica and Carl Jeiss Jena in Lisbon.

He refereed his final Football League game between European Champions Nottingham Forest and Coventry at the City Ground on May 2, 1981. It was a poignant occasion, though Pat's complete and utter respect in the game was marked after the final whistle when he was invited to the Forest boardroom to be presented with a pair of cut glass flower bowls, which he admits, brought more than one tear to his eye.

Partridge still had the no-small matter of a British championship clash between Scotland and Northern Ireland to referee, and he was delighted afterwards when both John Robertson and Martin O'Neill from the respective international sides presented him with their match shirts.

Soon afterwards Pat flew out to Vienna for the important World Cup qualifier between Austria and Bulgaria. This was his last professional match as a referee. He was well known and respected on the Continent and, afterwards, Hans Krankl from the Austria team presented him with his shirt, while Pat received an autographed match ball from the Bulgarians.

During a remarkable refereeing career, much of which had come at the highest possible level, Pat took charge of around 2,500 games.

While Pat's refereeing days were now over, his wealth of experience was not lost to sport. In fact he has been as busy as ever over the past 20 years. After retiring, he came a referee's assessor for the FA and held this position until the mid-1990s. He has also been adviser to the FA for the Northumberland and Durham counties since 1978.

In 1982 he toured Zambia for three weeks as an FA staff referee instructor and this was to be the first of many trips abroad in which he has carried out this role. Later that year he was appointed the northern region chairman of the Sports Aid Foundation and held this post for 14 years.

Partridge also became a referees observer and delegate for UEFA, which regularly takes him all over Europe. As an observer he looks at referees and their assistants, and provides reports for UEFA. As a delegate, he is responsible for recording the behaviour of players and also the crowd.

In the build up to Euro 2000, Pat's referee observing work took in most of the leading officials in the Continent. He watched Swedish referee Anders Frisk on three occasions and produced reports which could, possibly, have had a major bearing on the official being awarded the opportunity to take control of the Final in Rotterdam between France and Italy.

This UEFA work ensures that Pat is still fully involved with football at the highest level, though he also undertakes several other important roles in the community both as a magistrate in Teesdale and the Wear Valley, and as chairman of the board of visitors at Holme House Prison.

Throughout his life, Pat reckons his biggest critic, but also his biggest supporter, has been his wife Margaret, who has travelled everywhere with him during his illustrious refereeing career.

Pat continues to follow the Boro passionately, and one of the biggest pleasures he received from his involvement with the club was having the opportunity to meet his boyhood heroes Wilf Mannion and George Hardwick. In fact at one time he assisted Wilf with the refereeing section of his coaching badge.

Alan Peacock
Football

ALAN Peacock was a crucial link in the deadly Boro strike force with Brian Clough in the late 1950s and early 1960s, and went on to win four England caps.

Born in North Ormesby on October 29, 1937, he attended Lawson Street School and was soon making an impact in local football circles.

Alan quickly attracted the attention of Middlesbrough and signed professional forms for the club in November, 1954. He began his career in the tough world of the old North-eastern League which was packed with rugged miners and wily old ex-pros. Having learned to take care of himself in such tough company, Peacock made his first team debut for Boro in an embarrassing 7-2 away defeat at Bristol Rovers in the autumn of 1955. However he was pitched back into the side for a five-match run later in the season and scored his first two goals for the club in a 4-2 win at Nottingham Forest in March, 1956.

The same year, Alan was awarded England Youth honours, and was developing a fast-growing reputation as a good footballer and proficient header of the ball. However, his career in the mid-1950s was interrupted by national service when he was stationed at Catterick Camp.

When he returned full-time to Ayresome Park, Alan scored 15 goals in only 22 games in the 1957-58 season including a hat trick in a 4-1 win against Cardiff City. He helped to form one of the greatest twin spearheads in the history of the club when he quickly linked up with goal machine Brian Clough. Rumours that the pair did not get on were always vigorously denied by Peacock and between them from 1957-1961 they scored well over 200 goals, although it must be noted that even this prolific strike rate failed to gain Boro promotion back to the First Division.

When Clough left the Boro for local rivals Sunderland in the summer of 1961, Peacock was switched from inside-left to centre-forward.

Without Clough banging in the bulk of the goals, Peacock took over the major goalscoring mantle and

Boro centre-forward Alan Peacock was so highly rated that he was chosen for the 1962 World Cup.

passed 20 for the first time when scoring 24 times in season 1961-62.

Alan was so impressive, that he was chosen as part of England's World Cup squad for the 1962 tournament in Chile. It was a great moment for Peacock, and an honour for the club. He went on to play in two games, making his international debut in a 3-1 win against Argentina in Rancagua. He also played in a goalless

Middlesbrough FC 1961-62. Although Alan Peacock, middle, centre row, scored 141 goals during his fine Boro career, the club were never able to achieve promotion back to the First Division.

draw against Bulgaria at the same venue.

Alan won another two caps that same year, both in Home International matches. He played in a 3-1 win against Northern Ireland in Belfast in the October, and then scored twice in a 4-0 win against Wales at Wembley the following month. Despite breaking his goal duck, it was to be his last international appearance.

The goals were still coming thick and fast at club level, and Alan grabbed a remarkable 31 goals in only 40 appearances in 1962-63 season thanks to a useful contribution from winger Arthur Kaye, who provided much of the ammunition. But Boro just missed out on promotion, despite a dramatic late surge, and finished fourth.

In February, 1964, Middlesbrough born Don Revie signed Peacock for Leeds United in a record breaking deal costing £55,000. Alan had played 238 games for Boro and scored an impressive 141 goals, not a bad record for a man who often had to play second fiddle to Clough in the headline stakes.

At Elland Road, Peacock won a Second Division Championship medal and played in the 1965 FA Cup Final at Wembley against Liverpool, which Leeds lost 2-1 after extra time.

Unfortunately Alan picked up a bad knee injury while playing for Leeds in a friendly match in East Germany and was still occasionally troubled by the problem when he began playing again,

In 1967 he`moved to the South-west to link up with Plymouth Argyle but his career was cut short by the troublesome knee. He announced his retirement from football in March, 1968.

Alan returned to Teesside and became a successful businessman. He now lives in Carlton near Stokesley.

John Pearce

Boxing

JOHN Pearce was one of Britain's leading amateur boxers at the end of the millennium, winning the Commonwealth middleweight gold medal in Kuala Lumpur in 1998.

He was also ABA champion on two occasions, and was a regular England international who would almost certainly have been heading for the Sydney Olympics but for a troublesome eye injury.

Pearce was born in Middlesbrough on April 14, 1971 and educated at Brambles Farm primary and Keldholme schools. His father, also called John, had been a top amateur boxer himself who took part in 128 contests and won two National Association of Boys Clubs titles before turning professional and boxing as a featherweight.

John Snr was not keen, initially, to see his son follow in his footsteps, but young John fell in love with boxing from an early age and dad eventually taught him a few tips. John Junior joined North Ormesby ABC, where his talent was immediately spotted by coach John Dryden.

When Dryden left to form his own club at the Wellington ABC, Pearce followed him and the two have stayed together as a successful coach-boxer partnership throughout Pearce's career.

John emerged on the national stage in 1987, when he won an NABC title. He would certainly won more championships, but a shoulder problem which he first picked up as a 13-year-old caused occasional problems, as it has done throughout his career.

Once in the senior ranks, Pearce was determined to make his mark, but a combination of bad luck and illness thwarted his attempts to make a major impact in the ABA Championships.

He reached the North-east Counties Finals in 1991 and 1992, without making further progress. The following year John damaged a finger in an accident at work and was unable to contest the ABAs.

Worse was to follow in 1994 when he was hit on the side of the head by a brick thrown by a yob in the street and suffered a perforated eardrum. His hopes of fighting in the championships disappeared the next year when it was discovered he was suffering from a twisted spine, which was allowing liquid to seep into his lungs. Regular visits to an osteopath solved the problem, but John was unable to take part in any heavy training for 12 months.

His change of luck came in 1996. Even then, John almost dropped out of the championships because his wife Nikki was ill in hospital while she was carrying daughter Jade and worrying over his wife's health had decimated his training programme.

However Nikki encouraged John to box on and his pent-up emotion drove him through to the ABA middleweight final, which he won with something to spare. He stopped Wayne Elcock from Erdlington ABC after only one minute of the first round at the National Indoor Arena in Birmingham.

Elcock was forced to take three standing counts in that first minute after Pearce had put him under heavy pressure with some awesome punching.

A factory manager with the UPVC Window Centre in Middlesbrough, John was grateful for his employers for being given the time to maintain his tough training schedules and travel to compete in major events.

After his ABA success, Pearce was called up by England to box in a Multi Nations tournament in Liverpool. He did well in the early rounds, but had to settle for a silver medal despite being unbeaten. He overcame an Australian opponent in the semi-final but suffered a perforated eardrum and was not allowed by the doctor to box in the final.

Once fully recovered from his injury, John was one of only three English winners in an amateur international in Austria early in 1997. He stopped opponent Robert Mosar in the third round.

Later in the year he won a silver medal in a Multi Nations tournament in the Ukraine, when he was beaten in the final by the Frenchman Jean Paul Mendy, who was rated No.3 in the world at the time.

Pearce's medal winning performance was enough to earn him a place in the European Championships the following year, though he was unable to take part after picking up an infection from an insect bite while in the Ukraine, which resulted in him ending up in hospital on a drip.

John bounced back to pound his way to a second ABA title in 1998 despite carrying a muscle problem in his hand. He gained a emphatic points victory against the awkward southpaw Jim Twite from Coventry in the final at the National Indoor Arena. The fight was scored 28-13 on the judges' computerised system.

Pearce followed up with a gold medal winning performance in the Multi Nations event at Liverpool. In the final he won convincingly 22-8 against a Ukraine opponent who has since qualified to compete in the Sydney Olympics.

The Multi Nations tournament served as a very useful warm-up for the Commonwealth Games, and Pearce headed off to the Far East brim full of confidence.

In his first contest, he gained a comfortable 24-5 win against Dan Sackey from Ghana, and was then guaranteed a medal when receiving a walkover in the second round when the former Australian kick boxer Danny Green was forced to pull out because of injury. Pearce was paired with the British No.1 Brian Magee from Ireland in the semi-final and so received a lot of satisfaction when cruising to a 29-11 victory.

Pearce had been looking forward to this clash for some time and dominated the contest throughout to prove that the domestic rankings needed to be altered.

In the final, John crushed the Indian Jitender Kumar by 25-11 to win the gold medal. The tall Indian did cause some early problems with his extra reach, but Pearce had the measure of his opponent from the half-way mark and never looked back. In the last two rounds Pearce scored continually, to widen the points gap.

Early in 1999, Pearce was back on the ABA trail. He was pushed all the way by Stephen Swales from the Phil Thomas School of Boxing in the North-east finals at Redcar Bowl, but gained a points decision and looked set to go all the way to another title.

However his hopes of a hat trick were shattered in the quarter-finals at Coventry, when Pearce was forced to fight virtually one-handed because of injury to his hand, and bravely lost a narrow decision to Carl Froch from the Nottingham Phoenix Club.

In the summer, Pearce headed off to Houston in Texas with high hopes of making a big impact in the world

John Pearce, emphatic winner of the Commonwealth middleweight boxing gold medal in 1998.

championships. He was now fully recovered from the hand injury and was a member of an eight-strong English team.

It was a great experience to fight on a world stage, but John didn't do himself justice and was beaten in his first contest by a Lithuanian. John was sent on to the seat of his pants when walking straight into a left hand, but reasserted himself to come back in what turned out to be a scrappy contest. The final points scoring was 8-8, but John was beaten 43-41 on the countback.

At the end of the year, John was called up by England for the prestigious international against the United States at the Hilton Hotel in London. He was ahead and leading his opponent by 14-13 in the closing stages of the contest. However he was suffering from blurred vision as a result of having received a thumb in the eye and lost narrowly by 15-14. It was only his sixth defeat as a senior boxer in an outstanding boxing career throughout the Nineties.

It was later discovered that John had suffered a small fracture in a bone underneath his eye, and as a result his vision continued to be affected. It meant he was unable to box in any of the qualifying tournaments for the 2000 Olympics, and could not be included in the British team for Sydney. It was a bodyblow because John would surely have been selected but for the injury.

John continues to keep himself fit while he contemplates his future. He lives in Middlesbrough with his daughter Jade and wife Nikki, who was expecting their second child this year.

Fred Priest
Football

FRED Priest did eventually play professional football for his local club Middlesbrough, but it was as a dangerous goalscoring forward with Sheffield United that he made his name and earned a much deserved England cap.

Born Alfred Ernest Priest in Guisborough in 1875, his talent quickly blossomed in local football. He then played for Darlington and South Bank before being offered the chance to join Sheffield United in 1896.

Middlesbrough were not even in the Football League at that time, but United were a magnificent side and were one of the top three teams in the country during the late Victorian era. They won the Football League Championship in 1897-98 and finished runners-up on another two occasions.

Fred found himself among hallowed company, but his natural footballing ability helped him to force his way up through the ranks.

He made his league debut on September 5, 1896, scoring the only goal in a 1-0 win against Burnley. Eventually he won a regular place in this strong Blades team, and scored some vital goals during an illustrious career at Bramall Lane. He always operated on the left side, alternating between inside and outside-left.

Priest helped the Blades reach the FA Cup Final at Crystal Palace in 1899, where they met Derby County. Fred not only won a winner's medal, but also scored the last goal in the 89th minute as United trounced the unfortunate Rams by 4-1.

Fred had also been the hero for Sheffield in the semi-final against Liverpool, which was a mammoth affair needing three replays before the tie was eventually settled. In the fourth semi-final match, at Derby County, he scored the only goal of the game, and the 13th in all over the four matches, to send the Blades on their way to Crystal Palace.

His consistent displays finally earned Fred an England international call up on March 17, 1900, when he was outside-left in a 2-0 win against Ireland in Dublin.

Sheffield United were back in the FA Cup Final again in 1901, thanks mainly to the efforts of Priest. After United had been held by Aston Villa in the first semi-final clash, Fred scored twice in the 3-0 replay victory at Derby.

The Final grabbed the attention of the whole of the country, because Football League giants Sheffield United were lined up against Tottenham Hotspur, from the Southern League. The match was billed as North v South confrontation, and Fred silenced the largely southern based crowd at Crystal Palace by opening the scoring for the Blades after only ten minutes when he netted from 20 yards. However, United could not clinch victory on the day and were held to a 2-2 draw. The Guisborough lad also scored the first goal after 40 minutes in the replay, which was played at Bolton's Burnden Park, but it was not a good day for United because Spurs grabbed three second half goals to cruise to a 3-1 win.

Even so, Fred entered the record books by becoming the first player to score in three different Cup Finals. In fact he was the only player to achieve this feat until a modern day goal machine called Ian Rush equalled his record for Liverpool by scoring in the 1986, 1989 and 1992 Finals.

United again edged through to the FA Cup Final at Crystal Palace the following year to meet another Southern League side in Southampton. Fred, who by this time, had become a specialist match winner in FA Cup semi-finals, netted the only goal in a 1-0 replay win against Derby County at Nottingham Forest.

In the Final, the Blades were red hot favourites, especially as Fred helped form a very powerful three-pronged attack alongside South Bank-born centre-forward George Hedley and Alf Common, who was later to sign for Middlesbrough for a world record transfer fee £1,000. Once again there was the need for a replay, after the first match ended in a 1-1 draw.

The Blades led for a long time thanks to a goal from Common, but Saints grabbed a hotly disputed equaliser in the last minute. However, Fred had the last

Fred Priest, front row, second right, with Sheffield United's 1902 FA Cup winning side which also included, on his right, fellow Teessider George Hedley and future Boro star, Alf Common, front row, second left.

laugh by gaining his second winner's medal when the Blades triumphed in the replay by 2-1.

His last appearance for Sheffield United was in October, 1905, though he stayed with the club for the remainder of that season.

Fred's illustrious career at Bramall Lane finally came to an end on August 22, 1906, when he was 31. He had made 246 appearances and scored 86 goals for the Blades, but started out on a new career when he accepted an invitation to move back to his Teesside roots and join First Division Middlesbrough as their new player/coach.

Fred made his Boro debut in a 2-0 defeat at Woolwich Arsenal, but he failed to score and was quickly converted to a full-back. He made just 13 appearances for the club in that first season.

Guisborough's favourite son was unable to repeat his marvellous Sheffield days for the Boro, and his stint at Ayresome Park lasted only two years before he moved

on to become player/manager of Hartlepools United.

Fred was the first manager of Pools new professional club and was in charge until 1915, when he finally retired from football.

He settled in West Hartlepool and became the popular licensee of the Market Hotel in Lynn Street where he remained until his relatively early death on May 5, 1922 at the age of 47.

Recognising that he had been a great servant to Sheffield United, the Yorkshire club agreed to play in a benefit match at Hartlepools United for Fred's widow and family on October 11, 1922. Priest's reputation was further enhanced when former teammate and England international Alf Common volunteered to be the match referee.

As the first player player to score goals in three FA Cup Finals, Teesside born Fred Priest has a unique place in football history. It is an achievement which is unlikely to be broken.

Samantha Purvis
Swimming

SAMANTHA Purvis was a teenage swimming sensation who stormed to fifth place in the Olympic 200 metres butterfly final in Los Angeles in 1984, before winning a bronze medal in the 100m butterfly in the Commonwealth Games two years later.

She continued to stay at the forefront of British swimming and went on to compete in her second Olympics in Barcelona in 1992.

Samantha learned to swim as an eight-year-old in New Zealand, but later the family returned to England to live in Dale Street, Chilton, near Sedgefield. Eventually she linked up with Stockton Aquatics and also moved to live in the town, from where she achieved much of her sporting success.

After returning to England, Samantha had initially joined the Sedgefield District 75 swimming club, and her exploits earned her a place in the Esso England Youth team. At the age of 14, she won gold, silver and bronze medals at an international tournament in Chiasso in Switzerland.

In 1983, aged 15, she gained valuable experience when swimming the 100 and 200 metres backstroke for Great Britain in the European Championships in Rome.

Samantha had joined Stockton Aquatics in her bid to win a place in the Olympics, though initially it seemed that she had failed in her attempt. However, she was relieved to hear that she had squeezed into the team for Los Angeles when the British Olympic Association decided to allow extra places for the swimming team.

In June, 1984, Sam's family moved to Highfield Road in Hartburn in order that she could be much closer to Stockton swimming pool, where she was coached every day by Dave Bance.

Purvis warmed up for LA in style by smashing the British senior short course record for the women's 200m butterfly at the North-east Counties gala at Darlington. She set a new time of 2min 11.91sec, knocking two and a half seconds off the previous record. The time was good enough to put her in the top six in the world.

Samantha Purvis stormed onto the swimming scene at the 1984 Los Angeles Olympics.

Samantha flew out to Los Angeles at the end of July and made an immediate impact in the heats of the 200m butterfly, setting a new British record of 2min 11.97sec, which took more than two seconds off the previous best.

In the final, Samantha came up against the cream of the world's talent, and excelled herself to finish fifth. It was a remarkable achievement, especially as she was only a last minute addition to the British team.

Purvis returned to England after the Olympics and maintained her excellent form by winning the 100m

Edinburgh Commonwealth Games 1986. Samantha Purvis takes the bronze medal in the 100m butterfly.

and 200m butterfly titles in the ASA national championships at Blackpool.

She returned to America the following year to compete in the US international meet in Arkansas, and produced another superb performance when taking second place in the 200m butterfly behind the American Olympic champion Mary T Meagher. In the same month she won the 200m butterfly at the Speedo meet in Amersfoort in Holland, and was second in the 100m butterfly.

In the November, Samantha headed off to the United States to begin a four-year course in biochemistry at the Louisiana State University in Baton Rouge, with swimming very much on the agenda.

In 1986, Purvis was selected to swim for England in three events in the Edinburgh Commonwealth Games in the 100 and 200m butterfly and the 200m individual medley.

She had high hopes for a couple of medals, but had to settle for the bronze in the 100m butterfly.

Later in the year, she competed in the world championships in Madrid where, amidst very fierce competition, she finished out of the medals.

Increasingly, home sickness was beginning to take its toll, especially on her swimming performances, and in February, 1987, Samantha decided to leave her course at Baton Rouge university and return home to Stockton.

However, with her former coach Dave Bance now in Canada, Samantha linked up with Midlands coach Rick Bailey and joined the City of Birmingham club. The decision paid immediate dividends. The same year Samantha bounced back to top form by winning the

100m butterfly crown in the ASA national championships at Crystal Palace and finished runner-up in the 200m butterfly.

Her performances were enough to earn her a place in both events in the British team for the European Championships in Strasbourg.

A knee injury which occurred shortly before the championships failed to curb her competitive edge and Samantha went on to finish seventh in the finals of both events, clocking the fastest times of the year by a British woman. She also helped the GB medley relay team finish sixth in the final.

Immediately Samantha went into hospital for an operation on the knee, and then began the serious work of rehabilitation and building up her fitness again.

However her determined attempts to bounce back to peak form and qualify for the Seoul Olympics were thwarted when she suffered a virus attack shortly before the combined TSB national championships and Olympic trials in Leeds.

She made a brave bid to win a place in the top two, but the effects of the illness proved too much and Samantha could finish only sixth in the 200m butterfly final. She led at the halfway stage, but then her strength slowly ebbed away and she lost her way in the final 25 metres. Earlier she had failed to reach the finals of the 100m butterfly and 100m backstroke.

At the same time, Purvis decided to quit the City of Birmingham club and returned home briefly to Stockton, before joining the Wigan Wasps club.

The switch was not enough to earn her a place in the English team for the 1990 Commonwealth Games, so she returned to Stockton. However Samantha had lost none of her faith in her ability and immediately set her sights on the Barcelona Olympics.

This self belief and commitment paid dividends when she stormed into the team for Barcelona with a magnificent swim in the Olympic qualifiers at Sheffield. Purvis won the 200m butterfly in 2min 14.32sec, coming home three seconds clear of the field. Her time was her best for five years and she was selected to swim both the 100 and 200m in the Olympics.

The competition was hotter than ever in Barcelona, but Samantha swam well and recorded good times of 2min 14.47sec for the 200m and 62.94sec for the 100m.

Samantha continued with her swimming on her return home, but also moved into coaching. She had been working as a library assistant, but later started a sports science degree at Teesside University.

Alan Ransome
Table Tennis

ALAN Ransome has made a remarkable lifetime's commitment to table tennis, helping to develop top international players on Teesside and highlighting and promoting the game on a worldwide stage.

Throughout his life he has devoted up to 40 hours a week, every week, to playing, coaching, managing and eventually being elected to a series of senior international table tennis roles at the very nerve centre of the game. He built up the record breaking Ormesby club from scratch and has worked tirelessly in helping players at all levels of ability to enjoy the game and progress as far as possible. Without the incredible time and effort which he has devoted to the sport, local, national and international table tennis would be much poorer.

As a player Ransome was very good, but never great. As an organiser and a one-man table tennis crusader, he was very good, and always great.

Alan was the founder and driving force behind the development of the Ormesby club into one of the best in Europe, winning the English championship on ten consecutive occasions and carrying off the European club title in 1972.

Some of the players who were coached at Ormesby to international stardom by Alan include Carole Knight, Nicky Jarvis and Jimmy Walker.

He continues an active involvement at the highest level which is as hectic as ever, though has been forced to relinquish some of his local involvement.

That's because he is a member of the International Table Tennis Federation council, executive vice president of the European Union and chairman of the Commonwealth Federation, in addition to holding several other top ranked international posts.

As an added bonus, Alan is able to live and breathe table tennis through his business, Ransome Sporting Goods, which specialises in sports equipment.

Alan Edward Ransome was born in Middlesbrough on July 3, 1946. He attended Whinney Banks Juniors, Mill Hill and The Firs schools.

He was a keen all-round sportsman, playing for the school football and cricket teams, and also excelling at tennis. In fact he was under-17 tennis champion in the Middlesbrough, Redcar and Stockton tournaments all in the same summer.

However, by that time, table tennis was Alan's all abiding sporting love. His keen interest was spawned at Butlin's holiday camp at the age of 11, when he was nominated the camp's most promising player and won a free holiday. Ironically he had gone to Butlin's originally intending to concentrate on cricket. But there was no looking back for Alan, who proceeded to win eight free holidays in a row following his successes in the camp table tennis competitions.

He developed so quickly as a table tennis player that he was given England junior trials, landing his first major title in 1963 when he won the Yorkshire Open junior championship at the age of 16, beating Brian Marsden of Lancashire in the final. He also won the Essex Open.

A few months later Alan winning streak continued when he won the local North-east championships at Scarborough and rose to No.7 in the national junior rankings. It was no surprise when he earned England international selection against Scotland and the Scottish Open, both events taking place in Edinburgh. At the age of 12, Alan had joined the Grangetown Methodists team and then later became friendly with a lad called Denis Neale, who played for Newport Boys Club. The two already outshone most of the local players of their age, and began practising together, every night, for four hours a night, and six days a week. They progressed very quickly as a result of their passion and commitment and were members of the Middlesbrough junior and senior teams at the age of 14.

Alan's father Bob was already heavily involved in local sport at that time as secretary of the Middlesbrough Midweek Cricket League and the Middlesbrough Wednesday Football League.

He spotted the tremendous natural talent of both young

Through the commitment of Alan Ransome Ormesby became this country's leading table tennis club.

lads and converted an old chicken hut at the end of his garden in Church Lane, Ormesby, into a table tennis room for Alan and Denis to practise on every night. When their friends wanted to play, too, Bob replaced the chicken hut with an old quarry hut, which accommodated three tables. Suddenly Ormesby Table Tennis Club was born.

Alan became the new club's first secretary at the age of 13, but became frustrated during the summer when there was no competition when the local leagues closed down. So he decided to form his own league. Thus the North-east Summer Table Tennis League was inaugurated, initially with only five teams, though this total had swollen to 63 within four years.

When the Grangetown Methodists club closed, the members joined Ormesby. Suddenly Ormesby was the biggest club in the area, and also the best. Eventually, the old quarry hut had to be replaced by a brick building. And there it still stands, Ormesby Table Tennis Club, at the end of a back garden in Church Lane, and used every day.

When Denis Neale moved away from the area for a while, Alan was left with nobody with whom to practise, which was frustrating considering he was so much better than anybody else. So he played against the younger players, and began to teach and advise them during their games together. Within a year or so, the kids were beating Alan.

Ransom's commitment to table tennis was so deep rooted that, even as a teenager, he wanted to have an input into how the game was being run. So, at the age of 19, he canvassed throughout Durham County and was elected as their representative to the English National Council, the committee which governed the ETTA. There were shockwaves at committee level when this 'young revolutionary' was elected ahead of the previous representative who had spent 20 years in office. But Alan knew what he was doing, and began to promote and push his ideas at the highest level.

Maybe his devotion to the improvement and development of table tennis prevented him from progressing to become a top quality player nationally. He continued to play regularly and was one of the top players in the North without ever making the major breakthrough on to the international scene on a regular basis.

However he did represent England in 1971 in both the Commonwealth championships in Singapore and the world championships in Japan.

Alan had arranged to accompany the tour party as a paying spectator to study the different styles and techniques of the world's top players, to help him with his coaching and widen his knowledge of the game. However when England regulars Denis Neale and Chester Barnes both dropped out because of last minute alterations to the tour schedule, Alan was asked to deputise by team captain Bryan Merritt.

Remarkably Ransome reached the last 16 in the Commonwealth singles, despite a lack of match practice. When he next returned to the championships in Singapore in 1993, it was as chairman of the Commonwealth Federation.

Alan proved that he had benefitted considerably from his Far East experience by managing the Ormesby team to win the European Club Cup in 1972. It was a marvellous achievement because English table tennis lagged behind several of the top European nations.

However Ormesby won the cup convincingly, beating the Swedish champions Falkenburg over two legs in the final.

It was no cakewalk. Ormesby defeated top sides like Budapest Spartacus and Olympic Belgrade in the quarter and semi-finals in order to reach the final. They took a huge step towards winning the cup with a 6-3 away win in the first leg in Sweden, and made sure of victory by taking the first four matches in the return leg in only 64 minutes.

The best win of the evening was gained by Trevor Taylor, who beat the world champion Stellan Bengtsson by the incredible margin of 21-14, 21-19. The other members of the victorious team were Denis Neale and Nicky Jarvis.

Ormesby were not only the first British winners of the competition. They were also the first British team ever to get past the first round.

In 1973 Ransome presented the ETTA with a radical 14-page blueprint, recommending a total rethink of table tennis in Britain, and suggesting alterations for the future benefit of the game. His plans were not adopted in the way that Alan hoped, but there was a reluctant acceptance that there was a need for change. Gradually, as Alan produced more blueprints, he gathered more support.

By 1974 Alan was a member of England's selection and coaching committee, a member of the ETTA national council, national tournament organiser, chairman of the Northumberland, Durham, Yorkshire and Cleveland coaching panel, ETTA approved coaching assessor, general secretary of Cleveland table tennis, chairman of the Middlesbrough League and secretary of Ormesby, in addition to many other roles. Under Alan's guidance, Ormesby's success just seemed to go on and on. They were national champions ten years in succession. His major role within the club was on the coaching side. He wanted the kids from Teesside to be the best in England.

Ormesby produced seven internationals in seven years. There was Nicky Jarvis, Jimmy Walker, Dave Alderson, Linda Bashford, Carole Knight-Moore, Angela Tierney and Helen Robinson. It was no surprise that Ormesby's players swept all before them in regional competitions.

In 1976 Alan decided to turn his love of the sport to even better use, and opened his Tees Sport business in Zetland Place in Middlesbrough to sell table tennis equipment by mail order. Three years later he opened

Butterfly Table Tennis UK in Wood Street to sell supplies on a wholesale basis to sports shops.

In addition to having some sportswear made locally, he began importing goods from Japan, Germany and China.

Later he branched out into squash through the Unsquashable brand, then badminton with the Talbot brand and later basketball. Ransome Sporting Goods, the modern day company, is still based in Wood Street and is the major supplier of equipment in all these sports, though table tennis accounts for half of the gross sales. The company has flourished and now employs 30 staff.

At the same time, Ransome has continued to work in every possible capacity to maintain and help table tennis to progress. In July, 1980, he was presented with the Malcolm Scott Award for the greatest senior contribution to English table tennis over the previous 12 months. During this period he had been the major driving force behind the setting up of the national league. As a youngster, Alan had also received the Ivor Montague Award for up and coming players.

However during the past 20 years he has gradually edged away from operating in a local and national capacity to working largely at the very pinnacle of the sport's international governing bodies.

Alan was elected as a council member for the International Table Tennis Federation in 1986 and remains today one of Europe's nine representatives on this worldwide governing body. He also became general secretary of British Olympic table tennis in the same year.

He was appointed deputy chairman of the ETTA in 1987 and at this stage began to concentrate very heavily on working within the framework of the national and international side of the sport.

In July, 1988, Alan was made a life member of the ETTA. Three years later he finally reached the pinnacle of the sport in England, when he was elected ETTA chairman.

Throughout the Nineties Alan has continued to become increasingly involved at an administrative level. He was elected to the British Olympic Association committee in 1991 and executive vice president of the European Union in 1992, continuing in both roles today. He became chairman of the Commonwealth Federation in 1993 and also retains this position.

Ransome received a special honour when he was

July 1988. In recognition of many years of dedicated service Alan Ransome is made a life member of the English Table Tennis Association. He has since been awarded a further honour in 1996 when gaining an OBE.

appointed team manager of Great Britain's Olympic squad for the Atlanta Games in 1996. But there was an even bigger honour to come in the following year when he received the OBE for his lifetime services to table tennis.

Not surprisingly, Alan's commitment to table tennis is as strong than ever, especially as he regularly tours the world attending championships, meetings and conventions promoting the sport. One of his greatest moments in recent years was finally seeing table tennis introduced into the Commonwealth Games calendar for the first time in 2002.

Naturally, behind every successful man, there is a strong woman, and Alan has always received terrific support from his wife Jose.

That's no surprise considering that Jose is also steeped in table tennis. Born in London, she emigrated to Canada as a teenager and became chief executive of the Canadian table tennis association, and in 1977 was assistant director of the world championships when they were held in Britain.

Alan and Jose met several times in the 1970s and were eventually married, with Jose returning to England to live on Teesside. It's no surprise then, that Jose has maintained the family tradition and is the current secretary of Ormesby Table Tennis Club.

Andrew Raspin
Canoeing

ANDREW Raspin is an experienced Great Britain international who won a bronze medal in the European Championships in Prague in 1998.

He finished seventh overall in the World Cup series in 1994 and eighth in the world championship in 1995, while making his mark in domestic competition by winning the British Open three times.

Andrew was born at Middlesbrough General Hospital on October 22, 1969, and grew up in Skelton. It was a natural development for Andrew to become a paddler, because the sport was already an established tradition in his family.

His father Don was an all-round sportsman who had developed a strong interest in canoeing, and was a member of Tees Kayak Club, while elder brother Ian was already becoming proficient at the sport.

Andrew attended Skelton infants and junior schools and then moved on to Huntcliffe School in Saltburn, before attending Sir William Turner's sixth form college in Redcar.

He was in the school football team at Huntcliffe and also played some basketball.

Andrew developed a keen interest in surfing, initially competing at Saltburn, but then moving further afield to test the breakers at Bude and Newquay. He gained experience in small local tournaments before taking part in the North-east junior championships, where he made an inauspicious start, suffering a bloodied nose when his surfboard struck his face after being caught by a strong wave. However it did not put him off, and Andrew has continued to surf on occasions throughout his career.

However canoeing has always dominated his sporting involvement. He took time to work his way through the divisions as his built up his physical strength, but made the big breakthrough in 1984 when called up for a British junior training camp in Landeck in Austria.

The next year, he was one of the youngest competitors in the European junior championships at Spittal in Austria, which was won by his elder brother Ian.

Andrew continued to develop and proved his undoubted potential by winning the British Open youths' championship at Llangollen in Wales in 1986. The following year he took part in the European junior championships at Spittal and raced well throughout, taking the bronze medal and finishing just behind British teammate Shaun Pearce.

Raspin then moved on to the pre-world championships at La Seu d'Urgell, near the future Olympic course at Barcelona, and fared even better. He competed strongly to take the silver medal, again just behind Pearce.

Andrew found that the step up to the senior ranks was a huge one, and struggled for some time to make an impact in major events. He became an intermediate international and competed in different parts of the world, including several times in Czechoslovakia, but it was not until 1994 that he became a full senior international paddler.

In 1989 Raspin went to the United States to watch the world championships on the aptly named Savage River in Maryland, and then later was handed the opportunity to take part in a World Cup series race when fellow Teessider Russ Smith pulled out for a rest. Andrew's World Cup debut against top international opposition came at South Bend in Indiana and was a big success, because he finished 12th overall.

In the same year Andrew relocated to Nottingham to take advantage of the facilities at the white water course in the city, and started work on a foundation course in art and design at Clifton. After a year, he began a four years BA honours degree in furniture and product design at Nottingham Trent University.

Raspin finished second in the British Open in 1990, and also sixth in the pre-world championships at Tacen in Slovenia after leading until the closing stages of the event.

Andrew looked to have made the big breakthrough in 1991 when he was leading the national series going into the selection races, only to suffer misfortune during selection at Bala when his boat split along one

Andrew Raspin, winner of the British Open canoeing championships and a European bronze medal.

side and filled with water. Ironically his good friend Shaun Pearce did win selection and went on to win the world championships.

In 1992 Raspin won the first of his British Open titles and also competed in a World Cup race in Merano in Italy, finishing eighth overall.

The following year he retained his British Open crown and also finished third in the British slalom sprint championship, behind brother Ian. Both events took place at Llangollen. Andrew also travelled to Sheffield to win the inaugural national indoor pool slalom championship, clinching victory by just eight tenths of a second.

He also competed in several events in the World Cup, including two races in the United States in which he finished seventh and eighth. As a result he was given a world ranking of 15th, which indicated that his efforts were bringing some reward.

Finally, in 1994, Raspin became a senior international. It was also the year in which he graduated from university. He was awarded his 2:1 degree on a

Wednesday, and then took part in a World Cup series race in Nottingham two days later, finishing fourth overall. Later he finished fifth in Bourg St Maurice in France and sixth in Japan, and was seventh overall in the series.

The following year was another good one for Andrew. He benefitted from two months warm weather training in Chile in which he was accompanied by his partner Heather and a team of top European paddlers, including his brother Ian.

When he returned home he went on to win the British Open for the third time, and finished eighth in the world championships in Nottingham, which was a good performance, especially as he was the second British boat to finish behind the emerging Paul Radcliffe. Raspin missed a few World Cup series races that year, but finished 12th overall.

Andrew had targetted a place in the Atlanta Olympics and gave his best effort in the selection races. But he had to settle for a frustrating fourth place and was unable to win a place in the Great Britain squad.

However Andrew focussed on the World Cup that season and finished fourth in one event in Prague, going on to take ninth place overall.

Raspin returned to Chile for a similar training programme early in 1996 and was back in South America later in the year when he contested the final race of the World Cup in Brazil. He finished 13th, but did not paddle well and was disappointed with his performance.

Andrew loved the social part of canoeing, but not always the competitive side, and sat down to try to evaluate his performances during a poor 1997. He kept a written note of how things had gone wrong and worked out how to improve his mental attitude in the major competitions.

His self analysis paid massive dividends the following year when he produced his best ever performances in the selection races. He finished fifth in the first race at Grantully in Scotland, but then gained from faultless preparation by taking first and second in the follow up races to qualify comfortably for his international place. Andrew then set off for the European championships in Roudice in Czechoslovakia in an extremely positive frame of mind. He attacked the course strongly to take a marvellous third place and the bronze medal. It was the culmination of hard work and sheer determination to take something from a sport in which he had competed at top level for over 15 years.

Ian Raspin
Canoeing

IAN RASPIN is one of Teesside's top sporting ambassadors, having competed in two Olympic Games and won both gold and bronze medals at separate world championships.

The Skelton paddler is a regular British international, winning many national events and being rated No.2 in the world at the peak of his career.

He helped the British team to take the gold medal in the world championships in Brazil in 1997, having taken bronze in the same competition at Nottingham two years earlier.

Ian finished 17th in the Barcelona Olympics and had high hopes of a medal four years later in Atlanta, but had to settle for ninth place.

Ian Michael Raspin was born in Guisborough on March 31, 1967. He grew up in Skelton, where he attended Skelton primary school, before moving on to Huntcliffe School in Saltburn and later Sir William Turner's in Redcar.

His father Don, who became a PE teacher at Laurence Jackson School in Guisborough, had been a rugby player and athlete in his time, having once taken the bronze medal in the North of England 880 yards championships.

Don also became interested in canoeing and joined Tees Kayak Club in the early Seventies. Naturally Ian was eventually introduced to the sport, and had his first ride in a canoe at the age of two.

Ian took part in his first canoe slalom event at the age of seven, at Richmond, when he finished second in the under-10 class behind fellow Teessider Russ Smith.

Raspin went on to become a very useful athlete and swimmer at Huntcliffe School, but was already making a major impact in canoe slalom at the age of 13, when he joined a Great Britain junior squad which visited the site of the 1972 Munich Olympics course.

The following year he won a junior under-14 international at La Seu D'Urgell, close to the course which was eventually adopted for the 1992 Olympics. Ian took the national junior kayak title in Llangollen in North Wales at the age of 16, beating several older competitors. He continued to earn regular international call-ups, winning a grand prix event at Lofer in Austria.

He was then called up for the European junior championships in Spittal in Austria, and finished a highly creditable fifth. However, if not for picking up a five second penalty for touching a gate, he would otherwise have ended up in the silver medal position.

Raspin made amends for this error the following year, when winning the Europeans on the same water course at Spittal. This was the first year when the European championships were combined with the world championships, so he was effectively world junior champion.

In 1986 Ian stepped up to senior international level for the first time and combined with his Tees Kayak clubmate Russ Smith and Melvin Jones from the West Midlands to form the Great Britain B team which won the pre-world championships event at Bourg St Maurice in France. It was a marvellous achievement for Raspin, considering the wealth of international competition which he had faced.

The following year Ian was called up to compete in his first senior world championships, which also took place at Bourg St Maurice. However he picked up a 50 second penalty on his second run and finished well down the field.

Ian was beginning to find it tough as a senior and realised that it was not going to be as easy to establish himself at the highest level as he had originally hoped. However he finally achieved a high level of consistency in 1990 after three or four years of struggle, when he put the cap on a much improved season by winning the British Open at Llangollen.

Raspin won the British Open again the following year on the same river, his time of 1min 53sec over the 800 metres course earning him the crown by just one second. He was also called up for the world championships in Slovenia, which took place only days before the

Ian Raspin displays the grit and determination which made him one of Great Britain's outstanding paddlers. He competed in two Olympic Games and won gold and bronze medals at the canoeing world championships.

Balkans crisis which led to the gradual break up of Yugoslavia. In fact there was a belief at the time that the Slovenians deliberately delayed starting hostilities until the world championships were over!

The Slovenian course was artificial, and was very turbulent in parts, which made it unpredictable. But Ian finished in a highly creditable 15th position.

In fact he made a mistake at the second last gate on his second run which cost him dear. If Ian had been able to combine the best parts of his two runs he would have won the gold medal. The eventual winner was a Briton, Shaun Pearce, in his first senior international event.

By this time Ian had completed his education degree at Trent Polytechnic, gaining a 2:1 honours. He was now a full time paddler, living in Nottingham and based at the national watersports centre at Holme Pierrepont.

Canoe slalom was re-introduced to the Olympics in 1992. Ian, now ranked fifth in the world, qualified for the British team for Barcelona by winning the first of two selection races on the Olympic course at La Seu D'Urgell.

He warmed up for the Olympics by winning a race in the World Cup Series at Bourg St Maurice, which improved his world ranking to fourth.

However Ian suffered a major scare before the Olympics when he suddenly received a shooting pain in his neck during training. In addition to the pain, he had slight paralysis in his right arm.

There were initial problems with diagnosing the exact nature of the problem though it was eventually discovered that a disc had prolapsed slightly into his neck. The best treatment was rest, and Ian's Olympics preparations were suddenly shelved.

However he did travel with the team, initially watching them training from the river bank. It was at the last minute that he finally felt fit enough to race, and went on to take 17th position. He picked up a five second penalty on his first run and then made an error on the second which cost him dear because he had been the third fastest boat up until the half way point.

The following year Raspin combined with Shaun Pearce and Melvyn Jones to win the gold medal for Great Britain in the canoe slalom team event in an international in Merano in Northern Italy. His performances in the World Cup series, which included races in Europe, Canada and the United States, improved his world ranking to third, though he was out of luck in the world championships in Mezzanza in Italy.

He thought he had secured a magnificent fourth place, but was denied by a judge who claimed that his hand had touched a pole. He was handed a five seconds penalty which pushed him down to 22nd place. Ian lodged an immediate appeal, but it was overruled. Teammate Richard Fox won the event, while Mel Jones was third.

Back in Britain, Raspin bounced back to win the inaugural British Open slalom sprint championship at Llangollen, with brother Andrew in third place.

Early in 1994, Ian flew Down Under at the invitation of the Australian Federation to undertake coaching sessions with the national teams. While he was there, he won the Cataract Gorge competition at Launceston in Tasmania. He also finished second in the Australian Open at Melbourne.

Raspin did well in the World Cup Series, eventually finishing second overall following the final race in Japan. That result meant Ian was now ranked second in the world and celebrated by winning the British Open.

Ian failed to grab an individual medal in the world championships in Nottingham in 1995, but gained consolation by winning a bronze in the team event, along with brother Andrew and Shaun Pearce.

In the individual event, Ian had comfortably won the qualification race on the first day and had high hopes of another medal. But he unfortunately picked up two penalties on his first run and made a technical mistake on the second.

Ian's target was to compete in the Atlanta Olympics but he thought he had missed out on selection when he finished third in the trials on the River Tay, behind Paul Radcliffe and Shaun Pearce, and was handed only a reserve place for the British team.

However, because several other competing countries were not certain to take up their full quota of paddlers, Ian was told to stay in full training, just in case. Finally, following a couple of nail-biting weeks, he was offered a belated call-up for the British team.

He went to Atlanta in good heart and feeling no pressure. A good clear first run, without any penalties, put Ian in the top six and in contention for a medal place. However the wind gradually gained in strength during the second day, and disaster struck on his second run when the sixth gate was blown into him. Even so, Ian still finished ninth overall.

The 1997 world championships presented a fresh challenge, because this was a first time a major event had been held in Brazil. Ian flew out with Paul Radcliffe and Shaun Pearce for the competition at Tres Coras near Porto Alegre.

The trio were always in the running for victory in the team event, though it was close all the way with the Slovenians, Germans, Czechs and French providing stiff opposition.

Britain were the last team to leave the starting line, and Ian was the final paddler. When he reached the bank, he did not know the outcome. But when he was smothered by his two colleagues, he realised that the gold was in the bag.

It was a just reward for years of commitment and hard work, and the fact that Ian had finished 17th individually, hardly mattered.

The following year Ian finished ninth overall in the World Cup series, but was back in the world championships in 1999 when he gained his best ever result at the age of 32.

The event was held at La Seu D'Urgell and Ian finished sixth overall, having enjoyed two excellent runs. In fact he was only 0.9 of a second behind the gold medal winner, which was not bad going, considering that each of the two runs was 100 seconds long.

Since then Ian, who lives in Nottingham with his wife Linda, has been concentrating on maintaining his fitness and competitive edge throughout the Sydney Olympic trials.

Mary Reveley
Horse Racing

MARY Reveley has emerged over the last 20 years as one of the leading trainers both on the Flat and under National Hunt rules.

She rapidly became one of the dominant handful of trainers at Northern tracks throughout the Nineties, particularly with her National Hunt string and, in 2000, she saddled the 1,700th winner of her career.

Her success was based on a dogged determination to be successful, shrewdness, a natural horse sense, excellent training skills and the ability to place her horses to great effect and come home with the prize money.

Born Mary Allison in Lingdale, on September 22, 1940, she has lived in the Teesside area all her life.

Mary attended the local Lingdale School before transferring to The Towers in nearby Saltburn, where she particularly enjoyed the sporting curriculum and represented this all girls school at hockey.

However, it was only natural that the experience of living on a 170 acre mixed farm, where her father already bred a few racehorses, would help to foster Mary's keen interest in the sport of kings.

From an early age, she rode ponies around the farm and as a junior became a member of the Cleveland Pony Club competing in numerous northern gymkhanas. Although accumulating a fine collection of rosettes she surprisingly views her achievements with an understated assessment of: "No great shakes."

When she was only 15, Mary's father died. This unfortunate personal tragedy meant that she became much more involved with the busy day to day running of the family farm.

She did, however, continue riding, graduating through the local show jumping events before participating in point to point meetings throughout the North-east calendar.

In 1960 Mary married George Reveley from Stockton -on-Tees. They have two sons, Keith, who is now assistant trainer and John, who helps to manage the farm.

By 1979 Mary had begun training her own hunter chasers under permit and gained her first success with Lottie Lehman at Sedgefield in 1981. Following this breakthrough, and at the suggestion of one of her owners, John Fulton, who recognised her undoubted potential, she began training under licence in 1982.

She started with a small string of around 12 horses and made an immediate impact by walking into the winner's enclosure when her first runner, Legal Session, was successful at the first attempt at Cartmel. Since then she has never had to formally advertise for horses to fill her stables. Prospective owners have always come to her, and as a result the number of horses which she has had in training has continued to increase dramatically.

When asked to account for her success she reveals modestly that there is no great secret, just thorough preparation, attention to detail and careful placement of horses in appropriate races.

Such is her reputation that several of the leading National Hunt owners now have horses based in Lingdale including Peter Savill, chairman of the British Horseracing Board.

As consistent winning results were achieved on the tracks, so a steady expansion of the original training stables, which employed only three staff in 1982, has taken place. The modern facilities at Groundhill Farm now include purpose built gallops, 120 horse boxes and 35 full-time employees whose daily routine begins at around 6.30am with the first of three riding out sessions.

Although Mary is somewhat modest and unassuming about her own achievements she is certainly held in high regard by those within racing circles. In fact, such is her standing in the game that many of the leading riders have ridden her horses over the years and these include many of the greats like; Lester Piggott, Frankie Dettori, Pat Eddery, Steve Cauthen, Kieron Fallon, Kevin Darley, Richard Quinn, Peter Niven, Richard Dunwoody and Tony McCoy.

After starting from scratch in 1981, Lingdale based trainer Mary Reveley now has one of the country's leading horse racing stables with over 1,700 winners to her credit.

In a sport where observers are always looking for in-form stables, Mrs Reveley's horses are rarely out of form. This consistent level of performance helped her achieve the 1,000th winner of her training career when Hit the Canvas won at Ayr in June, 1995. That overall landmark was followed in November, 1999, when Robbo recorded her 1,000th victory over the sticks, again at Ayr.

Although Mary is yet to enter the winner's enclosure at the Cheltenham Festival, and the majority of her success has been achieved on her favourite northern tracks of Sedgefield, Wetherby, Kelso, Haydock and Redcar, she has still won some very prestigious races. These include, on the flat, the Cambridgeshire Handicap with Mellotie in 1991, the Cesarewitch, twice, at Newmarket with Old Red and Turnpole in 1995 and 1997, and the Zetland Gold Cup at Redcar in 1995 with Penny a Day.

It is a similar success story over the jumps, particularly at the famous Aintree Grand National meeting where she has won the Melling Chase in 1993 with Cab on Target and the Becher Chase in 1996 with Into The Red. At Doncaster the Great Yorkshire Chase, has been captured twice, with Carbisdale and Dalkey Sound, while both No More Hassle and Sad Mad Bad have returned from Haydock with the Victor Ladorum Trophy.

Another notable day in the training career of Mary Reveley occured on July 8, 1993, at Redcar when Kevin Darley partnered her first four runners on the racecard home to victory. It was the first time since the Second World War that the same combination of jockey and trainer had achieved this feat.

Recalling some of her great moments, she said: "I think Cab On Target winning a novice chase at Ascot was one of the best days, but Marello was brilliant, too. She was a good mare and it was a great thrill to train her."

At present Mary is concentrating heavily on pushing on towards her 2,000th winner, although she does hope in the future that her eldest son and assistant, Keith, will take over the reins on a full time basis when his family has grown up.

However, judging by recent results, it is not surprising that Mary intends to carry on training when she immediately followed last season's best ever National Hunt total of 105 winners, by carrying off the first major £50,000 prize of the New Millennium when Sad Mad Bad romped home in the UK Betting Dot Com Chase at Uttoxeter.

Don Revie

Football

DON Revie was one of the great managers of his era, transforming a struggling Leeds United side, who were languishing in the lower reaches of the Second Division, into one of the most powerful and efficient teams in Europe.

His achievements became legend at Elland Road, winning the Championship twice, the FA Cup and League Cup and also the European Fairs Cup on two occasions.

As a player, Revie had been involved in introducing the Revie Plan into football, which was founded on the Hungarian system of operating with a deep lying centre-forward. He played for Leicester City, Hull City, Manchester City, Sunderland and Leeds United in a 19 year career as an inside-forward, winning an FA Cup winner's medal with Manchester City in 1956.

The best six years of his playing career came at Maine Road, being named Player of the Year in 1955 and winning six international caps.

He was appointed manager of Leeds in 1961 and remained in charge until 1974, when he took over as manager of England. He held this post for three years before accepting a post as coach to the United Arab Emirates team.

Donald George Revie was born at No.13 Bell Street, Middlesbrough, close to Ayresome Park, on July 10, 1927. His early football experiences saw him play for Archibald School, Newport Boys Club and Middlesbrough Swifts. After leaving school at 14 he took up an apprenticeship as a bricklayer.

Don's potential was spotted by a Midlands scout while he was playing for Middlesbrough Swifts and he was invited to sign for Leicester City in August, 1944, at the age of 16. As a skillful inside-forward he made almost 100 appearances for the Foxes and is best remembered for the two goals he scored in the 1949 FA Cup semi-final against Portsmouth which ensured Leicester a much coveted Wembley appearance.

Although he was chosen to play in the final against Wolverhampton Wanderers, Revie had to miss the match when, on the eve of the game, he broke some blood vessels in his nose and the backroom staff couldn't stem the constant bleeding.

Surprisingly, he moved from Filbert Street in November, 1949, and joined Second Division Hull City, who were managed by Raich Carter. The former England inside-forward saw Revie as the man to help the Humberside club's push towards top flight football. Unfortunately the move failed to work out as Revie lost his form and moved across the Pennines to Manchester City in October, 1951.

It was at Maine Road where he enjoyed his most successful spell as a player when he was used as a deep-lying Continental style centre-forward to good effect. The formation, termed the Revie Plan, was based on the innovative tactics used by Hungary in their 6-3 thrashing of England at Wembley in 1953. His consistent performances during that period were acknowledged with the Player of the Year Award in 1955, the acquisition of six England caps and the pleasure of scoring on his debut against Northern Ireland.

He also appeared in two successive FA Cup Finals, losing 3-1 to Newcastle United in 1955, but earning a winner's medal the following year when he starred in City's 3-1 victory over Birmingham City.

An unproductive two year spell at Sunderland was then followed by a move to Leeds United in December, 1958. Leeds was a club in gradual decline since the heyday of the great John Charles, who went to Juventus in the summer of 1957 for a then British transfer fee of £65,000.

In 1960, Leeds were relegated to the Second Division and with the directors desperate to improve the club's ailing fortunes they asked Revie to take over as player-manager from Jack Taylor on March 24, 1961. Shortly after his appointment it became apparent that Revie was not afraid to ask the best for advice and this included the legendary Matt Busby of Manchester United. From the outset of his appointment it was

Although Don Revie turned ailing Leeds United into one of the most efficient and successful football teams of the modern era, he could not repeat his achievements with England.

obvious that he intended to make a success of this management opportunity.

He instigated many changes at Elland Road and one of the first was to change the strip from blue and gold to the all white of Real Madrid. Revie was determined that his players should aspire to the greatness of the Spanish champions and he emphasised that anybody who didn't think that way had no future at Leeds. There was also to be no more penny pinching on third class travel. In future the team would have nothing but the best in order to boost the morale of the players.

During his first full season in charge he managed to avoid relegation from the Division Two and set about developing a youth policy which in later years was to provide Leeds with a rich source of home grown talent. Initially he built his team around the combative Scot Bobby Collins, who had been signed from Everton in March, 1962, for £22,500. Collins possessed all the attributes of dedication and professionalism which Revie admired and was keen to instill into his team. The pocket-sized general Collins fulfilled Revie's role perfectly by guiding Leeds to the Second Division title in 1963-64, losing only three games in the process.

They also made an immediate impact on the top flight, finishing runners up to Manchester United on goal difference and quickly earned a reputation for being well-organised and difficult to beat.

In fact, at times their rather uncompromising and robust style, typified by players like the firebrand Billy Bremner, Norman Hunter and Jack Charlton, coupled with accusations of blatant gamesmanship, won them few friends outside Yorkshire. The atmosphere within Revie's Elland Road, however, was very protective and was built around a close knit 'family' togetherness both on and off the pitch. Few clubs would ever rival this unique kinship and it was this unity of purpose which was to be the platform of their success. Around the country Leeds United never received anything above a grudging admiration for their achievements but that attitude only seemed to harden their resolve.

Another shrewd Revie signing was the purchase of experienced Irishman Johnny Giles from Manchester United to add both creativity and steel to the midfield. Once back in the First Division, Leeds United were always challenging for the championship but they managed to clinch the top prize only twice in 1968-69 and 1973-74. In fact they were often the bridesmaids, finishing runners up in the title race on no less than four other occasions.

The outstanding title winning season of 1968-69 saw Leeds lose only two league games during the whole campaign and establish a record points total of 67. This success added to their 1-0 triumph over Arsenal in the League Cup Final at Wembley, the previous year.

They also reached four FA Cup Finals but were only successful in the 1972 showpiece, again defeating Arsenal 1-0 with a goal from Allan Clarke. The following year, however, celebration turned to despair when they were sensationally beaten 1-0 by Second Division Sunderland in one of the biggest upsets in the history of the competition.

Under Revie, Leeds made an excellent impact in Europe, winning the Fairs Cup in 1968 and 1971, the latter against Italian giants Juventus. They also appeared in the final of the Cup Winners Cup in 1973, losing 1-0 to AC Milan. These achievements were recognised when Revie was awarded the OBE for services to football.

In 1974 Alf Ramsey resigned as England manager after failing to qualify for the World Cup in Germany and Don Revie, now at the height of his powers, accepted the opportunity to lead his country. It was a decision which was to change people's perception of him forever.

Away from the cosseted environment of Elland Road he found it hard to reproduce the dressing room atmosphere of the Yorkshire club at international level. In fact some of his innovations, such as preparing bulging dossiers on the opposition for the players to read, were positively mocked in some quarters.

Under his leadership England failed to make the finals of Euro 76 and were struggling to make the 1978 World Cup in Argentina when Revie sensationally resigned and took up a position as director of coaching in the United Arab Emirates.

When it was later revealed that secret negotiations had been going on for some time without the knowledge of his employers, the Football Association, Revie's reputation was left in tatters. This was further compounded when he inadvisedly sold his story to the press. His public credibility evaporated overnight and he was charged with breach of contract and bringing the game into disrepute. He was eventually banned from English football for ten years.

Although Don later won an appeal in the High Court against the punishment, the damage to his reputation was already done. When he also had to deny allegations of fixing Leeds United matches, his fate was sealed.

Revie worked in the UAE until 1980 and then coached briefly in Egypt before being struck down by motor neurone disease, a debilitating and incurable condition which eventually confined him to a wheelchair.

Don Revie was undoubtedly one of the great club managers of his era, transforming a struggling Second Division outfit into one of the most powerful teams in Europe. His achievements made him a legend at Elland Road and it was no coincidence that Leeds United's fortunes went into decline after his departure.

He is held in high regard by his former players, including ex-Middlesbrough manager Jack Charlton, who has always claimed that Revie's sound advice was partly responsible for his success in management.

Charlton said: "Don Revie was most important influence on my football life. He taught me how to conduct myself as a player and I adopted many of his practices with Ireland and the other clubs I managed."

Don Revie died in Edinburgh on May 26, 1989, and despite the controversy which surrounded his tenure of England, the church for his funeral service was packed with leading figures from the world of football.

Peter Richardson
Boxing

PETER Richardson was one of the top boxers ever produced by Teesside. He was an outstanding amateur and a gold medallist in the 1994 Commonwealth Games in Canada who would surely have won titles as a professional but for a series of injuries.

Peter grew up living at Ormesby Bank, in Ormesby, and attended Keldholme School. It was obvious from an early age at Joe Walton's Amateur Boxing Club that he had a special talent.

This was proven when he won a national schoolboys title at the first attempt at the age of 12, when stopping Steve Green from Essex in the second round of the final at Derby. Peter broke Green's nose in the process, and this was the fifth time he had broken the nose of his opponent in 13 contests.

Two years later Peter won another schoolboys title, and was selected to box for England for the first time in the schoolboys international against Wales at Port Talbot.

In 1986 Peter won his third schoolboys crown, and also won a Junior ABA title when beating Alan Guiver from West Ham on unanimous points in the final at Wembley. His performance earned him a special ABA champion of champions accolade.

The following year, Peter completed a nap hand of national successes when winning a second Junior ABA title, beating Danny Marks from Repton on unanimous points at Milton Keynes.

Richardson later switched clubs and joined the Phil Thomas School of Boxing, from where he took his sixth title when gaining a unanimous points win over David Redgrave from Billericay in the National Association of Boys Clubs final at the Grosvenor House in London.

In May, 1989, Peter moved out of the junior ranks to win a senior ABA title at the first attempt. Still only 18, he made a tentative start in the first round but went on to outbox the Welshman John Williams to take the featherweight title on points at Wembley Arena.

The victory was enough to earn Peter his first senior England vest in the Canada Cup in Ottawa. His trip across the Atlantic may have been mainly for experience, but Peter fought his heart out, boxing four times in five days, to come back with the silver medal. Richardson was selected to box again for England in a multi nations tournament in Finland, but he was forced to drop out at the last minute because of increasing weight problems.

He stepped up immediately to lightweight, even though it could affect his hopes of competing in the Commonwealth Games in Auckland, New Zealand.

Peter need not have worried. ABA lightweight champion Mark Ramsey announced he was turning professional, and Peter was selected to take his place for the trip to the Commonwealth Games. In doing so, Peter became the first boxer from Teesside to compete in the Games.

He warmed up by beating Irishman Charlie Brown in an international at Coventry, and set off for the Games in January, 1990. Unfortunately Peter did not get the luck of the draw in Auckland. He was paired with the favourite, Scotsman Dave Anderson, in the quarter finals and lost a pulsating contest by 59-58 on the cards of all three judges.

Peter gained some consolation six months later when he won the silver medal in the Acropolis Cup in Athens, though there was a price to pay. He received a hairline fracture of the jaw when stopped in the second round of the final by the Frenchman Jean Checlet.

Further weight problems followed as Peter's physical frame continued to grow, and this time he stepped up to light-welterweight. However he was still very strong at the weight, and gained valuable experience when reaching the quarter-finals of the world championships in Sydney, Australia.

The 1992 Barcelona Olympics were now Richardson's target. He took a huge step towards booking his place when beating a Yugoslav opponent to earn a top six rating in a qualifying competition in Venice.

He returned home to Teesside to discover that he had

Unfortunately, after winning the 1994 Commonwealth light-welterweight gold medal in style, talented Boro boxer Peter Richardson's realistic hopes of being a professional champion were dashed by injury.

been selected for the Olympics, and took the difficult decision of quitting his job as a van driver with an engineering company in order to train full-time.

Ronnie Cave, his coach for many years, launched a public appeal for sponsorship, and Dunnes Stores in Billingham made an initial donation of £1,000.

Peter warmed up in the Canada Cup in Ottawa, and set off for the Olympics in the August. He battled his way through to the last eight and stood just nine minutes away from a certain medal. However Peter's hopes were ended by the stocky Romanian Leonard Doroftei. Richardson was then involved in controversy after the contest when he was one of three English boxers who became involved in a scuffle with a group of Iranian wrestlers outside of the Games village. However it was later accepted that the English men played no part in sparking the incident and Peter won libel damages against the newspaper which had accused him of starting the fight.

Peter then received several offers to turn professional, but decided to box on as an amateur. His decision was justified when he won his second ABA title when beating his Royal Navy opponent Rob Wileman with an awesome display of punching after just 90 seconds of their light-welterweight final at Birmingham.

The pro-fight managers were still queueing up, but Richardson went on to box in the European championships in Turkey, before losing narrowly to the home boxer Nurhan Suleymanoglu by 8-6.

In December, 1993, Peter had a lucky escape when he was involved in a car accident. Three days later he was back in a Middlesbrough hospital when he was stabbed nine times in the stomach after an attack at a birthday party.

The injury robbed Richardson of the opportunity to defend his ABA crown, but he returned to the ring to guarantee selection for his second Commonwealth Games when he won the gold medal and the best boxer award at a multi nations tournament in Liverpool. He beat the Italian Christian Giantomassio by 8-5.

Peter was duly selected for the English team as captain, and made amends for his disappointments from four years earlier by winning the light-welterweight gold medal in the Games in Victoria in Canada.

The 24-year-old made certain of at least a bronze medal when he outpointed the Zambian Daniel Fulanse by 10-6 in the quarter-finals. Then he outpointed the Ghanaian Tijani Moro by 11-7 in the semis.

In the final, Peter was paired with Mark Winters from Northern Ireland. It was a gruelling contest, especially as both men were already tired following their exertions in reaching the final. However Peter was determined not to let this opportunity slip away and brought back the gold medal to Teesside.

Now was the time to turn pro, and Richardson signed a contract with Frank Maloney, the manager of Lennox Lewis. He decided to base himself in London and moved in with his sister at Maida Vale, from where he travelled to work out daily at the Peacock Gym at Canary Wharf under the watchful eye of trainer Darkie Smith.

Peter won his first pro contest at Southwark on December 23, 1995, when he stopped John Johnson in the fifth round. In his first 18 months as a pro he won ten contests, including seven inside the distance.

He was lined up for a British light-welterweight eliminator against Scotsman Alan McDowell in November, 1996, but the contest had to be postponed when Richardson suffered a badly gashed eye in a warm-up against the Lithuanian, Ribvadas Bilius. The cut ended his unbeaten record.

When Peter returned to the ring in the January, he met Bilius again and this time recorded a comfortable points victory. He followed up by beating John Smith at Liverpool and then ground out one of the best wins of his career when beating Birmingham's Mark Ramsey over eight rounds. However Peter suffered another gashed eye which needed eight stitches.

Richardson had been lined up for a possible Commonwealth title tilt against Bernard Paul, but increasing weight problems forced him to step up to welterweight.

Immediately, he was nominated for a British title eliminator, and met Welshman Michael Smyth at the Grundy Park Leisure Centre in Hertfordshire on August 30, 1997.

Disaster struck when Richardson suffered another bad gash in only the second round, and although the Teessider was well ahead on points, he lost the fight when referee Richie Davies was forced to call a halt in the fifth round. It was only the second defeat of Peter's pro career, both coming on cuts. This time he needed 20 stitches to close the wound.

In February, 1998, Richardson returned to the ring when he met Dennis Berry from Birmingham at the Elephant and Castle.

It should have produced a comfortable win for the Teessider, but he suddenly began to suffer severe pains in his shoulder in the second round. He tried to fight on, but had to drop out in the next round because he could no longer lift his arm. He was rushed to hospital where it was discovered he had dislocated his shoulder.

It was another frustrating injury and one which forced Richardson to consider his future in the sport.

However in 2000 he began to consider making a comeback, and began training at the Hull gym run by Steve Pollard.

Stan Rickaby
Football

THE unexpected intervention of both Lady Luck and the fickle finger of fate often plays a major role in the level of professional sporting achievement attained by an individual, and the football career of Stan Rickaby is a prime example of those contrasting fortunes.

After making only ten appearances for Middlesbrough Football Club in a little over three years, he chose to leave Teesside and move to the Midlands, where he signed for West Bromwich Albion.

The change of club proved to be the perfect stimulus as Stan developed into a solid and reliable full-back who was eventually capped by England and represented the Football League. However, fate delivered him a cruel blow just as he was about to make a major impact in the game.

Born in Stockton-on-Tees on March 12, 1924, Stanley Rickaby's football career began in the local schools league before he graduated to South Bank Juniors.

At the end of the Second World War, Middlesbrough, who had been carefully monitoring his progress at their nursery club, were sufficiently impressed by the young defender to offer him a professional contract at Ayresome Park in June, 1946.

Opportunities at the Boro, however, were rare as the two full-back positions at that time were occupied by England captain George Hardwick, and England squad member Dickie Robinson. In fact Stan had to wait almost two years before making his Boro debut against Derby County on March 20, 1948, just a few days after celebrating his 24th birthday.

But his call up proved to be a false dawn and in order to secure regular first team football he was eventually tempted to move to West Brom in February, 1950, by Albion manager Jack Smith for a fee of £8,000.

At The Hawthorns, his career quickly flourished and he developed into a popular, dependable and almost ever present right-back, whose great attributes were his ability on the ball and his acute positional sense.

During his time with the Albion, the team gradually became a major force to be reckoned with in the First

Stan Rickaby's decision to leave the Boro for West Brom paid dividends with international recognition.

Division and the season 1953-54 was to prove pivotal for both the Throstles and Stan Rickaby.

The campaign started well with West Brom challenging Billy Wright's Wolverhampton Wanderers for the league title before they eventually finished runners-up, only four points adrift of the champions and local rivals from the Black Country.

Stan's consistent performances in a successful side were also rewarded with an international call-up on November 11, 1953, when he proved himself to be an able deputy for Alf Ramsey as England defeated Northern Ireland 3-1 at Goodison Park.

At this point, Stan's career appeared to be progressing very well. But heartache was just around the corner.

In the spring of 1954, West Bromwich reached the semi-final of the FA Cup, where they met Port Vale at Villa Park. Unfortunately during the tie, which West

Middlesbrough 1948. Stan Rickaby, back row, second right, found it difficult to break into this highly talented Ayresome Park team which included Wilf Mannion, front row, first right, and Micky Fenton, front row, centre.

Brom won 2-1, Stan received a very bad thigh injury which resulted in him missing a thrilling Wembley showpiece as The Albion defeated Tom Finney's Preston North End 3-2 in the final.

As if sitting out the Cup Final wasn't bad enough, the deep seated injury also delivered another hammer blow to Rickaby when it ruled him out of any possible selection for England's 1954 World Cup squad to compete in Switzerland.

Although he regained his place in the Albion side for the 1954-55 season, worse was to follow when new manager Vic Buckingham dropped him after a series of poor results which saw West Brom near the foot of the First Division table.

The 30-year-old Rickaby was shocked and deeply hurt by the treatment he had received but he continued to maintain an excellent attitude.

However he did not believe that there was a long term future for him at The Hawthorns and he made the decision to leave the club in July, 1955, after 205 appearances, and began a four year stint as player-manager of Poole Town.

Stan began his managerial career by immediately causing a sensation when he audaciously signed his former Middlesbrough colleague Wilf Mannion from Hull City. Although now past his mercurial best, the Golden Boy's surprise appearance for the Dorset club created a real stir and put an extra 5,000 on the gate. By 1960, Stan had moved down the south coast to Weymouth before eventually retiring from the game after a period with Newton Abbot Spurs in 1963.

Following his retirement from football he returned to the Birmingham area where he worked for a life insurance company.

In 1969 Stan decided to emigrate to Perth in Western Australia, where he still lives in 2000. He does however, closely follow the ever changing fortunes of Middlesbrough and West Bromwich Albion.

Stuart Ripley
Football

STUART Ripley is a strong running home produced winger who broke into Bruce Rioch's young side in the late 1980s and went on to win England international caps while with Blackburn Rovers.

He was born in Middlesbrough on November 20, 1967 and was a member of the Boro Boys side which shared the English Schools FA Trophy with Sunderland. He had trials with Manchester City and Chelsea before joining his home-town club as an apprentice.

Ripley made rapid progress through the junior ranks and made his Boro debut as a substitute in a Second Division match against Oldham Athletic in February, 1985. The following year he had a successful loan spell with Bolton Wanderers, scoring on his debut, which gave him the confidence to make an impact at league level.

He returned to Ayresome Park and earned a run of eight games in the latter part of the 1985-86 relegation campaign as Rioch began to bring in the younger players. He suffered the unfortunate experience of having Boro's demotion to Division Three confirmed while he was on tour abroad with the England Youth team in China.

Following the liquidation saga in the summer of 1986, Ripley established himself immediately in the Boro first team as a raiding teenage winger, playing more than 40 games as Boro gained promotion back to Division Two.

As the Boro rollercoaster gathered momentum Stuart became an integral part of a second successive promotion campaign, with his ability to get to the goal-line and cross into the box bringing many goals for strikers Bernie Slaven, Archie Stephens, Alan Kernaghan and later Trevor Senior.

Ripley also had a spell as an orthodox striker, scoring his first league hat trick in April, 1988, against Sheffield United. Boro went on to confound all the odds and Stuart helped the club regain their top flight status via nerve-wracking play-off wins against Bradford City and Chelsea.

The incisive wing play of Stuart Ripley undoubtedly contributed to the Boro's revival after liquidation.

Middlesbrough 1988. Under the shrewd management of Bruce Rioch, Stuart Ripley, middle row, third left, was part of a Boro team which gained promotion in successive years and restored the club's credibility.

In recognition of his consistent wing play, Stuart was awarded the first of his seven Under-21 caps that summer when, along with teammate Colin Cooper, he represented England in games against Russia and France in the Toulon tournament.

Further caps followed during a 12-month period in which Ripley played three games for England in the UEFA Under-21 Championships, scoring in a 2-1 win against Albania in Shkoder.

In the same season, Ripley was a virtual ever present as he tasted life in the hurly-burly world of the First Division for the first time, scoring four goals. However Boro fell away very badly in the second half of the season as Rioch's young side struggled to cope, and they were finally relegated following a 1-0 defeat at Hillsborough against Sheffield Wednesday in their last game.

Ripley stayed loyal to the club and, after a rocky period which saw him used as a frequent substitute by Rioch and his successor Colin Todd, he regained a regular place under Lennie Lawrence as the former Charlton boss took his new charges into the inaugural FA Premier League and an appearance in the semi-final of the League Cup against Manchester United. In fact Ripley scored the crucial goal in the fifth round replay

against Peterborough United which sent Boro on their way to a two legged showdown with United.

As a result of his overall contribution in helping Boro to achieve promotion, Ripley attracted the attention of Blackburn Rovers boss Kenny Dalglish. After some negotiation, Dalglish eventually paid £1.3m to take the blond winger to Ewood Park and make Ripley only the third Boro player in history to be transferred for a million pounds following the departures of Gary Pallister and Tony Mowbray to Manchester United and Celtic respectively.

Stuart had played 295 games, including substitute appearances, for Boro and nobody could deny him the opportunity to further his career at a new club.

Although his time with Rovers was plagued by injury, he did enough to earn the first of his two international caps against San Marino in 1994. This was followed by a very consistent season in 1995 when he supplied the ammunition for Alan Shearer to score the goals which helped Blackburn secure the Premiership title.

During the summer of 1998, and having played more than 200 games for Rovers, Stuart moved to Southampton for £1m where, despite the occasional injury problems, he has consistently proved himself to be one of the most effective wingers in the Premier League.

Eleanor Robinson
Athletics

ELEANOR Robinson is a stamina saturated athlete virtually without equal, having compiled a hugely impressive collection of ultra long distance running records which led to her being named the Female Ultra Runner of the Millennium.

At one time the Middlesbrough-born runner held 40 world records at the same time, and has set many more during her remarkable career. In 1990 she entered the Guinness Book of Records' Hall of Fame for holding the most world records at any one time.

She has won seven world championships, over 24 and 48 hours, twice at 100 kilometres, over 1,000 miles and also two veterans world events at 100k and the marathon.

Six day events, and races of up to 1,000 miles have never presented the fleet-footed Eleanor with too many problems.

She has won the gruelling 635 miles Sydney to Melbourne race on four occasions, and holds the world record for both men and women for the legendary Death Valley Run.

Yet arguably her best achievement came at the age of 50, in 1998, when she set 18 world records from 900 kilometres upwards in the tortuous Nanango Foot Race in blazing heat and humidity in Queensland, Australia, Born Eleanor Mary Puckrin in Middlesbrough, on November 20, 1947, she grew up in Willows Road, Linthorpe, and attended Beechwood and Green Lane primary schools.

Her sporting prowess developed at Middlesbrough High School, where she excelled at netball and athletics and also played hockey for North Riding Schools.

Her strongest sport, however, was on the athletics track, where she ran the 880 yards and became Yorkshire Schools half-mile champion. At the age of 16, she qualified for the English schools championships at 880 yards, but failed to progress past the heats.

However it was over the longer distances where Eleanor really came into her own. She had joined Middlesbrough and Cleveland Harriers at the age of 14

Eleanor Robinson's amazing achievements earned her the title Female Ultra Runner of the Millennium.

and, although competition was limited, always looked to race in the longest possible event.

As a result, she excelled at cross country and represented the North in the national championships. At the age of 16 she finished fourth in the national 'junior' cross country championships, which was really a senior event as it excluded the country's more experienced runners. Thirty years later she was still representing the Northern Counties at the half marathon and cross country.

After leaving school, Eleanor went to teacher training college in Coventry to study to become a PE teacher. She chose her destination carefully, because it was the only college with an attached running track.

In fact Eleanor can claim to have been one of the first people to organise official jogging sessions, having started a cross country club at the college, mainly for those students who were otherwise not involved in physical activities. The team which she put together was proficient enough to compete in the Gloucester Cross Country League, having earlier been turned

189

down by the Midlands League because they did not fancy the idea of competing against students.

Eleanor also established strong links with Coventry Godiva Harriers, which was one of the top athletics clubs in the country at that time. Whenever she returned home she continued running for Middlesbrough and Cleveland Harriers in all possible competitions and events, including briefly, the javelin and the long jump.

Later Eleanor took her first teaching job in Driffield in the East Riding and joined the Hull Achilles club, before moving on to Alfreton after 12 months.

Eventually she was married, and became Eleanor Adams. She went on to have three children, Kathryn, Stephen and Joanna, and hung up her running shoes to concentrate on bringing up her family. As a result, she stopped athletics completely, and never did any at all for ten years.

Joanna was born with dislocated hips, which caused a lot of family distress, especially as she was in and out of hospital and needed several operations. Fortunately the operations eventually proved to be successful, but it had a been a trying time for Eleanor and her own health had suffered badly.

Finally, she decided to do a bit of jogging simply to improve her own state of mental and physical well-being. As Eleanor said: "I started jogging because it was the easiest thing to do. The beauty of running is that it is so simple. I didn't need any special clothes or equipment, or leisure centres or facilities. It was just a case of open the door, and out you go."

Eleanor started jogging late at night, when it was dark and the children were asleep. Her first attempted run was a complete disaster. She ran 400 yards uphill, and collapsed on to a well-positioned bench, with "lungs heaving, and legs like rhubarb".

However she persevered, and built up her fitness gradually. At that time her brother Richard was competing in marathons, and Eleanor decided to join him in the Notts Ten Miles road race. She arrived believing that the women would run along with the men, and so was a little surprised to find herself in a separate five-miles race alongside a collection of young women. She was even more surprised to finish sixth. But it was a momentous occasion. Suddenly her competitive edge was rekindled.

Eleanor joined Sutton in Ashfield Harriers and entered the first People's Marathon in Birmingham. She had always felt comfortable running long distances and had no problems in dealing with her first 26-miler, going on to finish second in 3hr 24min. A series of marathon runs followed and within two years, Eleanor had knocked more than half an hour off this time. Not only that, but she was now rated in the top 15 women marathon runners in Britain.

Her determination to get even better was bolstered by the fact that she was approaching the age of 35, and would be classed as a veteran. This would open the door to her being potentially successful in the older, less competitive age group.

At this point, Eleanor discovered that a six-day race was being staged in Nottingham. She did not know much about the event, but went down to watch. She was asked to help with the lap recording, but when she was not required for this job, she began lapping the track herself and found that she thoroughly enjoyed it. Her big breakthrough came in 1982 when Eleanor entered her first ultra marathon, in Nottingham. She agreed to join a team, the members of which were expected to try to run 63 miles in 12 hours.

Eleanor took to the event like a duck to water. She soon developed into a rhythm and was lapping the track with confidence and strength. Fortunately the official lap recorder was also an athletics statistician. He had spotted how well she was running and consulted his book of facts and figures. The result was breathtaking. He informed Eleanor that if she kept going at the same pace, she would set a new world track record for 50 miles.

It was not a situation which Eleanor was prepared to allow to pass her by. She steadily built up her pace, and sprinted the last lap, finishing in 6hr 41min 2sec, which was quite clearly a new world record. However there was another shock in store. As she stood there gasping for breath, she was told that she must run another six laps in case of officials' error.

After completing those extra laps, Eleanor was 'out for the count' and doubled up in pain. Eventually she retired to her tent, where she changed into dry clothing. However the worst was yet to come. Eleanor was then told by a fellow team member that she needed to return to the track to run another 11 miles for the sake of the team, though he pointed out that she had five hours left in which to complete this task. -

At first Eleanor could hardly move, having stiffened up completely. But she returned to the track and began to walk around. However boredom took over and Eleanor ran the remaining laps.

In 1990, Eleanor Robinson entered the Guinness Hall of Fame for holding the most world running records.

Later she received a call to inform her that, not only had she set a new 50 miles world record, but she had shattered the 50k and 40 miles world records as well. Her life was changed overnight. Immediately the invitations began arriving on her doormat offering her the opportunity to compete in ultra races throughout the world.

First of all, Eleanor had to qualify for these top races by running 100 miles in a 24 hour race, which she achieved on her 35th birthday. In fact not only did she become the first woman to win a mixed race of this kind, but she also broke the world record as well.

From that moment Eleanor was hooked on the challenge of long distance running and very quickly developed into the finest female ultra-distance runner in the world, breaking records virtually every time she was in action.

Her first overseas race was a 24 hours run in Austria and soon she was running much further afield. Her work as a supply teacher was perfectly suited to enable her to accept the mouth-watering all expenses-paid invitations to run in these testing races.

In 1983, Eleanor ran in the first Spartathlon in Greece, which followed the same route across the mountains which Phidippaedes had taken.

The following year, she flew out to Australia to win the first of three consecutive runs in the Sydney to Melbourne race, which was the world's longest race at the time, being set at 635 miles. She had not known what to expect, but discovered that she was allotted a support team in a following van, which took away most of the dangers which she would have anticipated from running in unpopulated areas.

However this prestigious run was staged along the main highway between the two cities. This did present major problems, mainly as a result the weird sense of humour of the Australian truck drivers, who tried to get as close to the runners as possible without actually hitting them.

Unfortunately one driver eventually got too close. When a runner was killed during Eleanor's third win in 1986, she declined the following year's invitation, insisting that the route was too dangerous. In particular, she was not prepared to endanger her support crew.

Eventually the Australian race officials decided to take the event away from the major highway, and Eleanor returned to win it again in 1988 on a new course.

She visited Australia on several occasions, running in the Colac Race, a six days event near Melbourne. She also won 24 hours races in Adelaide and Melbourne, where she set a world record of 240 kilometres and 169 metres, which is 149 and a quarter miles. She enjoyed the Colac race, but it did prove to be a major problem, especially when gangs of Australian youths turned up to watch the event and amused themselves by throwing beer cans at the athletes.

All the time the world records kept coming. Eleanor's records ranged in distance from 30 miles to becoming the first woman to cover 500 miles in a six-day race. She created the record for running 500 miles in 143:11.23 in 1986 and later completed 1,000 miles on the road in 16 days 22.51.00 in 1987.

When Eleanor had run in the Sydney to Melbourne event for the first time, she was also the first woman to achieve this feat. She flew the first flag for her sex in many of her runs, and in doing so she opened the door for more women to take part.

She was always looking for a new strength sapping challenge, and the more unusual the event, the better. If the world record was up for grabs, then better still.

In 1987 Eleanor took on male ultra distance runner Malcolm Campbell in a 1000 miles British road challenge which was dubbed the 'Battle of the Sexes' by the athletics press.

Initially the race was regarded by both athletes as preparation for a much bigger test, in which they were due to run around Lake Michigan. Malcolm had recently run in an event from coast to coast in the United States.

However the British race did not work out as planned. When Eleanor realised that Malcolm was out to win, her competitive edge soon took over. As a result it became a non-contest. Eleanor hammered the hapless Malcolm by more than 18 hours.

The duo started off in Nottingham and ran up to Middlesbrough and on to Newcastle, then across to Carlisle and all the way down the West side to Bristol. From there they ran on to Brighton and then up to Peterborough via London.

They arrived in Peterborough on the day of the Great Eastern Run in the town. This race was a half marathon and Eleanor and Malcolm agreed to run in it, starting at the back. In the event Eleanor completed the run in 1hr 50min, after dodging her way through hundreds of assorted runners in fancy dress in the early stages.

Afterwards the duo returned to the Battle of the Sexes and ran back to Nottingham, via Derby. Ironically, the planned Lake Michigan Run never took place.

However Eleanor did go on to achieve another tremendous feat in the Death Valley Run, in which she set a record for both men and women. This race involved starting at Badwater, 280 feet below sea level in Death Valley, and running through the searing heat before leaving the Valley behind to run over a mountain range and then eventually finishing at the top of Mount Whitney, which is 14,500 feet high.

This race can only be attempted when the sun is at its hottest, otherwise it does not count in the record books. Thus it is only run officially in July or August. Eleanor somehow managed to survive the 40 degrees-plus temperatures, in addition to the final stages of the 'run', which ended with her scrambling on her hands and knees to reach the top of the mountain, which was covered in snow. She travelled the undulating 146 miles of the Run in 53 hours.

In 1990 Eleanor remarried and became Eleanor Mary Robinson. In doing so, she and her husband Nigel moved to live in Cumbria, close to Haltwhistle. Eleanor had fallen in love with the area while running across the Military Road during the Battle of the Sexes. But it was also a perfect move for Nigel, who is a fell runner and ultra runner.

In the same year Eleanor won her first two world championships, taking the 24 hour event in Milton Keynes and flying out to Duluth in Minnesota to win the 100k crown. She retained the 100k title the following year in Faenza in Northern Italy.

1991 was also the year in which her fourth child, Myles, was born, and as a result Eleanor was out of competitive action for about a year.

She was soon tramping the fells of Cumbria again and looking for new challenges. She went on to win her fourth world championship in 1994, this time in France, in the 48 hour race.

However she was happy to devote much of her time to Myles' upbringing and cut down dramatically on her overseas travelling, though she did fly out to the Philippines to run the Manila Marathon on behalf of the British Heart Foundation.

Remarkably, arguably her best ever achievement was still to come. At the age of 50, in 1998, she took on the blazing heat of Queensland in Australia, and set an astonishing 15 world records at distances of 900 kilometres upwards in the tortuous 1,000 miles Nanango Foot Race.

In temperatures which occasionally reached 40 degrees centigrade, Eleanor completed the distance in 13 days 1hr 54min 2sec to slice an amazing 32 hours off the previous world record. The run was all the more remarkable because it was the first time that Eleanor had run in such dense humidity.

Later she travelled to Winschoten in Holland to carry off another world title, in the veterans 100k.

The world championship victories continued to come in. In 1999 she was the world veterans' marathon winner at Gateshead.

By this time Mr and Mrs Robinson had returned to live in the Midlands. Nigel found a new job as a graphic designer and they settled in Riddings, near Alfreton, where Eleanor again started working as a supply teacher in some of the same schools she had taught in years before.

It was no surprise, at the start of 2000, to see Eleanor named as the Female Ultra Runner of the Millennium and the top athlete in history by the International Association of Ultrarunners.

During the early part of the year, Eleanor suffered from a niggling ankle problem which restricted her competitive runs in major events. However with so many more miles still to come on the clock, Eleanor just keeps on running.

Denise Ross
Athletics

DENISE Ross overcame the permanent handicap of losing her eyesight as a teenager to win a gold medal in the discus at the Seoul Paralympics, in addition to collecting European medals and dozens of national trophies.

She has been by far the outstanding competitor in the discus in Great Britain for 20 years, and also briefly held the world record in 1985.

In addition to the discus, Denise has made her mark at all the field sports, especially at the shot putt and javelin, in which she has earned many more medals.

Remarkably Denise took part in virtually no sport at all, until she was introduced to the facilities at Stockton Sports Centre at the age of 25.

She tried her hand at several different events, but discovered that she had a natural affinity with the throwing events. His special talents were noted by coach Roger Mason, who helped her to develop her basic techniques.

In 1980 she travelled to London to compete in the Metro Games for the visually impaired, despite having just three months of serious training work behind her. Yet she performed so well that she returned home with two gold medals from the shot and discus and a silver from the javelin. She also smashed the championship record for the discus.

Denise followed up by entering the long jump for the first time in the Manchester Games for the visually impaired and won the gold medal. It was only one of her four successes, because she also won the shot, discus and javelin.

The following year Denise proudly wore a Great Britain vest for the first time when she was selected to throw the discus in the European Disabled Games in Fulda in Germany. It was a great learning experience, but she found the competition very tough at that level, and finished out of the medals.

However from that point on, Denise began to dominate the domestic competitions over the next few years, setting the national records for the discus, javelin and shot and proving almost unbeatable.

She also had a change of coach, because Roger Mason emigrated to Australia. As a result, Barbara Rennison took over and began to guide Denise to new heights.

She worked hard to win selection for the 1984 Paralympics, which were held in Long Island, and believed that she had done enough to earn her place on the flight. But she was surprisingly overlooked in favour of another athlete from the South.

However, in 1985, Denise was called up for the European Games in Rome, competing for Great Britain in both shot and discus. She hit top form, breaking her national records in both events, and returning home with a pair of silver medals.

Ironically, she also broke the world record for the discus, but held it for only a matter of three minutes. Her throw of 25.14 metres was a new world record, but it was smashed again by the Russian competitor who followed Denise into the throwing circle.

The following year the Thornaby athlete was called up for the World Games for the Disabled in Gothenburg in Sweden. Thanks to the fund raising efforts of local clubs and organisations she was able to make the trip, and her journey was not in vain. Denise won the bronze medals in both the shot and discus, and was fourth in the javelin.

Denise continued to go from strength to strength and maintained her domination in British competition. As a result, she was selected to contest the European Games in Moscow in 1987, but suffered a huge disappointment when she was unable to take part.

She had been travelling to Dublin for the Irish Games when she was changing trains at Chester. A misunderstanding over the 'advice' given by a railway worker led to her falling and trapping her left leg between the train and the platform.

Later she suffered a thrombosis in her leg which needed an operation. When she left hospital, Denise was still very keen to travel to Moscow, but was refused permission by the specialist who had treated her.

However Ross's main target all along had been the 1988 Paralympics at Seoul, and she worked hard to regain full fitness and reach a peak for the tournament. Once again several local pubs pulled together to ensure that she was able to make the long trip to South Korea, while she also received sponsorship from Camerons Brewery. Denise was at the peak of her abilities at this stage of her career and she pulled out all the stops to take the gold medal in the discus.

It was a great moment for the Teessider, especially as she competed in the discus event first, and still had the shot and javelin to come. She went on to carry off the silver in the shot and was fourth in the javelin, being pipped by the bronze medal winner by just two centimetres.

Denise returned home to a massive celebration from friends and family and was also given an official reception by Stockton Council.

The following year she contested the European Games again and had to settle for two bronze medals, from the discus and the shot.

In 1991 she was beginning her build up to the Barcelona Paralympics and went to the European Games in Caan in France, where she again had to settle for the bronze medals in the discus and shot.

She continued to make a massive impact in domestic competitions and, at the age of 37, was selected to compete in the pre-Olympics invitation tournament at Barcelona's Olympic stadium.

Ross was well aware of the fact that the competition was becoming much more intense, but she dug deep to produce another superb display of throwing and she took the bronze in the discus. She was also fifth in the shot.

Denise was unable to repeat her medal winning feat in the 1992 Paralympics, but she was only a fraction away from returning home with more medals when finishing fourth in both the discus and the shot.

Since then, Denise has not competed internationally though she still travels to London for the Metro Games every year and regularly returns with the gold medals. She achieves these feats despite undertaking minimal training, but relies heavily on her natural technique and strength.

Away from athletics, she also took up cycling and competed for several years in the Tulip Bowl tandem marathon event in Lincolnshire.

Denise was not born in the North-east, but is very much an adopted Teessider. She was born in Barnsley

In 1988 Denise Ross won the women's discus gold medal at the Paralympics in Seoul.

on October 14, 1953, and attended The Derby School in Fulwood, Preston, and later the Henshaw School in Manchester.

She was born with a congenital eye problem and lost the sight of one eye at the age of 11. Seven years later she lost the sight of her other eye.

Denise was still determined to make a success of her life and went to college at Shrewsbury to train as a shorthand typist.

She met her future husband while at Shrewsbury and moved to Thornaby in 1976. She is the mother of two boys, David and Chris, and now lives in Stockton. Chris is a former sprinter with Mandale Harriers and was the youngest ever winner of the UK Chess Championships for the visually impaired. He is currently studying for a degree in German at Sheffield University.

Denise has attended Teesside University to earn a degree in accountancy and occasionally teaches braille to the visually impaired.

Mike Russell
Billiards

MIKE Russell is a wizard of the green baize who won the world billiards championship for the first time in 1989 at the age of only 20, before going on to carry off the world crown on another three occasions over the following ten years.

In fact he has failed to reach the world final just once since his first appearance.

Overall, Mike has won an amazing 31 major ranking titles, including the World Open, the World Matchplay four times and the United Kingdom Championship on seven occasions.

He proudly holds the world record break of 957 made in competitive play under the baulkline rule, though his best ever unbroken run is a massive 2018 which was made in practice play against Mark Wildman.

In 2000 Mike is playing as well as ever and continues to win major tournaments, though he is now expanding his interests into coaching and promoting the sport in the hope of generating a TV breakthrough in the west.

Michael John Russell was born in Middlesbrough on June 3, 1969, and grew up in Marske, where he attended Errington infants and junior schools before moving on to Bydales School.

His initial sporting talents shone forth on the cricket field, where he was a prodigious young talent with the bat. He joined North Yorkshire and South Durham League club Marske and played for all their junior age group sides, while also progressing to play for Cleveland County Under-15 and Under-17s. Remarkably, he made his debut in Marske's NYSD 'A' Division side at the age of 15.

Mike compiled an exceptional individual tally when playing for the county under-17s in the Joe Lumb Trophy, when he made 149. Not surprisingly, the county side won the competition that year.

However cricket was increasingly at odds with billiards as Mike entered his late teens. His interest in billiards had developed almost by accident, when his cricket match was rained off one day. His father Graham, who was friendly with the manager of the Marske Workingmen's Club team in the Teesside Boys Billiards League, suggested that Mike paid a visit to the club to try his hand at the sport.

Mike immediately gained an affinity for billiards and, after a few months of practice, was drafted into the team. He made a bright start, being unbeaten in ten games in his first season, and this was to sow the seeds for his future successes.

Mike began to practise on the club tables at every opportunity, usually on the way home from school. The Marske Workingmen's team was one of the top sides in the Boys Billiards League and Mike's illustrious teammates included Stephen Naisby, who went on to become British Isles champion at under-16 and under-19 level.

Mike learned a great deal about the game from Stephen and became a leading player in his own right. In fact he remained unbeaten for three years before contesting the British Under-16 Championships, which he won in 1985.

He also set a record for the Boys Billiards League when amassing an astonishing 307 points in only half an hour at the table. This record stands to this day.

Twelve months after his success at under-16 level, Mike won the British Isles Under-19 crown. At the same time he made a brave attempt to win the English amateur billiards championship at the age of only 15. He beat several top competitors on the way and forced his way through to the final, where he was pipped by the vastly experienced Ken Shirley at Bramhall in Cheshire.

Shirley, from Cannock, won the best of five frames final by 3-1, after Russell had taken the first frame by 300-163. Shirley was narrowly ahead by ten points in the crucial fourth frame, which he secured with an unfinished break of 94.

In May, 1987, Mike took the plunge by turning professional at the age of 17, after his father had driven him to Peterborough for discussions with Mark

In 1989 Mike Russell was only 20 when he won the World Billiards Championship at his first attempt.

Wildman, the chairman of the World Professional Billiards Association. Wildman's advice to the Russells was that Mike had an uncanny talent and should commit himself full-time to the sport in order to develop more quickly.

Mike did not take very long to make a major impact. He reached the European Championships quarter-finals and also the semi-finals of the United Kingdom Championships. Within 12 months he had become the youngest billiards player this century to win a pro title, at the age of 18, when he landed the European title.

Russell beat world champion Norman Dagley by 7-4 in the final at Antwerp, after hitting back from a 3-1 deficit.

The following year he won the UK Professional crown, by beating Hartlepool's Bob Close in the final at Marton Hotel and Country Club. Mike reached the final by crushing Dagley by 4-0 in the semis, and then demolished Close by 7-0.

Russell was determined to continue to learn the finer points of the game, and by this time was making regular visits to stay at the home of the legendary Jack Karnehm and his wife Jean in Berkskire.

Mike says: "Jack has been my main influence. He has more knowledge than anybody I have ever met and he taught me the real art of the game."

In July, 1989, Mike set off to Leura in New South Wales to contest the world championships for the first time, which were organised by the top snooker player Eddie Charlton. It was to be a memorable occasion for the 20-year-old Russell, when he landed the crown at his first attempt.

In the quarter-finals, Russell overcame Ian Williamson from Leeds by 1155-857, and then he beat his old rival Dagley in the semi-finals.

It set the scene for an all-Teesside showdown in the final, because Russell was paired with his good pal, 21-year-old Peter Gilchrist from Middlesbrough.

Gilchrist, who had beaten Charlton in the semis, was quickest off the mark, but once Russell had taken the lead there was no looking back and the Marske man went on to triumph by 2242-1347. In winning the crown, Mike produced remarkable breaks of 457 and 593, the latter winning him an extra £1,000 for the highest break of the tournament.

Russell pocketed his best ever pay cheque of £5,000 for winning the event, while Gilchrist would be satisfied with the second prize of £3,400.

The following year Russell achieved a further milestone when he won the World Matchplay Championship, beating the skillful Indian Geet Sethi at the Soviet Army Officers Club in Moscow. The event took place in a huge basketball arena and attracted 4,000 interested Russians, though even then the building was only half full.

Russell made a great start and seemed to be home and dry when leading 6-1 in the best of 13 frames final. But Gethi hit back to draw level at 6-6 before Russell won a tense last frame decider.

There was no world championship in 1990, but Russell retained his title the following year in India, when he

By 2000, Mike Russell has won an amazing 31 major billiards titles including the World Open Championship, the World Matchplay and the United Kingdom Championship.

overcame the rugged Australian Robbie Foldvari by 1352-957 in Delhi.

Foldvari worked hard to push Russell all the way, and at one time the Aussie was in front. But Russell took command with a break of 263, made in just ten minutes, and with the aid of a further three 200-plus breaks gradually pulled away.

Mike was back in Bombay in 1992, seeking a third consecutive world title. He beat his fellow Teessider Peter Gilchrist in the semi-finals to qualify for a showdown against Sethi in the final.

Russell played well, but on the day the Indian was in magnificent form, and it was Sethi who took the title. The result was the same the following year when Sethi again beat Russell in the world final in Bombay. However the match was totally different to the previous year's affair as Russell came away wondering how he had lost it.

At one time the man from Marske was 700 points clear and looking set to regain his crown. Sethi was struggling at that time, but then the Indian took advantage of a fluke shot to go on and put together a run of 700 which pulled him right back into the match. In fact he compiled another 300-plus break on his next visit and Russell spent the best part of an hour and a half sitting in his chair watching the title slip away.

The 1994 world championship final in Bombay saw Russell come up against his good pal Peter Gilchrist in the final. Unfortunately Mike failed to get his game into gear and was never in the hunt following a poor second session, which Peter won comfortably by 887-209. The final result was 1539-645 to Gilchrist, who gained revenge for his world final defeat by Russell in 1989.

The year of 1995 was not a particularly good one for Mike, especially as it was the only time he had failed to reach the world championship final since he won it for the first time in 1989. He was beaten by Roxton Chapman from Peterborough in the quarter-finals.

Mike also lost in the final of the Golden Cue tournament against former world snooker champion Steve Davis. The competition was played in Delhi and was a novel event, encompassing billiards, snooker, pool and a cue sport called carom which is popular on the sub-Continent. The tournament was a bit of fun, but there was a very strong international field, and Mike did well to reach the final.

Russell bounced back in style by winning the world championship for the third time the following year, when overcoming his old rival Sethi in the five-hour final.

The Marske man took control from the start and established a lead of 1,500 after four hours which Sethi had little chance of retrieving. As a result Mike was able to relax for the final hour and enjoy the scent of victory.

He had been in top form throughout the competition, recording a mammoth break of 770 under the baulk-line rule in the semi-finals against David Causier. Mike recorded a second big win in India that year when snatching the World Open in Onissa, beating Roxton Chapman in the final. He took command with a break of 640 and then recorded two more huge breaks in quick succession which left Chapman with little chance. However it was still a notable victory because Chapman had been in electric form earlier in the competition, having recorded a break of 600-plus in beating Sethi in the semis.

There were no world championships in 1997, but Mike was back in the final the following year, only to lose by 385 points to Geet Sethi, in the Indian's home town of Ahmedabad.

Mike had gone into the final in good form, having earlier compiled the highest break in the tournament when making 489 against Robbie Foldvari in the semi-finals.

However he did not play well in the final, and found it hard going, especially as he was very much the underdog. All the supporters were feverishly backing Sethi in his home town, but the Indian didn't play too well either and in the end it was a close run thing until the closing stages.

In the same year Russell beat Sethi in the UK Championships at Harrogate, when recording a massive world record break of 957 under the baulkline rule in the final.

Mike also produced one of his best ever performances in the British Open at Liverpool when he overcame Chris Shutt from Stockton in the final. Mike played consistently well and recorded an average of 168 per table visit including successive breaks of 850 and 500-plus.

Mike maintained this fine form the following year by carrying off the world crown for the fourth time, beating Peter Gilchrist in the final at Madras.

The final was played 2000-up, and was not a classic. But Mike always held the edge to win comfortably by more than 1000 points.

In March 2000, the duo met again the the final of the World Matchplay Championship at Bath. The match was played 1500-up and Peter came out on top by 1500-1200.

Mike and Peter are teaming up again, this time to launch a coaching initiative which they hope will give billiards a shot in the arm for the New Millennium.

They plan to take their billiards roadshow to a series of national venues to re-introduce people to the joys and skills of the game.

In addition Mike has ambitions to see billiards featured on mainstream television in a series of half hour programmes. He wants to emulate the former Pot Black programme, which introduced many viewers to snooker several years ago. Mike has been working hard to devise a format which might appeal to television programme makers.

In addition, Mike intends to return to his roots and start playing cricket again, though not at a serious level. His brother Neil is already an accomplished cricket player and, after spending many years successfully at Marske, was appointed professional for Normanby Hall in the 2000 season. Neil also works as a sports development officer for Redcar and Cleveland Council.

Mike, who has two sons, Karl and Luke, has lived in various parts of the country over the past ten years, including Birmingham, Clacton and Peterborough. But for the time being he is once again happily settled in Marske.

Keith Schellenberg
Bobsleigh

BOBSLEIGH racing, rugby union, motor cycling and motor racing not mention ski-ing - these are just a few of the sports in which the extraordinary adventurer Keith Schellenberg has excelled.

Primarily, he will always be best known as a record breaking motor racing driver who became captain of the British Olympic bobsleigh team. But few sports were not encompassed by his thirst for danger and excitement. If there was a challenge involved, there was nothing that Keith was not prepared to take part in.

Clifford Keith Wain Schellenberg was born in Marton on March 13, 1929. His father, C R Schellenberg, was managing director of the Cleveland Product Company, where Keith eventually became works manager.

The Schellenberg family originally came from Wurtemberg, in South Bavaria, in the middle of the Nineteenth Century, and made their home in Teesside shortly before the end of Queen Victoria's reign.

Although he took part in sport at his preparatory school and at Oundle School, Keith was a fairly slight youngster in his early teens, but developed quickly and was a hefty wing forward by the time he joined Middlesbrough Rugby Club.

He played for the Middlesbrough club for several seasons and became captain in 1954, when the team lost only three matches in the whole season. Later he went on to represent Yorkshire, making his debut against Cumberland and Westmorland at Kendal in 1959. He became captain the following year and won eight caps altogether.

On leaving school, Keith had joined the Royal Artillery and, after taking his commission, became sports officer of a unit in Scottish Command. The job embraced such diverse activities as running a motor cycle stunt team to organising ski-ing trips, while he also laid out a speedway track and virtually wrecked two bikes in his attempts to lower the track record.

It was apparent from an early age that the quest for speed and adventure was a great lure, and it was to dominate Schellenberg's life. After leaving the Gunners, he bought his first racing car, a supercharged Ulster Austin Seven in 1950, but later purchased the famous Riley Nine which the legendary Freddie Dixon had raced in the 1930s.

With Freddie's help, Keith developed a full understanding of motor engines and began to win races. He set two class records, as well as winning an international hill climb at Bo'ness and a national 1500cc sports car race at Charterhill in May, 1953. In the latter race he had been lying second following a neck and neck battle with the Scot Ian Hopper, whose challenge ended when he lost a wheel close to the finishing line. But Schellenberg deserved his stroke of luck because he was driving the only vintage car in the race, and also the one with the smallest capacity.

His next car, a vintage four and a half litre Bentley, was highly successful and Schellenberg proved his love of danger when winning the international race on the icebound lake at St Moritz.

He also acquired an eight litre Bentley Barnato-Hassan, which had set the track record of 144mph at Brooklands before the Second World War. This car was tough, quick and very impressive, and Keith won races at Silverstone, Aintree and Charterhall behind the wheel.

In front of an estimated crowd of 20,000, Keith entered the mighty Bentley in the popular Redcar Sand Races in 1954. He streaked past the finishing line to set a new record for the standing mile, clocking 76.9mph to beat the 19-year-old record of 75mph which had been held by Londoner E J Moore.

Initially, Schellenberg's interest in ski-ing was purely for pleasure, because he built up a series of strong friendships from his regular trips to St Moritz. However he excelled at ski-ing, and eventually began to take winter sports seriously, putting up the best downhill time for Britain in a competition at St Moritz. Tobogganing came just as easy to Schellenberg. Once again it was the high speeds and the scent of danger. After only three days' practice on the Cresta Run at St

Multi-talented sportsman Keith Schellenberg not only represented Great Britain in the Olympic bobsleigh and tobogganing but he also excelled in many other activities including rugby union, ski-ing and motor sport.

Moritz, he made a name for himself when he finished a close second in the classic Macklin Cup handicap race behind the veteran millionaire American Edmund Nelson from Honolulu. Nelson conceded 7.2 seconds to Schellenberg over the three heats of the race, and squeezed home by only 0.8sec after the third heat. The American Olympic captain, Fairchild Macarthy, was

pushed into a distant third place.

Keith was placed in several other races in 1950, and was awarded the Crammond Cup for the best performance without an actual win.

The switch from one-man tobogganing to the more popular two and four-man bobsleigh racing was a natural step, and Schellenberg was given the perfect grounding in the sport as 'brake' to his old rival Nelson. Keith braked for the four-man team which won the Waller Cup and, in 1953, he had enough experience to begin to drive the bobsleigh.

Schellenberg steered his team to victory in several club races before taking second place in the Grand Prix at St Moritz, and third place in the Swiss championships. In January 1955, Keith combined with former British ski-ing champion Stewart Parkinson to achieve 11th position in the two-man event in the world bobsleigh championships at St Moritz. They achieved an aggregate time of 5min 42.35sec over the four runs of the 1,749 yards Olympic course.

Seven days later Schellenberg drove the British bobsleigh to a highly commendable eighth position in the team event at the championships, clocking an aggregate 5min 17.83sec over the four runs.

At the end of the season Schellenberg was asked to captain the British four-man bobsleigh team for the Winter Olympics in Cortina D'ampezzo in Northern Italy in January, 1956. It was a great honour, especially as Keith was asked to undertake much of the preparatory work and organise training.

There was a great deal of work involved and, as a result, Keith was forced to relinquish his role as captain and secretary of Middlesbrough Rugby Club for the 1955-56 season.

Keith helped to organise the fine-tuning of Britain's two four-man bobsleighs, including a brand new one costing around £750 which was donated by Stavros Niarchos, the Greek oil tanker millionaire. The British Motor Company also kindly provided a lorry for the transportation of the equipment.

Although Keith and the rest of the team arrived in Italy in good time, the facilities for training were not available. So the Britons had to keep fit by playing scratch football matches with local teams.

It was hardly the ideal preparation for an Olympic competition, but Britain raced well and Schellenberg guided the team to 11th place. Their secret weapon of using plastic attachments on the runners of the sled was not a success, and they were removed after the first run. As a result, the British team were able to improve their time for their second run by more than three seconds, and clearly would have finished higher than 11th without the attachments.

Keith promised to fare much better in the two-man bobsleigh with his partner John Rainforth when they were lying third after the first run. However they lost two seconds on a poor second run, and dropped to 11th. The following two runs were more successful but there was too much ground to make up.

In February 1957, Schellenberg again guided the British team to 11th place in the world championships in St Moritz, though he fared better in the two-man boblet, combining with Chris Williams to take sixth place.

Keith was again playing rugby for Middlesbrough by this time, and continued to develop his interest in motor racing.

This general interest was to lead to a more practical involvement when Schellenberg became managing director of Nesham Garages Ltd in 1961. At the time he was driving a 1920 Model T Ford around Teesside, though he still retained his two Bentleys and also a legendary Ferrari which had previously been owned by his very good friend the Marquis de Portago before his untimely death in the Mille Miglia race.

Keith was also instrumental in the opening of the Croft Autodrome racing track, where he became a founder director.

Power boat racing had become one of Keith's new passions by this time, and in June, 1963, he partnered William Shand-Kydd of London to win the Sussex off shore race, which was one of the top three races of its kind.

The duo were competing in their newly acquired boat, the 31-foot Blue Moppie, which held the record for the 1,200 miles New York to Miami race when owned by the American Dick Bertram.

Not that Keith had lost his love of snow and ice. In the same year he competed in the world toboggan championships at Imes, in Austria, and was the highest placed Briton, finishing 59th.

As a result, he was selected to represent Britain in his second Winter Olympics in 1964. This time the event was held at Innsbruck in Austria. The Continental opposition in particular was hot, but Keith did well and improved dramatically on his performance at Imes when finishing in 25th position.

Schellenberg became chairman of the Middlesbrough Liberal Association in 1962, and was twice selected to fight the Richmond parliamentary seat in consecutive general elections on behalf of the Liberals. However he was unsuccessful in his attempts to become a Member of Parliament.

Ever looking for fresh challenges on the sporting front, Schellenberg flew out to Africa to compete in the

Angolan Grand Prix, and later decided to use the experience to good use by entering his 1930 Bentley Sports tourer in the London-Sydney marathon. Keith had bought the 140mph eight-litre car in 1963.

He left London with his co-drivers Patrick Lindsay from London and Norman Barclay from Glasgow in November, 1968, with a target of travelling 1,000 miles a day on the way to Bombay, from where they would be shipped on to Western Australia for the final part of the race.

The trio made a good start and hopes were high as they sped through Europe. However they lost five hours in Turkey when an oil-pipe snapped, and were forced out of the race the following day. En route for Teheran, the dirt road crumbled under the weight of the three-ton Bentley, which slid into a 20-foot gully. Lindsay broke his collarbone in the accident, but Schellenberg was unhurt.

Keith had bought the Whitby Whitehall shipyard in 1965 and was developing it as a yachting centre. It was the base for a series of yachting and powerboat events off the coast of Whitby, while Schellenberg also commissioned the building of a new boat which he entered in the round-Britain powerboat race.

The 27-foot craft was named Botany Bay Express and was built at a cost of £5,500. The boat was lying 22nd after six legs, despite developing a hole in the hull which the crew filled with clothing in order to stay afloat. They thought they had solved the problem at the start of the seventh leg, from Dundee to Whitby, but the boat began shipping water again and they had to return to Dundee and retire from the event.

Despite passing his 40th year, Schellenberg was still playing rugby whenever possible, turning out for the Middlesbrough lower sides.

However he was now living in Scotland, in Udny Castle in Aberdeenshire, and was taking a keen interest in the different way of life around him.

Ever looking for something new to test his levels of sporting endurance, Schellenberg took part in the rugged Scottish Six-Day Motor Cycle Trial in the Scottish Highlands in 1973. He rode a Montesa machine in his first ever competitive motor-cycle event, but was forced to drop out at the end of the second day with wheel trouble.

The same year, Schellenberg bought the 300-ton steam yacht Scharnhorn, which was reputedly built for Kaiser William in 1907. There was danger afloat for Keith simply bringing her to England, from Cuxhaven,

because the old vessel had to struggle manfully through a force nine gale. It must have been a worrying time, especially as the Scharnhorn was making the longest journey of her life.

In 1974 Schellenberg was back in his Bentley to compete in the World Cup Rally, which was planned as a three-week trek, starting from London, and covering Europe, North Africa and Asia. Having been joined by co-driver Hamish Moffat, Schellenberg suffered a disaster on the first day when the entire wiring loom on the Bentley burned out and left them in last place at the end of the first leg.

They decided to continue with the race and crossed Europe, albeit in the minor placings, before reaching the North African coast. They found it increasingly difficult as they crossed the Sahara and, along with many of the other crews, were unable to complete the race.

In 1975 Schellenberg became a Scottish laird when he paid £265,000 to buy the island of Eigg, after outbidding the Highlands and Islands Development Board. The 8,000 acre island, which is south of Skye, is the second largest of the Small Islands, which also include Rhum, Canna and Muck.

Keith immediately set about reviving the island's economy, and introduced many revolutionary plans to reverse the population drift. Sport was ever on his mind, and he arranged inter-island hockey matches. He also inaugurated the Eigg Island Games, which involved every man, woman and child on the isle, and also many of his friends from the St Moritz Tobogganing Club!

The Round Britain Powerboat race was revived in 1984, so Schellenberg, now aged 55, felt compelled to enter. He competed along with co driver David Dunnell in one of the smallest craft in the event, a 25ft Class III boat.

There was no rest for the intrepid adventurer. The following year, Keith turned his attention back to bobsleigh when a series of events were organised to celebrate the 100th year of the Cresta Run. Keith headed off for St Moritz with his family and eight litre Bentley to race the car on ice, and also compete in nostalgic bobsleigh events. It was fitting that Keith should take part in one of his last serious sporting contests on the ice at St Moritz.

Schellenberg reluctantly sold Eigg in 1995 and returned to the mainland, since when he has devoted his time to his family, friends, cars and writing.

Ronnie Sewell
Football

WALTER Ronald Sewell was one of the outstanding goalkeepers of his time. He was an FA Cup winner with Burnley in 1914, before belatedly winning his one and only England cap at the age of 33, a decade later with Blackburn Rovers.

Born in Middlesbrough on July 19, 1890, Ronnie was playing for Wingate Albion in the old North Eastern League when he was offered the opportunity to join Gainsborough Trinity in 1911. Gainsborough were in the Second Division at the time, but their stay in the Football League was not to last much longer because they failed to win re-election and were demoted to the Midland League in 1912.

However, in February 1913 after an impressive display in a second round FA Cuptie at Turf Moor, Ronnie was signed by Burnley, as understudy to Jerry Dawson, the future England goalkeeper. In fact his move was the start of a procession, because shortly afterwards, half of the Trinity side followed him to Burnley and also signed for the progressive Lancashire club.

The next season saw Sewell quickly make his mark as a solid goalkeeper who was cool under pressure. He deputised for the injured Dawson during the Clarets outstanding cup run and kept a clean sheet at Crystal Palace as Burnley beat Liverpool 1-0 in their first ever FA Cup Final appearance. This was also the first showpiece at which a reigning monarch, King George V, had presented the trophy.

Despite helping Burnley make history the amiable Teessider soon found the presence of Dawson restricting his opportunities at Turf Moor. So, when league football resumed after the Great War, Sewell switched his Lancashire allegiance and signed for Blackburn Rovers in February, 1920. He had only made 27 first team appearances for Burnley. During the next two seasons Ronnie missed only a couple of matches and helped to stabilise a previously indifferent Rovers defence. His consistent performances were rewarded with an England call up for the 2-1 international defeat by Wales at Ewood Park on March 3, 1924.

Middlesbrough-born Ronnie Sewell was an FA Cup winner with Burnley in 1914.

Sewell eventually became a very popular figure at Blackburn with both supporters and players alike and was particularly renowned for his marvellous sense of humour, which was always guaranteed to raise dressing room morale.

Unfortunately, after 248 appearances for Rovers, his career came to an abrupt end when he broke a leg in September, 1926. And, despite an abortive attempt at a comeback, the serious nature of the injury forced his retirement from the professional game at the end of that season.

In September, 1927, Ronnie's playing career finally turned full circle when he returned to Lincolnshire to once more link up with non league Gainsborough Trinity. Like many other footballers he later became the popular licensee of a local public house and continued in this profession until his death on February 4, 1945.

Norma Shaw

Bowls

NORMA Shaw is one of Britain's outstanding bowls players of all time, and as tough an opponent for male rivals as she is for female.

She learned to play the sport on Teesside greens and progressed quickly, reaching the pinnacle of her sport in Toronto in 1981, when she became world singles champion.

Norma then went on to win a remarkable collection of medals, many of them at the world championships.

She won world silver medals in the triples in 1988 and 2000, took silver in the fours in 1988, bronze in the singles in 1981, 1985 and 1988, bronze in the triples in 1992 and bronze in the fours in 1996.

In addition she helped the English team to win the overall world team trophy in 1981, 1988 and 2000.

At the Commonwealth Games, Norma won a triples bronze at Brisbane in 1982, a bronze in the singles in Victoria, Canada, in 1994 and a fours bronze in Kuala Lumpur, Malaysia, in 1998.

Norma has also excelled in the Atlantic Rim Games. She won a gold medal in the singles and a silver in the pairs in Florida in 1993, while also helping England to win the team trophy.

In Durban in 1995, Norma won silvers in the singles and pairs, and also took silver again when the Atlantic Rim Games returned to S. Africa at Cape Town in 1999. She also excelled on the indoor greens, taking the world singles title at Llanelli in Wales in 1997, before being beaten in the final in a strong bid to retain her crown at the same venue the following year.

Norma was awarded the MBE in 1985 for her magnificent contribution to the sport.

Born in the village of Stanley, near Wakefield, on June 8, 1937, Norma is a Yorkshire girl born and bred. She moved to live in Norton when in her early twenties and has been a great ambassador for the area as a whole, and is very much an adopted Teessider.

Norma attended The Grove primary and Stanley Secondary schools, and later started work as a cake decorator, latterly for Wm Jackson and Son Ltd.

She first became involved in the alternative game of Crown Green bowls because her husband Dennis played for the Post Office team in the Wakefield League.

However Norma was not particularly interested in the game and it was not until Dennis's work with the Post Office brought him to the Station Road office in Billingham that she started out on a bowls career which was to prove to be one of the most successful of all time.

Dennis and Norma had gone out for a walk and just happened to stop and watch the bowls players on the Norton green. They entered into conversation and were invited to join the club, which they did.

Rapidly, Norma emerged as a top quality player in the late 1960s. She began to win the first of a series of domestic titles at Teesside Indoor Bowls Club, where she was given support and encouragement from the great Tom Fleming to start entering national competitions. Norma also joined the nearby Ropner Park club for the higher standard of competition, but also continued to play for Norton.

In 1975, Norma appeared on a national stage for the first time when she forced her way through to the final of the English Indoor singles championship, and was back in the final again two years later. However, on both occasions, she was beaten in the final. There was some consolation when Norma helped Ropner Park take the outdoor fours at Leamington Spa, though she did lose another final when beaten by Betty Stubbings from York in the national four woods singles event.

At the same time, Norma was learning and progressing, and she had attracted the attention of the England selectors, who called her up to compete in the home international series.

The national title mould was finally broken in 1978, when Norma beat Jean Lord from Dartford in the women's singles final at Rugby, finishing strongly to win 21-14.

She followed up by landing the British Isles indoor

Norma Shaw's outstanding international bowling career was capped in 1981 when she became World Singles Champion. Even top class male bowlers such as David Bryant, above, found it tough going playing Norma.

crown, after recovering from a 9-6 deficit against Scotland's Margaret Ross to record 15 points without reply and lift the trophy by 21-9.

The year marked Norma's arrival on the national stage. She won the English Women's Bowling Association's two woods singles championship at Leamington Spa in the August, beating W Fletcher of Dorset 17-10 in the final.

There was no stopping Norma now. In 1980, she beat Pamela Ward from Croydon by 21-20 in the English women's indoor final, and then combined with her Teesside colleague Phoebe Spence to beat J Sweet and M Wessier from the King George club in the pairs final. It was only the beginning. Norma confirmed her status as the top indoor player in Britain by going on to win the British title, beating Frances Whyte from Paisley 21-8 in the final at Cardiff. Then she again combined with Phoebe Spence to win the pairs, beating Margaret Pomeroy and Shirley Proctor from Wales 20-10 in the final.

Outdoors, Norma ticked off another title when winning the national pairs title with Myra Burnett from Billingham.

Norma reached a pinnacle in 1981 when she took the singles title at the world championships in Toronto, making sure of the gold medal by winning 15 of her 17 matches. Flo Kennedy from Zimbabwe took the silver with 13 wins.

Victory was extra special because the quality of the greens was a bit disappointing. They had been iced up during the winter and had not been run in before the championships. It meant that they were heavy. But Norma quickly adapted to the conditions and was in top form right from the start.

She did not feel the pressure until the final game, when she played badly, while all the time being told by other competitors that she was guaranteed the gold whatever happened in her last match.

Characteristically, she snapped out of her poor form and finished strongly to win her final game.

Norma also took the bronze medal in the pairs, when partnering Irene Molyneux. She had started the event in partnership with Gloria Thomas from Cornwall, but Gloria was taken ill and had to drop out. The world bowls authorities kindly allowed Irene, who was the team's manager, to take Gloria's place for the final games. After the tournament, Norma, Irene and Gloria were all presented with bronze medals.

Early in 1982, the awards followed. Norma was named Vaux Sportswoman of the Year for the North, and then later picked up the Cleveland Sports Personality of the Year Award.

The highlight of 1982 was the Commonwealth Games in Brisbane, and Norma did not return empty handed. She combined with Mavis Steele and Betty Stubbings to win the bronze medal in the triples.

The trio took some time to come to terms with the greens, which were covered in a type of Canadian weed which grew sideways rather than upwards. However they went on to win ten and draw two of their 15 games, and were very close to snatching the silver medal. However they were held 17-17 in their final match against Swaziland, knowing that one more shot would have edged them ahead of silver medallists New Zealand.

The gold went to Zimbabwe, who had met the English trio in the very first match. Ironically the English ladies had led 12-5 at one time, but went on to lose the match 22-16.

The following year Norma won the English indoor crown for a record fourth time when she beat Betty Stubbings by 21-16 in the final at Scunthorpe, after coming back strongly from 16-15 down. Then Norma combined with Phoebe Spence to win the pairs for the fourth time, beating B Hall and G Lamb from London by 29-13 in the final.

In the summer, Norma won the English two-wood singles title by beating Joan Plackett of Worthing by 16-9 in the final at Leamington Spa. Once again Norma came from behind, having trailed 8-6 at the half-way stage.

In 1985, Norma flew out to Melbourne to defend her world singles crown. She was always in contention but knew that she could not win the gold medal by the time the event reached its last day.

The final match was a major disappointment for Norma, who lost 21-7 to new champion Merle Richardson from Australia, who had always looked the strongest player in the competition. Norma had been looking forward to the meeting with Merle, though she was disappointed when the date of their clash was moved, and the new date coincided with a spell of bad weather. Norma could not adapt to the gale conditions and was well beaten.

Fiji's Maraia Lum On took advantage of Norma's defeat to take second place, while Norma was edged out of the bronze position by New Zealand's Rhoda Ryan.

So Shaw had to settle for fourth place, though she did have some consolation, after taking the bronze in the pairs with her partner Jean Valls from Surrey.

Norma was still the outstanding English player, and won the national women's indoor title for the fifth time in 1987 when she comfortably overcame Barbara Till from Portsmouth by 21-6 in the final at Northampton. The following year she repeated the feat, this time beating Edna Bessell from Yeovil in a cliffhanger by 21-20 in the final at Manchester, after coming back typically from 20-18 down.

Earlier Shaw had teamed up with her Teesside club colleagues Phoebe Spence and Jenny Berry to win the triples title by beating the Cherwell team from Oxford by 25-8.

In 1988, Norma travelled to the world championships in Auckland in New Zealand, where she scooped silver medals in both the triples and fours. She also helped England to win the team trophy.

Sadly, husband Dennis died in 1989, but Norma had the support of a large number of friends in the bowls community in the area. She had already put down strong roots in Norton and continued to play for the local teams.

The world championships were held in Ayr in Scotland in 1992 and Norma took bronze medals in the singles and the triples.

The following year, the Atlantic Rim Games were held in the United States and Norma flew out to Florida for this inaugural event. She hit sparkling form, taking the gold medal in the singles and silver in the pairs.

In 1994, Norma was back on Commonwealth Games duty again in Victoria in Canada, this time taking the bronze medal in the singles.

The Atlantic Rim Games moved to Durban in S. Africa the following year and Norma returned to Teesside with a couple of silvers, from the singles and the pairs. She had to settle for bronze again in the world championships at Leamington Spa in 1996, this time in the fours.

Norma Shaw displays one of the many bowling medals she has won throughout her remarkable career. No other female bowler has managed to attain the same high level of consistency which has hallmarked her success.

Norma earned another Commonwealth Games medal in 1998, when she took the bronze in the fours event in Kuala Lumpur in Malaysia.

This medal was very hard earned, because the humidity was stifling at times, and all the bowlers had to regularly intake liquid to prevent dehydration.

In addition, all five greens played differently to each other, and so the English quartet of Shaw, Katherine Anton and Mandy Jacklin from Peterborough and Shirley Page from Hertfordshire did well to adapt and finish in the medals.

In the same year, Norma completed a full set of bowling honours when she won the national singles championship at Leamington Spa. It was the only event she had previously failed to win, having taken the two wood, pairs, triples and fours.

She also picked yet another award when named Daily Telegraph bowler of the year.

The Atlantic Rim Games returned to South Africa the following year and Norma flew out to Cape Town. She played well, and took silver in the singles.

In 2000 Norma was still competing at a high level and travelled to Moama, near Melbourne, for the world championships. She enjoyed a successful run in the triples, eventually settling for the silver medal and was part of a trio along with Katherine Hawes from Oxford and Jill Polley from Essex which finished top of their section to qualify for a showdown in the final with New Zealand.

Unfortunately Jill was unable to take her place in the final because of a leg injury, so manager Norma May stepped in. The Kiwi ladies held the upper hand on the day to win 21-16.

Norma also played in the fours and was not too disappointed with a fifth place, while the trip ended in success when England won the overall team trophy.

Harold Shepherdson
Football

HAROLD Shepherdson never pulled up any trees as a professional footballer but he achieved international recognition as England's trainer when the World Cup was famously won at Wembley in 1966.

Along with his outstanding career with England, he also served his home town club, Middlesbrough, with distinction in a variety of capacities for more than half a century.

Shepherdson was born in Elm Street, Middlesbrough, on October 28, 1918, and attended Marton Grove School, from where he won a scholarship to Hugh Bell Grammar. Academically proficient, he gained school certificates in a wide variety of subjects, including maths, English and French, and also became head boy. Young Harold was a very gifted all-round sportsman, playing football for Hugh Bell School and having the distinction of playing both cricket and football for Middlesbrough and Yorkshire Boys in the same year.

He was a big strong lad for his age and was signed by Middlesbrough on amateur forms in 1932 after some commanding performances at centre-half for South Bank East End. Like most local lads of his generation his ambition was to become a full-time professional with the Boro and this he achieved four years later, leaving his job as an office boy with the Richard Hill Wire Works Company behind him.

However, opportunities to stake a claim for a place in the first team were few and far between and Harold played for the Boro only 14 times before the outbreak of the World War Two. One of his appearances was particularly noteworthy because he marked the great goal machine Dixie Dean out of the game. So much so that after the game the usually prolific Everton centre-forward congratulated Harold on his performance.

Harold joined the Green Howards in 1939, but because of his football background was quickly transferred to the Army Physical Training Corps at Aldershot. There he studied physiology and anatomy before eventually becoming a staff sergeant instructor. Once fully qualified, he went on to Bedford Barracks and worked in the convalescent department, re-establishing the physical fitness and mental confidence of the men returning from the evacuation of Dunkirk.

As a result of this academic training he was to become one of the new wave of backroom staff whose modern methods would eventually sweep through the post-war English game.

After the hostilities were over he made only three more appearances for the Boro before being transferred to Southend United in May 1947. This move proved to be an unhappy experience for Harold because before he had even kicked a ball in anger for the Shrimpers, a serious knee injury brought a premature end to his playing career.

He returned to Teesside and on the recommendation of the retiring and long-serving trainer Charlie Cole he joined the backroom staff at Ayresome Park as assistant to new trainer Tom Mayson. He took over the mantle of head trainer in the early 1950s. Once in charge he was able to implement his own ideas and make the training regime less reliant on building fitness and stamina and more ball skills orientated.

Shepherdson was appointed England trainer in 1957, for the match against Wales at Cardiff, serving under Walter Winterbottom and later Sir Alf Ramsey when he became England manager in 1963. Harold participated in four World Cup Final campaigns and attended to needs of the players through a record 171 games. He was justly awarded the MBE for his services to football in 1969. The Football Association also awarded him a testimonial match and this was held at Ayresome Park in May 1973.

Back at Ayresome Park he became assistant manager to Stan Anderson in 1966 and then Jack Charlton, whose single-minded determination he admired greatly. During his time at Middlesbrough, Harold took over as caretaker manager four times but made it clear he had no desire to undertake the job on a full-time basis, preferring to work behind the scenes.

Harold Shepherdson served Middlesbrough and England with great distinction for over 50 years. He was England's trainer in July 1966 when they won the World Cup Final beating West Germany 4-2 at Wembley.

In October 1983 he retired as Middlesbrough's chief executive of football and pursued a part-time career in the media covering football for the local station, Radio Cleveland.

Over the ensuing years he spoke at many functions, both locally and nationally, always generously donating his fees to the diabetic centre at Middlesbrough General Hospital because he himself had become a diabetic and was grateful for the help and support he had received from the medical staff.

In the early 1990s he was invited to return to Middlesbrough FC as a matchday host, firstly at Ayresome Park and then at the BT Cellnet Riverside Stadium.

Harold died suddenly on September 13, 1995. His funeral was held at St Cuthbert's Church, Marton in Cleveland, and was attended by many of the greatest names in British football.

In his honour, the road leading to Middlesbrough's new Cellnet Riverside Stadium has been named Harold Shepherdson Way. It is a fitting memorial to a loyal and respected club servant.

Kendra Slawinski
Netball

KENDRA Slawinski is England's most capped netball player, having made 128 appearances for her country between 1982 and 1995.

She captained the England team in her fourth world championships in 1995, having previously played in 1983, 1987 and 1991, and has continued her involvement with the sport since her retirement by coaching at the highest level. In fact her charismatic personality and dedicated work have done much to raise the profile of netball over the past decade.

Born Kendra Lowe at Sedgefield on November 11, 1962, she grew up in Billingham among a sporting family.

Her father Kenneth had played football for Boro Juniors, her mother Lilian played netball and contested the high jump, while her elder brother Ken went on to win England semi-professional football caps.

Kendra attended Pentland Junior School and later Northfield School, and took part in hockey, netball and athletics to district and county standard.

In fact she could easily have concentrated on athletics instead of netball, having gained a bronze medal in the shot putt in the English schools championships in 1980. In all she contested the schools finals on five occasions, latterly as captain of the team.

Kendra also dabbled with the pentathlon for a while, but began to concentrate her energies into netball when she won England Under-18 international recognition in the winter of 1980.

Kendra started her career as goal attack, but reverted to goal defence and went on to make this position her own throughout her career.

She grew quickly and became a formidable netball opponent, reaching almost six feet in height and eleven and a half stones in weight. It was her strength and power, allied to her natural talent and unique determination, which quickly earned her the captaincy of the England Under-18 side, which she held for two years.

Throughout the following three years, Kendra played for the England Under-21 side, but she was also promoted to the England senior side at the age of 19 in 1982 and established herself immediately.

Her first senior tour with England was to the world championships in Singapore in 1983, when she helped the team reach a creditable fourth place. Kendra had fully expected to be sitting on the bench, but she had trained hard and was very fit, so she warranted her place in the team.

England qualified for the semi-finals via the group games, but were beaten by New Zealand in the battle for a place in the final. This left England contesting the third and fourth place play offs, and they lost again, this time to Trinidad and Tobago.

Back in England, Kendra started a degree course at Bedford PE College which was eventually to lead to a 2:2 honours degree. During each of her four years at the college, she helped Bedford to win the British Colleges Championship.

Kendra was also playing for the East Region and attending the centre of excellence, where she received expert coaching from England coach Heather Crouch. These sessions turned out to be significant in helping her career development.

In 1985 Kendra toured Australia with England and the team played in the Australia Games in Melbourne, where they again had to settle for fourth place, again being beaten in the play-offs by Trinidad and Tobago. However the final result was a major disappointment because England had been winning by seven points and looking set for the bronze medals, until their goal shooter was 'taken out'. This affected the whole balance of the side and they lost by a couple of points. On their return to England, the team competed in the World Games in London and were fourth again, this time being beaten by Jamaica.

Kendra's first job upon leaving college was a teaching position at a school Rickmansworth. She also joined the Hertfordshire county side and helped them to victory in the Inter Counties KO Cup.

Former England captain, Kendra Slawinski, did much to raise the profile of netball during her record breaking 128 international appearances which included participating in four world championship tournaments.

Twelve months later she moved to her current school, the Cardinal Newman RC School in Luton, where she eventually became head of PE.

Kendra toured Fiji and New Zealand with England in 1987, in the build up to the world championships, and they recorded a notable draw against the Kiwis.

However the New Zealand women gained revenge in the semi-finals of the world championships in Glasgow, winning by ten points. There was further disappointment for Kendra and England when they went down by four points to Australia in the third and fourth place play off.

In 1989 England did well in the World Games for non-

Olympic sports in Karlsruhl in Germany, when they finished third.

On her return home, Kendra was promoted to captain of the England team and held this position until her retirement.

The captaincy offered Kendra the opportunity to be involved in the selection process and to express her opinion at top level.

Kendra returned Down Under again in 1990, leading England in a Tri Test series against Australia and New Zealand, though the English women finished third.

The following winter Kendra suffered a major injury setback when she tore her cruciate ligament and dislocated her knee when she landed awkwardly during a game for the East Region. She was in plaster for a total of five weeks, and sidelined from the game for over nine months, during which time she was given constant and extensive physiotherapy.

It was assumed that she would not be fit for England's trip to New Zealand in May, 1991, but she made a remarkable recovery and announced her return to full fitness shortly before the team was due to leave.

Kendra played in the first two Tests, but suffered another setback when she aggravated a cartilage problem in the Second Test and was rushed to hospital in New Zealand for an operation.

The cartilage had apparently been damaged at the time of her initial knee injury, but had been left lying loose in its joint.

It seemed highly unlikely that Kendra would now have any chance of competing in the world championships in 1991, but she had other ideas. She was naturally a quick healer, but she was also a totally dedicated trainer. In fact she managed to build up the muscles in her knee in lightning quick time.

As a result, she came through a very thorough medical examination in Sydney, prior to the championships beginning, and was passed fit, much to the amazement of the England selectors.

Naturally she was a key player during the championships, but England again had to settle for fourth place, being beaten by Jamaica in the play-offs.

Kendra led England to great success in 1993 when they toured Jamaica and won the Test series by 3-0. It was England's first Test series win for 20 years.

Later, they took part in the World Games in The Hague, but surprisingly lost in the play-offs to Jamaica - by just two points - and had to settle for fourth place. The same year Kendra Lowe became Kendra

Slawinski, when she married husband Tim, whom she had met at college.

Later in the year there was another cause for celebration when Kendra earned her 100th England cap in the Second Test against Trinidad and Tobago at Birmingham. Even better, it was part of an England clean sweep as the home country won 4-0.

Kendra toured New Zealand with England the following year, but all three Tests were lost, while there was even more disappointment in the world championships in Birmingham when England again finished fourth, losing to New Zealand in the play-off. In all four world championships in which Kendra played with England, the team never failed to reach the semi-finals. But they lost them all, and also lost the ensuing play-off matches, having to settle for fourth place on every occasion.

In November 1995, Kendra officially announced her retirement at the end of a Test series against the Cook Islands, which England won 2-1. By the December, she was already assisting with coaching the England Under-15s in addition to coaching at county and regional level.

The following year she coached the England Talent Development Squad, and since then has worked with the England 2000 squad which was working towards the World Youth Cup in Cardiff. In 1999 she went to Australia as assistant coach to the England Under-21 touring team.

Kendra played regular club netball throughout her career. She had started with Stockton Pioneers as a teenager and went on to play for Vauxhall Golds for 15 years. While with the Golds, she doubled up and also represented the Linden team from Birmingham, helping them to three national club championships from 1987-89.

Kendra joined the Bedfordshire county side at the same time as she moved to the Cardinal Newman School in 1986, and played for them until 1998. She was also player-coach of Bedfordshire for five years, helping them to win the national league championship in 1996.

Her commitment to the sport was rewarded when she was awarded the OBE in the 1996 New Year Honours List for her services to netball.

Kendra and Tim now have a son, two years old Ben, but Kendra still finds time to serve on various netball committees in addition to undertaking a hectic programme of coaching.

Bobby Smith

Football

BOBBY Smith was the epitome of what was traditionally known as "a typical old-fashioned centre-forward". Big, bustling and brave.

He made his name at one of football's glamour clubs, Tottenham Hotspur, during the 1950s and 60s, playing a prominent part in helping them to win, in quick succession, the League Championship, the FA Cup on two occasions, and the European Cup Winners Cup.

Robert Alfred Smith was born on February 22, 1933, in Scarth Street, Lingdale, which was the village where George Hardwick also spent his formative years. Bobby was the son of a miner.

As a youngster he played for Lingdale Council School, Redcar Boys Club and Redcar United before attracting the attention of Chelsea scout Tommy Robinson. Tommy recommended the burly forward to the Blues manager, former Boro star Billy Birrell, who eventually signed Smith on amateur forms in May, 1947.

Bobby, on his own admission, was not the prettiest of footballers to watch but his tough, muscular, battering ram style often intimidated defenders and goalkeepers alike, and it was this hard physical approach to the game which helped him secure a professional contract at Stamford Bridge in May, 1950.

He made his debut for the Blues at the age of 17, eventually scoring 30 goals in 86 senior appearances. But personality clashes with new manager Ted Drake resulted in a lack of consistent first team opportunities. However, in December 1955, Bobby Smith's career was turned completely on its head.

Tottenham Hotspur, who were then surprisingly languishing near the foot of the Division One table, signed Smith to solve their goalscoring problems, for a fee of £16,000.

He was an immediate success, quickly scoring the vital goals necessary to only just maintain Spurs' status in the top flight, before going on to play a leading role in what were to be the club's glory years.

During the 1957-58 season Bobby scored 36 goals, which equalled the White Hart Lane club's league record, and by 1960 he was finding the back of the net with such regularity that he'd also become Spurs' highest aggregate goalscorer.

His prolific performances for his club were eventually acknowledged at international level when he was awarded his first England cap in October, 1960. Not surprisingly, he made a scoring debut in a 5-2 victory against Northern Ireland in Belfast, a game which, coincidently, also saw the debut of Middlesbrough full-back Mick McNeil.

In all, Smith scored a commendable 13 goals in 15 appearances for his country.

During the famous Spurs double winning year of 1960-61 Bobby was the club's top scorer, hitting some crucial cup goals, including the first in the FA Cup Final against Leicester City. The following year he repeated the feat at Wembley when Spurs retained the trophy with a 3-1 victory over Burnley.

In 1962 Spurs signed the mercurial Jimmy Greaves from Italy, and together with the combative Smith their contrasting styles formed the most feared striking partnership in English football at that time. The following season Tottenham conquered Europe by winning the Cup Winners Cup by 5-1 against Atletico Madrid with the Spaniards finding the imposing physical presence of Smith impossible to handle.

Rather surprisingly, however, at the end of the 1963-64 season, with Smith now turned 30, Spurs highly respected manager, Bill Nicholson, decided that Frank Saul would partner Greaves up front. So, after 358 games, during which time he'd scored an amazing 251 goals, Bobby Smith was sold to Brighton for £5,000.

Again he was an immediate success, scoring 18 times as the South Coast club stormed to the Fourth Division title. However, a series of inappropriate newspaper comments made during the close season saw him sacked from the Seagulls.

In October, 1965, he joined Hastings United and spent an 18 months spell with them in non-league football. By the late 1960s however, Bobby was increasingly

Bobby Smith, right, was an old style, robust centre-forward whose keen eye for goal played a significant part in Tottenham Hotspur's double winning success of 1961-62.

troubled by old injuries which were a painful legacy of his whole-hearted style. Apart from a brief period in 1968 playing for Banbury United, he was forced to retire from the game.

Unfortunately once out of the football spotlight, and with no time-served trade or skills to fall back on, Bobby had a series of jobs including painting and decorating and driving in order to support his wife and three sons. In 2000, having endured a hip replacement operation, he lives in retirement in Palmers Green, London.

He will, however, always be remembered with great affection by the Spurs supporters as a player from the North-east whose totally committed attitude helped to make Tottenham Hotspur England's most successful league club of the early 1960s.

Jackie Smith
Parachuting

RED Devil Jackie Smith took to the air and entered the Guinness Book of Records by becoming the first person ever to achieve ten perfect jumps in winning the world parachuting accuracy championships.

She dropped in from the dizzy heights in Zagreb in Yugoslavia in 1978 to land perfectly on a target no bigger than a beer mat and beat the cream of the world's top parachutists.

Jackie was the first woman ever enrolled by the Red Devils and went on to compete all over the world, jumping in several world championships and winning a silver medal in the team event in 1979. She also won a silver in the World Cup in 1983.

In 1986, she was asked to open the Commonwealth Games in Edinburgh by dropping into the stadium from the sky.

Belatedly, her achievements were recognised in 1999 when she received the Royal Aero Club's gold award from Prince Andrew at a special ceremony in London.

Jacqueline Smith was born at No.6, George Street, South Bank, on March 29, 1952, and grew up in Bevanlee Road with her two brothers and two sisters. She attended Middlesbrough Road and Napier Street schools, before going on to St Anne's Secondary Modern. She was sports mad as a schoolgirl and competed in everything possible. She was the mainstay of the netball team and also swam for the school.

Her life was changed overnight when a recruiting sergeant from the Women's Royal Army Corps arrived at the school and revealed the full extent of the sporting facilities which were available to people in the forces. Jackie immediately wanted to be a physical training instructor and joined the WRAC on her 17th birthday.

She had to learn a trade in the army and started out as a telephonist at Aldershot, but was keen to take part in physical events and enrolled on a parachuting course. She had never been in the air before, never mind in a parachute, but she immediately displayed uncanny talents.

In 1971, when she was only 19, Smith won the novice section of the Army's free-fall championships at Netheravon Airfield in Wiltshire, making six jumps over the week-long event and beating seven male rivals to land the title.

Jackie was then asked to train to with the Red Devils, the Parachute Regiment's daring free-fall team, and began to learn the finer skills of the sport. After successfully completing more than 100 jumps and taking part in a training programme in Germany, she officially became part of the 24-strong team. She was the only female member.

Jackie suffered a minor scare in May, 1972, when her main parachute failed to open during a 4,000 feet jump at a Red Devils display at Swansea. She had bent the top pin on her back pack on the top of the door as she was leaving the plane.

At the time she was falling at speeds of up to 200mph. Fortunately the reserve parachute opened at 1,200 feet, even though 13 of the 22 panels had split, and Smith was able to steer herself away from the Welsh city, landing 400 yards out into the sea in Swansea Bay. Immediately she inflated her lifejacket and was picked up from the ice-cold water by a rescue boat.

At the time, Jackie said: "I was coming down so fast that, if I had not fallen into the sea, I would have been killed. I don't remember feeling frightened. I just looked up, saw that the reserve parachute had opened, and I said 'thank you'."

On another occasion, she had a major problem when her head whiplashed and smashed her altimeter, but Jackie survived the incident and was undeterred.

She finished third in the Army championships at Weston on the Green in Oxfordshire in May, 1973 and was the only female competitor. Later in the year she became the first female to be awarded the coveted Red Devils beret following a 5,000 feet skydive on to a parade ground at Aldershot.

Smith's remarkable talents were rewarded in 1974 when she was selected along with three male colleagues

Jackie Smith was the first woman to be enrolled in the Red Devils elite parachute team.

from the Red Devils to compete in the world championships in Hungary. She did not feature in the top 20, but it was invaluable experience for the South Bank woman.

Jackie was promoted to sergeant in 1975, and the following year she completed her 1,000th jump, celebrating soon afterwards when being selected to compete for Great Britain in the world championships in Rome. She was in with a chance of a medal at one stage, but a disappointing jump ended her hopes.

In 1977, when she was 25, Jackie decided to leave the army to concentrate on developing her involvement with parachuting. She found work in the personnel department of a company in Farnborough, Hampshire, and later headed off to Pope Valley in California for six weeks training with the Symbiosis parachuting team.

The same year she was the only woman selected to jump for Britain in a major competition in Brisbane in Australia, following the Symbiosis team's victory in the eight-man event at the British national championships. She found work as a secretary in Sydney, and stayed on for several months.

Jackie's success in the British championships at Bridlington in 1978, when she won the women's section and was fourth overall, earned her a place in the fourth world championships in Yugoslavia. It was to lead to the biggest moment of her career.

Smith made two trips to the United States as part of her training programme and it paid immense dividends. She leapt ten times from the aircraft in Yugoslavia and gained full marks on all ten occasions, for making perfect landings on a tiny disc which was her target. It was the first time in history that anyone had ever recorded ten consecutive perfect landings.

Jackie went into the tournament full of confidence, but suffered a nervous time between her ninth and tenth jumps when the championships were suspended for three days because of bad weather. She was just one perfect jump away from creating history, but also knew that her major rivals were only a few centimetres behind her, and a poor final jump could even leave her out of the medals.

Fortunately Jackie made no mistake with her tenth effort when the competition resumed, winning the women's world free-fall parachuting accuracy championship and a first ever gold medal for Britain in the sport. She beat off competition from sky divers from more than 30 other nations, including the crack parachutists from the USA and the Eastern bloc.

However Jackie discovered that her life did not change for the better despite having won a world title for Britain.

She was unable to find temporary secretarial work when she returned to Britain because of the recession and was struggling to pay her way in parachuting, having poured all her spare money into winning the world crown. Eventually she took the very difficult decision to sell all of her sky diving clothes and equipment to raise cash.

Her financial plight did not go unheeded on Teesside and Langbaurgh Council stepped in with a vital grant, which meant that Smith was able to prepare properly to compete in the world team championships in Chateau Roux in France the following year.

She spent three weeks training in California before returning to win two team first places in the British championships in Wiltshire. She toned up for the world event with another trip to the States, and helped the British four-man team to take second place at Chateau Roux.

Unfortunately she never had the chance to defend her world individual accuracy title the following year because she could not afford to attend the training camp in the United States.

In 1978 South Bank's Jackie Smith made history when she completed ten perfect parachute jumps in the world accuracy championships. Her amazing feat was recorded for posterity in the Guinness Book of Records.

Between 1980 and 1981, Jackie found work in the United States, where she parachuted every night into the Kings Island theme park in Cincinatti, Ohio. This gave her enough cash to continue with her training.

As a result she again made the British team for the world championships in Zephyr Hills in Florida in 1981, and helped them into fourth place.

She suffered a blow the following year when she was involved in an accident when she was sitting in a stationary vehicle which was rammed in the back by another car. As a result she had to wear a collar for nine months and needed ultra sound treatment on a hip injury. However Jackie made a full recovery and made the British team again for the World Cup in Graz in Austria in 1983, winning a silver medal in the accuracy event.

Later Jackie found work as a courses clerk in the joint services department at the parachute centre at Netheravon, which enabled her to carry on practising her jumping in her free time. At the same time, she also met her future husband.

She won a major competition in Germany in 1985 and was proud to accept an invitation to open the Commonwealth Games by jumping into the Meadowbank Stadium the following year.

At the time, Jackie was three months pregnant with her first son, Scott. She was 34 when Scott was born and had a second son, Ross, 20 months later.

As a result, she devoted her time to bringing up her boys and did not jump for five years. However she did return to jumping and it was not until 1999 that she eventually decided to fold up her parachute for the final time, having completed more than 4,000 jumps in her career.

Finally, Jackie received full recognition for her remarkable achievements as a parachutist when she travelled to London to accept the Royal Aero Club gold award in 1999 which added her name to an esteemed list of previous winners which included the Wright Brothers and Amy Johnson.

Despite having given up parachuting, Jackie has discovered the joys of ski-ing, and travels abroad with her sons to improve her skills whenever possible. At home, she is still highly competitive, and plays badminton regularly.

She now lives in Salisbury and works as a school secretary, but visits Teesside occasionally to visit her sisters Marion and Jeanne.

Maxie Smith
Boxing

MAXIE Smith staked his claims for a slice of boxing history after winning the ABA light-heavyweight crown in 1967.

The stylish Stockton boxer had all the necessary attributes to make a big impact in the professional ranks, and so it proved.

He took on, and defeated, some of Europe's top light-heavyweights and moved to the verge of the British title at a time when world class boxers like John Conteh and Chris Finnegan were ruling the roost.

However the big break which Maxie so richly deserved finally deserted him, and the pinnacle of his career was an unsuccessful attempt to try to win the Commonwealth light-heavyweight crown in 1975.

Donald Maxwell Smith was born in Leeds on November 3, 1942, but arrived in Teesside with his family at the age of six and grew up in Stockton. He was educated at Oxbridge primary school and then Stockton Grammar School. He swam and ran the cross country at school, but never adapted his competitive edge to team sports.

When he left school, Maxie joined the Royal Marines. It was to be the most significant decision of his life. His nine years and 11 months' stint with the Marines helped him develop his basic boxing skills, but more importantly it gave him the discipline and self respect to stay fit and look after his body. In fact Maxie has taken part in some form of physical exercise virtually every day since he quit boxing 25 years ago.

Smith was initially stationed in Malta after completing his basic training with the Marines. He dabbled with boxing within the confines of the unit while in Malta and lost his first two contests. The following year he had another two contests, and lost both of them as well. Maxie made the decision to box on until he won a fight, and then intended to hang up his gloves. But his first win in 1963 was the forerunner to more victories and suddenly he began to develop a feel for the sport. In his third year as a boxer he took on an experienced trainer, who altered his full-blooded aggressive style by introducing basic boxing skills.

By 1966, Maxie had moved up from middleweight to light-heavyweight and had developed a successful style. He won the Middle East Land Forces Championship, while stationed in Aden, and also made a major impact in domestic competitions.

The following year he had established himself as one of the best amateur boxers in Britain and made a strong bid to win the Senior ABA Championships.

Luck seemed to have deserted him at the quarter-final stage when Maxie fell ill with a burst appendix and was rushed to hospital to undergo an operation. Amazingly, the boxing authorities knew nothing of the operation, and Maxie somehow managed to get himself back into the ring again and went on to reach the ABA finals, where he outpointed Richard Owens at Wembley to take the title on a majority decision. It was an incredible victory, especially as Maxie knew that his level of fitness was well below par.

Smith's battling victory was enough to earn him a place in the British boxing squad which was training for the 1968 Olympic Games in Mexico.

However he suffered major disappointment when he was informed that he was one of only two ABA champions who would not be selected for the trip to Mexico. Even so, he would probably never have made the trip even if selected. He broke his hand in a sparring session with the heavyweight champion and suffered recurring hand problems as a result of the injury. Smith was given some recompense when representing England in internationals against Scotland and Ireland, knocking out both opponents. He dispatched the Scot, D Frape, in the first round at the Albert Hall, and then beat the Irishman Pat Long in the third round in Dublin.

Maxie was also selected to box for England against Russia, but was withdrawn by the Royal Marines because members of the British forces were not allowed to compete in communist countries at that time. Maxie looked set to retain his ABA crown in 1968 when making a strong burst through the early rounds. But he broke his hand again, when beating Willie Stack in the semi-finals, and was forced to withdraw.

In November that year, Smith turned professional, even though he was still a Royal Marine. His rather sceptical commanding officers were initially not too happy, though Maxie attracted plenty of publicity for the Marines, which helped to compensate.

He signed for London manager Arthur Boggis, who was a butcher by trade, and made an immediate impact in the pro ranks. He won seven of his first ten fights, dropping a decision only to the up and coming Welshman Roy John. As a result, Maxie rose very quickly to No.7 light-heavyweight in Britain.

Maxie loved the life and the camaraderie between the pros, but continued to suffer from recurring setbacks with his hands. He decided that he could not overcome the problem and announced his retirement. However he had one more fight against the tough heavyweight Bunny Johnson in March, 1970, in order to earn enough money to pay off a tax bill, before hanging up his gloves.

When Maxie left the Marines, he returned to Teesside and took up a job with the Gas Board. He was offered the chance of a gym at Stillington, which he gratefully accepted. It gave him the chance not only to maintain his high level of fitness, but to help anybody else who wanted to benefit from the facilities.

Fortunately Maxie made a full recovery from his hand problems and the lure of the ring began to prove irresistible again. He decided to re-apply for his licence, and intended to manage himself. His comeback fight was in January 1973, when he stopped the much travelled Harry Scott from Bootle in the fifth round in Stoke. It was a polished performance, and proved to Maxie that he had lost none of his ability. However his hardest fight came afterwards, when there was almost another punch-up as he battled for his purse.

Smith then linked up with promoter Tommy Miller and had a busy first year back in the ring, winning all nine fights. He also earned a bit of useful cash which he used to improve the quality of his gym.

Maxie's progress was so dramatic that he was nominated for a British title eliminator after beating fourth ranked Briton Graham Sines from Wandsworth on points in a top of the bill eight rounder in Blackpool.

However he improved on that performance with a battling victory in a non-title fight against reigning British middleweight champion Bunny Sterling at Earls Court. The win was noted by many top boxing people because it came on the undercard of the Joe Bugner-Joe Frazier bill. Smith had a reach advantage over Sterling and used it to great advantage to outscore him.

In October, 1973, Smith outclassed the experienced American Ed Duncan, who had previously inflicted the only defeat of his career on Britain's leading light-heavyweight John Conteh, who was the current European, Commonwealth and British champion. Smith met Duncan at Belle Vue, Manchester, and Maxie was a convincing winner by six rounds to one, with three drawn. Duncan started each round strongly but Smith was too busy for him and always finished in control.

The following month he was back in the ring again as a last minute replacement opponent for return meeting with the tough Welshman Roy John, who had been beaten in a British title challenge by Chris Finnegan earlier in the year. Maxie met John, the third ranked Briton, on his home territory of Sophia Gardens in Cardiff, but silenced the fervent Welsh crowd by gaining a revenge win on points.

Smith was immediately promoted to No.2 in the British rankings and was being touted as a potential title contender. He managed to fit in another fight before the end of the year, stopping Bob Tuckett of Leeds in seven rounds at the Anglo American Sporting Club in Manchester.

On February 1, 1974, Maxie earned a decent pay night when travelling to Hamburg to take on the 26-year-old German Karl-Heinz Klein, who was world ranked. However the Stockton man was controversially stopped in the seventh round with a cut eye.

Maxie was ahead at the time when he was blatantly head butted by the German. The cut which resulted was later described by Maxie as the "smallest cut I had ever known in my life". But it was enough to bring a home town decision.

Smith bounced back by pulling off a superb win at Wembley in March, when he beat southern area light-heavyweight champion Pat McCann. The 22-year-old southpaw from Harrow had won 19 of his previous 20 fights and was widely expected to make a big name for himself in the fight game. McCann still gave Smith one of his toughest fights, but the Teessider dug in to take the decision.

Maxie then met foreign opposition again when flying out to Africa to take on the Zambian champion George

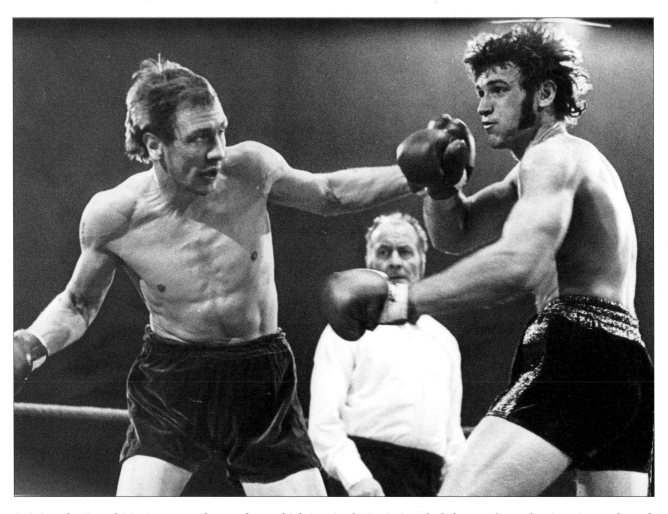

Joining the Royal Marines was the catalyst which inspired Maxie Smith, left, to take up boxing. As a talented amateur he won the ABA light-heavyweight title, but professional championships were to prove elusive.

Chisenga in Lusaka. Maxie floored Chisenga in the fifth and sixth rounds and had his man down on another three occasions before the referee intervened to stop the fight in the seventh.

Maxie had flown out to Africa with experienced Glaswegian middleweight Don McMillan, who was due to fight Zambian Hugo Chasa in Kitwe. Maxie watched the fight from ringside, and was alarmed to hear stories that McMillan's opponent had previously suffered fits and blackouts.

The Scot won the fight by knocking out Chasa in the fifth round. McMillan and Smith were later sitting on the plane in Lusaka, waiting to fly home, when they were arrested by the Zambian authorities. It emerged that McMillan's opponent had died after the fight. McMillan eventually missed the flight, but Smith returned to explain the whole story to the foreign office and pave the way for his colleague's eventual release.

However Maxie had returned to England without his pay cheque and it took several months of haggling before the promoter paid him part of the original agreed purse.

There was no movement on the title front, but Smith kept busy. He travelled to Vienna in the June but was stopped by Ave Peralta in the third round. Then he flew back to Africa, this time to Johannesburg, and recorded a stirring fifth round knockout win against Jan Kies.

Five weeks later Maxie stepped in as a last minute replacement for Phil Matthews at Manny Shinwell's 90th birthday boxing evening at the World Sporting Club in London, and beat the Argentinian Raul Loyola on points over ten rounds. Smith had just recovered from a bout of flu and didn't expect to win. But he was always in control and won by five rounds.

Remarkably, at the age of 31, Smith was still awaiting

to box in his first fight in the North-east. But a dearth of suitable promotions, and a lack of boxing halls, had forced Tommy Miller to accept fights elsewhere.

In December, 1974, Smith seemed to be on the verge of a major breakthrough when he was nominated to fight holder John Conteh for the British light-heavyweight title. There was an added incentive because Conteh was now world champion and, according to British Boxing Board rules, Conteh's world crown would also be on the line.

Naturally it seemed very likely that Conteh would relinquish his British title, but it also inferred that Smith would then be nominated to box for the vacant crown, possibly against former holder Chris Finnegan. Sure enough, Conteh abdicated his British crown soon afterwards, and plans were made for Smith to meet southpaw Finnegan for the vacant title. The British Boxing Board announced that the winner would also be nominated to fight for Conteh's Commonwealth light-heavyweight crown.

Smith's clash with Finnegan was set for February 19, at Belle Vue in Manchester, but there was a bodyblow for the Stockton man and his supporters when Finnegan pulled out less than a month before the fight was to take place. Finnegan had strained ligaments in his leg during a sparring session with the Scotsman Tom Imrie.

A replacement opponent was needed quickly, and promoter Mickey Duff brought in tough 20-year-old Hungarian-born Australian Steve Aczel, who had won 11 of his 12 professional fights inside the distance. The fight was billed an an official eliminator for Conteh's Commonwealth crown.

On February 11, Conteh also relinquished his Commonwealth crown - and Smith was matched with Aczel for the title.

The officially sanctioned title fight was great news for success-starved boxing fans on Teesside, who bought £2,000 of tickets for the big night.

Smith trained solidly up to the big fight showdown, fitting in his training around his regular job as a gas board collector. Two days before the fight he made 114 collections.

Maxie could not have been fitter, but he fought the wrong tactics on the night and was hammered to defeat by the strong punching of the Australian. The Stockton man was stopped just two seconds from the end of the third round, after taking a lot of punishment.

Smith had known absolutely nothing about his opponent before the fight. Maxie was encouraged to go forward by his corner, which was contrary to his individual boxing style because he was always a counter puncher. Unfortunately Aczel was taller, with a longer reach and the Australian fought a Smith-style fight to win comfortably on the night.

Maxie admitted later that he had fallen into the same trap as many of his own opponents in the past. He had also been a hot favourite to win, whereas he was usually the underdog and always planned his fights accordingly.

After the fight Smith suffered from severe concussion and a trapped nerve in his back, and announced his retirement.

He could not solve the back problem with regular medicine, so went back to the gym and developed his own remedial therapy. Then he began to train harder than ever and eventually got down to middleweight.

Maxie felt fitter than ever at this stage and decided to re-apply for his licence, but his application was not supported by the British Boxing Board.

It was the end of his boxing career, but by no means the end of the story. Maxie continued to develop his gym facilities and managed several local boxers, including Reg Long and Tony Kelsey. Later he linked up with local promoter John Spensley, and the duo provided local boxers with the opportunity to achieve something for themselves.

Maxie has since run several different gyms, and has never been without one. He has always been happy to continue to provide the facilities for himself and the people of Teesside. His latest gym is at the Acklam Hotel in Newport Road.

Several boxers have come through his hands, but at no time has Maxie ever encouraged people to go into the sport. He says: " Boxing is a seriously dangerous sport and I would never suggest that anybody should do it. But I know that it is something that some people just have to do. In those situations I can help to ensure that their energies and efforts are channelled in the right direction."

Women's boxing is a relatively new sport with which Maxie has beeen involved and he has helped to develop the skills of local boxer Jan Wild.

Maxie retired from the Gas Board in 1996, and has since continued to run his gyms and work as a doorman at pubs and hotels in the area. He lives in Stockton with his wife Julie and daughters Laura and Emily.

Russ Smith
Canoeing

RUSS Smith was a top slalom canoeist from Acklam who paddled his way right to the top of his sport and won the world championship in 1987.

He was also British and Commonwealth champion and a seasoned international who competed all over the world.

John Russell Smith was born in Middlesbrough on November 12, 1963, and was introduced to canoes at the same time as he started Kader primary school.

His father Len was a keen canoeist who was coach to Tees Kayak Club, and he made Russ's first canoe himself. Russ later attended Oaklands School and played a bit of football and ran cross countries, but mainly to tone up his fitness levels for his canoeing. He eventually moved on to Acklam Sixth Form College in Middlesbrough and was grateful for the support of the headteachers of both Oaklands and the sixth form college, who gave him Wednesdays off to attend the regional canoe centre of excellence at Leeds. By the time Russ was 16, he was already a very accomplished paddler and was selected for the Great Britain team for the European youth championships in Germany and Austria. He made a big impression in the tournament, finishing 11th out of 165. He picked up a series of penalty points, which cost him the chance to take second place. However he was second best British finisher.

The following year, with a wealth of experience behind him, Russ returned to the European youth championships to take the bronze medal in the individual event. However he did even better in the team event, linking up with Mike Druce and Andy Gladwin to take the gold medal.

As soon as he had returned to England, Russ set off for the regional event in the English Open youths' championship at Harrogate, where he won the individual race.

Russ went on to totally dominate the Open, taking five of the six races and finishing second in the other. He clinched the championship with a win in the final event in Wales. Not to be outdone, he also finished 11th in the British senior championships.

Russ broke through into the senior international ranks in 1982 when making his Great Britain debut in an international in Litovsky-Miklaus in Czechoslovakia. Smith finished 15th overall, while he joined the Great Britain A trio to finish fourth overall in the team event. He had a chance of making the British team for the Barcelona Olympics, but missed out by just three tenths of a second in the qualifying race.

The following year Russ was studying for his A Levels and this affected his training programme, though he still carried off the national indoor slalom at Crystal Palace.

In the summer, Russ set off for the Swedish Open Championships and won the individual event. The following year he gained tremendous experience by being selected to compete in the American International Canoe Grand Prix on the man-made Thunder River near St Louis, Missouri. However Russ was not content to fly to the United States simply for the experience. He won the gold medal in the individual event, beating many top slalom canoeists. He also did it the hard way, because he was not allowed to take his own canoe on to the plane. So he had to borrow one from another paddler when he arrived in St Louis.

The same year Russ picked up a prestigious award when he was named Cleveland sports personality of the year.

Smith was selected to compete in the Europa Cup in 1984 and made a great start in the first leg in Czechoslovakia, when he took third place, finishing just five seconds behind the winner, world champion Richard Fox from Staffordshire.

In the second leg, in Germany, Russ did not enjoy the best of luck. He picked up two penalties for going through gates sideways, and it had a big effect on his final placing, leaving him well down the field.

Russ teamed up with Ian Raspin from Skelton and

In 1987, canoeist Russ Smith, achieved his ultimate ambition when he became World Slalom Champion.

Melvin Jones from the West Midlands to form the Great Britain B team which won the canoe slalom in the pre-world championships event at Bourg St Maurice in France. However Russ did not fare so well in the individual event, finishing 22nd.

He quickly made amends when he defied an attack of flu to become British Open slalom champion at the National Watersports Centre at Holme Pierrepont, near Nottingham. Soon afterwards, he followed up with a victory in the national closed championships.

In 1987, Russ achieved his long term ambition when he won the world championship at Bourg St Maurice. He did make much of an impact on his first run and it looked as though he could finish out of the medals. But Russ was not fazed by the situation, and dug deep to produce a phenomenal effort in his second run to clinch the world title.

When he returned to Britain, he journeyed up to Scotland to contest the Commonwealth championships at Grantully. Both runs were excellent and Russ returned to Teesside with another title.

The following year he took part in the European championships, which consisted of two runs, one on the River Liffy in Ireland and the other at Holme Pierrepont at Nottingham. He finished seventh in Ireland and fourth in Nottingham, which was good enough for fourth place overall.

During the winter Russ headed off for Australia, where he defended his Commonwealth title just outside Perth, and was successful in retaining the crown. He also stayed Down Under for some time, as a guest of the Australian Canoe Federation, and coached the top young Aussie paddlers.

At this time Russ had moved to Barnard Castle to open the Four Seasons shop, which specialises in canoes and other outdoor pursuits equipment.

Running a business began to eat into Russ's training time, but he still qualified for the world championships on the River Savage in Maryland in 1989, and finished 26th overall.

This was his last major tournament, and he settled down to concentrate on running his business and also increase his coaching commitments. He has coached many top young paddlers over the past ten years, including Anthony Brown from Durham, who has won a place in the British team for the World Cup, and also under-23 international Simon Jackson.

Father Len has coached at the highest level since Russ first took to the water, and was coach to the British junior team for many years. All the top British paddlers of the new generation have come through his hands. In addition Len continued to coach Teesside-based paddlers, and at one time was coaching 13 paddlers at the same time on Hemlington Lake, all of whom were members of different national squads.

Len and Russ combined their talents at the launch of the white water course on the Tees Barrage in 1995 and have together run the canoeing and rafting activities since that time.

The opening of the white water course made Russ realise that there was the chance of a comeback, especially he had such top class training facilities at his fingertips. So he began training hard with a view to trying to win a place in the British squad for the Atlanta Olympics.

However his hopes were ruined when he suffered a broken leg in an accident on the Upper Tees in 1995. Russ has settled in Barnard Castle, where he lives with his wife Juliette and children Jack, and Katie.

Dick Spooner
Cricket

RICHARD Thompson Spooner was one of the biggest names in County Championship cricket in the 1950s, making seven Test appearances for England.

Dick was born in Stockton-on-Tees on December 30, 1919, and was a forceful left handed opening batsman and wicketkeeper.

Spooner began his cricket education as a junior player in the North Yorkshire and South Durham League at Thornaby. Later he moved the short distance to Norton, where his father Bob was a more than useful wicketkeeper before becoming a respected member of the Norton committee.

In 1936, Dick won the Crosby Cup award as Norton's young player of the year. Two years later he was a regular member of the first team, keeping wicket and scoring plenty of runs.

Before the Second World War, Dick served his apprenticeship as a fitter with Head Wrightson at Thornaby, and rejoined them after serving in RAF.

Dick also linked up with Norton again after the War and scored 110 not out in an unbroken opening partnership of 181 with Harry Thompson in a Kerridge Cup victory against Thornaby which was achieved with several overs to spare.

He started playing Minor Counties cricket for Durham in the same year, 1946, and was a crucial member of the side for two seasons. In 17 matches he compiled 473 runs at an average of 22.52, with his top score being 89. This was one of three half centuries Dick scored for Durham. He also took 12 catches and made 21 stumpings.

Spooner was a rather diminutive figure, only 5ft 7in tall, but his athleticism behind the stumps and his ability to amass big scores alerted Warwickshire CCC.

In 1947 Spooner became the first Norton batsman ever to score more than 1,000 league runs in a season, and he turned professional with the Midlands county the following year. He was already 28 when he made his county debut against Nottinghamshire at Trent Bridge, but he went on to make 312 appearances over the next 12 years. His batting was as important for Warwickshire as his wicketkeeping, and he amassed 1,000 runs in a season on six occasions.

His best season, both with the bat and behind the stumps, was in 1951, when he formed a formidable opening partnership with Fred Gardner and helped Warwickshire to win the County Championship for the first time for 40 years. He scored 1,767 runs and dismissed 73 victims, 53 of them caught and the rest stumped.

Not surprisingly, his performances earned him a place in England's winter tour to India, Pakistan and Sri Lanka. He had gained valuable experience in India as part of a Commonwealth team only 12 months earlier, and was selected by England to keep stumps in all five Test matches against India.

His finest moment came in the Third Test at Calcutta, when he compiled scores of 71 and a career Test best of 92 after being promoted up the order to open the innings. However, the Test was drawn, like the previous two in Delhi and Bombay.

Spooner eventually tasted Test success for the first time when helping England beat India in the Fourth Test at Kanpur. However, he was not so successful with the bat, making 21 and nought as England won by eight wickets.

India squared the series when England lost the Fifth Test by an innings and eight runs in Madras, though Spooner played well and hit 66 in the first innings. During the series he took eight catches and made two stumpings.

The following season Dick weighed in with 70 scalps for Warwickshire in the Championship, of which 54 were caught and the remainder stumped.

Spooner returned to the international arena in 1953 when he was called up for the winter tour of the West Indies. However, he was selected to play in just one of the Tests, the fourth in Port of Spain, making scores of 19 and 16 in a drawn match.

His last game for England came in the Fifth Test

Top international wicketkeeper, Dick Spooner, middle row, second left, began his distinguished cricket career with Norton C.C. who were NY & SD League Champions and Kerridge Cup Winners in 1937 and 1938.

against South Africa at The Oval in August 1955. Dick was drafted in as a wicketkeeper batsman for a match England had to win if they were to win the series. Unfortunately the match was something of a personal nightmare for Spooner, who was bowled for a duck in both innings by Hugh Tayfield, the brilliant off-spinner from Natal. Two catches in the South African first innings was little consolation, though at least Spooner had the satisfaction of finishing on the winning side. England won by 92 runs.

In Warwickshire's three-day match against the tourists earlier in the month, Spooner had fared little better with the bat, scoring two and 28. However, it was his immaculate display behind the stumps which had earned him his final Test call-up.

Dick was still a prolific run-getter for the county side. His career total of runs in the Championship was 12,014, at an average of 26.88. He also scored 11 centuries for Warwickshire. His total number of victims was 682, including 527 catches and 155 stumpings.

In 1957, Spooner was handed a well deserved benefit by Warwickshire and at the same time recorded a career-best six catches in an innings against Nottinghamshire at Edgbaston. In his final season he took eight catches in a match against Leicestershire, also at Edgbaston.

During the early 1950s, Dick also developed a sideline giving talks at cricket dinners, in addition to lectures and demonstrations.

He retired from cricket in 1959 and worked as an area sales a manager for Head Wrightson, initially in the Birmingham area and then later from Brixham in Devon.

Dick passed away in Torbay Hospital on December 20, 1997, aged 77, and was laid to rest at the local Torbay crematorium.

Harold Stephenson
Cricket

ONE of the best wicketkeeper batsmen of the 20th century was Harold William Stephenson.

Harold, who was an excellent middle order right hand batsman and possessed tremendous agility behind the stumps, made his name on the county cricket circuit at Somerset, where he took a county record 1,007 dismissals. He was one of the county's longest serving players, making 429 First Class appearances between 1948 and 1964.

He stands alone, statistically, as Somerset's finest wicketkeeper and the only major disappointment from his career was that Test recognition passed him by.

Stephenson was born at Haverton Hill on July 18, 1920 and attended Mill Lane School in Stockton before beginning work as a sheet iron worker in Billingham in 1936. He started his cricket career in the same year with Stockton in the North Yorkshire and South Durham League, having been awarded a three-year cricket scholarship by the club.

Harold was called up for the first time by Durham in 1944, but made only seven appearances for the Minor County over four seasons. This was because of the tremendous form of Durham stalwart wicketkeeper and club teammate Arthur Austin, who played 60 times for Durham between 1936-54. Stephenson later moved on to Billingham Synthonia in order to be able to play regularly behind the stumps.

Harold had to win his Durham place as a batsman, which he eventually did, scoring 169 runs at a solid average of 33.8. His best innings being 79.

During the Second World War, Harold also made his name as a fine footballer, and was an inside-left with Darlington before becoming a prolific goalscorer with Billingham Synthonia in the Northern League.

However, he was always more likely to make the grade as a cricketer, and Harold's potential was noted by Somerset and in 1948 he moved to the South-west.

Stephenson made his debut the following year and wasted no time establishing himself as the county's No.1 wicketkeeper, ousting the experienced Wally Luckes. He went on to become a prolific taker of scalps, accounting for 83 victims in his first season, in addition to progressing quickly as a fine attacking batsman.

The record books claim that Harold specialised in the seemingly suicidal pursuit of quick runs, but this only identified the youthful alacrity with which he bounded out of his ground.

Stephenson scored 1,000 runs during a season on five occasions for Somerset, and also compiled seven Championship centuries. His overall career total was 12,473 runs, made at an average of 20.05. His highest individual score was 147 not out against Notts at Bath in 1962.

Harold's 1,007 career dismissals included 698 catches and 309 stumpings. He also set a Somerset record of 86 dismissals in 1954, including 50 catches and the remainder stumped. He took 83 scalps in 1949, and 79 during his penultimate season at the age of 43 in 1963.

At Bath, in 1962, Stephenson took six dismissals in a innings against Glamorgan, including five catches. The following year he took nine victims in a match against Yorkshire at Taunton, including eight catches.

Despite his consistency, Harold was unable to break into the Test team because of the marvellous form of the legendary Godfrey Evans, but gained international honours when selected to tour India and Ceylon with a Commonwealth team in 1950-51. He led the batting averages with 71, including six not outs.

The last five years of Harold's career at Somerset were spent as county captain, having taken over from Maurice Tremlett, and he helped them achieve third place in the Championship in 1963. In fact they were in with a definite chance of the title until the closing stages. Harold's contribution that season also included 79 victims.

Stephenson was known as a pragmatic rather than a daring captain, but he was very loyal to his fellow professionals and it was noted that he was inclined to bristle when his county officials implied that it was

With over 1,000 first class dismissals to his credit, Haverton Hill-born Harold Stephenson was one of the greatest wicketkeepers of all time.

time to bring in 'wet-behind-the-ear' vacation players at the expense of the regular team-men.

At the end of his very distinguished first class career with Somerset Harold joined Dorset and played in the Minor Counties league. He also continued to live in Taunton and worked as a representative for a local brewing company, Hall and Woodhouse of Blandford, with whom he was employed until he retired.

In 2000, Harold Stephenson was 80 years of age and living quietly in the South-west of England.

Johnny Summers
Boxing

PROBABLY the best pound-for-pound boxer ever produced in Middlesbrough over several generations was action man Johnny Summers, who won British titles at three different weights.

In fact, in the years leading up to the outbreak of the First World War, there were few better fighters in this country between the featherweight and welterweight divisions than the gritty and determined Teessider.

The only major disappointment was that Johnny had moved down south to London by the time he started fighting and that's where the majority of his career was concentrated.

Johnny was born Johnny Somers in Middlesbrough on February 1, 1884. His family moved to Canning Town when he was a young boy, and Johnny boxed most of his distinguished career in capital's famous halls. After a fine amateur career, he decided to join the ranks of the professionals in 1900 when Queen Victoria was still on the throne.

In the early days of boxing, when fighters regularly fought in different weight divisions, there were often several claimants to the various championships and, as a result, there are conflicting reports of which boxers held which titles and at what times.

However, no specialist boxing commentator ever writes Johnny Summers out of the equation. His fine career is always acknowledged to be one of the best in the early 20th century by those who keep historical records of the noble art.

Johnny's dedication and total commitment paid dividends when he won the British featherweight crown on January 29, 1906, beating his tough fellow North-easterner Frank Spike Robson on points over 20 rounds at the National Sporting Club. The fight had been billed at the time as the 9st Championship of England.

Although NSC officially recognised Johnny's victory, the featherweight title was still claimed by Salford's Joe Bowker, who had won the 8st 12lb crown by previously beating Robson. These results effectively

Middlesbrough-born boxer star Johnny Summers won three British titles at different weights.

meant that Summers could not be officially credited with the undisputed featherweight title by all the boxing bodies.

Any lingering hopes that Johnny held of staking any fresh claims to the undisputed crown soon disappeared when he was comprehensively beaten in only four rounds by South Shields-born Robson in a return match, again held at the National Sporting Club, on December 17, 1906.

However despite this defeat, Johnny continued to ply

his trade at the very top level and was now a big name in boxing circles.

On November 23, 1908, he moved up a division to lightweight and secured the British title after beating the much more experienced Jack Goldswain from Bermondsey when the referee stepped in to stop the fight in the 14th round of a gruelling contest which was billed as an official title fight by the National Sporting Club.

Again Johnny's title claims were not universally accepted. Prior to the bout, Goldswain, who was seen as the undisputed lightweight champion, had weighed in for his defence against Summers a few pounds over the required limit, at 10st 4lb, and therefore the result was not recognised.

In 1909 the NSC announced they were introducing the prestigious Lonsdale Belts for the winners of British title fights. The belts would be held by champions during their reign, though any champion who won three title fights at the same weight would be allowed to keep the belt indefinitely.

On November 8, 1909, Johnny defended his lightweight crown against Freddie Welsh from Pontypridd. It was a chance for the Teessider to put the first ever notch on a Lonsdale belt. However the night was to end in total disappointment. It was Welsh who was to make history, as Summers was beaten on points after 20 very close rounds.

One of Summers' biggest wins came at the Memorial Football Ground at West Ham in London's east end when he knocked out the great American Jimmy Britt. The fair-haired Britt, despite nearing the end of his illustrious career, was still a huge name in the sport and attracted thousands of fans to the football ground. Britt had held the undisputed world lightweight crown from 1902-5.

Among the crowd that day was a young Ted Kid Lewis, destined to become a world welterweight champion in later years.

Despite his ever increasing weight problems, Johnny continued to push for the very top title honours. On June 17, 1912, he captured the British welterweight title, and the coveted Lonsdale belt, by beating Chatham's Arthur Evernden in London when the referee stopped the contest in the thirteenth round. It was Summers' third title success at different weights and was undoubtedly one of the finest moments of his boxing career.

Summers was now a big celebrity in British sport and was in great demand not only by advertisers, but also as a turn on the music hall stage. He appeared in adverts promoting boxing gloves along with other notable pugilists of the time such as Welsh, Lewis and British bantamweight champion Digger Stanley from Norwich.

Johnny held on to the welterweight title for more than two years, including a much heralded defence when he beat Sid Burns on points.

During his reign, Summers also fought in Sydney, Australia, where he laid claim to the British Empire welterweight crown.

However, he lost the Empire crown to Tom McCormack on a close points decision in January, 1914, and then towards the end of the same year he relinquished his British title when he was surprisingly defeated in fourteen rounds by the appropriately named Johnny Basham on December 14, 1914 in London.

This defeat was a major disappointment for Summers, because he would have earned a Lonsdale Belt outright if he had won.

Basham, from Newport in Wales, later went on to make unsuccessful attempts to wrestle the European welterweight and middleweight crowns from the great Ted Kid Lewis.

Freddie Welsh eventually relinquished the lightweight championship after the First World War. It was his second stint as champion and he had held the title for seven years. During that period he had also gone on to win the world crown. So, Johnny was offered the opportunity to lose a few pounds and challenge once again for the British title.

It was June 23, 1919, and although Summers was now 36-years-old he had trained hard and was still rated as one of the top 10st men in the country.

Johnny was matched with a 27-year-old Londoner, named Bob Marriot, for the title, and he rolled back the years to give a great account of himself. However despite being well in control in the early stages of the fight, fate decreed it was not to be Summers' night. He lost the bout rather contentiously on a tenth round disqualification to bring down the final curtain on a quite remarkable boxing career.

Johnny Summers' sparkling career spanned no less than 179 contests, of which 104 were won. A further 29 were drawn, while there were 13 no decisions, one no contest and just 32 defeats.

He died in 1946 at the age of 63.

Phil Thomas

Boxing

AS an organiser, administrator and coach, Phil Thomas's immense contribution to amateur boxing over 59 years is unsurpassed.

From 1934 until his retirement in 1993, the Stockton official progressed from his role as trainer, matchmaker and secretary of Teesside boxing clubs to travelling all over the North of England attending major tournaments adjudicating, refereeing, and eventually assessing the capabilities of new officials.

He was the North-east's 'Mr Boxing', who was known to every official and every boxer at every club, and who also became a member of the Amateur Boxing Association's national executive.

Thomas was an active member of the North-east division of the North-east Counties ABA from 1954, going on to join the examining panel, becoming chairman and president of the North-east division from 1976-79. He later served a second three-year term in the same offices.

Phil also served two terms as president and chairman of the North-east Counties, overlording a vast area which covered hundreds of amateur boxing clubs and thousands of boxers stretching from Northumberland to Hull.

His career as a boxing judge began in 1954 and he officiated at Wembley finals and international tournaments. Four years later he qualified as a referee. Eventually, Phil graduated to examining prospective new officials, and became chairman of the North-east Counties Adjudicators. He travelled around the North assessing and giving lectures to referees, judges, timekeepers and MCs.

His work in North-east circles led to him eventually becoming a life vice president of the North-east Counties executive of the ABA.

Philip William Thomas was born in Paxton Street in Stockton on July 20, 1910. His father, also Philip William, who worked as a driller at Ropner's Shipyard, was a sportsman in his own right. He was a top sculler, who had won the prestigious Tyne Boat Handicap in 1908.

Phil Junior was one of a large family of seven children, and was educated at St James's Primary and later Bailey Street School.

He started boxing while still at school but, unlike his younger brother Jack, who went on to become a useful professional, he did not hang on to his gloves. Phil picked up a series of rib injuries and decided to pursue his boxing career outside of the ropes.

He became trainer of the Billingham Synthonia boxing club at the age of 24, and held this position until the Second World War. After the end of hostilities, Phil was coach and club secretary, before taking a job in Portugal for 18 months.

When he returned home to Teesside, Phil resumed his duties with Synthonia, but then started work at ICI Wilton as foreman of the boiler plant. Once there he wasted no time in forming a boxing section. He was match secretary at Billingham and Wilton at the same time before eventually deciding to concentrate his efforts at Wilton.

In 1954 Thomas became an active member of the ABA North-east divisional executive, a role which he carried out for the next 39 years. In the same year he passed the ABA judges examination, and progressed quickly, being appointed to the ABA Major Panel of Judges two years later.

He went on to judge and referee at many major finals and internationals, before becoming an adjudicator in 1969.

In 1964 Thomas became ABA North-east divisional secretary and was elected a life vice-president seven years later.

Thomas retired from ICI as process superintendent in 1972 and was now able to devote even more of his time to the sport he loved. Six years later he was elected to the ABA executive and served out this role for five years.

He was named as manager of the England team for internationals against Scotland and Ireland and also took a team of seven to a Multi Nations tournament in Finland in 1979.

His boxers on the trip, including eventual professional

Without a doubt nobody put more time and effort into the development of amateur boxing on Teesside in the 20th century than Phil Thomas. Here he is pictured with his wife Evelyn.

champions Tony Willis and Ray Gilbody, won five golds and two bronzes.

Ill health finally forced Phil to drop out of his national commitments, but he never eased down a gear in the North-east and continued with his labour of love.

In 1987, Phil received a very special honour, when a boxing club changed its name to his own, to recognise his remarkable contribution to amateur boxing on Teesside. Joe Waltons ABC, then based at the Middlesbrough Customs House, became The Phil Thomas School of Boxing. Phil had been chairman of the club.

So, Phil's name continued to be highlighted around the country by the Phil Thomas School boxers, several of whom became national champions, including the Commonwealth gold medallist Peter Richardson.

In the same year he received another distinction, when he was handed the National Association of Boys Clubs Keystone Gold Award, to mark his 37 years' contribution to boys clubs' work.

In 1993, aged 83, Thomas announced his retirement.

There was not a single official operating in amateur boxing in the North-east who had not been guided and advised by Phil at some time in his career.

And he acknowledged that he could never have reached the highest pinnacle of amateur boxing without the continued support of his wife Evelyn, who had travelled around with him attending every boxing show for 25 years.

Phil's lifetime commitment to amateur boxing was recognised at the age of 86 in 1997, when he was awarded an MBE in the Queen's Birthday Honours List. The award was presented by Sir Paul Nicholson, Lord Lieutenant of County Durham, at Stockton Town Hall the following January.

In 2000, Phil is still an active chairman of the Phil Thomas School of Boxing, but no longer watches tournaments. He is head of a large family, having brought up sons Jack and Philip and daughter Patricia, and has six grandchildren and two great-grandchildren.

Andrew Thornton
National Hunt Racing

"YOU don't have to be mad but it certainly helps," appears to be the character blueprint required to lead the high risk lifestyle of a jump jockey.

Anybody who is constantly fighting a battle with their weight, and travelling 100,000 miles a year to every national hunt course in the country in the knowledge that at any given moment they could be seriously injured, has to possess a special type of grit and determination in order to succeed.

For one such rider, Andrew Thornton, that total dedication and sacrifice was rewarded in March 1998 by winning the ultimate prize in national hunt racing, The Cheltenham Gold Cup.

Andrew Thornton was born on October 28, 1972 and brought up on West House Farm, Bishopton, near Stockton-on-Tees. He attended the local primary school before transferring to Hurworth House and Barnard Castle School.

As a boarder at "Barnie" he developed a keen interest in maths and geography and was a naturally gifted athlete competing in a variety of disciplines both on the track and across country. He also followed in the illustrious footsteps of England internationals Rory and Tony Underwood and Rob Andrew by representing the school at rugby where he was a promising stand-off half who was good enough to be selected for the Durham County under 16 side. In fact the school coaching staff thought so highly of his ability that they endeavoured to convince him he could have a future in the game, but Andrew had already set his heart on a career in horse racing.

The Thornton family had connections in the racing game with established trainers like Denys Smith because Andrew's grandfather Tommy, a former master of the South Durham hunt, was a successful owner with more than 70 winners to his credit, including the prolific Grey Steel who won on thirteen occasions.

From a very early age Andrew grew up with horses. He had ridden his own Shetland ponies around the family

In March 1998 Andrew Thornton achieved every jump jockey's dream by riding Cool Dawn to the win the Cheltenham Gold Cup.

farm and joined the Hurworth Pony Club where he gained valuable experience of showing jumping and team chasing in many local riding competitions

By the time he was fourteen, and with his parents full blessing, Andrew was spending his school holidays "living in" at the Leasingthorne yard of the respected trainer WA Stephenson and immersing himself in the daily routine of one of the norths leading jumping stables.

At sixteen he turned down the opportunity of a three week school rugby tour to South Africa in order to begin working full time for Stephenson.

After spending two hard years learning his trade he was granted an amateur licence and rode in his first race at Kelso in November 1990. Unfortunately it was to be a bitter experience as his horse, Brave Ruler, broke its leg only 50 yards from the finish when in second place.

In the early days rides were few and far between for young amateur trying to establish himself, but Andrew was determined to make the grade and his persistence

Maamur partnered by Andrew Thornton, on their way to success at the 1996 Cheltenham Festival.

was eventually rewarded with his first winner, Wrekin Hill, in a three mile chase at Sedgefield.

This breakthrough was the impetus that his race riding career needed and by 1992/93 Andrew was crowned National Hunt amateur champion with 26 winners.

Unfortunately the same year Andrew's mentor Arthur Stephenson died, so he took the major decision to turn professional and move to the Lambourn based stables of Kim Bailey prior to the start of the 1993/94 season. The move south was initially fraught with problems when, in an effort to adapt to a shorter riding style, Andrew began to lose confidence in his ability.

After two tough seasons trying to establish himself in the professional ranks, with limited success, Andrew's career seemed to be at the crossroads. So, after much discussion and soul-searching, particularly with those close to him who still believed he could succeed, he decided to go freelance.

It was an inspired decision which, by the end of the 1996 season, had seen him ride 52 winners (his best season to date) and record his first success at the prestigious Cheltenham Festival on Captain Tim Forster's, Maamur, in the Ritz Club Handicap Chase.

1996/97 saw Andrew ride his fair share of winners but it was to be the following season, when he won the King George VI Chase at Kempton Park's famous Boxing Day meeting on Paul Nichol's outstanding steeplechaser See More Business, which would raise his profile even further.

However, it was at the 1998 Cheltenham Festival where Andrew really hit the headlines and came to national prominence. Following a superb victory on Ferdy Murphy's highly promising but ill-fated hurdler French Holley in the Royal Sun Alliance Hurdle, he won the blue riband of steeplechasing, the Cheltenham Gold Cup.

Although the Grand National seems to carry more prestige with the public, those within the game know that to win the ultimate prize in jump racing is everyone's dream and Andrew Thornton, by guiding Robert Alner's 25-1 shot Cool Dawn to a stunning victory, had joined a very elite roll of honour indeed. He now had a place in history.

Following his Cheltenham success leading trainers such as Dorset based Alner, David Nicholson, Paul Webber and Philip Hobbs booked Andrew to partner their top rated horses. He was also riding with great confidence. Winning trebles were now appearing on the race cards of the major courses, including a four timer at Kempton Park.

Unfortunately, this purple patch was brought to an abrupt end when Andrew broke his left leg in a fall at Fontwell Park on Winspit. The brake was so bad that it required two plates and seventeen screws to affect a satisfactory recovery. For a time everything seemed to be progressing well, but remedial surgery to rectify a bone infection prolonged the time spent out of the saddle still further.

Inactivity through serious injury not only costs a jockey money but also enables others to benefit from riding their horses. That is an accepted hard fact of life. Thankfully, Andrew has now returned to full fitness and is working hard to re-establish in the top flight.

To date Andrew Thornton he has ridden 375 winners but at 5'11" he is rather tall for a jockey and fights a daily battle to control his weight, often spending many hours sweating off those excess pounds either in a hot bath or a sauna. The general public are rarely aware of the constant daily self sacrifice and total dedication required to succeed in such a dangerous profession but Andrew intends to continue for as long as he can. In the future he would like to pursue a career in the media or, if the opportunity arose, become a trainer.

Alan Townsend

Cricket

IT'S quite possible that if Alan Townsend hadn't been made redundant by a local Teesside engineering firm in 1946, as a consequence of the industrial recession which followed the Second World War, he may never have become a full-time cricketer.

As it was, he gratefully accepted the chance to earn a bit of extra cash as professional with Eppleton CC, and played so well that he attracted the attention of several County Championship sides.

After a series of trial matches with Northamptonshire Glamorgan and Warwickshire, Alan eventually linked up with Warwickshire, before going on to become the mainstay of the Midlands county side over the next 13 years and making a total of 340 appearances.

Alan Townsend was born on August 26, 1921, and as a youngster lived in Thornaby before the family moved the short distance to Middlesbrough, where he attended Marton Road School and Middlesbrough Tech. On his own admission, with the exception of sport, he did not find education an enjoyable experience. In fact he was happy to leave school early to begin an apprenticeship as a template maker at Head Wrightson Engineering in Stockton.

His consuming passion for sport was undoubtedly inherited from his father, Charlie, who for many years played cricket for Thornaby CC. In fact the pair were so keen that they once cycled from Teesside to Leeds and back in a day to see the great Don Bradman bat at Headingley in the Ashes series of 1934.

"What a great day that was," remembered Alan. "We got up at about 4.30am and arrived just before the start. It was the second day of the Test match and the Don had already scored over 300 runs the previous day. After about half an hour Yorkshire's Bill Bowes bowled him. What a roar went up when he was out.

"My other abiding memory was that we had to stand almost all day because the ground was so full. And even when we did eventually manage to get a seat I sat on my tomato sandwiches and crushed them."

Alan followed in his father's footsteps and played his

Alan Townsend spent 13 successful years as a county cricketer with Warwickshire.

junior cricket with Thornaby CC before graduating to their North Yorkshire and South Durham League side. During the winter months he also turned out for Bon Lea Football Club at centre-half.

He was good enough to play in a North Riding Junior Cup Final at Ayresome Park against the might of a South Bank St Peters team containing future Boro professionals like Paddy Nash. But it was to be as a cricketer that he would eventually make his name.

During his time with Thornaby he was a prolific runmaker, and a more than useful medium quick bowler, helping them to win both the league championship and Kerridge Cup.

In 1943, at the age of 21, he made the first of his 19 appearances for Durham. At the time a prophetic local reporter wrote: "A promising all-rounder made his debut for Durham and more should be heard of him." Becoming a professional cricketer didn't really cross

Townsend's mind until he was made redundant from Head Wrightson's in 1946. Initially life without a job was hard but thankfully he was offered the position of club professional with Eppleton CC at £2 10s per match. His performances in the competitive Durham Senior League and for the Durham Minor Counties side eventually led to a series of trials, firstly with Glamorgan where he made a creditable 60 runs against Gloucestershire seconds, who had the great Tom Graveney in their side.

Unfortunately, Alan wasn't offered a position on the Welsh county's groundstaff as the official letter he received claimed they were looking for bowlers. Alan found this reply somewhat puzzling because one of his colleagues had also received a similar rejection but which stated they were looking for batsmen!

Townsend continued to play his minor county cricket for Durham, compiling 393 runs at an average of 20.68. He hit his highest score of 86 for the county in a victory against Northumberland at Ashbrooke. He took ten wickets for Durham at an average of 21.6 including a best performance of 3-22.

Alan's disappointment at failing to make the grade with Glamorgan was short lived because following successful trials with Northants and Warwickshire, they both offered him full-time contracts. His choice was quite simple. He decided to join Warwickshire in 1948, "...because they were offering £50 a year more which was a lot of money in those days."

He made his Warwickshire debut in the same year against Nottinghamshire at Trent Bridge and quickly established himself, receiving his cap the same year.

Being a full time cricketer during the 1950s was certainly not a glamorous life, as Alan recalled, "There was no sponsorship deals 50 years ago and players were expected to buy all their own kit. We had to make a county sweater and cap last a minimum of five years. "I only had two pairs of whites during a season. While I was wearing one pair the others were in the wash. Even when we won the Championship all we got was a commemorative gold watch."

During an outstanding all round career Alan helped Warwickshire to win the County Championship in 1951 and played for the MCC at Lord's on two occasions. He accumulated almost 12,000 runs at an average of 24.93. He scored six centuries and topped 1,000 runs in a season on five separate occasions.

His highest individual score of 154 was made against Worcestershire at Dudley in 1957.

Townsend was known for occasionally having an eccentric approach to getting from one wicket to the other. One of the more unusual photographs in the Warwickshire library shows Alan and Tom Dollery blithely running down opposite sides of the wicket away from the camera towards the City End, each unaware the other was heading for the same crease.

He was just as effective with the ball as he was with the bat for Warwickshire, taking 323 wickets at 28.6 apiece including the two wickets of the famous Middlesex pair of Bill Edrich and Dennis Compton in three balls.

His best bowling performance came against Essex at Brentwood in 1949 when he took 7-84.

Alan was also a superbly athletic fielder with a good, safe pair of hands. He took 41 catches in 1951 and 42 two years later, both of which were Warwickshire records at that time. His total career catches of 409 was also a county record until it was overtaken by England captain MJK Smith.

In 1960 he was awarded a well-deserved testimonial season before being persuaded by an Edgbaston committee member, Maynard Mitchell, to become the professional of the local Mitchell and Butler Brewery CC. Alan made an instant impression on the local cricketing scene when he became the first ever batsman to score 1,000 runs in a Birmingham League season.

Following thirteen seasons as a player and three as a coach with the brewery side, Alan reluctantly retired from local competitive cricket to take up a position as a representative with a furniture company.

However, in 1982 he was enticed back to Edgbaston to become a member of the Warwickshire coaching staff at their indoor cricket school with special responsibility for the technical tuition of the club's young cricketers. He went on to identify new talent such as Tim Munton and Dominic Ostler and also recommended the teenage Graeme Hick to Warwickshire, but they were unable to sign the young Zimbabwean as the club already had their quota of overseas players.

Alan Townsend has given most of his life to playing and promoting the game he loves. In fact he was still enthusing youngsters with his passion for cricket when he finally retired at the age of 70.

In 2000, Alan lives quietly in the Birmingham suburb of Solihull, but continues to follow county cricket with great enthusiasm.

David Townsend

Cricket

DAVID Charles Humphrey Townsend holds the notable distinction of being the last 'stateless' cricketer to appear for England.

Born in Norton on April 20, 1912, he played in three Tests on the tour of the West Indies in 1934-35, yet never played for a first class county during his career. Instead, Townsend came to prominence as a powerful opening batsman with Oxford University, for whom he made 37 first class appearances.

David came from a strong cricketing background. His father, Charles Townsend, had been a fine Test all-rounder in 1899 when with Gloucestershire CCC. His grandfather Frank also played for the south-west county, and was a teammate of the legendary W G Grace. David's son Jonathan, who was born in 1942, was also to go on and play for Oxford University.

Educated at Winchester, ill health prevented Townsend from playing for the university in his first year but he made an unbeaten 72 on his debut against Yorkshire in 1933. He subsequently headed the University's batting averages, compiling at total of 734 runs and scoring three hundreds in the process.

David played in both of the Varsity matches of 1933 and 1934, scoring a brilliant 193 in the second game at Lord's. His game was based on a very sound defensive technique but he was also an elegant stroke maker who favoured the cut and the off-drive.

After finishing his studies Townsend was called up for international honours because of the remarkable impact he had made against the top county sides while at Oxford. He was regarded as one of the top young talents in the game.

David toured the Caribbean with Bob Wyatt's MCC team in 1934-35. He played in three Test matches for England against the West Indies, opening the batting with Wyatt. Although it was a great experience for the Norton man, he never finished on the winning side.

Townsend's international debut came in the Second Test in Port of Spain, making scores of five and 36 as England were crushed by 217 runs. Caught on a virtually unplayable wicket in Trinidad, England were bowled out for 107 in their second innings. With Leary Constantine making the ball whistle around their ears, the more established players like Wyatt, Hammond, Ames, Leyland and Hendren all succumbed cheaply, while Townsend's 36 in the adverse conditions was England's top score.

He did not fare so well in the ensuing Tests, achieving a top score of 16 in his other four innings. England drew the Third Test in Georgetown, but lost by an innings and 161 runs in Kingston, and David never again featured on the international scene.

On returning to the North-east, David decided on a career outside cricket and became a solicitor. He linked up with Norton CC in the North Yorkshire and South Durham League and became a prolific run scorer, taking over the club captaincy from his brother Peter. He went on to make over 9,000 runs in league games alone for Norton, and scored eight centuries.

It is generally accepted that Townsend was the best captain to have ever played in the North Yorkshire and South Durham League, leading Norton for 19 years and winning the championship on six occasions and the Kerridge Cup four times.

He was fortunate to inherit a good team which he moulded into a strong side that probably could have beaten many Minor Counties sides.

Townsend's most outstanding innings for Norton was at Blackhall in 1935, when he scored 149 not out in a little over two hours to win the match by nine wickets. David signed for Durham at the same time as he returned to Norton, and played for the Minor Counties side over a 16 year period between 1935 and 1950.

Ironically, Townsend made his Durham debut in a high profile match against the South African tourists at Ashbrooke. However, it was not a memorable debut, because the tourists were very strong at the time and bundled Durham out for 45 and 141 to win by an innings and 45 runs.

David skippered Durham from 1937 to 1947 but

England Test batsman David Townsend, front row, centre, is generally regarded as the best captain to have played in the NY & SD league. Here he is pictured with the 1951 Norton side which won the championship.

played in only 40 matches, his work as a solicitor limiting his appearances. He still scored 1,451 runs at an average of 27.90. He made four centuries and five half-centuries.

Yet again he proved his potential on the big stage by making a top score of 138 not out against the touring New Zealanders at Ashbrooke in 1937. It was a great captain's innings and at one time Durham were favourites to win the match. However 67 from the Kiwis' ninth batsman, Jack Kerr, proved costly for Durham and paved the way for a battling draw.

In four games against different touring sides, David aggregated 240 runs in five innings at an average of 48, to illustrate his ability to play competitively at the highest level.

However Durham were massacred in their final tourist game against the Australians before the war, being beaten by an innings. Townsend made scores of 25 and 11, and was one of few Durham players to reach double figures in either innings.

In 1938, David was available to captain Durham in every game and enjoyed a golden August, scoring three centuries in the wins against Northumberland, Staffordshire and Lancashire Seconds.

Townsend was on active service during the Second World War and when Durham played their first fixture against a touring side after the conflict against India in 1946, David was one of three survivors from the pre-war game against the Aussies, along with Jack Carr and Jimmy Grigor.

David was also used as an occasional bowler by Durham, taking nine wickets at a respectable average of 21.11, though as a batsman he was always one of the mainstays of the side.

Unfortunately a broken wrist was to lead to Townsend missing the whole of the 1947 season, which was his last as captain. However he played on for a further three seasons before retiring from Minor Counties cricket at the age of 38.

David Townsend was undoubtedly one of the most talented local cricketers of the 20th century. He died on January 17, 1997.

Bob Turnbull
Football

ROBERT Turnbull was another of the great footballing sons of South Bank who went on to become a full international with England.

A fast and direct orthodox outside-right, he first came to prominence as a young footballer, scoring 80 goals in one season in Teesside schools football.

Bob was born in December 17, 1895, and it was to be his brilliant footwork with South Bank Schools that would eventually earn him the chance to join the renowned South Bank East End club.

While in the services during the World War One he played for the Army and when the hostilities neared an end, Boro were red hot favourites to secure the signature of the gifted winger. But they were denied their target through a bizarre set of circumstances.

In January 1918, Bradford PA, who were then in the First Division, had arrived on Teesside to play in a benefit match for the relatives of former Boro full-back, Donald McLeod, who had been killed in action. Shortly before kick-off, however, Park Avenue discovered that they were a man short and Bob Turnbull was persuaded to make up their number. Given this unexpected opportunity to display his talented wing play he proceeded to demonstrate the full repertoire of his close control skills.

The management of Bradford were so impressed with his performance that they signed him immediately following the game right from under the noses of his hometown club.

Turnbull made a sensational debut for his new side in the wartime league, when he scored five times against local rivals Barnsley. His direct attacking style quickly came to the attention of the England selectors, and he was chosen to play in three Victory Internationals before making his full debut against Ireland in October 1919 alongside Boro star Jack Carr, who was also a fellow resident of South Bank. The match, in Belfast, ended in a 1-1 draw.

Further recognition was to follow when he was included in the FA party which toured S.Africa the next season.

Bob Turnbull was signed by Bradford PA right from under the noses of the Boro, after playing in a benefit match against his hometown club.

Unfortunately, by 1923, Bradford's league status, not to mention Turnbull's international career, took a dramatic dive when they were relegated in successive seasons to the Third Division North. However, Bob must still have enjoyed the distinction of scoring the winner in a 1-0 victory against Middlesbrough in the first round of the FA Cup in January, 1925.

In May of the same year, Leeds United resurrected Turnbull's flagging career, and in a seven year spell at Elland Road, which saw him make 215 appearances and score 46 goals, his consistent wing play made him a firm favourite with the Yorkshire crowd. Life however, was never dull, as Leeds were twice relegated and promoted during that period.

In 1929 he toured S. Africa for a second time with the FA. After 14 years as a professional, Bob Turnbull moved to non-league Rhyl in September 1932 before finally retiring from football the following year.

He returned to his native Teesside to work for Dorman, Long and Company in the steel industry and died in Middlesbrough on March 19, 1952.

Rory Underwood
Rugby Union

RORY Underwood's lifelong ambition was not to play rugby union for England at Twickenham. It was to fulfil an early childhood dream and fly fast jets for the Royal Air Force.

However, owing to the extremely exacting performance standards required by the RAF, there were times when his choice of occupation, and remarkable parallel career of international and club rugby star, proved difficult to pursue.

It is therefore to Rory's great credit, and a measure of his determination and character, that he managed for over a dozen years, to combine the continual arduous requirements of both those careers to become England's most capped rugby player and all time leading try scorer.

His memorable exploits on the rugby pitch have rewritten the statistics books. He was the first English player to win 50 caps and by the end of the 1995 World Cup had scored 46 international tries, including a record five in a match against Fiji in November 1989. Primarily a left winger, Rory could play with equal facility on the opposite wing or at full-back. He won the first of his 85 caps in 1984 and played in the inaugural World Cup in Australia-New Zealand in 1987. He was also an ever present member of both the victorious 1989 British Lions team in Australia and the side defeated by the All Blacks in 1993.

At the age of 28, after helping England to their second successive Grand Slam in 1992 and receiving the MBE, Rory announced his international retirement. However, he reversed what was generally regarded as a premature decision early the following season and made himself available once again for selection and add considerably to his list of achievements.

Born in Middlesbrough General Hospital on June 19,1963, Rory was named after the cowboy matinee idol Rory Calhoun. His film buff father James Ashley Underwood, whose family roots were on Teesside, had been an officer in the Merchant Navy before joining Harrison Lister Engineering. And it was while he was based in Malaysia that he met local girl, Annie Tan, in the company's headquarters. Their relationship blossomed and following their marriage in 1962, Rory was the first of four children.

Due to his father's business commitments, the early years of Rory's life were spent in the expatriate community of Ipoh, a mining town 100 miles north of Kuala Lumpur. Then, as the political tensions in the region increased, the family moved to the capital itself. In 1971 Rory and his brother Gary returned to England and, supervised by their grandparents from Middlesbrough, continued their education at Brignall Grange and Barnard Castle School in County Durham. Initially, holidays were spent returning to Malaysia before the family settled, some years later, in the village of Startforth near to the school.

On his own admission, Rory was not particularly academically orientated, referring to himself as "a standard could do better pupil". However, after spending many hours travelling back and forth to Asia, and being allowed on to the aircraft flight deck by a variety of kindly captains, he developed a very keen interest in flying and eventually set his heart on a career in the RAF.

In order to achieve this ambition, he became a member of the Combined Cadet Force while still at school. This enabled him to visit many of the country's leading airbases and gain valuable experience of training flights. By the time he was 18, Rory's results in the RAF aptitude tests were high enough to earn him a flying scholarship and obtain his private pilot's licence after 35 hours of flying in a Cessna 150.

Running parallel with his burgeoning interest in aviation was Underwood's keen interest in sport. He was a good all rounder representing his school at rugby, cricket and swimming. A contemporary of his at 'Barnie' was the future England rugby fly half Rob Andrew with whom he struck up an instant rapport. They have been friends and team colleagues throughout their careers.

Future England winger Rory Underwood first played for Middlesbrough RUFC as a schoolboy in 1980.

From an early age Rory possessed the innate ability to run with genuine pace. This gift was undoubtedly inherited from his mother, who had been no mean sprinter herself as a youngster.

The school rugby coach, John Oates, was the first influence on the flying wing's rugby career, helping to nurture the latent prowess which would eventually score an amazing 41 tries during one spectacular schoolboy season.

This notable achievement brought Rory to the attention of the leading local rugby clubs and in 1980, following an impressive performance in a school game against their colts team, Middlesbrough RUFC invited him to Acklam Park to play for the Wasps.

Rory was quite surprised at the invitation because it had never crossed his mind that he might be talented enough to play rugby for a team which often featured on BBC television's Grandstand results service. But, encouraged by John Oates, he accepted Middlesbrough's invitation.

The fleet-footed sixth former made an immediate impression and, after only three games, was swiftly promoted to the 1st XV where he played with distinction for the next four seasons, enjoying the club's laissez-faire playing philosophy by noting: 'We just went out and did it'.

In 1981 Rory decided to leave school, with his parents' blessing, to await a place on an RAF training course. To gain some work experience he joined a Youth Opportunities Scheme and became an assistant to a local pewtersmith, Tom Neal. It was a job he enjoyed immensely.

At that time his rugby potential was acknowledged at an even higher level when he gave an outstanding four-try performance for the Rest against Durham in a county trial match. This significant feat led to his selection for the full county side and a hat trick of touchdowns in a victory over Cheshire during his debut season.

Underwood's first representative honour was then followed in March, 1982, with a call up to the England Colts and inclusion on the England Under-23 tour to Italy that summer.

At a time when everything appeared to be progressing so well on the rugby field, Rory's life was suddenly hit by an unexpected personal tragedy. His father, who was known affectionately to his family and friends as Ash, died at the relatively young age of 54. As the eldest child, Rory took on all responsibility for the funeral arrangements and acknowledges that dealing with the family crisis helped him mature appreciably as a person.

By September, 1982, his rugby career was further enhanced when he was chosen by the Northern Division to play against the Fijians at Workington, in Cumbria. This selection was quickly followed by an appearance for the England B side in December in Ireland. During this hectic season Rory switched his county allegiance from Durham to Yorkshire, concluding the first of five championship campaigns with the Tykes by scoring two tries as the White Rose

During an outstanding international career which lasted for over a decade, Middlesbrough born rugby union star, Rory Underwood, scored a record 46 tries in 85 matches for England.

XV defeated Middlesex 18-7 in their first County Final for almost 20 years.

Early in the new year, the moment that Rory had been waiting for since he was a youngster finally arrived when his application to join the RAF was accepted. He enrolled on the 18 week initial officer training course at Cranwell in February, 1983. This change of location also necessitated moving rugby clubs. So, after four happy seasons and 37 appearances for Middlesbrough,

he joined, on the recommendation of fellow Teessider and England international Alan Old, the highly regarded Leicester RUFC. To begin with, like most new recruits, he served his apprenticeship in the seconds before gaining a place in the Welford Road senior side on the left wing. This was a position which he would hold for more than a decade .

After successfully completing his initial flight training, Acting Pilot Officer Underwood stayed at Cranwell to before being posted to Swinderby near Lincoln as a Flight Commander. On his own admission, Rory found the training courses very demanding but his dogged determination and persistence to succeed ensured that by 1985 he would achieve his life's ambition and earn his wings as an RAF pilot.

However, juggling an important career in the services with his rugby ambitions became quite difficult for the Teessider. In fact, the thought did cross his mind on more than one occasion to "give rugby away" as his flying commitments intensified. That conflict of interests was highlighted during one particular conversation with his squadron leader when, after informing his commanding officer that he might be required to play rugby rather more frequently, he was told somewhat candidly: "You're a complete waste of space."

Fortunately, Underwood's personal malaise with regard to his professional career did not translate itself on to the pitch. Following impressive performances for Leicester in the autumn of 1983, particularly in the traditional Christmas fixture against the Barbarians, he received a phonecall in the officers mess. It was from the England chairman of selectors Derek Morgan, who broke the news that Underwood had been chosen to make his international debut against Ireland in Dublin on February 18,1984.

It was to be the beginning of a sparkling international career which would last for 11 years and end with the Middlesbrough-born player becoming his country's all time leading try scorer and maintaining the remarkable record of never being dropped.

As his international career began to flourish, Rory and the RAF were able to balance both his sporting and career commitments. Occasionally he was not available for overseas tours as he received no special favours from his employers.

However it was widely recognised that having a famous international sportsman in the services presented a very positive public image for both the game itself and the Royal Air Force. Over the years Rory has repaid the RAF's support by playing in numerous Combined Services and RAF matches on their behalf.

In terms of try scoring, Underwood's England career began rather slowly with only four touchdowns in 22 appearances. But on November 4, 1989, he equalled Dan Lambert's 1907 record of scoring five times in a match when he achieved this nap hand against Fiji in a 58-23 victory at Twickenham. He was also an integral part of the highly efficient England team which, under the cool, calculating captaincy of Will Carling, achieved back to back Grand Slams in 1991 and 1992 and was also narrowly beaten by Australia 12-6 in the World Cup Final at Twickenham in November, 1991.

Despite his undoubted success on the international stage, Rory has always taken his county, divisional, services and club rugby very seriously indeed. Throughout his career he has constantly played at all levels of the game, managing to avoid serious injury, and in making 239 appearances for Leicester he helped the Tigers win the English club championship in 1988 and 1995 and the Pilkington Cup in 1993.

In November, 1989, there was another great moment for the Underwood family when younger brother Tony joined Rory in the Barbarians side on the opposite wing against the All Blacks at Twickenham. It was the beginning of a partnership which would proudly flourish in later years with England.

Following the World Cup in South Africa in 1995, where England were blown apart by New Zealand's human battering ram of a winger, Jonah Lomu, in a rather one-sided semi-final, Underwood played in the 1996 Five Nations before announcing his retirement from the international scene after a truly illustrious career.

He continued to play club rugby for Leicester until 1997 before moving to Bedford for a couple of seasons. In 2000 he is a happily married with two daughters and intends to remain in the RAF as a flight lieutenant until June, 2001, when his commission is finally finished. Although he has attained an air transport pilot's licence, which would enable him to fly commercially, Underwood seems set to pursue a career in business after having already established his own management training company with colleagues.

Held in high regard by all his teammates and totally respected by his opponents Rory Underwood's achievements in a modern game noted for its constant and unrelenting highly competitive physical demands, are quite remarkable.

He succeeded in an era when the game of rugby became much more professional in its approach as it vainly attempted to meet the ever increasing standards set by teams from the southern hemisphere. To perform as well as he did, for as long as he did and also become a fighter pilot into the bargain, is testament to his determination, dedication and ability.

Michael Walford
Cricket and Hockey

TEESSIDE has produced few better sportsmen than the talented all-rounder and Olympic silver medallist Michael Moore Walford, who was born at Norton on November 27, 1915.

As a youngster he played both cricket and hockey for his home town club, before coming to national prominence as a sporting Jack of all trades at Oxford University.

It was there, between 1935 and 1938, he enjoyed the rare distinction of gaining a triple blue at rugby union, cricket and hockey. Initially it was his performances on the cricket field which caught the eye for Oxford, where he followed in the footsteps of another old Nortonian, David Townsend.

After completing his degree, a professional career in cricket beckoned for the prodigious talent with the ice cool temperament. But instead, Michael opted for security and took up a history teaching post at Sherbourne Public School, in Dorset. Once he had chosen to work in education his sporting exploits were carefully arranged around his professional life.

Together with his academic commitments at Sherbourne, Walford also coached cricket and one of his pupils was the future Bishop of Liverpool, the Rev David Sheppard. When Sheppard eventually opened the batting for England in the 1960s he readily acknowledged the debt of gratitude he owed his former schoolmaster.

During the Second World War, Walford saw action overseas with the 11th Army Division and 4th Army Brigade, where he rose to the rank of major.

Between 1946-53, despite playing full time cricket only during the school holidays, he still progressed to County Championship standard, eventually playing 52 matches for Somerset, scoring an undefeated century on his debut. His successes earned him a place on the MCC tour of Canada in 1951.

He was an attacking right-hand opening batsman and slow left-arm bowler, who also excelled in the field at cover point.

Educated at Rugby School, Walford had broken into the Durham County side when he was only 19, and played Minor Counties cricket for three years. In the winter of 1938-39 he toured Jamaica with a combined Oxford and Cambridge universities side.

In his first season with Durham, Michael topped the averages with 199 runs, including a top score of 72, at an average of 33.16. He was awarded his county cap after only four games.

Michael also holds the distinction of having compiled one of the highest scores in Somerset history, when he hammered 264 off the Hampshire attack at Weston-super-Mare in 1947. At the time, it was Somerset's second highest individual score ever, and the highest for 51 years. His only other double century came while he was at Oxford.

During his time with Somerset, and despite the restrictions placed on his availability by the demands of the school curriculum, Walford still managed to accumulate 3,395 runs, including seven centuries, at a very respectable average of 40.90.

The end of his first class career with Somerset was handled in a rather ham-fisted and tactless manner when he was asked to relinquish his special registration in 1954 so that it could be used for someone else. He did, however, continue to play representative cricket, and spent nine seasons in the Minor Counties with Dorset from 1954-62.

It is a widely held opinion throughout the game that if Michael Walford had devoted all his time to cricket, there is no doubt he would have been selected for England.

While cricket was his summer love, Michael also played rugby union and hockey during the winter month to a very high standard. He was an outstanding rugby three-quarter who played in final England trials and wartime internationals and represented Norton, Sherbourne and Taunton Vale at hockey.

On the hockey field he was a formidable right-half who not only played 17 times for England but also

Michael Walford, front, centre, was an outstanding county cricketer who also helped Great Britain win the hockey silver medal at the London Olympics of 1948. Brother David is on his left in this 1949 England team.

captained his country on six occasions from 1947-51. In three of his international matches he was joined in the England team by his younger brother David, who played centre-forward. As far as it is known they were the first brothers to play hockey for England, and at the time it was quite a coup for Norton Hockey Club where Michael had started his career and David still played.

However, the pinnacle of Michael Walford's sporting career was achieved when he was chosen in Great Britain's Olympic hockey team for the London Games of 1948. As the tournament progressed he played in all of his side's five matches, including the final where the team won silver medals following their 4-0 defeat by India.

As an all-round sportsman Walford's quite remarkable record of achievement speaks for itself. But what makes this unassuming man unique, is the fact that he attained such high standards playing on a part-time basis while preferring to devote himself to a career in education.

In 2000, Michael Walford, after spending his working life at Sherbourne School, still lives in Dorset in quiet retirement.

Colin Walker
Athletics

COLIN Walker is one of Britain's all time top 3000 metres steeplechasers who won a bronze medal in the Commonwealth Games in Auckland in 1990.

He reached the semi-finals of the Barcelona Olympics in 1992, and was twice a semi-finalist in the world championships.

Colin won another bronze medal in helping Great Britain into third place in the world road relays in 1992, while he was narrowly edged out of the chance of a second Commonwealth Games medal when finishing fourth in Canada in 1994.

On the domestic scene, he was AAAs 3000 metres steeplechase champion on four occasions and also won the AAAs Half Marathon Championship.

Colin Frederick Walker was born in Stockton on October 29, 1962, and attended Hardwick infants and juniors before moving on to Sheraton Comprehensive School. In his last year at Sheraton he competed in the English schools cross country championships at Newark. However it was not until he left school, that Colin's interest in athletics took off in a big way. He joined Mandale Harriers, who trained at Tilery Sports Centre at the time, and ran initially in the middle distance events and also the 400 metres hurdles, which eventually led to a natural progression to the steeplechase.

When Mandale switched to Clairville Stadium, Colin was introduced to the top coach Gordon Surtees, who had guided Dennis Coates throughout his career and was coaching Ian Gilmore at the time.

Steeplechase competition was very limited in the North-east, so Colin concentrated on the 1500 metres in regional events and began to make his mark. As he developed and gained in physical strength, Colin switched clubs and joined Gateshead Harriers in 1983 for the higher level of competition.

This was also the year in which he made his initial national breakthrough, winning the AAAs 2000 metres steeplechase indoor title at RAF Cosford in 1983. He recorded a personal best time of 5min 38.45sec, which he was later to improve by a further 15 seconds. Colin

also won his first outdoor title when taking the Scottish AAAs 3000 metres steeplechase crown.

Walker retained the AAAs indoor title in the following two seasons, and also began to make a much bigger impact on the outdoor track by taking second place in consecutive years in the 3000 metres steeplechase at the UK Championships.

He was called up for his international debut in 1985 when selected for England Under-23s in the home countries tournament at Swansea, finishing second in the steeplechase to Irishman Peter McColgan.

Colin then stepped up to the Great Britain B team for an international in Le Tourquet in France, before travelling with the British Under-23 squad on a tour of China which took in events in Beijing and Nanking.

When he left school, Colin had trained as a bricklayer. But, unhappy at working outdoors in the bitterly cold weather in the winter, he applied to become a prison officer. He trained initially at Durham but was then posted to Pentonville Prison in London in 1985.

This did not affect his training, and he was back in the North-east the following year for his full international debut. He was called up to run for Great Britain in a special match against the Commonwealth at Gateshead which followed the Commonwealth Games in Edinburgh.

In 1987 Walker took the steeplechase crown at the UK Championships and was fourth in the AAAs the following year. In between, he returned to live and work in the North-east when he was transferred back from Pentonville to Durham Prison to continue his career as a prison officer.

Colin took part in his first major championship in 1989 when competing in the European Indoors at The Hague. However he was suffering from a heavy cold shortly before the meeting took place and was unable to do himself justice, failing to progress beyond the heats. Walker then suffered a blow when he returned to The Hague for a major half marathon when he tore a calf muscle and was sidelined for ten weeks. He was

Steeplechaser Colin Walker won the AAAs title on four occasions and a Commonwealth Games bronze medal in 1990. He also represented Great Britain at the World Athletics Championships and Olympic Games.

worried that he might not be fully fit for the AAAs Championships, but made a full recovery and went on to win the steeplechase, which guaranteed his place for the Commonwealth Games in Auckland the following year.

In New Zealand Colin was competing against the Olympic champion, Julius Kariuki, among several other top runners, and knew that he needed to run a personal best if he was to have any chance of getting among the medals. As a result Colin decided to take on the field and increased the pace over the final 1000 metres to try to run the sting out of the top runners. He raced clear and held the lead for some time, before being caught and overtaken by two Kenyans, Kariuki and Joshua Kipkemboi, on the back straight.

Now it was a case of digging in to stay in the bronze medal position. Colin continued to chase the Kenyans and held sway in the home straight, managing to fight off a concerted challenge from Canadian Graeme Fell in the closing metres. Colin would not be denied and came home triumphantly in the bronze medal position behind the winner Kariuki and silver medalist Kipkemboi.

Kariuki set a Games record time of 8min 20.64sec, while Walker achieved a personal best time of 8min 26.50sec.

Later in the year Colin travelled to Spilt with the British team for the European championships, but the overall competition was much tougher than he had encountered in the Commonwealth Games and he did not progress beyond the semi-finals.

In 1991 Colin contested the world championships in Tokio. It was a great experience but he found the humidity difficult to cope with, being eliminated in the semi-finals. On the domestic scene, he won the AAAs title at Birmingham for the second time.

His AAAs success was enough to ensure that Colin was selected for the Barcelona Olympics, especially as he achieved the qualifying standard. It was a proud moment for the Stockton man to reach the pinnacle of his sport, and he prepared thoroughly as ever for the trip to Spain. However the competition was very, very tough and, although Colin comfortably came through the heats to reach the semi-finals, he did not qualify for a place in the final.

It was a busy year for Walker. He flew out to Madeira to help Great Britain take a superb third place in the World Road Relays in Funchal, coming home behind Kenya and Portugal and edging Ethiopia into fourth place.

The race was held over a full marathon course, with Colin running the fourth of the six stages. Britain were third when Colin took the bracelet and he held this position for the final two runners to maintain. The other members of the team of six were Dave Lewis, John Mayock, Dave Clarke, John Sherburn and Carl Udell. Colin was running well at this stage and carried off a quartet of titles, in the AAAs, the UK, the AAAs Half Marathon and the Northern cross country championships. He also finished fifth in the World Cup in Havana, again running well despite heavy humidity. His superb contribution helped Great Britain to finish second overall. The following year Walker ran in the semi-finals of the world championships in Stuttgart. He was in contention for a place in the final with 700 metres to go but hit a barrier and fell, impeding an American runner at the same time. He did pick himself up to finish the race, but was disqualified anyway.

On the domestic scene, Colin retained his AAAs crown which ensured that he was named in the English team for the Commonwealth Games in Victoria, Canada, in 1994.

Once again Colin was determined to test the field, and decided to take them on in an attempt to repeat his medal winning feat from Auckland. The race developed a similar pattern to the one in New Zealand. He made a positive break but was again eventually overhauled by the two Kenyan runners. Unfortunately this time Colin was also overtaken by the Canadian runner Fell with only 60 metres to go and had to settle for a frustrating fourth place.

In the same year Colin finished fourth in the World Cup at Crystal Palace, having been unable to fully prepare for the race. He could not get extra time off work, so he flew from Newcastle to Heathrow, ran his race in wet and windy conditions, and then returned immediately to Heathrow to fly home again.

Colin's winning run in the AAAs championship also came to an end when he finished fourth, though he recorded a good win on the road when winning the Morpeth to Newcastle race.

At that stage of his career he decided to quit the track and fully concentrate on his road running, but he was developing problems with his left knee and eventually decided to retire from top level athletics.

In 2000 Colin still runs for fun and also enjoys the occasional round of golf. He lives in County Durham with his wife Alison and son Byron Colin.

Peter Whiteside
Modern Pentathlon

PETER WHITESIDE was a very strong swimmer who took up the testing sport of modern pentathlon while serving in the Royal Air Force and went on to compete with distinction for Great Britain in the 1980 Olympics in Moscow.

He was British champion in 1985 and was runner-up on four occasions, while he was shortlisted for a further two Olympics and also finished 16th in the world championships in Budapest in 1979.

Peter was born in Middlesbrough on June 23, 1952, and grew up in Marton Road, attending Hugh Bell Boys School.

His introduction to swimming came quite by accident. He was visiting Middlesbrough swimming baths to watch his sister Agnes in action in the pool. As a schoolboy prank, he pushed a friend into the pool, but lost his balance at the same time and ended up in the water alongside him.

The problem was that Peter was fully clothed. Once he had clambered out, the baths officials offered to dry his clothes, while giving him free swimming time while he was waiting. Peter borrowed a pair of swimming trunks and stayed in the water for three full sessions while his clothes dried out, and so learned to swim.

He proved to be a natural in the water, and he joined Middlesbrough Swimming Club, for whom he competed in many galas and also in sea swimming races. His competitive edge was remarkable, but it did lead to physical problems and later on he went on to suffer from stress asthma, which curtailed some of his swimming events.

Upon leaving school, Peter became an apprentice motor mechanic with Robinson's Dairies, and carried out his swimming training on a lunchtime at Thornaby Baths.

When his girlfriend of the time announced she was joining the RAF, Peter applied as well. He was accepted, but his girlfriend threw a spanner in the works when she changed her mind about joining. However Peter had already made the commitment, and went on to train as an aircraft technician at RAF Fairford.

Whiteside had not competed as a swimmer for two years, but he was encouraged to take to the water again at Fairford and went on to sweep the board in both the regional and the national RAF championships.

A chance meeting with another serviceman in a NAAFI bar led to Peter hearing about the multi-discipline sport of modern pentathlon, though initially he was attracted only by the fencing.

He went to the gym at his RAF base for fencing lessons and met up with the head of physical education, David Gibbs, who was himself a former international pentathlete.

Gibbs immediately spotted Whiteside's all-round potential and introduced him to running and pistol shooting as well as fencing.

After a while Peter entered the RAF tetrathlon championships, which covered swimming, fencing, running and shooting, and he finished second overall. It was a remarkable achievement after so little preparation, and he was immediately marked down as a modern pentathlete of the future.

Lessons in the fifth pentathlon discipline, which was horse riding, soon followed. As a result, Whiteside was called up within months to make his Great Britain Under-21 international debut in Germany. He did not make a major impact overall, but finished third in the swimming and returned home with a medal.

Swimming was always Peter's best discipline, throughout his competitive career, but he was making dramatic improvements in the other four sports at that time and quickly progressed to become a senior British international.

In 1974 he finished sixth in the British championships. The following year he took second place, just 250 points behind Jim Fox, who went on to win a gold medal with the British team in the 1976 Olympics.

Peter was continuing to improve day by day, and was now one of the top British international competitors.

Peter Whiteside was British pentathlon champion in 1985 and was in the British Olympic team of 1980.

He enjoyed an excellent year of competition in 1977 and finished second in the British championships, recording his best ever aggregate points tally of 5,546. The winner, Danny Nightingale, set a new national record of 5,601.

Even so, there was a major disappointment for Peter when he was left out of the British squad for the world championships in San Antonio, Texas, in the October. He lost out to men whom he had been beating consistently in British events, and complained bitterly to the selection committee to no avail.

However his international prospects improved further when he took the advice of Jim Fox and left the RAF to join the Army.

He became a regular attender at the national modern pentathlon training headquarters at Arborfield in Berkshire. With the benefit of the intensive training programme, which usually involved between nine and ten hours of hard work, for five days a week, Peter continued competing in international events and gaining valuable experience of top level competition.

His regular daily work usually involved two hours swimming before breakfast, followed by shooting and fencing practice until lunch.

Much of the afternoon was spent on horseback, culminating in a 90-minute ten-miles run. Three of the evenings were often spent toning up his fencing at London's De Beaumont Centre in Hammersmith, while the other evenings normally involved another dip in the swimming baths.

Jim Fox also arranged for Peter to fly out to the United States and train with the American modern pentathlon squad at their base in San Antonio, and this proved to be a great learning experience.

In 1979 Peter achieved his highest international placing of eighth in a major event in Warendorf in Germany, and followed up by winning his place in the world championships in Budapest in Hungary.

He finished 16th overall and was the best placed of the three-man British team, equalling his personal best total number of points. Whiteside helped the team to 12th position overall. In fact Britain would have done much better had Nightingale not drawn a horse in the afternoon session which had suffered a bad fall in the morning resulting in it refusing to run for him.

Peter was more fortunate with his horse, and was delighted to gain a maximum 1,100 points at riding, which had been his weakest event. He also recorded his best ever shoot in an international of 1,022.

In June, 1980, Whiteside finished 20th in the Debenhams International modern pentathlon at Crystal Palace, but was fourth best Briton. It was enough to win him a place in Britain's four man squad for the Moscow Olympics, along with Nightingale (Loughborough), Nigel Clark (Rickmansworth) and the reserve Tim Kenealy (Portsmouth).

The British team were defending the gold medal in Moscow but got off to a bad start in the riding event, and were lying tenth overall at the end of this discipline. One of the problems in the riding is that the horses are unknown to the riders beforehand, and often the luck of the draw is crucial. Peter drew a reasonable but excitable horse, and was satisfied with his haul of 1040 points, which included two knockdowns.

Unfortunately the team was unable to make up much ground in the fencing, where they also finished tenth. The major problem over the 16 hours was that Clark was not happy with his swords, and switched from one to the other in a vain attempt to produce some consistency.

The British team finished ninth in the shooting, but there was an improved showing in the swimming, which produced sixth place overall. This was still Peter's strongest event, and he was determined to do well.

However he was nervous at the start and felt that he had gone off too fast. It was to work in his favour, even though he did try to alter his pace, because he went on to set a personal best of 3min 25sec and was beaten by a fingertip by a Russian competitor who later took the overall gold medal.

Nightingale and Clark were strong runners and the British trio lifted themselves again to finish second in the final event, which was the cross country. Whiteside ran well, but felt completely drained over the closing stages, which were run on a soft, sandy surface. He did not know it at the time but it was the first signs of the illness ME, which was to hit him hard in later years.

Despite their fine efforts at the cross country, the British boys had to settle for eighth place overall.

Peter still retained high hopes of winning a medal in the world championships and the 1984 Olympics, and continued to work towards those two goals.

He had become a sporting celebrity for his exploits in Russia, and was initially in demand as a public speaker. His first ever talk was made in a local school, and it went so well that he expanded his oratory abilities.

There was also the no-small matter of trying to attain the military qualifications to become a sergeant in the Army, and this occupied a great deal of Whiteside's time over the next two years.

His life was then changed forever in June, 1983, when Peter was involved in a tragic accident which led to the death of one of his best friends and colleagues.

He was practising his fencing with Flight Lieutenant John Warburn at the De Beaumount Centre when the safety tip on Peter's epee bent and snapped off as he lunged forward. The blade entered a small gap under John's protective bib and severed the main artery in his neck. Warburn was mortally wounded and died within minutes.

It was a complete and utter accident, and Peter was entirely vindicated at the inquest which followed. However the catastrophe was such a harrowing experience that it took Peter many years to come to terms with it.

As a result of the accident, the fencing authorities took action and the equipment has been changed universally. Bibs are now thicker and longer, while the sword blades have been refined and are less likely to snap.

It was no surprise when Peter was omitted from the British modern pentathlon team selected to compete in the world championships three weeks later. No doubt the selectors believed that he needed time to improve his mental condition.

Peter had not performed very well in some of the internationals leading up to the championships, while he was continually being affected by bouts of tiredness. The following year he failed to win selection for the Los Angeles Olympics.

Whiteside did move into coaching and was considering announcing his retirement in 1985, but felt well enough to have a stab at the British championships. Remarkably he won the event, for the first time in his career, after previously finishing second on four occasions.

He stayed in full training for another two years, but continued to be affected on occasions by ME and finally called it a day.

Peter went into coaching at Arborfield and played a major part in the success of the initial British ladies team. He took the ladies to the world championships in Canada and was delighted when one of the team, Wendy Norman, finished fourth overall. She was just pipped for the bronze medal.

Later, another member of the team, Sarah Cox, finished fourth in the European championships.

Peter then coached the British Under-21 team, before widening his horizons to coach triathlete Stacey Robinson at the modern pentathlon centre. Robinson went to the world championships and, but for a major setback when his saddle came loose during the cycling, might have won a medal.

Whiteside was introduced to health foods in the 1990s which helped his ME considerably. In fact he entered a triathlon in 1994 and not only was he amazed to finish second, but it qualified him for a place in the world championships in his age group.

Peter flew out to Mexico the following year and enjoyed the experience, finishing 23rd overall.

He left the Army in October, 1996, and started up in business himself, initially as a fencing coach in schools in the Berkshire area.

Then, having qualified as a sports masseur some time earlier, he opened his own therapy centre near Wokingham. Later he introduced the Bowen soft touch therapy method from Australia, which has been described as acupuncture without needles, and has proved remarkably successful.

Both businesses are thriving and Peter is enjoying life away from the armed forces. He and his wife Linda are also developing a nutritional foods company, with football clubs and other sporting organisations among their increasing list of customers.

Harry Whitfield
Speedway

HARRY Whitfield was one of the kings of the cinder track when speedway was developing in Britain and he journeyed Down Under to win the unofficial world championship in Australia in 1932.

Born in the centre of industrial Middlesbrough on May 9, 1908, Harry was frail and delicate as a boy and so his parents reacted to medical advice by sending him to live on a farm at the age of eight.

He made his home at Stanley Grange Farm at Great Ayton and stayed there with foster parents for over ten years, gradually gaining in physical strength. In addition to a two-miles walk to school every day, Harry became involved with the day-to-day farm work, which could often be very heavy going.

His introduction to farm ways also brought him into direct contact with motor cycles for the first time, and was to lead to him becoming one of the biggest names on two wheels in the 1930s.

Harry was often sent into Middlesbrough on farm business and eventually his foster parents bought him an ex-Army, belt driven Douglas motor cycle to speed up his trips. He regularly raced the bike on the rough terrain at the farm and gradually built up a sound mechanical knowledge of the machine.

When Harry returned to live in the town again, he joined Middlesbrough Motor Club and made an immediate impact in sand racing and grasstrack events.

After he had been riding as an amateur for three years, he was spotted at a North Ormesby grasstrack meeting by the Australian John S Hoskins, who was regarded as the leading exponent of speedway racing in this country.

Hoskins offered Harry the opportunity to race at Wembley Stadium and it was an offer the Middlesbrough man could hardly refuse. In 1929 he rode in the first speedway meeting ever held at Wembley Stadium, taking on a host of celebrity riders from several countries including New Zealand, Australia, Canada and the United States.

Even though Whitfield was only 21 at the time, and

Speedway ace Harry Whitfield proudly displays the Scottish Open 500cc Championship Trophy.

giving away years of experience to most of his rivals, he won the first ever scratch race at the stadium and received the Dominion Plate, valued at £100. In the races which followed in the stadium's inaugural week, he also won £280.

When the Wembley team was eventually formed, Harry became a regular member of the line-up for seven years.

On several occasions he was selected to ride for England, and was a member of the English team which visited Australia in 1932. Apart from a speedway trip it was also a honeymoon, because Harry was married at a few days notice before setting sail for Sydney.

The Aussie trip turned out to be a great moment in Harry's life because the unofficial world championships were staged at the Sydney Royal Showground and Harry stormed his way to winning the crown.

At the height of his career, Whitfield once rode in nine meetings in ten days throughout England and Scotland and collected £550 in prize money - not a bad financial

In 1932 Harry Whitfield, seen here astride a JAP 500, travelled to Australia and won the world speedway championship. It is also accepted that he was the first rider to adopt a forward leg position when cornering.

haul in the troubled times of the Thirties. In those ten days he also gathered a few trophies, including winning the Scottish Open 500cc Championship at Marine Gardens in Edinburgh and South Coast Championship at Southampton.

The large Scottish trophy was 3ft 6in high and Whitfield was allowed to keep it. However it was a close run thing in the final, with Harry just pipping the legendary American Sprouts Elder by a half a bike's length. Harry was immediately challenged to a return match with Elder one week later and won again, though the Teessider was sensible not to put the trophy at stake.

Throughout his career, Harry was thrown off his machine on many occasions and suffered several broken bones, but was fortunate that he was involved in only one particularly bad fall, when he received permanent scars from facial wounds inflicted by the cinders on the track.

Whitfield's knowledge of speedway was so highly regarded by Wembley that they occasionally sent him on scouting trips to Spain and other parts of Europe to inspect the latest riding trends.

In 1936 he decided to hang up his helmet, but was enticed out of retirement two years later by his friend Bluey Wilkinson, to ride for Sheffield.

However all sport came to a standstill the following year because of the Second World War and Harry put his mechanical skill to excellent use by joining the RAF. During his time spent in Italy, he organised speedway tracks for the entertainment of the troops.

Not surprisingly, he took note of the most impressive riders and signed them up for teams in Britain at the end of the hostilities.

Once peace was fully restored, and speedway leagues were reformed., Harry became managing director of the Borough Bears speedway team and was a popular figure at Cleveland Park Stadium.

After his retirement, Harry became an RAC/ACU examiner and continued to be involved with Middlesbrough Motor Club, starting a training scheme for learner motor cyclists. He was also a keen golfer.

Harry Whitfield died on September 14, 1988 but is remembered with great affection by all speedway fans.

Marrie Wieczorek
Football

MARRIE Wieczorek was a highly talented central defender and midfielder who won three England international caps in 1980 and is now making her mark as a coach.

She joined the Cleveland Spartans at the team's formation in 1976 and quickly emerged as one of the top players in the North of England.

She played representative football at all levels and won several league championship medals before later going on to coach and manage Middlesbrough Ladies in a 24-year ongoing association with the club.

Marrie was born at home in Victoria Road, Middlesbrough, on July 5, 1957, and attended Sacred Heart School in the shadow of Ayresome Park, and later went to St Thomas's School before switching to St Mary's Convent Grammar School at the age of 13.

She played hockey at St Mary's and swam in school galas, but it was football which had always been her No.1 love.

In fact Marrie had been asked to play for the Sacred Heart School football team but had declined, because she was rather shy. However she never missed the chance to support the school team in action every Saturday morning.

Marrie spent most of her teenage years playing football at every opportunity, usually with a group of friends on the land behind the former bowling alley in Linthorpe Road.

When she left school she took a secretarial course at Kirby College of Further Education and also passed an A Level in English Language, later finding employment as a typist at Teesside Polytechnic.

However she gave up the job to spend a summer season at Pontin's Holiday Camp, and went on to spend four consecutive summers at Pontin's - two at Lowestoft and two at Chichester. In between she had various jobs, including working in a hotel in Notting Hill and British Home Stores in Oxford Street, both in London, in addition to working at Middlesbrough telephone exchange and also for Hill's the Bakers.

She was still at Pontin's in the September of 1976 when she was informed that an advert had been placed in the Evening Gazette by Cleveland Spartans, who were looking for new players as they prepared to join the Northern Counties League.

Marrie returned early from Pontin's and went along to the Spartans trials on a hard gravel pitch in Church Lane in Acklam. She was not an immediate success.

She recalled: "I was wearing a pair of £1.99 sandshoes and a baseball shirt, with my jeans rolled up to my knees. Most of the other girls were wearing boots. I didn't even own a pair. I got sore feet and I felt really embarrassed."

However Marrie was kitted out when she returned for the second trial, which was held indoors, and she never looked back.

After one season in the Northern Counties League, the Spartans joined the Nottingham League, where they came into competition against the best teams in the North, including the Doncaster Belles.

The Spartans had a good team at that time, including the likes of Theresa Murphy and Anne Duffy. Marrie was also one of the leading players, operating either at right back, centre-back or in midfield. Spartans went from strength to strength over the next few years and were national five a side champions in 1979.

They also enjoyed several good runs in the FA Cup, including reaching the semi-final in 1980 when they outplayed Preston but could not score and went down by 1-0.

They finally reached the FA Cup Final in 1982, after beating the crack Southampton side in the semi-finals. Spartans drew 1-1 at Fratton Park against the Southampton side which contained six internationals, and then beat them by 2-1 in the replay at Feethams, Darlington.

In the cup final, Spartans travelled to meet Lowestoft on the artificial turf at Queen's Park Rangers' Loftus Road ground. Unfortunately, Lowestoft had packed the superior footwear and Spartans produced a

Marrie Wieczorek was at the forefront of women's football on Teesside winning 3 England caps in 1980.

unfortunately she never again received international recognition, despite playing a lot of regional football.

Throughout the Eighties and early Nineties, the Spartans changed their leagues and also their name on several occasions.

They won several Northern Counties titles in the Eighties and also won the Yorkshire and Humberside League crown on three occasions, finishing runners-up twice.

In 1987, Marrie played in a Northern Counties League Cup Final when she was five months pregnant, carrying her son Danny. However she helped the Spartans to beat Filey by 6-1 and scored one of her speciality free kicks.

At one time Spartans became Boro Electronics, and then Madison Ladies. It was as Madison that they first visited Italy in 1990 when they played two matches against Czechoslovakian sides. The following year they returned to Italy and played Czech opposition again in a tournament at Modena.

They became Middlesbrough Ladies in the early Nineties and have since received valuable sponsorship from Boro chairman Steve Gibson.

Marrie became captain of the team in 1987, and held this position for five seasons, until she stepped up to player manager. She had taken her FA preliminary badge in 1989, when she was one of few people to pass on a course which was dominated by male entrants.

In recent years the Ladies have narrowly failed on three occasions to reach the Division One North, through the play offs. They now play in the Northern Combination.

They played at Wembley in 1997, meeting Chelsea Ladies in a six-a side match before Boro's FA Cup Final against Chelsea. The Boro Ladies won their game by 3-2.

Marrie gained her first official coaching experience away from the Ladies team when she worked for Middlesbrough Council at Southlands Leisure Centre. A chance conversation with current Boro coach David Geddis led to her joining him on the Middlesbrough Football Club's community programme as women's football development officer in 1993. She has now graduated to the Middlesbrough Football Club Community Centre at Eston.

In 2000 Marrie still manages Middlesbrough Ladies but has not played for two seasons due to persistent knee trouble, which needs an operation. She lives locally with her partner Arthur and son Danny.

disappointing display in going down by 2-0.

By this time Marrie had already played in three full international games for England.

She progressed through the Nottingham League side and also the Midlands Region, before earning an international trial at Warminster along with clubmate Theresa Murphy.

Afterwards Marrie received her call up for England's game against Belgium in Ostend and experienced one of the biggest moments of her life when taking part in the match. However England lost 2-1.

A couple of weeks later Marrie played the first half of England's 6-1 rout of Wales at Warminster. Her third cap came when she came on as a second half substitute in England's 1-1 draw against Sweden at Leicester City's Filbert Street.

Marrie continued to gain in power and experience, but

Tim Williamson
Football

LEGENDARY goalkeeper Tim Williamson holds a record which may never be beaten. He is the only Middlesbrough FC player ever to play in more than 600 league and cup games for the club.

His 602 appearances were made during a remarkable one-club career which stretched from 1902-1923. Throughout this period he was a regular in the side.

Tim was Boro's first ever England international when he made his debut against Ireland on February 25, 1905, and he went on to win a further six caps, only finishing on the losing side on one occasion.

Reginald Garnet Williamson was known as Tim from an early age, and also Tiny, throughout his life because, at 5ft 9in tall, he was considered rather small to be a goalkeeper even by the turn of the 20th Century standards.

He was born in North Ormesby on June 6, 1884, and attended House Street Junior School. His early football was played with Coatham Grammar School, Redcar Juniors and Redcar Crusaders, where he came to prominence as a progressive goalkeeper with special attributes.

Tim's talents were spotted by the Middlesbrough directors and he was invited to keep goal for Middlesbrough in a friendly against the Irish side Cliftonville. His coolness under pressure and safe hands impressed the management of his home town club because he was immediately offered professional forms, and duly signed for the Boro in April, 1901. However Tim was dubious about taking the plunge into unknown territory, and eventually signed only on the understanding that he could continue his interest in becoming a qualified draughtsman.

Williamson's first competitive game for the club was against Crook Town in the Northern Alliance League on New Year's Day, 1902, before going on to make his league debut against Bristol City at Middlesbrough's old Linthorpe Road ground on April 19 of the same year. Not surprisingly he recorded a clean sheet.

This was to the first of 602 league and cup

Tim Williamson made a remarkable 602 appearances for Middlesbrough in a career lasting over 20 years.

appearances which still stands today as a club record and is unlikely to be beaten in these days of diminishing player loyalty.

During the early part of his career, Tim was understudy to the experienced Scotsman Rab Macfarlane. However, he broke back into the team on January, 3, 1903, playing in a 3-0 defeat at Everton. Clearly he was in no way to blame for any of the goals because he went on to establish himself as a first team regular and became ever present for more than 20 years.

Remarkably, only two of Tim's appearances came in the Second Division. Following his debut against Bristol City, he kept another clean sheet in a 2-0 win at Blackpool as Boro made certain of promotion to the top flight. Never again did he play outside of the First Division.

Unusually, for a goalkeeper, Tim also scored two goals,

The Boro squad of 1912-13 with Tim Williamson, centre, middle row, in front of Ayresome Park's old north stand. The next season they would finish third in the First Division, Boro's highest ever league position.

both of them coming from the penalty spot. He netted in a 2-2 home draw against Liverpool in April, 1910, and in a 3-0 home win against Bristol City the following September.

Williamson suffered the misfortune of scoring an own goal on his England debut against Ireland at Ayresome Park in February, 1905. The game ended in a 1-1 draw. Tim had to wait another six years for his second cap, but then made half a dozen appearances for England in a two year spell in the pre-Great War years.

In February, 1911, he played his part in helping England to record a 2-1 win against Ireland at the Baseball Ground at Derby, and then kept his first international clean sheet in a 3-0 win against Wales at Millwall. The same season, Tim completed a Home International clean sweep when playing for England against the Scots in a 1-1 draw at Goodison Park.

Williamson achieved another international shut-out in March, 1912, when helping England to win 2-0 against Wales at Wrexham, and then travelled with England to meet the Scots at Glasgow, again featuring in a 1-1 draw.

In his final international, against Ireland in Belfast on February 15, 1913, Tim tasted defeat for the first and only time for England, when the Irish won by 2-1.

Williamson was in goal during the most successful season in the history of the club, when they finished third in the First Division in 1913-14. If not for the fact that the Boro won just one of their first 11 games that season, they would surely have won the title.

Tim was exempt from the forces in World War One because of his reserved occupation but continued to play for Middlesbrough after the end of hostilities. However he was denied a benefit match by the Football League on the grounds that the war years did not count as service.

Williamson was a much respected and appreciated goalkeeper at away grounds throughout the country, often receiving a personal ovation as he took his place between the sticks. He eventually retired, aged 39, at the end of the 1922-23 season but continued to play in the local amateur leagues.

His other interests outside football included riding his motorbike, playing golf and game shooting which he continued to follow passionately.

Tim died on August 2, 1943, in North Ormesby Hospital shortly after an operation. He is buried in Coatham Churchyard near Redcar.